D0256767

Time to Declare
MY AUTOBIOGRAPHY

Also by Michael Vaughan

A Year in the Sun
Calling the Shots

Time to Declare
MY AUTOBIOGRAPHY

MICHAEL VAUGHAN

with Mike Dickson

HODDER &
STOUGHTON

First published in Great Britain in 2009 by Hodder & Stoughton
An Hachette UK company

2

Copyright © Michael Vaughan 2009

The right of Michael Vaughan to be identified as the
Author of the Work has been asserted by him in accordance
with the Copyright, Designs and Patents Act 1988.

All rights reserved. No part of this publication may be
reproduced, stored in a retrieval system, or transmitted, in any form
or by any means without the prior written permission of the publisher,
nor be otherwise circulated in any form of binding or cover other
than that in which it is published and without a similar condition
being imposed on the subsequent purchaser.

A CIP catalogue record for this title
is available from the British Library

Hardback ISBN 978 0 340 91932 3
Trade Paperback ISBN 978 0 340 91934 7

Typeset in Sabon by Ellipsis Books Limited, Glasgow

Printed and bound by Clays Ltd, St Ives plc

Hodder & Stoughton policy is to use papers that are natural, renewable
and recyclable products and made from wood grown in sustainable forests.
The logging and manufacturing processes are expected to conform to the
environmental regulations of the country of origin.

Hodder & Stoughton Ltd
338 Euston Road
London NW1 3BH

www.hodder.co.uk

For Nichola, Archie and Talulla

Contents

Acknowledgements ix

Photographic Acknowledgements x

Preface xi

1 The Best Job in the World 1

2 Crossing the Pennines 9

3 Learning the Trade 24

4 I Never Saw Phil Tufnell Eat 44

5 Playing Myself In 58

6 Time to Deliver 74

7 In the Runs 89

8 Year in the Sun 98

9 The One-Day Job 117

10 Stepping Up 131

11 The Need for Change 148

12 Laying the Foundations 161

13 Upping the Run Rate 176

14 The Final Pieces 190

15 On Captaincy 205

16 The Run-up to the Ashes 221

17 Golden Summer   235

18 After the Lord Mayor's Show   262

19 Looking On   277

20 Revolving Doors   291

21 Feeling the Pressure   308

22 There May be Trouble Ahead   327

23 Changing of the Guard   343

24 Twenty20 Vision   359

25 The Decision to Go   374

26 Last Chances   392

27 Time to Declare   404

28 The Final Chapter   416

    Career Statistics   428

    Index   460

Acknowledgements

First and foremost I would like to thank my family for their unfailing support at all times. Without the understanding of my wife Nichola, there would have been much less success in my life. My children Talulla and Archie are also an inspiration, and my mum and dad deserve unqualified praise for the way they brought me up.

This is a book that I have been planning to write for some time, and my diaries have proved incredibly helpful; however I was sensible enough to approach Mike Dickson at an early stage to help me structure my thoughts and present my overall story in the most readable way. Mike is a good friend as well as being a highly respected sports writer and his involvement has hugely improved the readability of my book.

Too many people to mention here have been helpful to me at one stage or another during my life, but a good number are included in the book itself.

I would like to thank the team at Hodder & Stoughton for their assistance in producing this book – my publisher Roddy Bloomfield for his patience and trust, and Sarah Hammond for working so hard to see that *Time to Declare* was published so soon after I made my declaration!

Photographic Acknowledgements

The author and publisher would like to thank the following for permission to reproduce photographs:

Alessandro Abbonizio/AFP/Getty Images, Matthew Ashton/ Empics Sport, Mark Baker/Reuters/Action Images, Hamish Blair/Getty Images, Philip Brown, John Buckle/Empics Sport, Graham Chadwick/Getty Images, Paul Childs/Action Images, David Davies/PA, Kieran Doherty/Reuters/Action Images, Patrick Eagar, Mike Egerton/Empics Sport, Paul Ellis/AFP/Getty Images, Matthew Fearn/PA, Mike Finn-Kelcey, Stu Forster/ Getty Images, Paul Gilham/Getty Images, Laurence Griffiths/ Getty Images, Fiona Hansen/AFP/Getty Images, Martin Hayhow/ AFP/Getty Images, Owen Humphreys/PA, Tom Jenkins/ Guardian News & Media, Christopher Lee/Getty Images, David Munden/Popperfoto/Getty Images, Rebecca Naden/PA, Phil Noble/PA, Ross Parry Agency, Ben Radford/Getty Images, Clive Rose/Getty Images, Tom Shaw/Getty Images, Neal Simpson/ Empics Sport, Bob Thomas/Getty Images, Dave Thompson/ AP/PA, Rui Vieira/PA, Andrew Yates/AFP/Getty Images, Obed Zilwa/AP/PA.

All other photographs are from private collections.

Preface

26 June 2009

It was a familiar enough situation to me by now, being the most recognisable face in the team and therefore attracting the attentions of the comedians and/or drunks in the crowd. We were playing at Grace Road, homely ground of Leicestershire, and on this early Friday evening Yorkshire were in the penultimate match of their Twenty20 Cup qualifying section, trying to make it through to the quarter-finals.

'You're rubbish, Vaughan!' was one cry. 'You'll never make it back into the England team, no chance!' was another. A lot of professional cricketers, as they get older, become less tolerant of this kind of thing and are more inclined to have a dart back. It really did not bother me, one way or the other, although I was tempted to respond 'You're right, mate, I won't be playing for England again, because I'm about to announce my retirement.' That would have been true, as my career would soon be coming to an end, although I did not realise quite how soon. There was another Twenty20 match on Sunday and the plan was to play in some NatWest Pro40 matches later in the season before departing for good.

I had decided to retire from first-class cricket exactly a week previously, because my wider hopes of playing against Australia later in the summer were clearly not going to materialise. Squads for the series had been announced without my name in them, my body was rebelling and I could see that it was not meant to be.

I had gradually come to that decision while fielding at New Road on the last day of our Championship match against Worcestershire. There I was at this picturesque outpost of English cricket, and all I could think about was the US Open golf, the second round of which was going on at the same time. For some reason I kept turning over in my head the chances of golfers I knew, such as Lee Westwood and Rory McIlroy, wondering how they would get on, and I felt completely detached from the cricket. The game was petering out and my mind was wandering hopelessly. At one point I actually burst out laughing at the absurdity of it all. It was the latest in a stream of messages – some obvious, others less so – telling me that at the age of 34 my time was up.

I had kept my decision pretty much to myself, although I did let Yorkshire coach Martyn Moxon know my thinking, and so here we were at Leicester with plenty to play for. Two victories in our remaining games would ensure qualification for the latter stages and there was a determination to win on this gloomy late afternoon. They made 164 and we looked as if we were going to win after putting on 104 for the first wicket in response. I had found the Twenty20 competition very enjoyable, I still loved representing Yorkshire and I really wanted us to win. I had even passed up an offer to fly to South Africa on a private jet to watch the British Lions. My contribution was 17, bowled by veteran seamer Andrew Harris as I tried to hit a boundary, and I thought I had done OK, considering I could hardly see the ball in that light. Walking off with 29 left to get to be greeted by my friends in the crowd, I still thought we would get over the line. But we blew it, losing by nine runs.

Afterwards, we sat in that horrible away dressing room at Grace Road for the post-mortem. That is what happens when you are losing, you have lots of meetings to find out where you are going wrong. You talk about training, preparation, the work ethic, then some people try to come up with their explanations as to why it has all gone wrong and the others have to listen. It is generally, as was the case in this match, because a couple of players have stuffed up, taken the wrong options in their batting. It happens.

It came round to me and I pointed out that we seemed to have inquests every week, but that really it boils down to individuals taking responsibility to get us the win. What I always wanted as a captain was for people to make their own decisions, think for themselves and be mature and responsible. So much of it is about character and having the right mix of personalities in the team.

Another defeat, another inquest. And afterwards I did what county pros usually do after the business is done: I got in the car and pointed it towards the motorway.

1

The Best Job in the World

12 September 2005

The best moments of all, better than any open-top bus ride or even the lap of honour around The Oval, came after the ground had emptied and dusk had fallen. As I sat in the corner of the dressing room in my whites and floppy hat, bottle of beer in hand, there was the sheer bliss of everything sinking in. Private words were exchanged, as well as the odd hug, one of them with Duncan Fletcher. This had been more than two years in the preparation. All the stress, the setbacks and hard decisions – and now there was the brilliant clarity that it had all been worth it. The congratulatory messages were coming thick and fast, from the Queen and Prime Minister among others, and Elton John had a crate of champagne delivered to us. It was the ultimate Happy Hour. People came up and talked, and I just wanted to drink everything in. Paul Collingwood was getting stick from the other lads for nipping in at the last minute and gatecrashing the Ashes.

There is a big, old-fashioned bath at The Oval and everyone was in there singing and drinking. Freddie Flintoff was DJ-ing, getting some tunes on. These are the best things about sport, and what I will miss the most – when you are finished you cannot ring up 15 mates and say, let's get pissed and jump in a bath together and talk about what we have just done. So where were we going to go? Would we carry on the celebrations back in the hotel, or go out to the nightclub that our sponsors Vodafone had laid on? Better be careful not to get compromised, a few of the lads pointed out, the paparazzi are likely to be around. That one fell on deaf ears.

In the last few seasons, not a minute or hour had gone by without me thinking about beating Australia. I briefly went into their dressing room to shake hands and had a quick chat with Shane Warne. The Australians are brilliant to play against; they have an incredible culture in their sport that marries enjoyment and commitment and makes for a potent opponent. It was a warm enough encounter, but our dressing room was where I wanted to be.

A few dignitaries came in, which was fair enough, but my only desire was to be with the team and the backroom staff. I wanted to make sure I shared a nice bottle of Sauvignon Blanc with the latter group, as I considered them a massive part of our success and had ordered them to join in our lap of honour. For that moment in time, Team England was one big happy family.

3 August 2008

For the last year of my captaincy I had been carrying a little black book with me. In it I kept a diary, not so much to record things that had been happening, but more as a kind of confessional device, somewhere I could put down exactly what I was feeling at any given time. It might have been anything from my irritation with Peter Moores, to my periodic losses of self-confidence, to reminders of things I needed to do. I was certainly no Samuel Pepys, and often my scribblings were just a haphazard collection of random thoughts, but I found it helped.

For all that time, I felt I was wearing a mask, desperately trying to act the England captain who always kept his head. Now, on the morning after I had resigned the England captaincy, the mask was well and truly slipping. My entry for the morning of 3 August shows how much:

Cried all morning.
First to Nichola.
Then to Richard Bevan. Then to Craig.
Then to my dad.
Very emotional, not because I wasn't sure but because I was relieved it was ending.

So my wife, long-time confidant Bevan, Craig Sackfield from my management company and my father had all had a sneak preview of what the wider public were going to witness that afternoon. And all from someone who had always been averse to revealing his inner self.

I had known it was all over the previous day when, with South Africa needing 20 more runs to beat us at Edgbaston and clinch the Test series, Graeme Smith hit one back past me at mid-on and my mind was totally elsewhere. The feeling was one of gathering relief, and I was weighing things up – do I let the players know by announcing it tonight? It was a measure of how my sentiment towards my South African opposite number had changed that I was thinking I did not want to do anything to detract from his magnificent innings and take away his headlines.

It was all passing me by when Smith pulled KP to midwicket for the winning boundary. Some of their team ran out of the pavilion and I did the necessary handshakes, thanking the players for their efforts in the game, and walked off. I knew I must have been doing the right thing because I felt a total lack of emotion, completely calm as I went in to congratulate the South Africans and then talk to the press.

Although I tried not to give much away to the media when I sat before them, a few undoubtedly suspected something was up and, in fairness, they usually had good antennae for when things were not right. Before the match I had given a slightly tetchy interview to Jonathan Agnew of the BBC and had a semi-dig at him. This was taken by some to suggest that the odd crack was starting to show, and they had read that right. Me and Aggers had got on pretty well in that situation, so it was a bit unusual.

I gave a fairly measured press conference and by the time I came back into the dressing room a lot of the lads were packing up the bags and looking at me as if they were expecting an address. So I gave a quick speech, along the lines of we will bounce back, it has been a difficult series, South Africa have played good cricket and we should not be too harsh on ourselves and so on. I told them that I thought we should have won and that we needed to keep our minds together for the last big match at The Oval. I didn't give them any indication of my decision at this point, not wanting to do anything to add to the disappointment they were feeling.

After I'd spoken to the players, Peter Moores asked to have a word with me in the coach's room. He wanted to discuss how we were going to practise ahead of The Oval and decide which day to have off. After 30 seconds I stopped him and told him I was going to stand down straight away. I explained that I had come to the end of the road and that it was time for someone else to come in. He asked if I was sure I was making the right decision. I told him, 'I know I am, because I don't feel upset, in fact I feel very relieved. I'm quite happy with what I have achieved and I don't have any more mental energy left.'

We shook hands, he thanked me and we talked about who might take on the job. I was limited in what I could say because nobody else knew about Colly's decision to stand down from the one-day captaincy at the time and he was going to tell the required people later. In my mind there was only one candidate who could do both jobs and so we talked about Kevin Pietersen. I said I thought he was a bit of a maverick and that, at the time, I had not seen that many leadership qualities in Kev, but maybe that was what the team needed, something a bit different. He asked me about Fred and I replied that, while I thought he had matured, I was not sure he would want to take it. Strauss I really rated, but he could not justify his place in the one-day team and I reiterated my belief that it had to be one man doing both jobs. It was very cordial, and while I asked if he could generally keep it quiet I understood he wanted to tell the selectors.

Within half an hour Ashley Giles had rung and asked me what I thought I was doing. I said, 'Ash, I'm gone.' He asked if it was down to problems with the new regime – though the regime was hardly that new now – and I replied that it might not have helped, but that, basically, after five and a bit years I had come to the end of my tether, particularly after everything I had gone through with my rehab from injury.

Nichola was waiting for me back at the hotel, and as we had a babysitter we went and had a few drinks in the bar. I told Mark Garaway and Mark Saxby, good friends from the backroom staff, and Fred as well. They appeared saddened to hear it, but I think they all knew that the job had got to me in the end. I was disappointed to hear from someone that, with me and Colly having resigned, Peter had described it as 'an exciting time'.

The one thing I never wanted was for the players to see me on a real downward curve, as had maybe happened with Fletch. I suspected that a lot of them remembered him from his last six months, and not from the really good times that had come in the seven years before that. I did not want things to disintegrate after five years and for me to become someone they did not recognise.

Despite the relief, I barely slept that night. I had downed quite a few glasses of wine and did not feel great the next morning. I could hardly get out of bed and called Richard Bevan, who pretty much knew about my decision two days before, and he said he would come over. Nichola burst out crying and I joined in, saying that it would probably be best if she went home and left me to it. I told her that these were not tears of sorrow, but of relief. Embarrassingly, I started crying when Bev came over. Then Craig Sackfield, who was taking me over to Loughborough for the press conference, came up to my room while I was packing my bags and I started blubbing again. By that stage a notification had gone out to the media about an announcement being made that afternoon at the academy in Loughborough and my phone was starting to go into meltdown. Even a few South African players were leaving messages. Then I had to ring my dad. He said that he thought I was making the right decision, and that I could be proud. More tears.

I went down to reception and Freddie was lying on the floor playing with his kids. I reckon I had 150 text messages, either offering congratulations or commiserations, or trying to persuade me not to do it.

I was so nervous about the press conference. There was no

script; I had just written down a few headings with a list of people to thank. I arrived at Loughborough and went into the office. Hugh Morris took me into a room and thanked me for what I had done. In response, I said that I thought that the England captaincy was the most important job in English cricket and that, whoever was to succeed me, it was important that he got all the support he wanted.

Chief selector Geoff Miller and Moores then took me into another room. I had said to Pete the night before that it was best if I was not picked for The Oval. Then, in a moment of bravado, I said maybe I should play after all because I could get runs, but I was hoping they were not going to pick me. I also felt that as I had been captain for so long, it would be easier for the next man if I was not there. I had not found it very easy having Nasser around two days after he had resigned. If I had gone to The Oval, so much of the attention would have been on me. I was also beginning to think that my missing the India tour at the end of 2008 might be a good thing for KP, because it would guarantee him nearly six months to get established without me around.

I was very calm by now after the tears of the morning, but what pushed me to the brink again was when Gus Fraser, formerly of England and then of the *Independent* newspaper, came up and gave me a big bear hug and some heartfelt words. That is what started me off. It's not a great feeling knowing you are about to go on live national television and radio and burst into tears.

When I went into the press conference I thought, 'I've got to be me. I haven't been me for such a long time, so now is the time to be me again.' All those years of keeping on the mask of positivity – and now it really does not matter. No more having to put an angle on things, trying to avoid hurting someone's feelings, trying to put across a coded word to a player. No more bloody diplomacy.

I have not seen the press conference to this day, and people have said I did OK, but at the time I did not really care. Even the *Daily Telegraph*'s Derek Pringle, who had taken numerous pops at me in the previous 12 months, appeared to be impressed, writing: 'Vaughan, now 33, was the mastermind behind England's famous 2005 Ashes victory, but in recognising his descent as a human being and taking the only true recourse possible, this makes him a far bigger man than the one who won the country's admiration three years ago.'

I was also humbled and grateful for what Mike Atherton and Nasser wrote in their newspaper columns, Athers insisting that I was the one who should be thanked, rather than the other way round. As Athers put it, 'There comes a time when you don't want to spend every evening at dinner ignoring your companions, or your family, thinking about where your next run is coming from, who should be opening the bowling the following morning, or how to tell your mate that he is no longer good enough to be in the team.' He and Nasser were in an exclusive club that would have understood what I had been through.

Straight afterwards I drove home and we had a barbecue with a few friends and family that Nichola had organised. It was the perfect antidote. Within an hour of getting back, KP rang up and said that he has just been offered the captaincy, asking what I reckoned. Without hesitation I said to him, 'Kev, you will never get a better chance in your life; it's the best job in the world . . .'

2

Crossing the Pennines

There was a remarkable personal symmetry about the fact that when I started playing for England in matches at Old Trafford we would stay at the Marriott hotel in Worsley. It was in this Manchester suburb that I had spent the first years of my life, and here where I came close to death before I had even picked up a cricket bat in anger.

It was about half a mile up the road from the hotel where, at the age of six, I was on my way to play football with a mate. A car flew round the corner and knocked me over at speed. Passers-by moved me up against a tree while the ambulance was called, and it turned out my grandparents were in the queue of traffic that backed up as a result. I do not remember much about it beyond waking up in hospital with a huge cast on my left leg, but it was a lucky escape and the most serious of the physical mishaps that seem to have dogged me throughout my life.

According to the many specialists I have seen over the years it is unlikely, but possible, that the accident is connected with the problems I have had with my knees and other parts of my anatomy. However, even now I still get the odd unexplained ache in my left leg where it was originally broken.

But good things can come out of bad, and this first – and

sadly not last – spell of rehabilitation was the time when, laid up for weeks on end, I began to watch Test cricket on television. It also led to me getting my first bat, one that my father, Graham, got signed by the late David Bairstow at a benefit function that his company was supporting.

My dad originally comes from Coventry but moved up to Manchester, where his father's job had taken him, and settled down with my mum, Dee, in Worsley, where her family has been for generations. When I was a sports-mad small boy, playing constantly with my brother David – two years my senior – we could never have envisaged what a wider talking point my origins would become. Soon after the accident, we moved across the Pennines to Sheffield, and the fact that I was born Lancastrian would cause Yorkshire to adapt their age-old rules on who was eligible to play for the White Rose.

And just to add spice to the question, I was not descended from any old Lancastrian family, but from one of the most celebrated to have played cricket for the county. There is even now a suite at Old Trafford named after my ancestors. In all, there were six members of the extended Tyldesley family who played for the Red Rose over a period of more than 40 years leading up to the Second World War. The most famous were brothers J.T. and Ernest, both of whom were to play for England and who began their cricket days at Roe Green, just up the road from Worsley. Between them they scored more than 66,000 runs for Lancashire, before Ernest finally retired in 1936 aged 47.

He was my great-great-uncle, the brother of my mum's grandmother Ada. I would like to say that all this information was etched on my mind from an early age, but it was something I was largely unaware of. My mother can remember Ernest coming to visit when she was a girl and she can remember him as a quiet and unassuming man before his death in 1962. He was not much talked about in the family, and pretty much the only thing that made me vaguely aware of the Tyldesleys was the glass ornament we used to keep on the window ledge of the sitting room at home. It was the 1928 commemorative rose bowl that was given to all the players who took part in Lancashire's Championship triumph that year, and it had been handed down to us.

There were some decent sporting genes on that side of the family. My grandmother played hockey for Lancashire and my mother was a good player, too, and the champion athlete at her school. My dad has always been more of an enthusiast than a blinding talent, and captained Worsley cricket club's third XI, a stalwart of the club who dropped down to the thirds in order to have a hand in developing the junior players. My early sporting memories are of messing around on the boundary while he was playing and Mum was doing the teas. The only hint of any early promise from me was that, at a very young age, it was remarked upon that I could throw a ball from one side of the bowling green to the other and properly clear it.

In 1982 Dad, an engineer by trade, was offered a management job by his employers, Presto Pressing Tools, over in Sheffield, so we left Manchester behind. By then my brother David was showing potential as a footballer, playing for Salford Boys, and that was the sport that had captured my interest.

It was only when we moved to Dore, just outside Sheffield, that I began to play any kind of organised cricket as our house was within a mile of Abbeydale Park, where Yorkshire used to play one or two first-class fixtures per season. David, who was also pretty good at cricket and could probably have taken his sport further if he had been so inclined, wasted little time in getting involved in the nets with Sheffield Collegiate, whose home it was. At first, my main focus was on playing junior football for Porter FC, but my conspicuous talent at that stage was for ending up in hospital after various mishaps.

On one occasion I was in the street with a friend and informed him that I had the power to walk with my eyes shut and know where I was going. This was all well and good, but when I attempted a demonstration I walked straight into a lamp post and the wound needed stitching up. An early sign of dopiness? During the Los Angeles Olympics of 1984 David and I became so enthused that we set up a high jump in the garden using bamboo canes, only for one of my attempted Fosbury Flops to end with a length of cane sticking into my thigh. Luckily a nurse lived across the road and she told us we needed to get to the hospital quick to have it removed.

As children David and I were both sports nuts, with every spare minute devoted to some form of energetic activity. There was football on the front drive and cricket in the road, with a lamp post as the wicket and the neighbours' patience sorely tested by us hitting the ball into their properties. We set up a little net to play tennis in the garden and there was a sandpit in a nearby field where we practised the long jump. My dad's boss at work was Bert McGee, who was also chairman of Sheffield Wednesday, so we would go to every home game, particularly because Presto were club sponsors.

Meanwhile, I had started going down to the nets at Abbeydale Park and was swiftly showing an aptitude for the game. Occasionally I would also accompany David back over to Old Trafford for nets, because in our family we just took it as read that neither he nor I would be able to play for Yorkshire. But the county side's visits to Abbeydale were major occasions, and from the start I would always go and watch with my mates and my brother.

One time Worcestershire were the opposition, with Phil Neale – later to be the England cricket team's manager – and Ian Botham in attendance. As members, we were able to get into the pavilion, and at night we would sneak into the visitors' dressing room and try out all the gloves and bats for size. At one point we discussed stealing one of Beefy's bats, but we were basically far too nice boys to do that.

I saved up to visit Cole Brothers in Sheffield and buy my first bat at the age of 10, a Gunn & Moore Skipper, and I have been with the same manufacturer ever since, although these days the money goes in the opposite direction. My growing affection for cricket meant that I would sometimes score matches off the television, and I can remember Mike Atherton, later to become someone I had so much respect for as a colleague, being the first player I really took an interest in.

All sport fascinated me to the exclusion of most other things. One weekend, en route to an early age-group cricket match, I was so keen to find the football results that I asked Dad to stop at the newsagents so I could buy a paper to check them all on the journey. I chose the *Sunday Sport*, innocently thinking that, given its title, it would be full of all the information and reports I wanted. After I'd brought it back to the car, he became aware of me and my fellow young passengers sitting in the back giggling away at pictures that were not necessarily of footballers scoring goals, and advised us that we might have got the wrong publication.

My fledgling sporting career was halted abruptly at the age of 12 when it was decided that I needed an operation on a hereditary toe condition called Charcot-Marie-Tooth disease, which affected both me and my father. The chief feature is that your toes fold back into the foot – not a particularly pretty sight – and it was decided then that I needed to have them straightened out. I missed a lot of the summer and was convinced my burgeoning dreams of being a cricketer were at an end. In this case, the specialists believe that the condition probably is linked to the problems I have suffered in my knees and legs, just because I have never walked as normally as I should have done.

From the age of 12 to 18 my big toes were totally numb and I still do not have complete feeling in them even now. I had pins put in and, eight years after the operation, the screws came jutting out of my right big toe of their own accord. It was agony, although I was used to going through various types of pain by then. At least some good came out of it. The specialist who treated me, Dr Tom Smith, went out to India to perform the operation on children out there and when I got picked for England he borrowed photographs of me to take along as reassurance for the cricket-mad kids that you could undergo this treatment and come out the other side capable of making it in top-class sport.

In my case the operation had broadly been a success and I became fit again to pursue my goals of either playing cricket, or football for Sheffield Wednesday, although the former was starting to overtake the latter. With David and I so sports-mad, my parents became like a sporting taxi service, ferrying us around to whatever activities we were doing, and they continued to do so throughout our teenage years. Parents are the unsung heroes of the sporting world and we were very blessed to be brought up in our happy and secure middle-class environment, and to have such a supportive mother and father.

I loved playing for Porter FC, and I turned down offers to play for stronger teams in the area just so that I could remain with my mates. That was the big difference between my attitude to football and cricket. If the opportunity had arisen for some reason to further my cricket career beyond Sheffield Collegiate, I know I would have grabbed it, but I was not quite as passionate about soccer.

Push came to shove at the age of 13 when I attended trials for my beloved Wednesday. The format was a bit like some modern reality-TV show, with a week-long trial starting on a Monday and a percentage of the youngsters (I was a striker or right-sided midfield player) being told that they were no longer required at the end of each day. And the answer was . . . shove off! By the end of the Tuesday I had been told my services would not be required for the remainder of the week. There were no tears from me, in fact I was really not bothered at all, despite my love of football and Wednesday. My dad told me later that he was secretly pleased because he always felt you make better mates in cricket than in football. Anyway, I was not good enough and, as it turned out, my knees would not have been up to it anyway.

While I was gaining a reputation within Sheffield Collegiate as a decent youngster, I was still not part of the Yorkshire junior set-up. The coach at Collegiate was Jack Bethel, a man who really knew his stuff and was pretty selective over who he gave his time to, depending on their ability. After moving to Sheffield, Dad had asked him if he would like any help with coaching the youngsters, to be bluntly told 'No thanks'. Fortunately I was one of those he thought had some ability, although I was regarded then as an all-rounder who bowled medium pace and batted in the middle order. The process that would lead to me becoming integrated into Yorkshire cricket only really started moving after a fateful visit to Abbeydale Park to watch the annual county match when I was 14 and already not far from getting a call-up for the Collegiate first XI in the Yorkshire League.

I was playing on the outfield in front of the pavilion during the lunch break with a group of mates and Doug Padgett, the Yorkshire first-team coach, happened to be watching while I was having a bat. I did not think much of it when he put his cup of tea down, came out shortly afterwards and pulled me to one side to ask me who I was and where I was from. He wanted our phone number because he thought I should be getting some coaching up at Headingley. It always amazes me that some counties these days no longer allow kids to play on the outfield during breaks, even when it is perfectly dry. I came to have good reason to be thankful that the tradition was still flourishing at Sheffield back then.

Doug made a note of our number and a few days later Joe Lister, then Yorkshire secretary, rang my dad to tell him that I had been spotted and that they wanted me to go up to the county headquarters for a trial. It was not a particularly long conversation, however. After a few pleasantries Dad reckoned he ought to come clean: 'I should say that my son was born in Manchester and we have only moved to the area in the past few years,' he admitted, at which point Lister promptly put the phone down! Such were the diehard attitudes at Yorkshire in those days, although there were already straws in the wind suggesting that they would need to relax their bar against incomers.

Apparently Doug persisted behind the scenes, supported by Steve Oldham and Martyn Moxon, trying to convince the club's main committee that they had to be more open to outsiders. The arrival of Chris Hassall as chief executive also suggested attitudes were changing. By the time I was 15 we had taken their word that change was afoot and I was on my way to getting absorbed into Yorkshire's system and their academy. Apart from a brief attempt by exiled Yorkshiremen Steve

Coverdale and David Ripley to lure me down to Northampton-shire a couple of years later, where I went for a couple of week-ends' nets, I have been with my adopted county ever since.

Then began the period when my parents' selfless support really came into its own, with constant trips up to Leeds in the evenings for county nets, the kind of journeys many cricketing mothers and fathers will be familiar with. Often it was my mum driving me up there and sometimes I would catch the bus from school to my dad's office near Hillsborough, where I would wait for him to finish work before he would take me.

I have to say, though, that it was my early years in the first team at Sheffield Collegiate that provided me with the sharpest part of my cricketing education, helping shape my whole outlook towards the game. It was a fantastic club with some very decent cricketers, and from the age of 14 I had the chance to face some pretty scary bowling in the nets.

We had Kenny Benjamin, the West Indian bowler, playing for us around that time and it was priceless experience to have to summon up the courage to face him for 10 or 15 minutes twice a week in the summer. West Indian Ian Bishop was also on the scene, and among the other players were Nick Gaywood, who played for Somerset, Neil Priestley, the captain of Lincolnshire, Simon Myles, who had played some very good cricket in Australia, and our legendary captain, Andy Tasker, from whom I learned a lot. I am sure that it was the tough-ening experience of playing with the likes of them at such a young age that helped me cope with fast bowling when it came to the big time.

I made my first XI debut at 14 in the middle order and started opening the following season, learning not just about cricket but about so many other facets of life. 'Bitter or lager?' Andy would ask before play began, in order to get preparations in hand for the post-match rituals. I was not going to miss out on that, even at a tender age, and would order my pint of bitter for the close of play along with everyone else. I learned to mix with older people as I waited in the bar for whoever would be giving me a lift home. Seeing things such as adult magazines strewn around the changing rooms was also a bit of an eye-opener. Even at that age, I loved the banter among the lads and the sheer enjoyment of playing hard on the pitch and having a laugh with your team-mates off it has stayed with me throughout my career, whatever level it has been at. It is perhaps why I have always been comfortable in bars and why I will probably never be a new-age puritan.

Being sledged and facing some sharp bowling in the Yorkshire League made it quite a hard school, but it meant that scoring runs at my real school was pretty easy by comparison. The following year I was named *Daily Telegraph* Under-15 player of the year for my run-scoring feats at Silverdale Comprehensive, beating off competition mainly from the independent sector. The prize was £1,000 worth of Duncan Fearnley cricket equipment for my school, although Silverdale asked my dad if he would mind if they requested £1,000 worth of books instead. That, unfortunately, can be the standing of cricket in state schools.

That season I was also starting to make some significant contributions at Collegiate. In a national knockout competition we reached the quarter-finals and I took a bus up with the rest of the team to Gateshead, where there was a big crowd. I scored 80 and took three wickets as we went through to the last four, where we were beaten by Walsall.

I was starting to gain wider recognition and was named in the England Under-15 team that summer at the Bunbury Festival that took place at Oundle School, a great event organised by the irrepressible David English. Gary Neville, who went on to make such a name for himself at football, was in the North team with me that year (as was his brother Phil a couple of years later) but broke his thumb. Cricket-wise we never saw Gary again, although we remain in contact as friends to this day.

School was never a great counter-attraction for me, although I enjoyed it enough and made a great set of friends. When we had moved over from Manchester my parents were keen to get us into Silverdale, which had the best reputation in the area we were settling in. So Dad went to see the headmaster, Tom Sanderson, who had been a professional footballer, to see if he could accommodate David, who was already playing good-standard boys' soccer. Mr Sanderson suggested that the best chance of getting in was to declare an interest in a specialist subject they might be able to cater for. So David suddenly developed a passion for Russian, and our future education plans were mapped out.

When I left Silverdale – prematurely, in order to embark on my cricket career – it had nothing to do with not liking the place. I was fairly average academically but managed seven GCSEs, and was reasonably accomplished at things like maths and metalwork. As would be a feature of my cricket career, my attention span was perfectly good when I thought I could learn something that would be of use to me in bettering myself. Hence economics was something I got into, because I reckoned it was bound to be helpful in later life.

I was not really a troublemaker, although I recall I did get sent out from science class once when I set fire to my friend's textbook with a Bunsen burner. Then there were the scraps we would have on the way home with the boys from King Egbert's, who were our rivals. Their school was nearer to where we lived, so we were generally outnumbered and got chased through Dore plenty of times, usually after an argument about girls or something. I still see a few of those lads now and we have a laugh about it.

Whatever different courses our lives have taken, my good mates from those times are still the same good mates now. You are obviously aware as a high-profile sportsman that people want to know you for all sorts of different reasons when you make it, and it is reassuring to still be close to the guys who knew me when I was barely a household name in my own home. I have made many friends through cricket and met some fantastic people, but there is still a hard core from way back. My best man, Matt Sanderson, is a gym owner, and my brother is an estate agent, and has helped me with some of my investments. Richard Kettleborough, now a first-class umpire, is probably my longest-standing friend that I played cricket with, but others have gone on to do a huge variety of jobs: financial adviser, running a carpet business, selling chickens, working for Boots, being an engineer in the army. Mates for life.

Together we did most things, and my initiation to drinking was playing stupid games round at each other's houses with cheap cans of Skol lager that we could buy four to the pound. I tried smoking but did not like it, in fact I tried most things while growing up, as you are supposed to, but the one thing I never had anything to do with was drugs.

In my second year at Silverdale a girl arrived at the school from Northern Ireland called Nichola Shannon. Immature as we were, my mates and I originally nicknamed her 'Petrol Bomb' for no other reason than that she was originally from the Province, which was a more troubled place then than it is now. She was in my class, very much one of the cleverer ones, and she took her studies more seriously than I did, as befitting someone who went on to become head girl. We were always reasonably friendly without being especially close and I occasionally saw her out and about away from school as she lived in the nearby village of Bradway. While I was making my way as a cricketer, she was carving out a successful career as an accountant in the National Health Service.

It was approaching the winter of 1998, by which time I was well established with Yorkshire, when I happened to go out on a Monday night in Sheffield – I was often out on strange nights of the week to fit in with my playing or training schedule – to Champs sports bar in the city. Nichola happened to be there with her sister and we started talking. She was not that interested in me at first because I had a bit of a reputation as a lad about town at the time, but I brought her round to my way of thinking in the end. Life is so often about random events and taking your chances when they present themselves. Who knows how differently life may have turned out for me if one of us had happened to go somewhere else that night?

I am glad we did both choose the sports bar, because a bit more than three years later I proposed on Christmas Day, by asking her to marry me in a message in her card. Fortunately Nichola agreed and in 2003 we got married at Chatsworth House, courtesy of its owners, the Duke and Duchess of Devonshire, who I had met through cricket. The Duke and Duchess were among the 200 guests who made it a fantastic day. Having a settled family life helped enormously in coping with the pressures of being captain of England – I am a lucky man.

But back at Silverdale, Nichola had been relatively in the background as, increasingly, I focused my attention on trying to make my way at Yorkshire's academy and onto the professional staff. I had elected to do two A-levels, perhaps not the most academically taxing ones in economics and sports studies, while effectively training part-time to be a cricketer. Around this time Yorkshire were formally accepting that they had to relax their rules on who was allowed to play for the county. Sachin Tendulkar was being lined up as the first ever overseas player, while an ever so slightly less proven talent from the other side of the Pennines – i.e. myself – was being talked about as the committee tried to push it through without suffering a backlash from hard-core members. In my case, the idea was that anyone who had been 'weaned' within Yorkshire would be eligible to play for them.

This contributed to my becoming more negligent about my studies and thinking more about a life in professional sport. I was very much semi-detached from Silverdale by now and doing my sports studies A-level at Norton College. I began with the best of intentions but they were never destined to bear fruit. I was a part-time student and forever missing lessons to attend nets that went from indoor to outdoor as the summer of 1991 came around. Sports studies was easy enough but, although I was interested in it, the economics was proving more tricky and I was not gifted enough to do it at anything less than 100 per cent.

My economics tutor from Silverdale, Paul Kent, was a huge cricket and Sheffield Wednesday fan, so we had a lot in common. He would come round to my house for private lessons and a pattern would develop. We would do half an hour's economics and then he would say, 'You're bored, aren't you?' and sheepishly I would admit that I was.

So it became not uncommon for us to walk up to the Devonshire Arms public house instead and start chatting about the things that really fascinated us over a beer. This was often on a Wednesday, which happened to be a big night at the

Sheffield's Leadmill club, and there were even a few times when we ended up doing a ring-round and getting a few lads to go down there. The Leadmill looked like a converted bus station and on Wednesdays, appropriately enough, you would often find Wednesday players there on a night out. I used to manage to sneak in by looking as grown up as possible and gaze at my heroes.

We had reached May when we came to the mutual realisation that my heart was not really in studying. Mum and Dad, who were always keen on me gaining qualifications, reluctantly agreed, so it was decided that my efforts should now be concentrated on turning professional. The studying was put on hold on the basis that I could always go back to it if things did not work out in cricket.

Adam Smith, John Maynard Keynes and other great economists never had much to fear from me. I was hoping that the same could not be said of the cricketers I would encounter.

3

Learning the Trade

It was the high summer in 1991 when I became more than just a professional cricketer – I was, officially . . . a Yorkshireman. With a princely £80 per week on offer, the deal required little more than a friend of Dad's to check the small print. On Friday 28 June, I became the first non-overseas player born outside the hallowed boundaries of the county to be signed up by the White Rose. The historic contract was signed, most appropriately, on the outfield at Abbeydale Park and I was inaugurated into the joys of giving a press conference to the media assembled for this unprecedented event.

So the leap had been taken from schoolboy to apprentice Yorkshire cricketer, which meant lodging with Mr and Mrs Barker on Cardigan Road at the back of the Headingley ground. They were a delightful couple who had taken in many young Yorkshire players and, before the new stand was built, you used to be able to see the pitch from their house. Mrs Barker was a great cook and would make slap-up breakfasts, which we would consume in the kitchen that looked out onto the road, eyeing up the students who walked past. I shared a room on the top floor with Gavin Hamilton, who was to play for both Scotland and England, and Steve Bethel, son of my Sheffield cricket coach. Downstairs in a single room was future England colleague Craig White, and we lived there on a full-board basis.

To start with, I was at the academy and although the wages were hardly enriching I enjoyed every minute of it, whether it was in the nets, out on the pitch or in the pub. It was a time of work hard, play hard, with a typical evening starting with karaoke at the Oak, a renowned pub in Headingley. Every time we were there the same bloke used to sing 'Light My Fire' and would cop some abuse from us. Then it was on to Mr Craig's Club in town, where it was cut-price for students. And that was just Monday night.

Every Monday morning I would be dropped off by Mum or Dad and then each day it was down to Bradford Park Avenue, where the academy was based. Former player Mike Bore was the head coach and the morning would be taken up with nets. About 11.30 the call would go out from Mike, often to me, 'Young 'un, go and get the fish-'n'-chip orders!' So I would get a pen and paper and scramble around asking everyone what they wanted. It did not matter whether they were in the middle of a net at the time or not, the batsmen would stop. The odd cry would go up of 'Don't forget the mushy peas!' Once the lunch list had been assembled, two of the younger players would go off to get everyone's grub at the chippie.

Having digested, it would be fielding and fitness in the afternoon, or middle practice or a game. There were times when we were not playing and had to do maintenance work, such as painting the walls. It was old-school. I used to get driven around by a lad called David Jarvis, a fellow Sheffielder who was a bit of a character and was known as 'Spaceman'. On one occasion we turned up at a club ground for a match and were told by the coaching staff that the wicket would be a dream for left-handers to bat on. So even though he was a natural right-hander, he went out there and batted left-handed.

When we got back to Mrs Barker's late in the afternoon we

would watch a movie called *Road House* repeatedly, so much so that by the end we knew all the dialogue. *Silence of the Lambs* was another that I virtually learned by heart. Then it would be out for the evening in Headingley or Leeds. Tuesday night's favourite was a place called Yell.

It was great fun. Some of the lads, including Richard Kettleborough, Alex Morris, Gary Keedy and Chris Silverwood, would go on to have professional careers to a greater or lesser extent, while sadly Bethel and Jarvis did not quite make it. Bethel was another character, who blotted his copybook when the academy played a match against a Yorkshire Legends team at Park Avenue. The oldies team had the likes of Fred Trueman and Brian Close in it, and we were under strict instructions to be tactful and restrained and not take advantage of their advancing years. Bethel responded to this by continually smacking Trueman clean out of the ground, earning himself a major bollocking afterwards for failing to show enough respect.

The academy was the bottom rung of being a professional, and everyone's aim was to earn a place in the second XI. So the big event of every week was waiting for the announcement of the team. My first call came in early August when, during an academy game at East Bierley, I was sitting on a wall feeling dejected after getting out for 20, only to be told that I was being promoted the next day.

Doug Padgett, a mentor and staunch supporter of mine, basically just threw me in to see what would happen, and I considered it the biggest step of my life. Jack Bethel had instilled in me my basic technique, but Doug was great at explaining the finer points of what was required to play at a higher level and was a great influence on me. This really was an era with the kind of quirks that are now largely dying out from the game. Doug suffered from stiff shoulders, and if you were in the viewing room he would ask you to give him a neck massage while watching the game. If you got a fifty he would send you round the ground with a hat to collect a bit of cash.

On 6 August 1991 I made my debut for the second team against Sussex at Headingley, and it felt like a sharp incline. Everything was bigger, stronger, faster and although we won by five wickets my contribution was a modest six and 11. You feel a bit of a big cheese, a legend in your mind, when you make it to the second team, but one thing I was always good at was observing and absorbing. Relatively young guys like Jeremy Batty and Paul Grayson were in the first team at the time and I was always looking at them to see what was required to make that even bigger step, probably the largest leap you ever take in your career. It might be even more daunting than going from being a county player to Test player. From seconds to firsts means you are going from club grounds and glorified club cricket with no spectators to proper arenas and people talking about you in the media and so on for the first time.

I loved all the banter and the fooling about, and, while I was ambitious and took it pretty seriously, if I am honest I only became really professional when I got to about 25 years of age. Up until then I saw it partly as a paid hobby, something to have fun with, and much of the time was spent talking about what we were going to do in the evenings. A lot of the chat was about who had pulled which girl, and at the academy it was about who could come back with the best story from the night before. Sometimes it was more like Freshers' Week than deadly serious professional sport.

We were chased out of a nightclub en masse once, and a regular dietary ritual was to round off the evening with pizza. Bethel's party piece was to come up behind you and smack the pizza box from underneath so it would go all over you. Boys will be boys and debaggings were an almost nightly occurrence. I was usually singled out for the treatment, being dragged around the floor by my underpants.

My cricket upbringing in Yorkshire is the root of my fondness for a certain amount of the old school, and why my philosophy has always been to try and mix the best of that more carefree approach with the best of more modern thinking. On the positive side, you could be instinctive, develop as a human being and learn to think for yourself without constant coaching, but on the downside there was not sufficient attention paid to things such as catching technique. I was basically never taught how to catch properly, which is a major reason why I dropped so many over the years. It was not until the latter stage of my career that I began to catch better and I didn't have such a terror of the ball coming to me. Clearly there was not much wrong with my hand–eye coordination, so a lot must have been down to technical deficiencies and the wrong habits getting ingrained.

There was quite a hierarchy among the players at Yorkshire, and we would have to knock on the first-team dressing room door before entering. A lot of the senior players would talk down to the youngsters and demand that you fetched their kit. 'Young 'un do this, young 'un do that, go and get us a cup of tea.' The late Phil Carrick, who I later learned a lot from, would try and get you to do his laundry. He once asked this of a young Darren Gough and was told in no uncertain terms what he could do with his laundry. Goughy regularly fell out with senior players because he would not take anything from any of them.

I tended to be more diplomatic and accepted that you had to earn respect, although one or two of the older players felt threatened by the younger ones and avoided passing any knowledge on. Opener Simon Kellett never seemed that keen on me, and Ashley Metcalfe was particularly unhelpful – he was probably right to be fearful, as I went on to take his spot in the team. But he was the exception and most were fine, including Carrick, who when he became second-team skipper always said that you should concentrate on spinning the ball as hard as you can, before focusing on control and accuracy later. You do not hear that so much these days, but in the modern game if you do not spin it much, you are not going to survive.

When Steve Oldham came in as coach the whole level of discipline upped considerably. He insisted on more professionalism and would not let you get away with much, being very hot on the everyday things, which looking back was a good thing. You would have to shave on a daily basis and wear your blazer at lunch, and he was a stickler for punctuality. He had his faults as well and could be a miserable sod, but the habits he began to instil stood me in good stead. I became a convert to being on time, and even now I do not like lateness in other people.

Second-team captain Kevin Sharp also knew how to be stern. I once turned up 15 minutes late for a game against Middlesex with my room-mate Mark Broadhurst because the alarm clock had not gone off and Kevin absolutely savaged us in front of everyone else to make sure we all got the message. It scared the life out of me at the time.

My first full year with the seconds was 1992, when I started making consistent runs at the lovely out-grounds where we used to play. I made a decent hundred at Harrogate that got me talked about and Todmorden was always a favourite, largely for the unparalleled quality of its bacon sandwiches. I was regarded very much as an all-rounder and was also taking my share of wickets, with Geoff Miller, later England's

...oming in to give me some specialist help with

...my early years with Yorkshire I was often involved
...ngland age-group cricket, which I loved, even though
t.. representative stuff was generally viewed with suspicion by
many within the club. The fear seemed to be that after meeting
up with the England lads you would come back a different
player, in a negative sense, but I found it only broadened your
horizons. Yorkshire might have resented it, but from the start
I was always very comfortable in whatever England set-up I
was in.

On the back of my second-team runs, I made my England
Under-19s debut at the start of a year of significant breakthrough for me, 1993. Shortly after the New Year dawned we
left for India on what was to prove a difficult tour, at least in
terms of how I felt. I had never really been away from home
before, certainly not for the best part of two months, and I
found that pretty hard to handle and really missed it. Outbreaks
of Delhi belly were something new as well. It was not that we
were staying in the lap of luxury, often going off the beaten
track to places like Ghaziabad, where we had a Test at the end
of January.

I was one of the younger players in a good set of lads led
by Matthew Walker of Kent, and did OK, making 43 in the
first match. Again there is the temptation to think you have
cracked it when you play for the England Under-19s, but history
shows that there is no automatic progression to senior honours.
Of the lads I played with on that trip the only other one to go
on to wear a senior England jersey was Glen Chapple, a considerable talent who won a solitary one-day cap against Ireland.

Chapple was among the group of us who got into mischief
after we had been taken out to the British High Commission

in Delhi on that trip. We were over-enthusiastic in availing ourselves of the free wine and when we got back to the Taj hotel, definitely one of the smarter places we stayed, we all jumped into the swimming pool in the early hours and got in trouble for it. We drew the series and I had my first experience of touring the subcontinent, something you had better come to terms with if you want to make it in cricket.

In the summer we played the West Indies and I made a hundred in the one-day series, followed by 119 in the first Test at Trent Bridge. After that innings I was in the dressing room when the phone rang and was passed to me. It was Steve Oldham, telling me that I was to report to Old Trafford for first-team duty the following week. They had suffered a batting collapse in their latest match and he and then skipper Martyn Moxon, always a great supporter of mine, had decided that it was worth throwing me into the Roses match. My heart rate doubled, and it was hard to concentrate on the rest of the game.

I had a couple of days at home with Mum and Dad before heading to the hotel in Manchester ahead of the game, as in those days you just rocked up the night before. Richie Richardson was there, Peter Hartley, Martyn and Goughy, who was very much the rising star at the time and being talked about as a certain England player for the future. He had already been in the team for a few years and that season, encouraged to bowl as quick as he could by Richie, he was really making his mark.

The next day I walked down to breakfast in my blazer to try and force down some food, although I was so nervous it was the last thing I wanted. I was thinking of the Lancashire attack, the likes of Wasim Akram, Phil DeFreitas and Peter Martin. I had never played in front of a crowd of nearly 10,000 people before and now I was about to walk out to open the innings with Martyn in the county of my birth, representing the enemy to whom I had defected.

Martyn was a very reassuring presence and there was nobody I would have been happier walking out with. I thought he was a brilliant player and used to look at him and wonder why he was not playing for England, thinking that if he could not make the national team then I had no chance. I flicked DeFreitas for four through midwicket to get off the mark and worked my way to double figures. Chapple told me afterwards that DeFreitas, knowing that we had played together in the Under-19s, had asked him what I was likely to do to the short ball. Chappy apparently told the bowler that it was certain I would do nothing more than duck. So he duly bounced me and I hooked him out of the ground for six, all the way onto the railway tracks. The bowler was not best pleased with his colleague's honest advice.

I had never faced anything like Wasim, who was on his way to taking 8–68. He absolutely peppered me, and the physio had to come out twice to perform running repairs on my bruised arm and body, but I was hanging in there while wickets fell at the other end. Neil Fairbrother, who was later to become my business manager, was fielding in the slips alongside Warren Hegg. He tells me that they turned to each other after a bit and agreed they had just seen a future England player. Battered and blue, I was eventually caught down the leg side for 64 and walked off feeling a mixture of disappointment and absolute exhilaration. It had been a real baptism on a quick deck, and I had loved the battle against one of history's great left-armers. What I found far more scary, not for the last time, was the fielding.

It was a fantastic week, and not just because we won what turned out to be a terrific match by 19 runs, with me making a total of 92, enough to convince myself that I could play at this level. The social side of first-team life was also quite a reve-lation, as after each day's play we would stop for a couple of pints on the way back to our hotel in Bowden, before heading into Hale village and its wine bars. In fact, I seem to recall that scoring-wise it was a fairly successful week in all sorts of ways. This was undoubtedly the way to play cricket, I decided.

Another tradition I was swiftly introduced to was the Saturday Night Club, which regularly took place prior to the Sunday League games. For my initiation I had to dress in a toga and walk through the hotel lobby and into a private room that looked like a scene from *I Claudius*. Everyone else was in a toga as well and for an hour our convention of Roman emperors/cricketers played drinking games, basically, with a whole series of toasts and silly forfeits such as trying to eat a certain amount of Jacob's Cream Crackers within two minutes. I had by now been christened Virgil, not so much due to a possible facial resemblance to the *Thunderbirds* character, but because I spoke quite slowly.

Every single team member had a toga on, there was no getting out of it, and that night we had the former England opener Barry Wood as special guest, as he was a friend of Oldham's. After the ceremonies everyone went up to their room to get changed before going out. We did not actually stay out partic-ularly late at night on all these occasions, but between 7.30 and 11 p.m. it always seemed to be one long Happy Hour. At the time it was very much the norm, part of the culture, and nobody really questioned it. Saturdays were always the biggest nights, which may partly explain why I was a slow starter in the short form of the game – I was usually hung-over on a Sunday.

*

As I was required for England age-group duties I played just one more Championship match that summer, and in the autumn was named as captain for the Under-19 trip to Sri Lanka scheduled for early 1994. This was the first time I properly came across Marcus Trescothick, my future opening partner for England, who was universally known then as 'Banger'. This was because of his addiction to sausages, and I noticed how much of his own food he brought on the trip because he was so suspicious of the local fare.

More pertinently, I noticed what a magnificent striker of a cricket ball he was. He had an incredibly natural swing of the bat, not much movement of the feet and was completely obsessed with the game, always wanting to fiddle with your bat and your grips. He was exactly the same then as he was when he became an established England star. We all loved the game but nobody but was quite as besotted with it as Marcus, and he was less inclined to treat it as a way for typical young lads to have extra-curricular fun.

We were in the bar of the Hilton in Colombo one night on that tour, separated into two booths, when we started throwing a few nuts at each other. Suddenly I was aware that we were getting pelted by a group of locals from another area of the bar. Then one of them came over, we assumed in a friendly manner, and without warning delivered a huge punch to Kevin Innes, latterly of Northamptonshire. Dean Conway, the big Welshman who was our physio, got up and started wrestling with about four of them and sent the main offender sprawling across a couple of tables. It all seemed so out of character for Sri Lankans, who normally seemed such gentle people. A few of us, including Glamorgan bowler Darren Thomas, chased them out with Dean and they ran off, but the unlucky Kevin was in a pretty bad way from the haymaker he received, his whole face swollen up with the force of the blow.

Even in my early days as a captain I tried to focus on thinking about how we could perform best as a unit, and a lot of my thinking was informed by what I had seen at Yorkshire. I had already noticed the strong element of self-preservation in county cricket, the divisions between factions that led to some negativity, particularly between a few of the older players and the younger ones. From the start I was against the one-size-fits-all mentality and tried to accommodate different characters in the team, making sure there was an inclusive atmosphere around the place.

As I was to do nearly 10 years later, I encouraged players to express themselves and be aggressive if they possibly could. At Yorkshire nobody seemed to mind you getting out as a batter as long as you were playing a defensive stroke when dismissed, but if you were out playing an attacking shot there was the allegation that you were playing 'like a millionaire'. Man-management was already a strong interest, but the only vague captaincy ambitions I had were to lead Yorkshire one day in the distant future. Given my fixation that if Martyn Moxon was not good enough for England then I would never be, full international cricket was the last thing on my mind, let alone as skipper.

What I found very helpful on that tour was the fact that I had already played first-team cricket for Yorkshire, which gave me a lot of kudos among the other lads. Making 64 against the legendary Wasim Akram in full flight on a quick bouncy wicket at Old Trafford on my debut in the Roses match was regarded with some awe by my fellow teenagers, and that imbued me with a certain authority.

That summer was to be my first as a fully fledged Yorkshire

player and the first that brought me 1,000 first-class runs. My maiden century came against Oxford University, which I kept in its proper perspective, and it meant far more when I made it into three figures against Somerset at Bradford. I had got to 96 and was struggling to control my nerves ahead of what would be my first authentic major achievement in the first team. Graham Rose came in to bowl and put one on a length, which I middled, but only straight to extra cover. My heart immediately sank, but the ball just kept on going and marginally cleared the fielder for four. I knew it was going to be my day.

It was nice to reach the landmark at Bradford, where I had started with the academy, and it was a massive boost to my confidence. These are the building blocks on which your career is constructed, and another was put in place when I made 117 at Luton against a Northants team containing Curtly Ambrose. I did not hit him for many but coped reasonably well with his relentless accuracy and bounce. My travelling partner by now was Ambrose's fellow West Indian Richie Richardson, who would drive me around in his big Mercedes. He took me under his wing, and was so laid-back it was untrue. I spent hours and hours in the car with Richie, far more than was necessary because he was always pulling into lay-bys to have an hour's nap. It once took us eight hours to get back from Kent. To the frustration of Martyn and Steve Oldham, I even tried to bat like him at one stage, cutting and pulling everything I could.

The season ended with 1,066 runs scored at 36.75 and me thinking that I had cracked it. Therefore it was probably a good thing when I was picked for the following winter's England A tour and had a bit of a shocker. We went to India and Bangladesh and I could not get into any form at all, probably the worst performer in the whole squad. I looked at players like Mark Ramprakash and realised that I still had a very long way to go. Mentally I was nowhere near ready to play for England, and I was due a setback to show me where I really stood.

Slightly chastened, I put together a better season in 1995, which resulted in me getting awarded my Yorkshire cap late on at Scarborough. The tradition was that you had to go out and buy six bottles of champagne to be consumed by everyone in the dressing room, which I duly did, and then you had to keep the corks. I think I might still have them somewhere.

Another solid if unspectacular season for Yorkshire after that got me picked for the A tour to Australia that took place late in 1996 under the captaincy of Adam Hollioake. Again I was hardly a standout performer, but it taught me a huge amount about the game and captaincy, and about how to engender a positive spirit around a group of lads. We did very well as a team on that tour, beating Australia's academy and two state sides, South Australia and Victoria.

Adam was a big influence, in that he showed me the value of creating fun on and off the field. He wanted us to have a go and be uninhibited whether we were batting, bowling or fielding. Mike Gatting was the coach and David Graveney the manager, and there was a real energy to the whole outfit – although Gatt's tendency to have a kip in the dressing room was not the most energetic thing about us. I got out in Melbourne against Victoria and walked in to find our coach fast asleep on the floor, only for him to talk me through how I had been dismissed an hour later. 'You can only have seen it on the video, mate!' I told him. Gatt loved his football to the extent that our warm-up kickabouts used to last about an hour. The physio Dean Conway had also graduated with me from the Under-19s to the As, and continued to mirror my career later on. He was a great tourist in every sense and ran quite a few of the social activities. He became a close confidant of Duncan Fletcher, and while they were very different characters, they complemented each other perfectly as extrovert and intro-vert.

Off the field that trip was like a stag do a lot of the time. We enjoyed ourselves so much that Grav once took to stationing himself in the hotel lobby to clock us coming in after an evening out, the only problem being that he did not stay up late enough. With no sign of us by 1 a.m. he assumed that we must have come back in, when in fact everyone was still out partying. We probably went over the top at times, but the end results seemed to justify the methods.

My career was motoring along decently enough with Yorkshire, although the progress was far from stratospheric as I struggled to pile on huge scores at a home ground that was not the easiest for batting. I was consistently just above or below the 1,000 runs-per-season mark as we moved into the late 1990s and the adjustments I was making to my technique were not quite doing the trick. It did not help that I was prob-ably not at the required level of professionalism, still happy to be the daft northern lad more regularly than I should have been.

I started studying the technique of the England batsmen to see what they were doing that I could try and emulate. The big difference between them and me was that they had significant trigger movements as they prepared their stroke, while I was trying to stand still at the crease until the last possible split second. When I examined myself I found that I was actually moving a little, and I was also more vulnerable to the ball nipping back from outside off stump than most batsmen. So I tried to develop more of a trigger, but a breakthrough was proving difficult to achieve.

One of the more notable matches came in 1998 when we played Durham at the Riverside and I spent every minute of the match on the field. We fielded first and then, as opener, I batted throughout our first innings for 177 before we fielded again and then knocked the runs off for the loss of one wicket with me still at the crease. A young Steve Harmison was playing in that match and bowled notably fast, while sometimes spraying it all over the place.

We had some titanic one-day battles with Lancashire around the mid to late 1990s, which was superb preparation for what, unbeknown to me, was going to be my future. In 1995 we played them in the NatWest quarter-finals at Headingley, which we won with three balls to spare thanks to one of those chasing masterclasses regularly handed out by Michael Bevan, our overseas player. We were having our team talk on the outfield from David Byas and I remember the odd Lancashire player in his tracksuit carrying a cup of tea onto the field, which gave off a terrible vibe. At that moment I knew we would beat them, and we duly won, only to bomb in the semi-finals against Northants.

The following year at Old Trafford the old enemy beat us by one wicket in the Benson & Hedges Cup semis. We seemed to have at least one of these humdingers per season and the grounds would be rammed full, creating an electric atmosphere. When we met them at Old Trafford again in the NatWest semis that same season – we lost again – they even had to segregate the crowd, with 3,000 Yorkshire fans in their own enclosure.

In truth I never felt that, out on the park, there was a particularly special edge to Roses encounters, certainly nothing like England–Australia, and the players got on pretty well off the pitch. If there was a bitter rivalry in my time at Yorkshire it was with Surrey, particularly during the time when Bingo Byas was skipper, because he absolutely hated them. He viewed them as the worst type of arrogant southerners and was not alone in being desperate to beat the boys from the metropolis. 'Just look at the way they walk,' he once said as they headed for the changing rooms, his voice dripping with venom about a team he used to refer to as the 'Brown Hatters'.

Our near misses continued when we fell in the B&H semis in 1998 to Essex, but we did manage to get to the short-lived B&H Super Cup final at Lord's in 1999, where we were downed by then one-day kings Gloucestershire.

We were a bit of a nearly team in the one-dayers and I was starting to wonder if I was going to be a nearly player. At Yorkshire we were desperate to play in a big final at Lord's but we seemed to have a psychological block whenever we got in sight of one. From a personal point of view, I was struggling to put together the kind of headline-grabbing sequence of scores to push my case for international recognition. I was aware that I was talked about as someone with unusual potential, but I could not translate that into the sort of mentions in the papers that all players look out for when they feel they are close to England.

It would be convenient if I could cite some seismic incident that changed my attitude towards cricket and made me become more professional, but that would be untrue. It was rather that around the summer of 1998 it gradually dawned on me that, nearly five years on from having tackled Wasim at Old Trafford on my debut, the time was coming when I really had to train on. There was no great revelation or heart-to-heart that changed things. About the nearest I came to those were when my mum would occasionally tell me off on the phone for playing some stupid shot and getting out. I would tell her where to get off but normally realise later that she was spot on.

I averaged over 40 for the first time in 1998 and was chosen to captain England A in Zimbabwe and South Africa. While still enjoying myself off the pitch, the big nights out were getting less frequent and the physical and mental preparation closer to what was required. In short I was maturing, to a degree. We went off to Africa in early 1999 and, with a young Andrew Flintoff and Steve Harmison in tow, we beat our Zimbabwe counterparts with me making 131 in the second match. Having won every game as skipper, I came back buoyed, resolving to put in the big season that would propel my career forwards.

The summer of 1999 was arguably when English cricket reached its nadir. The staging of the World Cup was by all accounts extremely inept and we, the host nation, bowed out in the group section, with Alec Stewart and David Lloyd paying for it with their jobs as captain and coach respectively. Then we had a series against a very beatable New Zealand team and, after starting well, quickly began to struggle. The whole England set-up was in a state of flux and it was obvious to any aspiring international player that there were going to be opportunities.

I had worked this out, and subsequently put undue pressure on myself to make a final thrust towards my goal. As is the case with many things in life, wanting something so badly is counter-productive and the closer you get to it, the more it seems to slip away. Apart from our match at Chelmsford, where I scored a hundred in each innings, I just could not string together a consistent run for Yorkshire, and it was really getting to me as I saw what was now Nasser Hussain's England team struggling against the Kiwis.

What probably did help me, in hindsight, was that I played a few nice one-day innings on the television, which is where Duncan Fletcher viewed most of his county cricket. Despite that, I started to get a little neurotic and selfish, blaming the pitches and even wondering if I needed to get away from Yorkshire to play on more batting-friendly surfaces. I should have been tougher with myself and knuckled down, but I was fretting and looking for excuses. In May I scored those 251 runs against Essex, which turned out to be not far off a third of my whole season's haul. I thought that might be lift-off, but my form began to mirror that of England in their concurrent Test series. That summer I was to average only 27.12, and so despite the clamour for change in the Test team in the wake of our loss to New Zealand, I had no inkling I would be among the new intake that was being called for.

On 30 August, fresh from making 2 and 2 in our Championship match against Nottinghamshire, I was sitting in my flat in Sheffield when the phone rang. It was David Graveney telling me that I was going to South Africa with England that winter. I was flabbergasted, having at best expected another stint of winter sunshine with the A team, which was about what my recent form deserved.

Instead, I was to be one of several new faces brought in supposedly to reinvigorate England after the disastrous summer the team had endured. Nasser and Duncan had met for only a few minutes before being unveiled as the new captain–coach partnership, making it one of the most intriguing blind dates you could imagine. And I was going to be part of the new adventure.

While I would have liked to have made it onto the full England scene rather sooner, this was just the right point in my life to make the breakthrough. I was about to turn 25, had really started to grow up and, most importantly from a pure cricketing point of view, I had experienced a lot. I had been a good boy, a bad boy, experimented with my technique, had some soaring highs, a few setbacks, phases of drift and frustration, been away for long periods and seen most of what the game could throw at you short of full international cricket. A lot of players are promoted before they are ready and suffer in the long run, but for me the timing was perfect.

Delighted and liberated after my call-up, I went out the next day and stroked a free-flowing 153 against Kent at Scarborough. Who says it is not a mental game?

4

I Never Saw
Phil Tufnell Eat

Duncan Fletcher was a very important figure in my career, but as I got on the plane to Johannesburg I had no idea how much I was in his debt even before I had got to know him. Later I found out that, while he had a limited input about selection for that squad, his main insistence had been that I be taken to South Africa. I was his personal pick, based on fairly fleeting glimpses of my batting, and very much the 17th man.

You will not hear me raising any objections when people talk about his famed eye for a player. In the summer of 1998 I had played against Glamorgan and, even though I did not make many, apparently Duncan had seen something he thought he could work with. It doubtless helped that for some reason I had always enjoyed a good record against the Welsh county and probably would have impressed them. Duncan listened a lot to the likes of Matthew Maynard about county cricketers, and I would have got a pretty decent report card. Who cares, Fletcher was obviously a genius! More seriously, I was always struck by how little time he needed to size batsmen up and assess whether he could develop them or not.

So it seemed I was hardly a unanimous pick, but as it was I felt very comfortable right from the start, even when we first assembled at the airport for the overnight flight. I looked around the other players and they were all guys I was familiar with – another advantage of having been round the block in county cricket several times. My mate from Yorkshire Gavin Hamilton, who had made quite an impact for Scotland in the World Cup, was among the several other new picks, as was Darren Maddy of Leicestershire and Graeme Swann, then of Northants. Later it was an aspect I looked at quite closely – those who seemed to be at ease in the new environment and did not have that startled-rabbit look about them because of where they were and the company they were in. I felt secure within myself as we flew down to Johannesburg, eagerly anticipating everything that lay ahead.

Early on in the tour we netted out at Centurion in Pretoria and Alan Mullally, then one of the more established bowlers, made sure he gave me a decent working over. He was relatively brisk in those days and peppered me a bit, possibly under orders, and as he tried to dig them in short I began to pull and hook him and give as good as I was getting. Duncan and Nasser hadn't had much chance to examine me before that but apparently liked what they saw.

Our first match was a one-dayer against Nicky Oppenheimer's XI, the diamond magnate who had his own opulent ground outside Johannesburg, and that was where I had my first stroke of luck. Mullally had a niggling injury and I was called up at the last minute to bat at number seven. We lost a few early wickets and I ended up making 59 not out, largely in the company of Mike Atherton, as we got ourselves to somewhere like respectability. The most significant thing about that match was that it was the last time Dean Headley played for England before he limped off with an ankle injury, but for me it seemed to be the passport to the number four spot. They had put out quite a strong side, including Pat Symcox and the then firebrand Nantie Hayward, and I had played all right.

I suppose it reinforced to me what high-level sport is all about – getting the opportunity and then having the ability to take it. I do not know what would have happened if I had not had the unexpected chance that day; I am just very glad I did. There is no doubt that luck plays its part, although I tend to be a believer in the cliché that you largely make your own.

Before the first-class warm-up games began there was another one-dayer in the Johannesburg suburbs at Benoni, and although I did not feature, that was where I learned the perils of Duncan's fielding drills. At the end of play those who had not partici-pated had to take 10 consecutive high catches and then do a crossover fielding drill which involved chasing three balls on two different sides. It was physically tough and I was evidently not as fit as I should have been, because it left me absolutely knackered. I had never done it before and it hit me hard, so much so that I threw up behind a tree at the side of the pitch. Duncan was very good at incorporating fitness work into cricket tasks and he thought it hilarious as I emptied my stomach. He knew I could do with some work on my conditioning, but at least I had put everything into his drills.

As ever, I was always observing and fascinated by different aspects of this new environment, one of the features being Mark Butcher and Phil Tufnell's fondness for a drink. I also loved the media attention at practice because with them watching it felt like a cup final to me, having come from county cricket. I liked being on show with all the kit on and the England bags lying around. I enjoyed doing the interviews and the sense that you were in the middle of something big. The whole circus was very exciting and had gripped me from the moment I had received my official England gear at home, coffin and all. We had joined up for a few preparatory training sessions and Nasser had stood up and said that anyone who did not want to come should say so there and then. I think he had the odd one in mind who had personal problems at the time, but I was totally up for it.

Overall, the set-up seemed much more professional than anything I had known and there was far more talk about strategy. There was also greater stress and pressure, but that was energising, and I loved things like going out for dinner with Athers and Nasser and joining in the talk while doing lots of watching and listening. It was a good bunch of lads on that tour, and we had plenty of golf with me and Gav taking Goughy and Nasser's money. Nasser used to sulk when he was beaten and accuse us of cheating, sometimes refusing to pay up.

I discovered how well you got treated, and that there were always people around willing to do you favours, such as the diamond dealer eager to give us a good price for his wares. Vodafone had a representative organising your social activities and you never seemed to have to pay for anything – it was almost like having a team concierge.

I did not quite know how to take Fletch at first, partly because I did not know whether he had picked me or if it had been the selectors as a whole. Straight away, though, he was working on my batting in the nets, which I took as a good sign.

It seems incredible now that, in addition to the initial nets and limited-over warm-ups, we had no fewer than three first-class four-day games before the opening Test on that trip. Within five or six years, preparation matches would be cut to the bone, but nobody could accuse us of being undercooked on this tour. These days, there is so much cricket that it would be impossible to have such a build-up and players have to become adept at visualising rather than working it out in the middle. Deep down, I do not think you will find the modern player complaining too much.

The first of the first-class games was in Cape Town, where I went in at number four ahead of Chris Adams and Maddy, both of whom would probably have assumed they were above me in the pecking order. We drew and went on to Bloemfontein before our final warm-up at Centurion against a very strong Northerns/Gauteng team. Nasser had indicated to me before the match that I was in line for my full England debut, which I already suspected but was happy to have confirmed. We had a good win and I made 85 as well as taking a few wickets and, not always predictably for me, some catches.

At the end of that match we had what will go down as one of the better nights I had on tour. We all assembled at the Butcher's Shop, a very public restaurant in a square by our hotel in Sandton, the fortified shopping and hotel complex where we were billeted. We had a great sing-song, with Chris Read excelling. This really appealed to the club cricketer/ Sunday-morning footballer in me from my younger days and I remain a great advocate of the team night out. How good is this, I thought to myself.

We were in a pretty good frame of mind, having seen off the Northerns team and made South Africa aware that we were unlikely to be pushovers. What I really noticed after that dinner was how the atmosphere changed in terms of the preparation, and how the senior players suddenly started to switch on properly. There was a whole different vibe at practice; everything was more serious, with more media around and a few supporters starting to come in. Someone like Butch was never a big one for warm-up games, but when it came to three days before the Tests you could see him tuning in.

We had now been in South Africa for a month, and the next day it would be my Test debut. The night before, I went into the square for a rather more sober feed with some of the lads. I did not sleep a great deal and at breakfast could hardly eat because of the tightness in my gut. I got on the bus thinking how dark it was, and it was already clear that the fulfilment of my Test dream would not be greeted by glorious sunshine. Nichola's dad Ray and his mate had travelled down to watch and the text messages were pouring in. Mum and Dad were due to come later on the tour.

When we reached the ground it was probably even more miserable, and after Nasser had formally presented me with my cap on the outfield I was bewildered to see him going out to toss up. I thought, hang on, this was the kind of light we might just have a go in on the county circuit – surely they must have different rules on the international scene. There was a slight fatalism about at the time, and we just assumed we would be batting in what were going to be horrible conditions.

All I can recall, however, was a huge sense of excitement that I was going to be batting for England that day – whatever the weather – and that I would be walking down that famous tunnel at the Wanderers into the bullring. These were the best sort of nerves, a buzz from thinking that you would probably be up against two all-time greats in Shaun Pollock and Allan Donald in their own backyard in conditions favourable to them. I thought it was going to be good fun.

Nasser duly lost the toss and the dressing room was very tense as I looked around. Atherton was in a corner putting on his scraggy pads with kit everywhere; Butch was cool as anything listening to some music; Nasser was playing with his grips, anxiously rehearsing in the mirror. And then out they strolled to bat. It was a relatively small crowd, hardly surprising

given the cold, and I was sitting in the comfy chairs outside
the dressing rooms wondering why on earth we were playing
in this light.

It is fair to say that the coach–captaincy ticket of Fletcher
and Hussain did not get off to a dream start in its first Test
together. In the borderline gloom Athers was bowled by Donald
with the second ball of the opening over, which was my cue to
stand up and stretch and play some strokes in the mirror to
check the bat was coming down straight. I do not know why
we do that because it is pretty obvious, but I used to like having
a look at myself.

I had barely got back out to the viewing area when Nasser
was out in the next over to Pollock. Showtime. The Wanderers
offers about the longest walk out to the wicket of any ground
on the international circuit. You have to go back into the
dressing room and out again, passing everybody on your way
twice before you walk along the grass verge and past the South
African dressing room. Then you walk down that long tunnel
and then, for this virgin Test batsman, you look up at the grey
sky and then at the scoreboard, which is telling you that it is
2–2.

It was the last ball of the over, so I knew I would have a
chance to look at what was happening before taking strike.
Unfortunately things had somewhat deteriorated by then, as
when I got round to taking strike we were 2–4, with Butch and
Alec both having been dispatched by Donald, who was
boomeranging it all over the place.

This might have seemed like a terrifying prospect, although
if I am honest it relieved some of the pressure on me because,
with our four big guns gone, I knew that I could not do any
worse. Much as I would like to portray my debut as having
been heroic under fire, the truth is that it is easier to come in

at 2–2 on your debut than at 200–2 on a flat wicket full of runs. Chris Adams came out at 2–4 and asked, 'What's it doing?' to which I replied, 'Don't ask me, I haven't faced an effing ball yet.' He then said, 'What do you reckon?' and I observed, 'Well, we can't do any worse.'

I felt remarkably calm, in fact, which was strange considering Boucher, Cronje, Klusener, Kirsten and Kallis were in the slip cordon waiting to snaffle me. Pollock was seaming it both ways and Donald was coming up with these massive in-duckers. Within a few balls I had flung my bat at a wide one on a full length from Donald that flew over gully for four and I was away. Then I edged one through the covers off Pollock for another boundary. Klusener and Cronje were light relief after those two, and when I whipped the latter through midwicket I was thinking this could be my day.

After Chris's departure to Donald for 16 Freddie Flintoff came in, a very familiar face but another virgin tourist at full level, and we started playing a few shots and having fun. Then on 33, with Pollock having come back on, I got an inside edge and was caught behind. Fun over and England 90–6. Ten minutes later I was sitting in the dressing room with my pads still on and Nasser came up, saying that if I applied myself like that I would play 50 Tests. I was replaced by Gavin, who went on to get a pair in his only Test match. He just never looked comfortable in this environment, a very different figure from the one with a bit of swagger I had known at Yorkshire, which was maybe a front after all.

We went on to be dismissed for 122, but not before I had learned a lesson about how much scrutiny you are under as an England player. Mullally, our hapless number 11, had come in at the end and somehow managed to top-edge Donald for six over square leg. Even the bowler saw a slightly funny side to this and on the balcony it was an opportunity for about our first laugh of the day, given our woeful predicament. In the next day's papers back in England a picture appeared of us all giggling at Al's great triumph with one headline reading: 'WHAT ARE YOU LOT LAUGHING AT?' On Yorkshire duty you could do anything while watching, but obviously not here.

The toss had been very important and, in any case, they were a better team than us. They batted positively and I dropped Klusener at gully, having lost the ball in the seats behind. We were out in the field for 138 overs, and that was another thing that really struck me about international cricket compared with the county game: I found it absolutely draining in the field and was unused to feeling that your every move was being watched.

We got rolled over in the second innings, and my contribution was a modest five, lbw to one from Donald that kept slightly low. We had not made them bat again, and over a couple of drinks at the end of the match I reflected on the intensity of the experience and how I had been completely zonked each night when I got back to the hotel. When playing for Yorkshire I would usually have the energy to go out and see what was around wherever we were, but in this match I just wanted to get my head down.

The relatively sedate pace of the tour compared with modern itineraries meant that there was a two-week gap before the next Test and time to take in a four-dayer against KwaZulu-Natal in Durban. It was there that I came across a tall off-spinner batting number nine called Kevin Pietersen. He bowled nearly 56 overs at us and I was among his four victims. Afterwards he came up to me and asked if Yorkshire were looking for a player – I do not think I was the only one he approached – and although I thought he had bowled very nicely, I did not think there was much potential for him at Headingley. I did actually pass on his name to the county, but they were not interested at that stage. The only memorable thing about that match was that when Nasser got 103 it was the first century that anyone had scored for England that year – and it was 4 December!

There was a lot of free time, and apart from playing golf there was plenty of opportunity for drinking. The most extra-ordinary thing was that I never saw Phil Tufnell eat on that whole tour apart from, that is, the peanuts and crisps on offer at the bar. I was once on *A Question of Sport* with him when he was a captain of one of the teams and we had a sandwich together. They were about the first solids I can remember witnessing going into his mouth, if you do not count cigarettes. I could not help laughing when Nasser told the Schofield Report that there was too much drinking among the England team around 2006–07 – it was nothing compared with my first tour! We did train hard, though, and I was really enjoying working with Fletcher and was so impressed by the highly organised net sessions and fielding drills, which were a step up from anything I had previously known. I was having a great time all round.

The next Test was at Port Elizabeth, where Fletch sat us down and told us that he had heard a lot about the English bulldog spirit, and that now he wanted to see it in action. That was pretty much all he said, and it seemed to do the trick. In response to their 450 we made 373, with Athers getting 108 in six hours and 20 minutes, an innings that taught me some more about international cricket.

He had bagged a pair at the Wanderers, but I had noticed that his reaction to that and to making a vital century remained more or less the same. It reinforced my belief that it was essen-tial to keep an even keel at this pressurised level and not to beat yourself up just because you had got out cheaply twice.

Another thing that was registering on my radar was the negative tendency that runs through South African cricket, as they
took more than 92 overs to get to 224–4 declared in their
second innings. They could have gone for the throat a lot more,
and we were able to bat out the 77 overs they left themselves
to bowl us out. I came in at 5–2 this time, and batted out two
and a half hours with Nasser before I was erroneously given
out caught behind down leg when the ball had clipped my backside. Fielding in the match was noticeably easier for me after
the hard labour of Johannesburg and I am sure it was partly
down to the presence of the Barmy Army. There was a song
they sang to take the mickey out of Allan Donald that greatly
amused me, about his famous run-out in the World Cup semi-
final, and it helped to pass the time.

It was an honourable draw for us and the caravan moved
on to the unprepossessing location of East London, where I
suffered the first injury setback of my England career. Garnett
Kruger, who later turned up in county cricket, hit me on the
end of my middle finger and broke it, ruling me out of the
Boxing Day Test at Durban, although it was only a small hairline fracture. Sitting it out allowed me to enjoy what was my
first ever warm Christmas, which was a pleasantly novel experience. Nichola came over and we had a sociable time, as we
relaxed in what seemed the slightly strange humidity.

Cape Town was a fantastic atmosphere for the new millen-
nium as thousands of fans flocked into town, although with
my finger repaired and the match starting on 2 January our
celebrations on the waterfront had to be restrained. The only
hammering going on was the one we received on the pitch
before the massed ranks of English support at glorious
Newlands. I had reached 40 not out overnight and was set for
a big one, only to get out early the next morning when Kirsten

caught me at short leg. From 213–3 we added only 45 runs, and that was the match effectively over.

We subsided badly in the second innings to 126 all out, with Klusener getting me for five and Freddie already homeward bound, unable to bat with a broken foot. Another innings loss saw us consigned to a series defeat, and we were particularly down because we had put on a poor show in a such a prestigious Test.

Quite often that would have meant a relatively uneventful end to the Test leg of the tour, with a solitary dead rubber to be played, but that final match at Centurion turned out to be anything but insignificant. There was another factor around at the time which meant that we had everything to play for. Central contracts were at last going to be introduced at the start of our summer, and there was a lot of talk about them among the lads. Nobody knew quite what they would entail or how much they would be worth – or at least I did not – but I did go into that last Test thinking that with a good performance I might be able to snare one for myself.

It was, to put it mildly, a strange old Test, with the build-up to it wrecked by constant bands of rain lashing the High Veld. As it happened, the match got off to a relatively prompt start, but then the bad weather set in and it looked as if we were just marking time – in my case before going home, because I was not involved in the one-day series. They batted first and in fairly ugly conditions we restricted them to 155–6 by the close of a shortened first day. And then it rained and rained, meaning that there was no play for the middle three days. We hardly even bothered making the long journey to the ground from Johannesburg, and I followed the pack at night, going out for dinner, with a fair bit of wine shifted. On the fourth night there was actually quite a session in the bar, spearheaded by Goughy, on the assumption that it was all over as a contest.

Nasser and I knew nothing of Hansie Cronje's ulterior motives; I was Steve Naive at that stage of my career, and when it became clear that there might be some sort of run chase created I was just delighted that there was going to be something at stake and thought nothing of it. In fact, I was put on to bowl at Klusener to speed up their run rate, but he kept punching me through the covers with such regularity that there was a danger of it getting out of hand.

I was as shocked as anyone when the truth about Cronje's intentions in that match emerged, and the game went through a period of blood-letting over the whole match-fixing issue. Has it disappeared from the game completely? All I will say is that I have seen things on isolated occasions in recent years which, as someone with plenty more experience than I had back then, have looked pretty suspicious to me. It is a difficult area, and one that is hard to talk about without getting m'learned friends from the legal profession involved. What I do think is important is that the game continues to be very vigilant on the matter, particularly with the proliferation of limited-over competitions on the subcontinent.

They set us 249 to win in about 75 overs, and I was thankful to have a relatively clear head that day because the innings I played marked a significant point in my career. With Stewy I formed the match-winning partnership and I showed off my repertoire of shots in a way I had not done before. Coming together at 102–4 we took it on to 228, and then I was out, infuriatingly, for 69 with us nine runs short of victory. Hitting Pieter Strydom over cover for my first Test fifty was a particularly sweet moment, a real milestone along the way. I honestly had no inkling that anything untoward was going on and it certainly felt pressurised out in the middle, whatever scheme it was that Cronje had hatched.

Goughy hit the winning runs through his hangover, confirming what a brilliant batter he was under pressure in tight situations at the end of an innings. It had been quite a tough tour and we celebrated as if we had won the World Cup, oblivious to the shenanigans that had gone on to bring about a most un-South African declaration. I was even made man of the match.

On the tour we had been beaten up as a team, but from a personal point of view I had answered a lot of questions I had posed myself beforehand. I now knew I could stand up to pressure situations at the highest level and was not going to freeze, which was the most pleasing thing. I had absolutely loved being around the England set-up and wanted more of it. Apart from anything, I had really enjoyed the company of the other lads and felt perfectly secure amongst them. I now felt confident that a proper Test career lay ahead of me and when I got home I found that my profile had risen considerably.

People wanted to speak to me, newspapers wanted interviews. I was a young lad and if I am honest I lapped up the attention. As soon as I got back into training and early-season matches with Yorkshire I felt a much better player and more motivated than ever, but my progress towards getting established was destined to be interrupted by the injury jinx again.

5

Playing Myself In

The start of the summer of 2000 was different from any early season I had known before – I was now Michael Vaughan, England cricketer, and it felt great. The first ever batch of central contracts had been handed out and I was on the list, admittedly on the bottom tier with the likes of Lancashire leg-spinner Chris Schofield, the main surprise pick, but it gave me a considerable boost being one of those guinea pigs in a system that had been a long time coming.

At Yorkshire it was remarked upon that my batting had clearly gone up a notch, and for that I could thank Duncan Fletcher for the technical work he had done, combined with the self-belief that came from making a start at Test level and being around those senior England players. From then on, I found I scored far more consistently and I could not have made a more emphatic start in our opening Championship game against Derbyshire at Headingley. I had romped to 155 when a sharply rising ball from Matt Cassar broke my hand and with it my hopes of consolidating my place in the England side.

The opening Test against Zimbabwe was only a fortnight away and, although they were a much better side than the sadly beleaguered outfit they were to become, I still had hopes that they would provide an opportunity for a first international hundred. Instead, I could do nothing for a month with another broken bone, adding to the one that Gloucestershire's Mike Smith had shattered when I was 20.

So, for neither the first nor the last time, it was back to rehab work, starting with the painful squeezing of tennis balls to strengthen the muscles in my hand. Then it is hitting tennis balls, then having throw-downs with tennis balls, then some soft work with cricket balls, then a proper net and then a second-team game and so on. Zimbabwe were long gone by the time I was available again and I wasn't able to make sufficient impression to be picked for the first Test of that summer's major series, against the West Indies.

England lost the opening game by an innings, and by the time the second one came around at Lord's on 29 June, Nasser had broken a finger and I found myself called up again under the temporary captaincy of Alec Stewart. He gave a stirring speech in the dressing room and talked of the importance of putting the West Indies under any form of pressure, as he felt they would be a totally different proposition if we could ever get on top of them, and he was right.

They were dismissed for 267 and when my turn came I had to face Curtly Ambrose, who was making his last visit to England in tandem with Courtney Walsh. I remember asking myself how on earth you could score off Ambrose – but not for long as he bowled me for four. We conceded a 133-run deficit on the first innings and it really did look as if we were heading for 2–0 down and yet another Test series defeat against a major nation. But then Andy Caddick and Dominic Cork got it to zip around under the cloud cover that was there for the three days the match lasted.

With the ball hooping round corners the Windies were routed for 54 in barely two hours, and suddenly we were only 188 runs from a victory that would mark the real start of the Fletcher era. Mark Ramprakash went early and I came in, now at number three, and played and missed so often at Ambrose that it was embarrassing. I was almost giggling at myself because here I was, in front of a full house at Lord's on a Saturday, and I could not get a bat on it. Athers, who I loved batting with for his calm demeanour, was at the other end and we were almost smirking at each other with mock embarrassment because of the difficulties in facing Walsh and his sparring partner.

I thought I had nothing to lose, so I finally tried to pull Ambrose, and it came off, managing to force him through mid-on. Eventually, praise be, Jimmy Adams replaced them with Reon King and Franklyn Rose, but when they came back Walsh got me caught behind with less than 100 needed and nine wickets standing. I had made an important 41 – not as important as I wanted it to be, mind – and it was left to Corky to take us home with a priceless unbeaten 33 accompanied by his fellow introvert Goughy, again proving his worth as a finisher, this time in the dark. Corky made a gesture to his wife in the stands that people were trying to work out, the sort of gesture that made him a lively presence in the dressing room. I was never quite sure how deep his confidence actually ran. He always seemed able to intimidate lesser opponents, but the bigger ones were not put off, and the Australians seemed to melt him.

Corky was quite an innovator, we were to find out during that match. He was the man who introduced the ice bath to the England cricket team, and it is a measure of how far thinking has come that when he first filled the Lord's bath with ice cubes one evening we all took the piss out of him. The jokes flowed about what it would do to your private parts and so on as nobody had any idea how this painful innovation could be so beneficial to your muscles. Within a few years everyone was jumping in and out of them.

But that day Corky was just plain tough, and this was where my love affair with Lord's started, a ground that was to yield me six Test centuries over the years. We were absolutely elated after that, and it was the best feeling I had had in cricket to date, followed by the headiest celebration in the capital. We knew straight away that it was a huge win for us, and historians will look back on it as a real turning point in the reign of Duncan and Nasser, even though the latter was not playing.

In those days the Test series were suspended while a triangular one-day tournament was held, so it was a month before we could rejoin battle. Whatever shortcomings there were in the calendar in my later days as captain, at least we did not have the ridiculous hiatus of that summer. So I went back to Yorkshire with us at 1–1 rather than 0–2, and when the third Test at Old Trafford eventually came round on 3 August I was kept on, dropping down to six to accommodate Nasser's return.

It was Alec's hundredth Test and, fittingly, he made a century in our first innings which was met by the northerners raucously applauding the card-carrying southerner for what seemed like an age. The match, which ended in a draw, was also notable for the behaviour of Brian Lara, who had come in shortly before lunch on the third day. Rather than retiring to the pavilion for lunch he went straight over to the nets, and we sat around in the dressing room watching the Channel Four pictures of him practising. We thought it might mean trouble and it did, because he came out afterwards and proceeded to smack it everywhere till he was run out for 112.

The match ended in a draw, and had lasted considerably longer than those on either side of it, especially the remarkable fourth Test at my home ground on 17 August. You will always find a few players whose careers see a meteoric rise, but mine was one of steadily higher platforms, such as this almost unprecedented two-dayer at Headingley.

Fifteen wickets fell on the first day, with us dismissing them for 172 and myself and nightwatchman Andy Caddick not out overnight, perilously poised on 105–5. The next morning I was joined by Graeme Hick and together we put on 98, the crucial partnership of the match.

Hick is another of those enigmas I played with from a generation that was often held back by the insecurities of being in and around the England team of the 1990s. He was such a nice bloke, and he treated me brilliantly as a young player in the team, although I personally found that to be the case with most of the senior guys. Graeme was particularly generous, but I have to say there was something about him that made me feel that I was the senior partner when we were out there together, despite it being only my seventh Test. There was very much a self-effacing element to his character and I recall thinking when he was made captain of Worcestershire that it would not work. A lot of people bracket him with Ramprakash and John Crawley as players who did not fulfil their potential at the highest level. Crawley was a great guy and brilliant in county cricket, but I thought his technique was always going to be limited outside the off stump against the very best. Ramps was simply too uptight to fulfil his enormous natural talent.

I consider myself lucky to have played when it was a good time to be an England cricketer. Players of Hicky's age group – and there was some real quality among them – came through a system that promoted selfishness and the desire to look after yourself because there were no central contracts. Selection in the 1990s was very inconsistent and you could understand the lack of a belonging feeling. One of my big theories about cricket, if I am being totally honest, is that your first 75 runs are for you, and that after that it is all for your team. By that stage you have already bought yourself two or three games, so from then on it is wholly about the team, as you have already made your personal mark. I felt that some of Hick's contemporaries might have subconsciously been inclined to relax a bit once they had got past a certain score because of the way things worked. Inevitably it led to cliques, and that was one of the things I wanted to stamp out when I became captain. You need to have a selfish streak in you as a batsman – all the best ones have it – but there has to be a balance.

Anyway, Graeme and I came together on 124–6 with Walsh and Ambrose proving difficult again, and it was at this time that I resolved to properly put into practice the advice that had been given to me by Darren Lehmann, who was a huge influence. Having seen the improvement in me after coming back from South Africa, he told me that I had all the shots and should give rein to them more often and that, crucially, I had to run harder between the wickets. I had a tendency to be one-paced and he reckoned I could nick eight or nine runs per session just by running harder, which over a day works out at nearly 30. I said to Hicky when he came in that we should try and run them ragged, and so the very first opportunity we got, with the ball trickling to third man, I hared it back for a second and that set the tone.

For the first time I really tried to dominate the bowling while playing for England, and I took Nixon McLean for 16 in one over as well as cracking Walsh to the boundary. My 76 was further proof to me that I belonged at this level, but the innings was rightfully overlooked after the carnage wreaked by Gough and Caddick when the West Indies came out to bat. In 127 minutes they were blown away, with only one dismissal being caught, and I am not sure I ever saw Gough bowl better, although Caddy got one more wicket than him.

. For me to see the Western Terrace going nuts, fancy dress and all, was fantastic and this was when Nasser started to get a very strong bowling attack around him. Despite not getting along that well off the field, Gough and Caddick complemented each other beautifully, and this was to be the first time since the era of Fred Trueman and Brian Statham that England had picked the same opening bowlers through a whole series. Cork was a wily swinger and at the time it was easily overlooked that Chalky (Craig White) was about the quickest bowler in the world. He went through a phase of being able to bowl at lightning pace, and I only wished he had been more at ease with being on the international stage. I thought he was a cracking cricketer and if he had a drawback it was, contrary to what you might think for one of Australian background, that he was very much the type that needed a supportive arm around the shoulder.

By the time we got to The Oval at the end of August our attack was absolutely flying and we faced the prospect of winning back the Wisden Trophy for the first time since the 1960s. This was not one of the greatest West Indian teams, but we knew that it was of historic importance to finally beat them again.

Crucial to the effort was to try and get Lara out early. The word has to be used sparingly, but he is a genius. So, too, in is own way is Fletcher when it comes to spotting things on a cricket field. We had made 281 in our first innings and then made a couple of early inroads when they replied, bringing the brilliant Lara to the crease. Fletch had noticed that he was inclined to jump across to off stump when he first came in against pace and so he came up with a tactic for us of firing a couple in short and then unleashing a yorker at leg stump. In fact, Chalky took route one, spearing one in first ball that completely did for him. You can have all the good plans in the world but you need the talent to execute them properly, and my Yorkshire mate was on great form at the time.

Whilst I loved Lord's, I have always thought The Oval is the best cricket wicket you can come across because it offers everything. You know that if you get a snick, it carries; if the sun comes out, it will be flat; if there is any kind of moisture or overhead conditions, the ball will zip around a bit. Perfect. For Ambrose and Walsh this was their swansong together and they bowled themselves into the ground. I hated facing Ambrose; I just never knew how I was going to score off him. In his career Atherton had the misfortune to coincide with him at his best, but in this match he scored a magnificent century in the second innings, which left the West Indies needing an unlikely 374 to win.

You could tell at this stage that Nasser was really feeling the pressure because it meant so much to him, and he was struggling with his batting. He got a pair in this match but at the same time was desperate to get a big series win under his belt. Now I can look back and see how all these things came together, because as a captain there is so much to fill your head to overflowing in these situations. He was at a very low ebb in the dressing room after getting out. When you are so desperate to win it can easily take the edge of your batting and when I was at my best I had two very separate hats that I could comfortably swap.

The lesson the series made clear to me was how crucial it was to have a settled unit and, particularly, a settled bowling line-up. We were becoming a real team and everyone seemed to know what made the other individuals tick. You can judge a team by how they click in the field and how smoothly things move around, and for that to happen there needs to be familiarity. There is nothing worse than when a team looks disjointed because nobody knows who is bowling or who needs to be where for a certain bowler.

We lifted the Wisden Trophy on the balcony, and that was my first experience of what a great feeling holding something aloft could be. Little did I know that I would be doing something similar myself at the same ground five years later. It was true that at Yorkshire I was known as FEC (Future England Captain), as Athers had been at Lancashire, but I genuinely never saw that. In my wildest dreams, I honestly never thought it would happen, nor in my wildest nights out, which was what the celebration that followed the Oval victory qualified as.

I had averaged just shy of 50 for Yorkshire that season but, despite having started to play more expansively for England, I was not seriously considered for the ICC Trophy one-day tournament in Kenya that would precede our three-match Test series against Pakistan in the winter.

It was now a year since I had set off with England for South Africa and I had managed eight Test matches, with my appearances restricted only by the regular occurrence of injuries, and in particular the susceptibility of my fingers and hands to breakages. I travelled to Asia convinced that I could consolidate my place in the team for the longer form of the game and was duly picked for the first two warm-ups, one in Rawalpindi and the other in Peshawar.

The latter destination is in the North-West Frontier Province which, since the events of September 2001, has sadly become very much off-limits for visiting teams. Given that Osama bin Laden is meant to be resident somewhere thereabouts, it is probably not the wisest place for English teams to head for. But it was certainly an interesting place to visit, and one of my few regrets about failing to partake in non-cricketing activities on tour was that I turned down a chance to visit the Khyber Pass while we were there. I would never claim to be a culture vulture, but I am slightly embarrassed to say that I chose to play golf on the serviceable enough garrison course there when the chance arose. If I had known how the world was going to evolve at the time, I would certainly have opted for the trip up into the tribal areas. Some of the lads and the accompanying media came back and said they had seen the house of this leader who was meant to have caves running under where he lived. My sole cultural expedition was to buy a carpet.

I was not fated to have a particularly fulfilling time there anyway, as I pulled my calf muscle in the four-day match that followed our day of leisure. The match had started with Nasser and Athers having a massive set-to on the field because the captain thought that he was having too much of a laugh and a joke in the slips. He wanted to instil the idea that we were a tough unit whatever the cricket, which I sympathise with, although Nasser might agree that it is also possible to take things too seriously. Having a bit of a laugh on the pitch between deliveries is fine as long as you are focusing on the ball. There was also a spat between Caddick and an umpire, who thought he had made derogatory remarks about his country. As with a lot of these things, they tend to happen when the umpiring is poor, and some of the locals in India and Pakistan were shockers.

My calf was tweaked there and I aggravated it again in training, and from then on I could see that I was likely to be doing more swimming than batting on this tour. We went to

Lahore for the first Test on 15 November and came away with a decent draw, which featured an excellent 93 from Chalky. I was sitting in the dressing room when he came in after being dismissed and I said, 'Brilliant, Chalky, well played.' He was shattered and replied, 'There's my chance gone.' I was amazed, but he thought he'd blown what would be his only opportunity of making a Test century. That boy never knew quite how good he was.

Between Tests we had a match at Bagh-e-Jinnah, the leafy park ground in Lahore where, five years later, the long-term problems with my knee were to begin in earnest. This time I tried out my calf again, but it was still not right despite the valiant efforts of our physio Dean Conway. Back to the swimming pool, then, and hours and hours of PlayStation games against Ashley Giles. Ashley did pretty well in Pakistan and proved an astute pick by Nasser, for whom this would be his best period as captain.

It was on this trip that I gained a real insight into Fletcher off the pitch and how clever he was in the area of game plans and tactics. I could not contribute much physically but again I was watching, listening and learning. Ashley started bowling over the wicket to restrict the batsmen, in fact he would get so tight in that he would almost be bowling wicket to wicket. Some other bowlers were encouraged to bowl lines outside off stump to packed fields in order to further test the batsmen's patience. And we had bowlers good enough to carry out the plans, with the result that we really put the squeeze on the opposition.

I was a spectator for the second Test in Faisalabad, and during our victory in the third and final Test at Karachi perhaps my most important contribution turned out to be moving the sightscreens. Freddie, myself and Hoggy were among those dispatched to help speed matters along as the Pakistanis desperately tried to slow the game up as we closed in on the 176 needed for victory. It was a fantastic achievement and the celebration was a reminder to me that you did not need to actually play to be able to share the joy of winning.

So injury was continuing to blight my drive to consolidate a place in the starting XI, although what appears to have been a personally unproductive trawl around the subcontinent was far from a waste of time. As we headed for Sri Lanka after Christmas for the second leg of the winter I resolved to try and get back in the team and, at the very least, improve myself as a player.

Something that I benefited from, along with other batsmen around that time, was Fletcher's theory on something he called the 'forward press'. Without wishing to anaesthetise any non-fanatic about cricket technique, this was a method he was keen on that involved pressing your front foot forward just before the bowler let go of the ball. It allowed you a bit of extra time to watch the ball and helped to get you lower so your eyes would be beneath the ball's trajectory, which made the length quicker to pick up. Another benefit was that it made the sweep shot easier.

He was the first batting coach I had ever listened to who spoke so well about playing spinners and he was always prepared to go against accepted theories. For instance, Duncan thought that playing off-spin back towards the bowler was as valuable as the usual trying to squirt it to leg all the time. He changed a lot of things in my game, and I know that other players of my era will also swear that there was a touch of coaching genius about him.

Sri Lanka is a place I always enjoyed touring, and while

I would love to have regained my spot I was not fooled into getting my hopes up by being picked for the first two warm-up matches. Hicky had done well in that run chase at Karachi and understandably they wanted to stick with him for the first Test at Galle on 22 February. Trescothick hit a superb hundred there but we went down, and I was forced to watch from the sidelines again as we fought back with great tenacity to win the very fractious match which followed at Kandy.

Again a lot of the disputes were down to appalling umpiring, and Nasser made a very gritty hundred in which he was actually out about half a dozen times but not given. We won by three wickets, setting up a decider in Colombo. By now Hicky was struggling again and Kandy turned out to be his final Test for England. One man's misfortune can be another man's boon and I found myself back in the team for the sixth and final Test of the winter.

I was itching to be allowed to have the improvements in my technique examined and who better to do it than Muttiah Muralitharan, tormentor of all those who visit his lovely island. Graham Thorpe was at the height of his powers and played him beautifully, and it was interesting that another left-hander, Trescothick, was also proving productive in that series. Murali had a massive off-spinner, but what he did not have back then was his doosra, which we found such a nightmare to face the next time we went there, in late 2003.

Everybody liked Murali as a character and I personally never had any problem with the legality of his action. I felt he was, overall, good for the game because his skill in landing the ball yards outside the off stump and bringing it back into you (as a right-hander) was beyond question. Of course his action is slightly suspect, but I thought his talent was fascinating and I did not want to get caught up in the arguments about him. In fact, when he developed the doosra, right-handers started playing him better. Up till then, Sri Lanka would pack the leg side and it was almost impossible to score; after the doosra, if you could pick the wrong 'un (at least sometimes), it would open up the off side. I think the left-handers found it correspondingly more difficult.

We again had huge reason to be grateful to Thorpe in that match, who made a brilliant unbeaten 113 in the first innings. I made 26 as part of a partnership of 86 with him and felt that I had played pretty well. The remarkable thing at Colombo, and I suppose something that is a continuing worry for Test cricket, is that our supporters seemed to outnumber theirs. It was great for us, though, and they had a famous victory to cheer as we skittled Sri Lanka for 81 in the second innings and then just about knocked off the 74 needed to win for the loss of six wickets. I made eight, having gone in at three because Nasser had a slight injury. Word had reached me that, in any case, Duncan was by then keen to get me up the order.

Sri Lanka had made a big mistake in that match by preparing a complete dust bowl of a wicket, because it brought our two spinners, Ashley and Robert Croft, right into the game. The one thing you do not want to see there is a flat wicket that nullifies your bowlers but hardly affects the impact of Murali. Goughy was absolutely brilliant that winter, among the best in the world at the time, and he won the man-of-the-series award in both Pakistan and Sri Lanka.

Injury meant that Nasser had to go home straight away with Thorpey promoted to captain in his place for the one-day series, a by-product of which was that I was called up to make my one-day international debut in Dambulla. In what was, perhaps, an omen of things to come, I scored just nine and we failed to make my debut last long enough for them to switch on the floodlights as we were beaten by five wickets. At the time I was pretty optimistic about my chances of having a successful career as a one-day cricketer, although it was not something I had been prepared for. At Yorkshire my coaching had been very much geared towards the longer form of the game, from the academy through the second XI to the first team.

I thought my technique would adapt, but if I am completely honest, in my heart I always saw limited-overs cricket as something secondary to the first-class game; I had just been brought up that way. I expect the opposite will be true for those following the path that I trod, and if I had my youth again I would be honing my skills for the short form as much as anything. In the intense heat that we encountered for that one-day series we got absolutely marmalised, not helped by the fact that, subconsciously, perhaps we thought our main job on the trip had been done.

Some supporters had short memories and we got barracked by a few of them in the hotel lobby in Colombo after our third and final heavy defeat. Things had deteriorated somewhat at the fag end of the tour and as we gathered in the hotel bar for a few beers ahead of the night journey home, we were ready for our final minibus journey. One of our number was caught short on the way to the airport and felt the need to relieve himself en route. He waited until we reached a supposedly quiet intersection before doing what he had to do out of the window, only for a coachload of supporters to pull up alongside us, which was the cue for some frantic scrambling about and much hilarity.

When we actually got to the airport we were ushered directly to the front of the check-in queue, which angered some of our more tetchy travelling fans who were having to stand patiently in a long line. One of them, in a robust northern accent, declared, 'You lot should be going home on a boat, not a bloody aeroplane.' At least they cared.

6

Time to Deliver

Despite my small part in the final Sri Lanka Test and the enjoyment of being involved in two outstanding series wins, featuring in just one out of six Test matches in the winter had not been part of my game plan. Eighteen months after a reasonably successful introduction to the England team I was still trying to establish myself, a process my body had tried its worst to stop.

Pakistan were our early-season visitors for the summer of 2001 and after joining up with the squad for what I was determined would be a breakthrough series I received the news I was hoping for. Duncan was being good to his word about pushing me up to number three, and that is where I would start for another examination by Wasim Akram, Waqar Younis and the furious pace of Shoaib Akhtar. I had batted at three in the second innings against Sri Lanka and, although now recovered from injury, Nasser had agreed to step down to number four to accommodate me. I was told that either three or opening was where they saw my future in the long term, and that was absolutely fine by me.

Even more exciting was that the Australians, as strong as they had ever been, were coming as the summer's main event, and after our outstanding winter, with Gough and Caddick proving such a potent new-ball attack, there were expectations that we could finally give them a game. I thought so too, but as warm-up acts go the Pakistanis were hardly shabby and none of us could afford to get too far ahead of ourselves.

The first Test at Lord's starting on 17 May hardly did anything to dampen down the hype about what might be possible that summer. With Ryan Sidebottom playing what turned out to be a very isolated debut match, we dispatched them by an innings and nine runs, our fearsome strike duo taking 16 wickets between them. I had got a decent start but was caught behind on 32 in our one innings.

Now on a considerable roll, we headed up to Old Trafford for the second and final Test confident of rounding off another series triumph to send us into Ashes battle in the best possible heart. I felt especially good, as after the opening match I had gone down to Taunton and won the man-of-the-match award by hammering an unbeaten 125 to put Yorkshire into the last four of the Benson & Hedges Cup. Even the one-day game was feeling easy. Checking into the Marriott at Worsley, such familiar territory, I felt sure I was ready to make my long-awaited significant impact, and by the end of the second day I was on the brink.

I had 84 runs against my name overnight as we replied to their 403 all out, the wicket was decent and I was absolutely desperate to get those remaining 16. So much so that I was bricking it, knowing that a Test hundred in what was now my eleventh match would finally establish that I was an authentic player at this level. The texts were pouring in, Mum and Dad would be in attendance, and I barely slept for thinking about the handful of boundaries that would get me to the magic mark. Try as I might to avoid it, I could not get out of my head how I was going to celebrate three figures and where was I going to raise my bat to. Was I going to be superficially cool or let my emotions all hang out?

In the nets the next morning I was shaking with nerves, wondering if I would get so close again if I blew the chance – this is how batsmen, often fearful of the future, can sometimes think when possessed by their demons. I carefully worked my way to 95 and then nibbled one down to wide of third man where Wasim was grazing. Immediately I made the decision that I would take him on for the second and, seeing this, he frantically winged the ball back way wide of the stumps and, with even the man backing up out of position, it sailed across for four overthrows, taking me to the landmark score. So much, though, for the classic celebration, because there was an awkward pause before people realised I had scored five to bring my hundred up. I almost wanted to tell them, 'You do know that I've made a century here, don't you!'

It was still a euphoric feeling, although, having crossed the great divide, I was angry not to go on and get a big one when I was out for 120, caught behind again, and we collapsed to 357 all out.

We ended up being set an unlikely 370 to win and the match became best known for its final afternoon, when umpire David Shepherd continually missed the Pakistan bowlers' overstepping of the crease. We were side-on, sitting on the Old Trafford balcony, and could see it from there, irate and shouting out as if we were playing a beer match in a public park. Fletch went down to the match referee but it seemed to take an age before Shep was alerted to what he was missing. It struck me as interesting that, although we were Test cricketers, our behaviour on the balcony was exactly the same as if we had been playing in the Yorkshire League. We were actually barracking poor old Shep like demented clubbies.

I was third out for 14, and we disintegrated after Marcus Trescothick was out for a century. Pakistan teams always seem to have it in them to have a mad session one way or the other that can totally change the game, which is why they are so dangerous. You never knew what they were going to do. We lost with 6.5 overs left to survive for what would have been a third series victory.

Our momentum was stopped and the one-day triangular series that followed against Pakistan and Australia was disastrous in pretty much every way imaginable, from both a team and personal point of view. I did get my first run in what was a somewhat experimental limited-over team, and my fortunes mirrored the thrashing we got, scoring the grand total of seven runs from four innings. Some of the Pakistan supporters were a disgrace and got a kick out of mounting mass pitch invasions, resulting in talk of the ECB having to employ alsatians to patrol the boundaries. In the last match I featured in, at Headingley, we actually had to concede the game after another invasion, although we were well on the way to losing it anyway.

It was around this time that my right knee started playing up again, causing sufficient soreness to warrant further examination. I had been wary of it since a small operation that had been required when I was 18, and now here it was again to haunt me just when I did not need it. A bit of cartilage had come loose and it was locking on occasions, so it was decided that I had to go under the knife again. It was a very low moment when they broke the news to me. Like so many others, I had dreamed of playing in the Ashes since I was a boy and after my innings at Old Trafford I felt that the time was right to pit myself against the best in the world.

So instead of lining up opposite Steve Waugh and his world champions at Edgbaston on 5 July for the first day of the series, I was having my knee sliced open again, that very same morning. All I could do was lie in bed afterwards and watch Shane Warne take his latest five-wicket haul. Geoff Boycott rang that day, just to wish me well and tell me not to worry, showing the undoubted pleasant and considerate aspect of his character that exists alongside his tendency towards self-obsession and self-promotion.

Thoughts of Ashes glory were replaced with tedious rehab work back at Yorkshire, and although I was about ready for the last Test I was not going to be rushed back in with the series long dead and buried. Mine was not the only injury among England players to have contributed to wrecking our hopes, but we would have been outclassed anyway. The sole consolation was a dead-rubber victory at Headingley sparked by a masterful knock from Mark Butcher.

The season was far from a write-off, however, thanks to Yorkshire's surge towards winning our first County Championship in 33 years. I was able to get in on the back end of it and the memory of clinching the title at Scarborough is up there with the warmest of my career. David Byas led the team, Darren Lehmann starred and we had some great emerging players who made crucial contributions, such as Steve Kirby, Richard Dawson and Matthew Wood. Kirby was as mad as a box of frogs, had plenty of pace and was the source of a million anecdotes; Dawson, the first university graduate our dressing room had come across in years, was a bit of misfit from that point of view but a popular figure nonetheless; Wood was a very good mate of mine. We were a very decent all-round team and it was great to be back spending time in the ranks.

There were about 8,000 at North Marine Road as Bingo Byas lifted the trophy, and I was very pleased for him, especially as this was very much his own backyard, or his own farmyard, given his heritage. Some of the lads were not mad about him and his sometimes abrupt manner, but I appreciated his complete straightforwardness. This being his home club ground, it was as if some things were just meant to happen. There were two sessions to spare as we finished off Glamorgan by an innings and 112 runs, and we chose the scenic route back to our hotel, embarking on a magnificent pub crawl. We had a few drinks and a sing-song in the dressing room, where Darren Lehmann spoke and became very emotional, saying how proud he was to play for Yorkshire before starting to cry. 'Boof' was a very sensitive guy in some ways and cared passionately about the club. There is much talk in the modern game, some of it justified, about 'Kolpak' and overseas players coming over and taking our cash, but to have a properly committed imported player in your team can be a great benefit to everyone. He was everything an overseas player ought to be and a huge influence on me.

To an extent we had always been prisoners of our own history during my time at Yorkshire, and this was when we broke out. It is a fantastic place to play, and a club followed with a passion that is unusual to find in any sport outside football. The man to whom I gave a lot of credit for that season was our Australian coach Wayne Clark, who had arrived the previous winter. He knew how much pressure the illustrious past of the club and the intensity that surrounds it brought to bear, and was keen to emphasise that we should make some history of our own.

There seem to be a lot of ghosts around Yorkshire cricket, not all of them dead. Some of the ex-players were legends of the sport, not just for their ability on the field but for their larger-than-life character, and I had formed different opinions about each one. Boycott has a kinder side than some might think, but he was also very much out for himself and always carving his niche as a controversialist. His constant criticisms of Duncan Fletcher as England coach were completely wide of the mark and seemed to be based more on personal dislike than anything else. I loved Brian Close, a real character with whom I invested my first pension at the club. I was generally fond, too, of Fred Trueman, who I would have loved to have had in my team. Ray Illingworth was a complete pain in the backside, always miserably chipping away at everybody in his newspaper column and bearing a grudge against anyone who does not come from Pudsey.

Wayne was aware of an atmosphere at the club that perhaps worked against achieving success, and consequently he tried to change a few things. He dropped the strict requirement that everyone had to shave every day before turning up at the ground, and we were allowed to wear tracksuits more often to away games. His style of coaching, which had brought the Pura Cup title to Western Australia, was a lot more carefree and tried to bring out self-expression. I liked what I saw when I was back at Yorkshire and the team that won the title was young enough to have stayed together and gone on to win other trophies.

Unfortunately the whole thing imploded in a very Yorkshire-type way. We were relegated the following season, Bingo left the club and there were the usual squabbles with the committee. Wayne left in February 2003, which I thought was a grievous loss.

Winning the title in 2001 was just the lift I needed. I think we went into every single pub in Scarborough the night we won and, in some ways, the hangover lasted a lot longer than we ever imgined.

Far beyond the narrow confines of Yorkshire cricket, the world was about to change as a result of the attacks on New York's twin towers that took place less than three weeks later. We were due to tour India before Christmas and in the prevailing atmosphere some of the players, particularly those with children, were anxious about going. My attitude was that I would listen to the security people and that if they said it was safe enough to go, then that would be good enough for me; I was sure they would err on the side of caution anyway. In the end Andy Caddick and Robert Croft decided not to tour, which was bound to make an already difficult assignment even harder.

Before that there was a one-day series in Zimbabwe, for which I was overlooked. The issue of touring there, which was to prove such an emotive one as time went on, had already started to bubble up in the summer because of the steadily deteriorating situation in that country. However, given the momentous occurrences in New York, most people had taken their eye off that particular ball for the moment.

We had some more new faces for the three-Test trip that had been planned to India, with a return after New Year for a one-day series en route to New Zealand. Before 9/11 Alec Stewart and Darren Gough had announced they wished to take the tour off – which ran contrary to Duncan's philosophy – and we had a new wicketkeeper in James Foster. My friend Richard Dawson had been called up after just nine first-class games, following his hefty contribution to Yorkshire's triumph; Richard Johnson, a talented pace bowler I had come across in schoolboy cricket, was going and so was Jimmy Ormond, another considerable talent, who was, shall we say, an old-fashioned type of cricketer and not quite in sync with modern fitness methods.

For the first Test starting on 3 December in Mohali, in the northern part of the country, we stuck largely with the group who had gone down in the Ashes, so I had to sit it out. I had played in the warm-up matches and done OK without capitalising on one of my several starts and going on to get a big score. Ramps had made a fine century against the Australians at The Oval at the end of the summer and was understandably being persisted with. My main duty for that part of the tour was, in company with Ashley Giles, to spend lots of time in Graham Thorpe's room to try and keep his mind occupied with endless games of PlayStation. He had a lot of personal problems back home and was in a complete state, so the idea was not to leave him on his own at any time.

We lost the first match, but despite that I travelled down to Ahmedabad, then one of the grimmest grounds on the international circuit, expecting to be surplus to requirements once more. The night before the Test I went to bed for a nerveless sleep and had dozed off when there was a knock on the door at midnight. It was Nasser in his tracksuit, telling me that I was playing because Thorpey was going home to try and deal with his marital issues. It would probably have been better to leave me in the land of nod, but I did not mind one bit. In fact, I had been half expecting it because of my team-mate's state of mind.

We pressurised them pretty well in that match, with Craig White getting the maiden Test hundred that his talents deserved. I made an unbeaten 31 in the second innings despite being one of several players to get a serious stomach upset of the type you dreaded in India. I remember having to lie down in the dressing room feeling like death warmed up before coming round and starting to feel a bit better after some medication. At that point I walked out to offer my services for fielding, but Nasser told me, in no uncertain terms, to get back because they could do without me. I traipsed off and the match ended in a creditable draw.

The final match was down in Bangalore just before Christmas, where I was to make some unwanted history. We

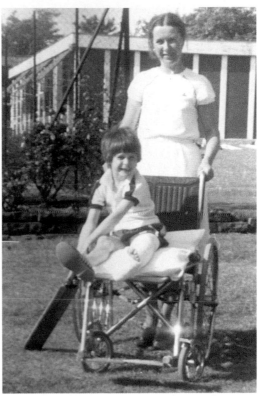

nest Tyldesley, one of Lancashire's great e-war batsmen, may have been sponsible for my sporting genes.

A serious road accident was not enough to stop me from holding a cricket bat.

ven my tendency towards childhood shaps, fireworks could have been quite ngerous.

With brother David, who also had plenty of sporting ability and against whom I honed my competitive instincts.

Presented with Yorkshire's 'Young Player of the Year' award by White Rose legend Ray Illingworth.

Craig White is a long-standing friend and another Yorkshire trainee who went on to become a full England player.

Sheffield Collegiate became a home from home once we moved across the Pennines. In this 1983 picture I am second left front row, with David far left back row.

eat Yorkshire coach Doug Padgett
otted me playing on the outfield at
effield and became a mentor.

Martyn Moxon was my opening partner on first
XI debut and someone I always looked up to.

e demon spinner in 1997 when I had
ious pretensions of being an all-
nder.

Hitting a trademark cover drive during the 1995
NatWest Trophy semi-final v Northants at
Headingley.

Above: My father, Graham, sees me off as I prepare to go away on tour with the full England team for the first time.

Right: I always enjoyed being at the other end from the phlegmatic Mike Atherton, as in the 2nd Test v South Africa at Port Elizabeth in 1999.

Below: Welcome to England top-order collapses. Shaun Pollock bounces me on debut in Johannesburg.

bove: Waiting for the rain to stop during the famous 5th Test v South Africa at Centurion in 000.

ight: Little did we know what Hansie Cronje, smissed here by Darren Gough, was up to at enturion.

elow: Chatting with some catering staff while tting out the 1999 tour match in East London outh Africa) with a broken finger.

The two-day Test at Headingley in 2000 v West Indies was also notable for having four Yorkshire players in the England team *(l-r)* Mathew Hoggard, Craig White, me and Darren Gough.

Winning the Championship with Yorkshire in 2001 was one of the most enjoyable moment of my career.

first Test hundred, made against Pakistan at Old Trafford in 2001, came after a night
worry.

Left: Warm-up at Kanpur in 2002 – cricket's gain was not really football's loss.

Below: Nasser Hussain's hundred against New Zealand at Christchurch 2002 was one of the finest innings I saw him play.

batted first and I was building an excellent partnership with Ramps to take us past 200 for the loss of three wickets. I had reached 64 and was playing their spinners with ease when I tried to sweep Sarandeep Singh and, down on one knee, got the ball jammed between my arm and my thigh. As it rolled away, for some reason I instinctively grabbed it with my right hand and flicked it away to short leg, possibly thinking in the heat of the moment that there was a chance it might spin back onto the stumps. They appealed and I was given out, becoming only the second Englishman after Graham Gooch and only the seventh in Test history to be dismissed in this way. I was a bit disappointed that they appealed at all and said so afterwards, but technically they were within their rights.

In that game Fletcher and Nasser came up with a ruthless plan to get Ashley to bowl just outside leg stump to a 7–2 field, and the resulting frustration saw Sachin Tendulkar dance up the wicket and get stumped for the first time in his career. Some people weren't happy with the tactic, likening it almost to Bodyline, but we just saw it as using our available resources in the most effective way. It was another example of Duncan's ability to think outside the box, and by giving Ashley the role of bowling tight in to the stumps and over the wicket he effectively brought him a whole Test career. If Ashley had just bowled round the wicket he would not have been half the bowler, because he did not rag it much, but as it was he became a crucial player as he allowed the seam bowlers to attack while he plugged away. Nothing used to annoy me more than criticism of Gilesy, a great team man and someone who could not be accused of failing to make the best of what he had.

We had the Indians in trouble, but on the third day the clouds started to come in and I said to Nasser, 'There is only one reason clouds come over in this part of the world and that is to dump rain.' It was a washout, and probably just as well for our opponents, who had escaped with a 1–0 series victory.

After a welcome break at home we returned to India with Goughy back – forgiven for his Test absence, although Duncan had a memory like an elephant for these things – as we embarked on a six-match 50-over series. A partly experimental squad had been taken to Zimbabwe and I was now picked as part of our latest search for a winning formula. There was a good spirit on that trip and we came away with a highly respectable 3–3 draw, the whole mini-tour being a great experience as we played to packed-out houses everywhere.

Marcus made a quite superb century in the first game at Calcutta in front of more than 100,000 at Eden Gardens, before getting sawn off by one of many dreadful umpiring decisions on that trip. We fell just short there but levelled things at Cuttack, where I top-scored with 63. We were to go 3–1 down, but then won by two runs in Delhi, despite me dropping a complete sitter at mid-off from Mohammad Kaif off Goughy.

I should come clean about this: I had a terrible tendency to drop catches in my career. I just never had confidence in my catching and, despite having an excellent eye, my technique was never up to scratch in this area. One of the definite improvements in modern coaching is that there is much more emphasis on catching methods but, incredibly with hindsight, I was never really taught properly how to do it at the right age. People say that you should be able to do it because it is something you practise every day, but I just never felt comfortable with the ball coming towards me. When my mentality was good I would back myself to snaffle the ball, and it was something that both Duncan Fletcher and Peter Moores improved in me.

I will admit, though, that as captain I would put myself in positions on the field where I did not think that catches would be offered. It was the worst part of the game for me and there were times after the odd spillage when I would dread going out to field and yearn for the ball not to come anywhere near me in the air. My reservoir of confidence was very shallow in that regard, although perversely I have also caught some blinders in addition to committing some terrible blunders. The time I was most susceptible was when I was concentrating intensely on the captaincy, but it was something that was with me even before I became a professional. The feeling of dropping a catch in front of a large crowd has to be one of the worst in cricket: there is no hole deep enough to fall into. You feel embarrassed and that you have let everyone down, from your team-mates to the supporters.

England's continual failure to win a trophy at one-day cricket is no accident, but there have been times when we have played well together and this was one of them. We just never seemed to be able to keep a good one-day outfit together long enough for some reason or other, often due to injuries. The younger generation now coming through, exposed to Twenty20 cricket, will hopefully change things, but even when I was playing we were still more culturally adjusted to the longer form of the game. We secured the drawn series with a last-gasp victory at Mumbai on 3 February when Freddie yorked Javagal Srinath at the death and celebrated by ripping his shirt off, capping a wonderful little excursion.

From there it was straight on to New Zealand, which turned out to be a much less happy experience for reasons far more profound than mere cricket.

I do not know if it was a reaction to suddenly being in a country with more obvious temptations, but the five-match limited-over series was one where we probably drank a little too much. After going down to a 3–2 defeat with a loss in the decider at Dunedin at the end of February we were drowning our sorrows when Collingwood came out with the classic remark 'This drinking team has got a cricket problem.'

It had been a particularly frustrating time for me because I had put my shoulder out and been able to play in just one of the matches, the fourth game in Auckland, where I made 59 and, glory be, held two catches. It had repaired itself by the start of the Test series in Christchurch on 13 March, where I was now put up to open alongside Marcus, with Butch going in at three and Nasser at four.

The pitch was like a paddy field, incredibly green, and after being stuck in we were soon in trouble when I got out for a brisk 27. Nasser was to make 106 and it was one of the best innings I ever saw him play. The ball was moving everywhere and his technique stood up to it brilliantly. Conditions got better as the match wore on, with Thorpey getting a double century, Freddie 137 (his maiden Test ton) and Nathan Astle an extra-ordinary 222. But it was Nasser's knock that I remember best for setting us up for a 98-run victory, our first in a 'live' Test since beating Pakistan early the previous summer.

Ben Hollioake had been with us on the one-day legs of the winter and it was during the second Test, before lunch on the third day, that I received a text saying 'Sorry to hear about Ben Hollioake'. Duncan heard me and Ashley talking about it, so he informed us that Ben had been killed in a car crash at his home in Perth. We were asked to keep it quiet until lunch so as not to disturb those waiting to go in to bat.

The news was totally numbing, and the Surrey contingent were naturally affected in particular. Ben was a good mate to all of us and I think the last time I saw him was when he came down to Queenstown in New Zealand after the one-day series was over, having chosen to stay on for a short holiday. We met him in a backpackers' bar, where we were drinking cocktails out of teapots, a bit like the way we used to secretly drink wine in restaurants in Pakistan.

Tragedy is a word that should be used carefully in relation to sport, but it really was a tragedy that we did not see him again. He had a carefree approach to his cricket and was a very gentle guy with a lovely, natural way about him. In all honesty, I think he would probably have done better in one-day cricket, but he was so talented he could yet have gone on to do well in the Test arena as well.

It was in New Zealand that certain things started to evolve in my cricket. I was getting off the mark with a flourish and pulling the ball more, while I was also developing my thinking about the strategies of the game. We had won the first Test and in the second at Wellington starting on 21 March we did not declare anything like early enough. Basically, we left them 356 runs to get in 84 overs and I felt we would have been better served by opening up the chances of defeat by 15 per cent in order to give us more time to bowl them out. It struck me that, with England's history of forever blowing hot and cold, when-ever you have a chance of actually winning a Test you should go after it more aggressively than was our tendency in that period. We were to make a similar mistake at Trent Bridge the following summer, being too conservative and failing to go for the win. Possibly Nasser and Duncan were a little too alike at times in their relatively cautious approach.

We drew the match in Wellington when, in fairness, there was good reason for everyone to be distracted from the busi-ness of winning a Test. We were still somewhat deflated for the final match in Auckland, a low-scoring affair dogged by bad light. The second day was abandoned for rain and to kill some time a few of us went onto the rugby field at the back to kick some goals like Jonny Wilkinson. Craig White slipped and did his groin quite badly, something that had to be hastily covered up.

We lost by 78 runs and in both innings I got a start and failed to go on to make a significant score, the fourth time it happened in six outings at the crease in that series. It was now April 2002, nearly two and half years and 16 Test matches since I had made my debut for England. I was averaging a shade over 31 and had scored 810 runs. Hardly disastrous, but I was getting worried that I was starting to be a nearly man, showing glimpses of decent potential at this level but not absolutely nailing down my place and making the kind of contributions that would decisively alter games. Without wanting to hark back too much to Hicky and Ramps, I did not want to be in the same bracket as them. It should also be stressed that I knew by now I was in an era when it was a more healthy environment for an England cricketer trying to establish himself than when they were starting out.

I had the sense that I was approaching a time when I was going to find out, one way or the other, what sort of England cricketer I was going to be. To borrow a baseball term, it was time to step up to the plate.

7

In the Runs

I placed high expectations on myself ahead of our early-summer series against Sri Lanka in 2002, but I would never have envisaged that by early September the season would have yielded 900 Test runs in seven matches at an average of exactly 90. True, I looked at our first visitors for the season and reckoned that I could take them for quite a few, but I did not believe I was starting on a path that would lead all the way to the England captaincy within barely a year.

Results-wise it had been a 12-month period of virtual stagnation for the team, with our progressive triumphs from the winter of 2000–01 stopped rudely in their tracks. Even though there had been a few extenuating circumstances in New Zealand, supporters were becoming impatient that this team was not delivering what it should. Playing Sri Lanka in early-summer English conditions largely alien to them ought to have been the perfect opportunity for us to get the momentum going again.

Particularly helpful was the fact that Murali was unfit for the first Test on 16 May, so the natives at Lord's became restless when we conceded 555 in the first innings and were then forced to follow on. I had top-scored with a relatively sedate 64, but received a few swipes about my failure again to go on to three figures. Around this time the Lord's wicket seemed to be morphing into a flat track full of runs and, although I had frustrated myself with another untimely exit, I had played well and felt sure I was on for some decent runs in the second innings.

I told myself to stick with it, and my first hundred at Lord's duly arrived as Marcus and I put on 168 for the first wicket. It has to be said that Aravinda de Silva's off-spin was not of quite the same quality as that of Murali, but they were a half-decent team all the same. Irrespective of that, getting your first hundred at Lord's is a very special moment, and as I ran past the wicket at the Nursery End for the single that took me to three figures I kept running in celebration. Can there be a better feeling in any sport than scoring a Test match hundred at the home of cricket? I suppose none of us can know, but I always consider it an achievement of real substance, something built over a period of time in which you are bound to have been tested.

Doing it for your team-mates is a fantastic feeling, and on this occasion my hundred, and that of Mark Butcher, made sure we would secure a draw. Still, overall it was not the result we wanted.

Murali was back for the second Test at the end of May, but our two southpaws, Thorpe and Trescothick, continued their great run against Sri Lanka with hundreds and we hammered them by an innings. Thorpey was already established as a masterful player of spin, but it was now emerging just how good Marcus was as well. He had so many options of scoring against the subcontinent teams and I spent many a happy hour watching from the non-striker's end or back in the shed as he would put in that big stride and slog or sweep them to the boundary.

Murali got me for 46, but we were starting to score hundreds galore, and two more of them came, to Alec Stewart and the now prolific Butcher, in the final match at Old Trafford that produced an almost Twenty20-style finish. It looked as if Sri Lanka were going to bat out the final afternoon for a draw when Ashley ran through their tail, giving us an unexpected target of 50 off six overs to win. Marcus and I sprinted off at the end of their innings to pad up – I particularly didn't want Nasser to get any ideas of promoting Stewart or Flintoff for first bite at the slog. In the event we dashed to victory with 11 balls to spare in an exhilarating flourish that saw us take Dilhara Fernando for 16 in one over.

My fluctuating one-day career saw me left out at the start of the subsequent triangular one-day series but brought back in for the last four matches, without making any huge impact. Probably the biggest splash I made was against Sri Lanka at Manchester on 7 July, where I returned 4–22 with my demon off-spin. Marcus dropped one on the boundary, so it could have been five – something I have struggled to forgive him for ever since.

I did, however, play in one of the great limited-over matches up to that time when India managed to overhaul our 325 at a packed Lord's with three balls to spare. It was in this match that Nasser made his famous gesture to the commentary boxes he now graces after scoring 115, pointing to the number three on his back in answer to criticism of his one-day batting. I just thought it quite amusing at the time, and was not then one of the younger players turned off by his constant grumpiness. In fact, when he was effing and blinding on the field it made me giggle. I liked playing under him, but I could see that his behaviour towards some of the lads was very inconsistent, and made a mental note of that. That was why I tried so hard to hide what I was feeling about individuals when I was captain, which I found a very tiring process. I would certainly come to understand the kind of pressures Nasser was under that led to the way he behaved.

When the Indians won at Lord's, Sourav Ganguly ripped his shirt off and waved it above his head, a riposte to Freddie, I presume, for his similar action in Mumbai earlier that year. Ganguly had an abrasive side to him but he got his team playing for him. Somehow I could never see him and Nasser fraternising too much over a few friendly beers.

The main part of the season was to be our Test series against India, and in the first innings of the opening match at Lord's at the end of July I spent quite a few hours batting, although sadly only a tiny portion of it was in the middle before an expectant crowd. In the second over Zaheer Khan nipped one back to trap me lbw, ensuring that what was, from a personal point of view, to be a watershed series for me began with a duck. My old problem of vulnerability against the ball nipping back from outside off seemed to be resurfacing, and after going back and watching a video I was reminded that I was not actually standing as still as I thought at the crease. I was moving just before the ball was bowled and failing to get my feet in the right position. My alignment against quick bowling was not quite right, whereas against spin I was using Duncan's 'forward press' and getting into the correct position.

So I asked our trainer, Nigel Stockill, to come round to the Lord's indoor school with me to operate the bowling machine, and started forward-pressing to the quicker balls as well. I spent two hours on it non-stop and resolved that I would use the technique of making that initial forward movement against all types of bowling. That decision, made in the quiet of the indoor school when I was furious at having missed out on what was going on in the main arena, was to transform my Test career.

Nasser had made 155 and, with Simon Jones taking two wickets on his debut, we had amassed a 266-run lead when I went out for the second dig. The new technique made me feel I had that fraction more time and the immediate benefit was that I started to pull the ball with increased confidence. My second Test hundred of the season came up in 141 balls, and one of the features of my batting that summer was that I scored at a very brisk rate. We set them a mammoth fourth-innings target and won by 170 runs.

There was another significant debut in the second match at Trent Bridge on 8 August, Steve Harmison replacing Simon, who had a side strain. We were already missing Marcus with a broken thumb and this time we were another experienced batter light, as more problems in his private life had forced Thorpe to withdraw from the team. I was 30 not out at lunch and then in the afternoon found myself in one of those glorious 'zones' that you sometimes discover, scoring all over the wicket at virtually a run a ball to get to 197. My downfall came shortly before the end when I flung my bat at Ajit Agarkar and was caught behind, the nearest I was to come to an elusive double hundred.

We were on our way to what should have been a match-winning total of 617 and people were now really starting to talk of me less in terms of being a new Mike Atherton – I considered that high enough praise anyway – and making other comparisons. Vic Marks, of England, Somerset and the *Observer*, became the first to draw comparisons with Peter May.

This was not my only magical experience of the match, as I also claimed the wicket of Sachin Tendulkar with my usually less than magical off-spin. I had thrown one up and he drove me through the covers for four, so I decided to throw one up further and wider the next time and managed to hit the rough patch, bringing it sharply back in to bowl the maestro. It was probably the worst thing that could have happened – I still have the ball in my snooker room at home and he kindly signed the stump for me afterwards – because people started to think I could be a proper spinner. Frankly, unless you have the doosra or an unbelievably clever change of pace, I would not recommend becoming an off-break bowler to too many young players. There is not much future in it, I am afraid.

I thought we should have gone more for the kill in that match, and in the end they held out for 424–8 in 115 overs.

Robert Key had come into the team then, one of the most amusing characters I have played with. At Nottingham he was fielding at first slip and Nasser felt he had to move him out of there because he was talking too much to Fred at second slip. Then in the next match, at Headingley, he found himself exiled to long-off while I was at backward point. The Indians were smacking it around ahead of their declaration on a massive 628–8 and the catches seemed likely to go where Rob was. He had dropped one earlier and asked if I would mind going up there and swapping. The next ball Ganguly hit it straight to backward point and he spilled it.

I made 61 in the first innings and thought I was on for another big one before chipping to cover. The pitch became more uneven as the match went on, and we succumbed to an innings defeat despite a typically defiant century from Nasser.

We headed straight to London for the decider at The Oval on 5 September. I was really into my stride now and unusually eager to get back at it so soon after a disappointing defeat. It had always been a dream of mine to bat through a day for

England and it finally came true after we had won the toss and opted to bat. It was one of those days when I thought I could hit every ball for four, and while I did not quite manage that I rattled along to score an unbeaten 182 by the close. I could not believe how easy I was finding it to play Harbhajan Singh and Anil Kumble and my confidence was so high it was virtually off the scale. When Anil started to come round and bowl into the rough I just danced down the pitch and flicked him over midwicket. If only the game could seem this simple all the time.

By the end of the day I was completely goosed and my knee was sore, this time my left knee rather than my right one. I declined to speak to the media and was allowed not to – something that would not have been permitted in other countries – and Duncan took the flak for it when, in fact, it was my decision. There was quite a kerfuffle about my refusal and in hindsight I was wrong. I should simply have been ordered to talk and that would have been that. I had become, after all, the first English batsman to hit four centuries in an English summer since Graham Gooch in 1990 and only the sixth in history, so there was plenty to talk about.

The next morning I hit a couple of boundaries and thought I was on for a monster score before Zaheer Khan, who was bowling pretty quickly, got me to edge one behind. Out for 195, in 279 balls. We made 515, and they got to within seven of it, combining with some bad weather to make it a draw in both the match and the series.

After Marcus and I had put on 114 at the start of the second innings the last day was a washout, and at the end I went into the dressing room, where I encountered a distraught Nasser. During the rain breaks the television had been on, and the Channel Four panel were filling the time by debating the party that should tour Australia in the coming winter. One or two of them had said that it might be time for Nasser to stand down. Sitting on the edge of the big bath, he was very tearful, but at that point I didn't fully understand what he was going through – the emotions of being captain, worrying about your own batting and then having the ex-players constantly picking and analysing. It had really got to Nasser, and if you had fast-forwarded to six years later I would have had complete sympathy with him. At the time, I thought that having a few old pros casting doubts about you could not be that bad.

As a rank-and-file player you at least feel very much in control of your own destiny, but you do not have that luxury as captain because you are largely dependent on the performances of others, which brings its own set of stresses. I thought about what I should do in this awkward situation but did not go over to console Nasser, partly because I was a bit shocked, as I had never seen him like that before, and partly because he was not especially approachable anyway. I wish I had known what I know now, but then that is something you could say about so many things in life.

At the time it never occurred to me, or to any of the other players for that matter, that it was possible for anyone but Nasser to be our captain. I think the same was true when I resigned: none of the others had much of a clue what I was going through or what my plan was.

I did feel we should have been a bit more ballsy in that series, and that the results during the Nasser–Duncan era would have been slightly more positive if a few more risks had been taken. Sometimes we would go 1–0 up in a series and thereafter it was as if we were a bit too keen to put 10 men behind the ball, so to speak. In the end, we had drawn against a decent enough Indian side, and there was the slight bonus, I suppose, that this time we had not unduly ramped up expectations that we would thump Australia in the upcoming tour.

At the end of the Oval match there was the usual traffic between the dressing rooms, and in the sometimes surprisingly frank conversations that can take place on these occasions two things stood out for me. Firstly, there was Rahul Dravid asking us, Englishmen, how we played spin, which was quite remarkable given his cricket upbringing and status as a player. He was impressed with our techniques, and again this was something that you could directly trace back to the coaching of Duncan. Dravid asking us about playing spin was a bit like Michael Owen asking how you find the back of the net.

I took the opportunity to speak with Sachin Tendulkar, especially as the Ashes would soon be upon us. After all, how often in life do you get the chance to tap the brains of an all-time legend, who just happens (like Dravid) to be a total gent as well? Sachin put forward the theory that, good as the likes of Glenn McGrath were at the time, some batsmen had the tendency to show them too much respect, and that it was necessary not to forget to mix caution with aggression. That confirmed to me what I had already been thinking about the winter to come: that I would not be holding back in taking them on. It turned out to be one of my better resolutions in life.

8

Year in the Sun

On 15 April 2003 I received a text message from Matt Sanderson, a great friend who was to be my best man. It read 'What is the world coming to? Wednesday are top of the league and you're the world's number one batsman!' Both things, incredibly, were true, as I had climbed to the top of the official batting rankings for Test cricket, usurping Matthew Hayden.

The series against India the previous summer had seen me reach the top 10 for the first time, and in September there was also the pleasing recognition of being awarded the Professional Cricketers' Association player-of-the-year award during their annual night at the Royal Albert Hall. But I was still a long way off the summit then, and even though I was so buoyed by the hundreds against India, the initial events of the winter that followed did not suggest that my form was about to perform its own follow-on.

The bridge between the India series and the Ashes was to be the ICC Trophy in Sri Lanka in September, one of those sporadic events which exist on the international calendar without any apparent reason. Whatever its status, I was not among those lucky folk heading for Colombo. The reason was that my left knee had been causing some soreness and after various scans the specialists decided that it needed a clean-out. I was relatively happy about this, both because I wanted to get my latest injury problem cleared up and, if I am honest, because I was not too disappointed to be missing out on three weeks playing limited-over cricket in Colombo.

It was not that I actively did not want a one-day career, far from it, but I can see now that subconsciously I was always focusing on being the best I could be in the longer form of the game. Regardless of the knee, I would have been quite content staying at home, resting up and getting my mind clear for the challenge that lay ahead, the biggest of my career to date.

When it came to our departure for Australia in October we gathered at the airport with about half of us looking as if we had just stepped out of the Crimean War. I was still limping and so was Goughy, while Fred was stiff and also clearly recuperating from his recent hernia surgery. The selectors had taken a real risk in picking players who were so obviously short of full health, but they thought it was worth doing so despite many a sceptical eyebrow being raised in the media. As we met up there was the usual buzz and a reasonable amount of optimism in the air. As far as our prospects on the tour went I did not share it, because I knew we were still short of being a top team, certainly well short of Australia, and that there was too much of the wrong mentality about, too.

My rational assessment was that we had no chance at all, purely based on the attitudes I was encountering. The name McGrath came up an unhealthy number of times in discussions among the players and I was constantly being asked how I was going to tackle him. 'I'm going to have a go,' I would tell my colleagues. Perhaps I was partly responsible for some of the talk about him, because I had been asking some of the more experienced players how you played Australia's premier pace bowler and they would just say, 'He puts it on a sixpence; you won't score off him.' I remember thinking that there was an element of giving in to him already. I would reassert that if the ball was there to be hit I was going to try and whack him and they would tell me, 'No chance; he just won't give you anything to hit.'

On it went: 'McGrath never bowls a bad ball, Hayden hits it harder than anyone else in the world, Warne spins it miles, Waugh is impossible to get out, Gillespie's bumper is unplayable, Lee's unbelievably rapid.' I suppose much of this was borne out, but to a degree these things are only as true as you allow them to be.

The defeatism was plain to me. If they were already thinking at the airport that there was no way they were going to get anything to hit, it was hardly surprising that they were going to get beaten up by him. That was shown to be the case throughout the series, and it must have got filed away in the memory bank because, later on as captain, I became fixated on the idea that some players were scarred by Australia after taking so many beatings from them. There was no doubt that it was to my advantage that I was going there as a first-time tourist, completely fresh, with the intention to just have a go. My head was somewhat clearer than some of my colleagues' and I was clearly more excited about the approaching challenge, perhaps understandably so.

In fact, there was a huge amount on that trip that got stored away at the back of my mind for the purposes of tackling Australia in the future. The basic lesson was that if you were going to stand up to the Australians you could not have anyone in the team who had this fear about them. One of the things I learned was that it only takes two players starting to talk them up an unhealthy amount for it to become contagious, spreading through the squad until you have half the team fearful about them.

This will sound arrogant, but I really quite fancied facing McGrath. If the ball was seaming he was a bit of a nightmare, but if it was swinging I found him quite juicy. I was more worried about the skiddier Gillespie on that tour. By the time we left for Australia McGrath had already paid me the compliment of being the Pom he was singling out as his series 'target'. He always picked someone from the opposition as a ritual and I came to view it as a bit of playful fun and harmless nonsense – as I am sure he did – but at the time it only served to give me a real confidence injection that he regarded me so highly.

One of the first things that hit me upon arriving in Australia was the coverage in their newspapers, which I had been warned about – though I was still taken aback. In the build-up to the first Test there was a double-page spread in the paper, with McGrath going through our whole team and openly saying what our weaknesses were and how we were going to meet our downfall: Vaughan doesn't play the short ball well; Trescothick doesn't move his feet and will edge the ball to our large slip cordon; Hussain plays with half a bat – we'll find his edge as well; Butcher is too cocky and will play rash shots; Crawley can't play on the off side; Stewart will play for himself; don't know too much about Craig White or if there's much worth knowing about him; the rest – we'll just knock 'em over.

I read this with a sense of incredulity and amusement, but there was a serious side to it as well. They were so open with the media and so self-assured, which I guess had come from a serious inner belief in their ability and having so much success behind them.

It had started as soon as we got to Perth – our first stop – with their media finding it hilarious that Freddie, me and Goughy were labouring around the boundary ropes of the WACA in our half-jog, half-walk. The rest of the squad did catching practice and as I recall there were about three spillages in the whole 45-minute session – all of which were captured on camera and appeared in the local paper under the headline 'ENGLAND DROP INTO PERTH'. If anything, the TV reports were even more scathing, essentially saying 'Look at these English idiots who have just arrived.'

The traditional opener back then was a one-dayer at a place called Lilac Hill outside Perth against a scratch XI in front of about 12,000 people. The most notable thing about the day is the amount of alcohol consumed around the cricket, with the police setting up roadblocks outside the ground to catch drink-drivers. This meant that about one in four of the spectators would be sober while the other three-quarters would be roaring drunk by the afternoon, and very keen to let us know their opinion of English cricket and England in general.

We lost there, and then drew against Western Australia at Perth in two further warm-ups, with me all the while trying to get back to full fitness in time for the first Test at the Gabba in Brisbane on 7 November. I was not too perturbed because of the form I had been in over the summer, and certainly happier than either Fred or Goughy, who were clearly still a long way short of full health and who had no chance of making it by the opening match.

My first outing was our last warm-up match at the Allan Border Field in a suburb of Brisbane, where our bowlers took another pummelling, this time from the formidable Queensland state team. Freddie was trying his best to bowl but was obviously too stiff, and while Martin Love was cranking up the pressure on the pitch by smacking us for 250 in their total of 582, there was some clever psychological stuff going on off the field as well.

The Australians were doing their meet-the-media session before the Test and chose to do it at the same ground where we happened to be getting thrashed. While we were out in the field desperately trying to dismiss Queensland, Steve Waugh turned up with his team in their tracksuits and made this imperious walk round the boundary, to applause, en route to their press conference in the gym. Waugh was the master of making a subtle point and the subliminal message was clear: 'You are struggling against this lot and here is a reminder that none of them is good enough to get into our team.'

They kept battering us until we were completely out of the game. The good news for me was that my form appeared to have seamlessly carried over from the summer and, despite the hiatus caused by injury, I put together a decent 127, although unfortunately there were few other grounds for optimism in our performance.

The appearance of Waugh and his men had been a clever ploy, but then I do not think we especially helped ourselves with our team meeting the night before the first Test. Again I felt that there was a bit too much building up the Australians into supermen, but then this was another habit of Nasser's. I think that emphasising how much we were up against it worked well for him personally, because he always responded positively to having that feeling of being backed into a corner. For the rest of us I was not so sure as we sat there hearing about how they ran between the wickets better than we did and so on. By the time I came out, I felt really nervous about what lay ahead, and the mood persisted when we arrived at the ground the following day.

The feeling of defensiveness probably had something to do with the notorious decision that morning to put the Australians in when we won the toss. I was in the dugout when it was done and just assumed that we would be batting, as with Shane Warne in their line-up there would have to be very strong reasons for doing otherwise. Then Alec Stewart turned round and said no, we were fielding, so I just presumed that there must have been sufficient in the pitch to encourage the thought that we would have them three or four down by lunch.

I found the unusual ritual of playing the national anthems before the game a bit of a strange experience. It involved us going out onto the field 15 minutes early, and for some reason it was a bit deflating and unsettling afterwards and I did not feel at my mental peak from the start. The whole day was to be pretty disastrous, both from a team and personal point of view. I let one through my legs on the very first ball of the series to give them a single and later dropped Hayden in the covers. Curiously, although my batting confidence was sky-high in that series, not for the first time it was quite the opposite in the field, where I spent most of the time dreading that the ball would come to me. It was nothing compared to the trauma suffered by Simon Jones, who badly damaged his knee ligaments when sliding on the outfield to try and stop the ball.

A less obvious indicator of our general mindset came early in the first session. Something we had talked about was all sticking together if there were any verbal confrontations flying about, whoever was involved. Andy Caddick was always fond of chirping the batters but was absolutely awful at it, and when he came out with a few of his very average one-liners, there was a tendency to giggle at what he had said. For this series we had agreed that if the atmosphere

became heated at least a few of us would pile in. In the first
few overs Caddy had a bit of a go after a play and miss by
Matthew Hayden and nobody backed him up, rather giving
the game away that we were not the united fighting force we
were trying to portray ourselves as. That was another aspect
that I drew upon when formulating our approach to the
following Ashes series.

There are loads of anecdotes about sledging in cricket but
in my experience most of it amounts to little more than the
kind of insults that dear old Caddy used to dole out. The
most effective sledging was of the more subtle type and the
Aussies, like Steve Waugh, were the masters of it. They would
walk past you between overs and just drop in the odd depth
charge to play with your mind, a lot of it centring on what
they had seen in the papers. Did you see that so-and-so wrote
that you can't play spin? I am sure they read the media specifically to find out what weaknesses they could poke fun at.
Outside the Australians, probably the best sledger was Sri
Lanka's wicketkeeper-batsman Kumar Sangakkara, but then
he is a qualified lawyer. Of the four or five Sri Lankans who
seemed to be permanently camped out under your nose he
was streets ahead.

Anyway, we had effectively lost that first Test match after
the opening day and although we fought back the next morning
it was too far to come back. Marcus and I did, however, have
quite a positive opening stand and I was true to my word in
trying to take the fight to McGrath in making a brisk 33 in
36 balls with a few drives and pulls. It did not add up to a lot,
but afterwards Warne came up to offer a few words of encouragement. It was the first time, he said, that he had seen an
England batsman really go out with aggressive intent against
McGrath.

Ultimately, though, it was a hammering, and things got worse when we went to Tasmania to face Australia A. Nasser had gone to Perth, where his wife was due to give birth to their child, and so Tres took over, which I did not give a second thought to as the captaincy seemed so far away at the time. In fact, I was vaguely aware that Marcus was Duncan's and Nasser's likely choice of successor at the time and more or less assumed that it would be him next. A few people took a dim view of Nasser's absence from that match, and the fact that he had originally flown out separately from the team, although I thought it was fair enough.

While he was away we were forced to follow on, with only Rob Key saving us from an innings defeat and getting us out of Hobart with a draw. Martin Love, not good enough for his national side, this time chipped in with a mere 201, instead of his 250 a fortnight before.

When we got to Adelaide to prepare for the second Test on 21 November I was immediately struck by the number of England supporters who were there, far more than in Brisbane. I presume they had come out because there were now two back-to-back games to watch, with us due to go back to Perth afterwards. They thronged around the nets and it seemed to make the likes of Harmison and Caddick steam in even quicker on what were very quick practice wickets, unlike the conditions in the middle. I was in the next net when Harmy, who was not bowling out of a sightscreen, hit Ashley Giles on the hand. That's another one out of the door, I thought. I was not wrong, as it turned out to be a break.

Not that I was without my own problems to worry about. My left knee had begun to lock again and I was sometimes unable to run, which made me consider myself a major doubt for the match. On the morning of the game it was still giving me trouble, so I went out into the nets to see if I could actually bat. Luckily, as it turned out, Nasser had already decided I was fit to play, and stuck my name down on the team sheet as he went out to toss. I was aware that there were rumours around that I was being high-maintenance, but a measure of my concern was that I was desperate for us to lose the toss so I could buy some time by being out in the field or having more treatment.

As it was, Nasser won, and so I was straight in there, just hoping that this locking-up of my knee was not going to occur again. The positive thing was that all the worry took my mind off the actual business of batting, so when I walked out on that most beautiful of grounds with its long straight boundaries and juicy short square ones I was just going to stand there and focus on the ball. As a result I started to play beautifully, that is before I drove the ball to Justin Langer at cover on what looked like a half-volley, with him claiming he had taken a catch. I thought it was probably out, but that there was enough doubt for me to be allowed to stand my ground. I ended up staying and got away with it, and I sometimes wonder what would have happened if that had gone against me, as it probably should have.

Langer did not speak to me for the rest of the series and I took a fearful sledging off his team-mates. 'You fucking cheat!' was fairly typical of what I got, and I responded in similar fashion. The usual sophisticated stuff. Warne, McGrath and Langer were really giving it to me, and in the background I could see Darren Lehmann, my old mate from Yorkshire, subtly grinning away to himself. He wanted to get involved but he obviously could not. I loved Boof. Craig White, who is his brother-in-law, had been round to his house a few days previously, and when he came out to bat was sporting a trophy from his visit. 'Bloody hell, those are my boots you're wearing!' said Lehmann, who was fielding at forward short leg. And they were.

There was little light-hearted stuff, though, and that day I found out why it is said that playing against Australia is far more mentally taxing than against any other team. They just never gave you a moment's peace and were always coming at you in different ways. Steve Waugh came on to bowl bouncers at me with a square field that was very tricky to handle, while Gillespie hit me on the shoulder and, although I did not know it at the time, broke it. I really got hold of McGrath after lunch and a couple of times I put Warne into the pavilion. This had been the ultimate examination of technique and temperament and I felt sure I could finish a wondrous day by being there at the end, only to nick their least scary bowler, Andy Bichel, just before the close. I walked off having made 177 out of 295–4, taking 306 balls over it, and had enjoyed some staunch support from Nasser.

I was virtually bandaged up like a mummy in the dressing room afterwards and had ice packs hanging off everywhere when there was a nice touch from Gillespie, who came in specially to congratulate me. I heard that Langer was still pissed off and that a few of his team-mates were telling him to let it lie because he would have done the same. I thought Langer was a weasel at that particular time, although as the series went on I could see that he was exactly the sort of bloke I would have liked to have in my team.

With my knee, ribs and shoulder very sore – we subsequently discovered that there was a hairline fracture in my shoulder – I could not field. I spent most of their first innings in the swimming pool trying to get the shoulder to ease up while they smashed us for 552. I managed to bat again in the second innings and made 41 before McGrath caught me with a sensational diving catch near square leg after I had slog-swept Warne. We were hammered by an innings and 51 runs and my body felt as if I had gone 15 rounds with Lennox Lewis.

We took an even worse beating at Perth, where I ran Butch out in the first innings and he returned the favour by doing the same to me in the second. My abiding memory of that Test were the six overs Tres and I had to face late on in the second day against Brett Lee bowling at the speed of lightning with the Fremantle Doctor – the prevailing wind in Perth – behind him. Marcus had a real dislike of facing McGrath and Gillespie and as we were walking out I said to him, 'Looks like Lee is going to be opening the bowling.' He was pleased: 'Thank God for that; I'd have him over one of those two any day,' he replied. 'Are you sure? He's got the Doctor behind him,' I said.

The first ball was a bit wide, and then the second absolutely flew and Marcus gloved it down the leg side. Bloody Hell, that was quick! Marcus departed in the seventh over of the innings to be replaced by my Yorkshire mate, the bespectacled graduate Richard Dawson, as nightwatchman. 'Have you got your glasses on properly, Daws, because you're bloody well going to need them here!' I said to him as he came in. McGrath was bowling into the wind and it was like facing another Yorkshire mate, Anthony McGrath, by comparison. Dawson showed considerable courage and we both managed to escape until the next morning, but then they peppered us again, with Alex Tudor taking a horrible blow on the head.

Lee was at his fastest then and it was one of those innings when everyone is sitting on the balcony and nobody is saying much because you all know you are thinking the same thing:

'Blimey, this is rapid!' When I got out, there was the odd ritual inquiry back in the dressing room from colleagues trying to feign nonchalance. Is it a bit quick, then? Erm, yes, just a bit. Tudor had been left to face Lee a little too early in the over by Alec Stewart for my liking. I really liked and respected Stewy and still do, but I did think that his reputation for batting for himself was not without foundation. He had been guilty of it in Adelaide in the previous Test as well, and I thought he was at it again in Sydney during the final Test. I could understand it to a point, because he was among those who had been beaten up by Australia so often that self-preservation would be to the fore, but for me it reinforced the fact that if we were ever going to beat them we had to have an all-for-one, gung-ho mentality.

This time the Ashes had been lost in less than 11 days of cricket, causing the usual inquests into where the whole English game was going wrong. There was a pattern emerging of us losing these matches early and then going on the sauce for a couple of days. I think Butch got run over by a car that night as we drowned our sorrows, although it was only a glancing blow and nothing serious. On what should have been the fifth day of the Perth Test, Butch, his dad Alan, me, Martin Bicknell and Chalky White ended up going down to Cottesloe Beach for a long seafood lunch with plenty of wine, coming back to the hotel slightly the worse for wear and being a bit loud in the foyer. Fletch found out and called us in the next day to give us a real rollocking. He was right – it was not that we had missed practice or anything, because these were 'clear' days, but it was not really appropriate, especially as there were loads of supporters about.

This tour was a strange one in that the one-day triangular series was to start prior to Christmas between the third and fourth Tests, allowing it to finish earlier than usual because there was a World Cup to prepare for in February. So those of us who were surplus to requirements were left behind in Perth while the rest of the squad headed off for a few one-dayers. Those 10 days were, in fact, fairly blissful, and we were pretty much left to our own devices. It was, in truth, a bit of a jolly. We slept in, trained in the afternoon and either watched the cricket on the TV at night or went out and enjoyed ourselves.

The serious business resumed in Melbourne on 26 December, as there never seemed much feeling of a 'dead' rubber about any of the Tests we played against Australia, even when the series was lost. I flew in to meet up with Nichola, who had come out with other wives and girlfriends, and, as it transpired, my enjoyable stay over in Western Australia with the likes of Butch and Dawson seemed to have done me no harm whatsoever.

We put in a much-improved performance for that match, and were really not far off beating them. My 145 in the second innings is a good memory, although the MCG would not go down as one of my favourite cricket grounds. Its size is very impressive and the dressing rooms, both the old and the new ones after its refurbishment, are massive because they have to accommodate Australian Rules football teams. The atmosphere on day one was fantastic when the traditional Boxing Day crowd flocked in, but after that the place was so big that the spectators tended to get lost in the sheer scale of the place. You had all the barrackers in Bay 13 and then everyone was spread out, although the Barmy Army managed to concentrate themselves quite well in the latter days.

It was in this Test that Matthew Hayden bowed to the crowd after getting another hundred against us, the latest outstanding knock in a series where he showed superb form. We had a great plan against him, to bowl bouncers at his right ear early doors because we knew he would have a go at them. He did on this occasion and sent up a skier to Harmy at fine leg – and the plan would have worked a treat if Harmy had not dropped it.

Fine player though he was, we did not have a great deal of time for Hayden, whose bowing and general behaviour was pretty disrespectful. I thought he was rather self-righteous and arrogant as an opponent, which made it all the sweeter when he struggled so badly against us in the next Ashes series. He used to talk as if the game was so easy – that you just stand there and hit it – when obviously it is not. In 2005 he was labouring with his grip, his gloves and his stance – and Hoggy had him on toast.

Off the pitch I did not mind him. When he retired in early 2009 I made sure I sent him a text message along the lines of 'You were a tosser to play against but I would have loved to have you in my team every time.'

I was gutted that I did not go on to a double hundred in that Melbourne match, and had I done so, I feel sure we could have won as they were very edgy even chasing just 107 to win. Steve Waugh was completely out of form and we actually had him caught behind on the last morning but, bizarrely, nobody appealed for it. There was a nice bit of captaincy from Nasser when he deliberately set a field to give Waugh's partner a single and get him down the striker's end for the start of the over. We had been bullied in the series and it was good just to empha-sise to the Australian captain that even the great man himself might have been human.

My feelings about Sydney Cricket Ground are very different to the MCG as it is about my favourite on earth. We arrived there on New Year's Eve and the Vodafone concierge service looked after us again with a boat trip on the harbour to see in 2003. Becoming England captain, I have to say, was not among the New Year's resolutions I made that night.

I could not wait for our final match to start, even though it was going to be a face-saving exercise. They say the pavilion at the SCG is the best nightclub in Sydney and it is amazing how the women dress up as if they are at the races, adding to its stylish ambience. There was a long-standing dressing room attendant there called Rocky who was a great character, who liked to leave amateur psychology messages for you on the board. 'What's your attitude, is it worth catching?' was one of them.

After getting nought in the first innings I was back on that wonderful plane in the second and I finished day three 113 not out, did the press conference and then raced back to the hotel. The reason was that Nichola and I and the Hoggards had booked a trip walking over the Sydney Harbour Bridge that night. A strange thing to do, you might think, in the middle of an innings, but I was absolutely buzzing. I was playing better than ever and we were in a position to finally win a Test, so it was a truly memorable evening and it felt as if I was on top of the world, almost literally, you might say.

The strain of the series was taking its toll on Nasser by then and, although it was a great effort to drive us on to that eventual victory, it was the first occasion that I thought his time as skipper might be coming to an end. His man-management skills were leaving a lot to be desired and he was being unnecessarily aggressive, to a degree that was counter-productive. We had set them a target of 451, which was millions on a wicket that had turned into a spitting cobra, and Hoggy walked down the steps to do some warm-ups before their second innings. Before all the public, Nasser shouted from the pavilion, 'Oi you, you ****, get back in here!' – and the bloke was just going out to prepare to do his job. Again, I understand it more now than I did then, but it was still pretty poor. Nasser had made 72 down the other end from me in our second innings and, whatever stress he was feeling, I thought he batted beautifully, not for the first time on that tour. I never quite bought this image of Nasser being a worker who got the most out of a limited ability. You could not pull Brett Lee in front of square like he did that day without having plenty of natural talent. The same gets said about Paul Collingwood, but make no mistake, he has ample ability as well.

Caddy bowled them out to win the Test, one notable for Waugh's brilliant return to form with a hundred when he was under huge pressure. I was actually very pleased for Nasser in particular, because he had borne the brunt of the abuse that had come our way. He is not a very social animal and we had been discouraged from having a post-match drink with the Australians throughout the series, which was contrary to my policy when captain. I thought it was good to get to know the opposition – particularly when they were a stronger team – because when you got up close to them it would show them to be human. You would realise they have the same body parts as everyone else. We were so distant from the Aussies on that tour that the only time we ever came across them was out in the middle, when they would just reinforce how much they were battering us.

After this match we made up for lost social time, drinking in their 'rooms', as they call them there, and then entertaining them for more beers back in ours. It went on well into the evening, and concluded when a number of us – me, Crawley,

Dawson, Butcher, James Foster – hijacked the golf cart that carried the drinks out onto the field, with Crawley driving it out of the main gates and onto the main road by the SCG. We got as far as the traffic lights and realised it was probably not such a good idea, so we ditched it on a bank outside the ground before getting a taxi home in our tracksuits. Creepy was a great tourist.

By now my stroke play had got me back into the one-day team, and I batted decently in the four matches that saw us get to the triangular final. But I was still thinking of what an incredible cricket education the Test series had been, one in which I made 633 runs that earned me the player-of-the-series accolade.

It also brought me the great compliment of becoming the first player ever to appear on the front cover of the *Wisden Cricketers' Almanack* as it changed its traditional appearance. Inside the big yellow bible, the *Sunday Telegraph*'s Scyld Berry was generous in his assessment of my contribution to the series. He wrote of me: 'His driving all round the wicket was reminiscent of Peter May; his pulling was equally brilliant. Vaughan's footwork had always been outstanding in a generation of England batsmen who either played on the crease or pushed half-forward. Now he used it to move into position to pull the short ball, as perhaps no tall batsman has done better.'

The Test series had been an education all right. Foremost was the insight into just how much an England–Australia series means to people. There was Test cricket, and then there was Ashes cricket. I was fascinated by just how much pressure they put on you, and the sheer exhaustion of playing against them. A day in the field against Australia was five times harder than against others. Every ball you felt the pressure; there was never any grazing in the field. The crowd, the media, everything had been totally different from any other series I had participated in. The next Ashes series, I concluded, would have to be won on character.

9

The One-Day Job

The start of what turned out to be a tumultuous 2003 World Cup campaign – and the latest in a line of crushing disappointments in the competition – was very much a case of the calm before the storm.

In Australia relations between the England and Wales Cricket Board and the squad had already become a little fractious because of the question of what to do in the week between our duties finishing Down Under and the date we would reassemble in South Africa. Most of us wanted to fly home for five days just to decompress and get out of each other's pockets for a brief while, but the Board made it clear they were not going to pay. After a few meetings it was decided we would head straight on to Africa and kill the necessary time at Sun City. In any case, the Zimbabwe issue seemed to be hotting up at home, and I am not sure how relaxing it would have been to be back there anyway. The wider point was that it was hardly a great schedule in terms of preparing for the most important limited-over event for four years.

So we flew across to Johannesburg and headed to the resort, where we had a perfectly pleasant few days chilling out. Freddie and I had a game of golf with Darren Clarke, our stablemate from International Sports Management, as he was out there preparing for a tournament. Nasser and I also played as part of some different fours, having our usual fallings-out, with him accusing everyone of cheating. In fact, the spirit was pretty good among us, which was fine because it was about to be sorely tested once we headed down to the Eastern Cape to begin our World Cup build-up in earnest.

While we played our low-key preparatory games there was no way of escaping the Zimbabwe issue, which was to continue to plague our sport throughout my England career. The draw had decreed that our first group game was to be in Harare, which was a case of Sod's Law if ever there was one. On one side the argument ran that Robert Mugabe's regime was so repugnant that we had no business setting foot there; the counter-argument was that there were plenty of governments where cricket was played that were not exactly perfect, and that British businesses were trading in Zimbabwe anyway, so why should it be left to the cricketers to make a stand?

I was a relatively young player at the time and did not feel qualified to take a lead on it, and wanted some guidance from senior players. Ronnie Irani was very vocal that we should go to Zimbabwe, and he said in the team meetings that we were cricketers and should stay out of political wranglings. I thought Nasser handled it all extremely well, certainly better than the ECB did, and it all boiled up into a climax while we were in Cape Town, where it got to a point where we actually ceased practising. He really tore a strip off Malcolm Speed, the International Cricket Council chief executive, in one of the endless meetings we had to endure. We completely lost our focus and, if we did train, it was mostly just games of football to work off a bit of frustration. Unusually for me, I started reading the papers front to back, rather than the other way round, to try and get informed, but I was still pretty young and unworldly.

Something that did not help was the fact that Duncan found it difficult to get involved. He still had family members in Zimbabwe and did not want to do anything that might make their lives more difficult, so he carefully kept himself out of it, which we could all understand. I was aware in the back of my mind that there were four World Cup points for the taking, and I also believed that we really had a chance in that competition. We were not far off being a decent one-day side.

As history now tells us, we did not go to Harare and so forfeited those four points that were probably the difference between us going through to the 'Super Sixes' and going home early. But who knows how things would have turned out? We would, I am sure, have been as safe as houses in 2003, but the threatening letter we received from a group calling themselves the Sons and Daughters of Zimbabwe certainly sent a chill through everyone, myself included. The worst bit was when they asked how safe we thought our families were back in England. If it was a hoax designed to scare people then that was certainly a good line to dream up and it hit the target. Matters were not helped by the mixed messages we were receiving from World Cup security personnel. For instance, it got back to us that a well-known ex-player and broadcaster had been privately told by a leading tournament official that the fixture would never be cancelled because of the harm it might do to South Africa's bid for the 2010 World Cup. The ECB's job was always going to be hard in this matter.

While we were in Cape Town we went to the event's opening ceremony and that really pushed us towards wanting to be a major part of the tournament. The crowd was big, we had a couple of beers beforehand and really enjoyed walking around

Newlands on that evening, getting a decent ovation from the crowd.

Maybe we should have gone to Harare, made a statement disassociating ourselves from the Mugabe regime or worn black armbands and got out of there as quickly as possible. The world would have moved on fast enough, but that is all looking back from afar. I think the whole episode had a big effect on Nasser, who by then I thought was coming to the end of the line, and this probably just tipped him over. As I know now, it would have been incredibly draining, and it was definitely harmful to our cricket.

Despite that, we played pretty well for a lot of the time. We beat Holland but then nearly came unstuck against Namibia, where Alec had to stand in for Nasser and Marcus made a bit of a mess of counting the overs because there was a Duckworth-Lewis situation. Our captain had a stomach complaint and I would not be surprised if there was some stress tied up with it all, because I know that is how it can get you. Ian Blackwell was in our squad and played in that match before limping off with a back problem, never to be seen again in the competition. I found him a fascinating tourist. He had absolutely bags of ability and the potential to be a real star in the game because he could hit it beautifully cleanly and bowl some canny spin. He was as nice as pie as a lad but strangely vacant on that trip, spending most of his time on his Tiger Woods golf game and ordering room service.

When we played Pakistan at Cape Town Shoaib Akhtar was bowling like lightning, to the extent that the speed gun registered 100 mph for a delivery at Nick Knight. I was actually sceptical about whether it was that fast, but whatever the exact speed it was pretty damn quick. Anyway, I was waiting to bat, very much with my game head on, and there was Blacky behind me getting his camera out and taking a few pictures. In Port Elizabeth the management committee had thought his lethargic attitude was starting to have a dragging effect on others, so Alec Stewart was deputed to have a quiet word with him about his professionalism. Alec reported back that he had done so.

We took Blackwell to the West Indies the following year and, while we were involved in quite a tense run chase, he was asking the lads to sign a few shirts. I was more amused than annoyed by it, but it did show that he was not quite as driven as some. It was a shame he did not feature more for England because he could have been quite a player.

In the Pakistan match Jimmy Anderson excelled, with the ball moving all over the place through the air under lights and, despite it being a good toss to win, we played well. We lost to India in Durban but knew we could still go through if we beat Australia in Port Elizabeth.

This was one of the most sickening defeats of my career, as we should have beaten them on a poor pitch. Michael Bevan was quite brilliant in chasing down what was, in the circumstances, a very competitive score of 204–8 largely forged by Alec and Freddie. When we had them 135–8 with only 12 overs left I really thought we were going through, but we could not get Bevan out and he was bravely supported by Andy Bichel. Nasser made the call of bowling the young Anderson in the penultimate over with 14 required ahead of the vastly more experienced Caddick. Unfortunately, Bichel hammered him for six and 12 were scored, leaving only two required off the last, to be bowled by Freddie. It was one of those calls that can make a captain look foolish or brilliant, but I could see nothing wrong with it.

Anderson had the exuberance of youth on his side and had bowled very well in the tournament, so it was a risk worth taking.

The tension was just about unbearable and with two still needed and three balls left I let the ball through my legs at mid-on. I was horrified and cannot explain why I did not do the basics right, an example of pressure eroding technique. Sick to the stomach, I was searching for a hole in St George's Park to swallow me up. You could make a DVD out of my fielding howlers with England, and probably have enough material left over for a sequel.

Bichel wrapped it up with a boundary off the next ball to send us, in effect, out of the World Cup and make it yet another disastrous campaign.

It was all the more harrowing because I felt that there were two stages when we were a pretty decent one-day side during my career and this was one of them. Australia had been destroying other opposition and here we were running them agonisingly close. The other time I felt it was all coming together in 50-over cricket was around the ICC Trophy in September 2004 – when we should have beaten the West Indies – and the Ashes the following summer. We just could not keep our teams together long enough, through injuries, loss of form or whatever. If you look at a lot of our tours, we would often play one-day series at the end of Test series and lose a couple of key players. The bottom line, I suppose, is that we never had a deep enough reservoir of quality limited-over players. We needed our best XI available all the time, otherwise we were found out.

Had we won in Port Elizabeth, we would only have needed to beat Kenya to make the semi-finals, and in those eliminators anything can happen. I really thought we could have reached the final, but instead our fate rested on Pakistan winning the final group match in Zimbabwe. We seemed to spend half our life in Port Elizabeth early that year, hanging out at a restaurant called Mauro's and playing rounds of golf at Humewood, an outstanding course.

It was a very strange situation to be in after that, as all we could do was wait around, powerless, for that last match to be played out in Harare. It was a horrible time and quite a few of us were by now tired and disillusioned after all the aggro over Zimbabwe and the setback against Australia.

I had a sense that Nasser's time as one-day captain would soon be drawing to a close, but made a conscious effort not to get involved in talking or thinking about who might be a replacement. Obviously I knew by now that my name would be in the frame but, apart from anything else, it has always been a bugbear of mine when players go looking for the captaincy. I am not sure that the people who actively seek out leadership are necessarily the right people to lead. Leaders should be spotted and their attributes weighed up. I have never understood players moving counties all over the place just to try and get a shot at captaincy.

Around that time Marcus did an interview in *Wisden* magazine stating what type of England captain he would be, which I did not think wise. He also did a newspaper column saying that all he wanted to do was go home, get away from cricket and have a good feed, sentiments I understood but did not think amounted to a very sensible job application.

If I am honest, I never thought he was the right person to captain England anyway. Marcus is such a nice bloke and, like a lot of very decent people, prone to high levels of worry and stress, and I always saw him as the perfect right-hand man or vice-captain, which he was. He is a great man to step in for the odd game because his ego is not so large that he will try and upset or change things in a detrimental fashion. He is also a great man to talk cricket with, a giving sort of person and excellent senior player for the younger ones to look up to, with his professionalism and sheer passion for the game.

Nasser had whispered it to a few people that he was going to step down, and word had got around the squad that something was going to happen. On the day that Pakistan played Zimbabwe I had a round of golf with him, Ashley and Colly and he was grumpy even by his own Olympian standards, just hitting the ball and walking off. Ashley, Colly and I tried to get a bit of banter going but he was not in the mood. At the time I thought, 'Come on, you miserable bastard, just switch off for five minutes from your job,' not knowing that it is never that simple. Word came through afterwards that rain had caused the abandonment of the match in Bulawayo and we were out.

Not long after we got back to our hotel we were summoned to the team room and Nasser announced that he was stepping down before Duncan spoke and thanked him for all his hard work. The tournament had been an example of sport at its harshest – for whatever reason, it was just not meant to be for all of us who had been there. I think Nasser would have resigned anyway, because there was a widespread sense that we needed to start planning for the future in one-day cricket, but it would only have taken a few small things to fall in a different way for him to go out on a much higher note.

Clearly the media were going to speculate about what would happen next. I did a carefully worded column in the *Daily Mail* stating that Marcus and I were good friends and would remain so, whoever got the job, but that if I was asked to do the captaincy I would accept. Mark Butcher and Adam Hollioake were also mentioned, but Marcus and I seemed to be the front runners. By now I was keen to be asked, although I could see no point in chasing it. The chairman of selectors was David Graveney, who I knew well, and I had captained before on an A tour, with many of the incoming players having already played under me.

Only a few days after getting back, Fletch rang me at home asking why I would want to be England one-day cricket captain. 'Because I think I could make a difference,' I replied. 'Anything else?' he asked. 'No,' I replied. I was happy to leave it at that. It was not a long conversation. Duncan asked how I thought it would affect my batting. 'Haven't got a clue; you don't know until you do it,' I said.

At the beginning of May, and after weeks of speculation, I was at Hillside Golf Club in Southport playing in a pro-am event with Darren Clarke, Chubby Chandler (who runs International Sports Management) and David O'Leary among others. I was on the patio in front of the clubhouse when Graveney rang on my mobile. He asked me the same questions as Duncan and I gave the same replies. 'OK, that'll do for me,' said Grav. An hour later he rang back and offered me the captaincy.

Was I elated? If I am honest, there were no whoops of cele-bration or laps of honour around the Hillside clubhouse, and not just because by now it was not a total surprise. I took it very much in my stride without too much fuss and immedi-ately started asking myself questions. How am I going to lead the team? How am I going to speak in front of all the players? How am I going to motivate them? How good am I going to be tactics-wise? Will it affect my batting? How should I deal with the media? Am I going to enjoy the higher profile? These cascaded through my head, not in a panic, but more as a sign that I wanted to get my head around the situation as fast as possible. My initial thought was that I needed to get a fairly fresh set of players in.

Once the news had sunk in I thought about it and came to the conclusion that I was just about in the ideal position. The one-day job would give me a chance to settle in and get used to things, and in the meantime my Test career would continue as normal under Nasser. At the time there was no expectation that he was going to quit that side of things. Indeed, he had done an article setting out his goals, including gaining the most Test wins as captain and most appearances in the job. A few people, such as Mike Gatting, had thought he was presumptuous saying that but I, for one, was keen for him to carry on for a while. I could learn, pick his brains, and then in a year or two, with everything having hopefully gone OK, I would be in line to take over in both forms of the game.

I had to go down to Lord's to do a press conference, but at the time my main preoccupation was maintaining my form in Tests because I had got back to England with this huge reputation. As it was, in the early-season series we went from the sublime to near ridiculous in terms of opposition as we were entertaining a now chronically weakened Zimbabwe. I only batted twice as we won both matches with supreme ease, making an eight and 20 that did not really reveal whether I was still in my Australian form or not. Much to my frustration, I was never to recapture that on a consistent basis.

My bow as one-day captain was to be taken on 17 June 2003 versus Pakistan at Manchester at the start of a three-match series of, frankly, very little consequence. The road to the next World Cup in the West Indies in 2007 seemed a very long one indeed. I thought that my first objective ought to be to make sure that those playing under me were really enjoying their cricket. Under Nasser I had the sense that we were not expressing ourselves out in the middle as much as we should have been. Perhaps there was a bit too much fear in the air, the kind that drove him on, and it was transmitting itself to the players.

I wanted the players to remember what it was like when they were playing as youngsters for the sheer enjoyment and glory of it. Of course, that is easier said than done in front of crowds of 20,000 wearing the three lions, but I still thought it would be worth trying to recapture some of that essence. I also wanted us to work hard on our physical fitness, more than we had been doing, although I was wary about trying to go too far too soon. It is easier to achieve change when you have some new players in, and in that team we had the likes of Warwickshire's Jim Troughton, Surrey's Rikki Clarke and Yorkshire's Anthony McGrath. In all, pretty different from the one that had lost at Port Elizabeth in such agonising fashion. Obviously not many of them were going to make it all the way to the Caribbean in 2007, but I thought they were a good group to start off with.

We were a young team and that really struck both me and Duncan when we arrived at Old Trafford, with the built-in benefit that they were all in good shape already. There was a lot of energy among what was a team of under-30s, with Darren Gough the only exception to that rule. There had been some debate about whether he should be included but I was keen to have him, not just for his limited-over know-how but also the bubbly personality he brings to the dressing room. He is not the ultra-confident guy that everyone might think from his exterior, in fact he is quite insecure in some ways, but he is terrific to have around a group of blokes in a dressing room.

I wanted us to look and act like a team that was having fun, and there is never much shortage of that when Goughy is in full flow.

I was so nervous on the morning of that match. Even though it was only on satellite television I thought that the whole country would be watching. Mum and Dad were there, but I could not escape the feeling that on my first day in the job everyone else would be examining my every move and all my mannerisms. How would I react when a bowler started getting smacked about? Nasser had this reputation for kicking the ground in frustration or looking away in disgust when someone did something wrong. Rather than setting out simply to do the exact opposite, I settled on a policy of just being myself. From the off, I decided that if we had prepared well and everyone had given 100 per cent, then there was no point in worrying too much about the result.

Just as well, as far as my debut match went, because we lost that day-nighter by two wickets. We made 204–8, which was probably about 40 short, but we then forced them to work really hard to get across the line. It took a gritty ninth-wicket partnership from Mohammad Sami and Abdul Razzaq to see them home with four wickets to spare.

Despite the result, I was pleased with how it went as I thought that we had looked like a team with a bit about us. Around that time I encouraged all the players to come up with their own ideas of what we should be doing. Although I was an inexperienced captain, it was not so much about needing their ideas as trying to get them thinking in the correct way about managing their own games and contributing to the team.

Marcus really produced the goods for me in the second and third matches. It was a fairly recurring pattern that if he did well at the top of the order and Freddie contributed in the middle then we would win. At The Oval, we won by seven wickets and then at Lord's by four wickets, to take the series.

So far, so good, as we headed into a triangular series against Zimbabwe and South Africa, who were to be the main event as far as Test matches went that summer. The first match against Zimbabwe took place only four days later, on 26 June, and brought my backside down to earth with a considerable bump. We lost by four wickets and it was a swift introduction to what it is like being on the end of biting criticism. Though I always did my best to be phlegmatic in the face of flak, I found this quite a painful experience. Try as you might to put the shield up, it is quite daunting when you first walk down to breakfast and see the headlines slating you and your team. I actually took it quite personally at the time, but I later learned, or tried to learn, not to.

We turned it round after that in pretty good style, including a win against South Africa at Birmingham in which I made 83. I had made a few starts and not managed to build on them in that series, and this put my mind at rest that I could make significant runs while being captain. Then at Lord's in the final on 12 July, in what was now my ninth match in charge in less than four weeks, we hammered South Africa by dismissing them for just 107 and knocking them off for the loss of three wickets. South Africa were a very decent outfit and we had done exceptionally well to beat them. We were a team who looked like we were enjoying it and wanted to be out there in the pressure situations. The relationship with Duncan was working well and the backroom staff seemed to be enjoying what we were doing.

On the way back from the press conference in the museum at Lord's to the dressing room Nasser rang to congratulate me, emphasising what a great effort it had been, which was good of him. It could hardly have been a more satisfactory start, beating Pakistan and then South Africa. Short of beating Australia, in fact, it could not have gone better. I was not to know, however, just how close I was coming to this captaincy thing being a full-time arrangement.

10

Stepping Up

When I turned up at Edgbaston a few days before our opening Test against South Africa on 24 July I did not have the sense that I was an overall captain-in-waiting, but apparently a few others did. What we had done in winning the triangular series – and perhaps more importantly the way we had done it – had sent the hare running around the track in terms of who should be skipper and there was little I could do about it. On the Sunday prior to the Test Nasser gave an interview to the *News of the World* stressing that he would hand over the captain's armband if that is what the selectors wanted, but that he felt there was no reason why he could not carry on and take the team to the West Indies in early 2004.

That was exactly how I felt, and as I turned off the motorway to arrive in Birmingham I was happy to assume that this would be the case. Pretty much a year as one-day captain to get a feel for things and a year to consolidate my new-found status as one of the world's top Test batsmen – that was still just about the perfect arrangement.

I checked into our hotel on Monday night ahead of the following morning's practice actually looking forward to not captaining for the week and being able to get back into my more selfish bubble. It was a very different set of lads from the one I had just been in charge of, with less than half of them being in the team for both forms of the game. Certainly I did not feel that the likes of Freddie, Tres, Anthony McGrath and Jimmy Anderson were looking at me any differently in the Test-match environment, although it turned out that Nasser perceived it otherwise. I did suspect that they might have had more of a sense of enjoyment in the one-dayers, but nobody had actually said that to me.

If Nasser felt that things had changed, it might have been down to a state of mind that naturally occurs when you wonder if you are coming to the end of your captaincy reign. You tend to feel more insecure and perhaps imagine that people are thinking things that are not necessarily so. In my last two Tests as captain I worried that players might be privately talking about my actions and decisions, although maybe they were not. In any case, by the end of that first Test against South Africa it was clear that Nasser was struggling with the thought that I was a vibrant young captain at the peak of my game and was somebody people were looking up to more than before.

Any insecurity that Nasser was feeling could only have been added to by the way we performed in the field during their first innings, and the manner in which South Africa racked up 594–5 in 145 overs. Our attack looked desperately placid as Graeme Smith – the man with the habit of finishing off England captains – put on 338 with Herschelle Gibbs. I did not exactly play my part by dropping the latter when he had made 125. We looked woefully short of firepower, and comparing the demeanour of the team with that in the one-dayers was an obvious angle for the media, especially when rain meant there was no play on the Friday and there were column inches to fill.

It was all added to when I made 156 on the Sunday in our first-innings reply to help us save the follow-on, batting with the same flair I had shown in Australia. That night – my last one in the ranks as it turned out – I still did not have the sense that seismic change was about to occur.

Perhaps I should have spotted that something was up on the Sunday night, due to Nasser's change from his regular routine. On the Sunday evening in Birmingham a bunch of us would usually go out to the Living Room, one of our favourite haunts, or a curry place to have a meal and he would come along. At Test matches, after coming out on Tuesdays when we arrived, Nasser would usually eat in his room and we would not see him of an evening until the Sunday, when he would join the rest of us. I just assumed that he fancied another curry night in, not realising that he was spending the evening on the phone, speaking to people about his future.

On the Monday morning I went down to the ground unusually early for me, arriving at about 8.30 a.m. because I was having some treatment. Nasser was always one of those, along with Darren Gough, who liked to get there early and have half an hour to relax and read the papers before getting ready for the day ahead. He looked very agitated and was on the phone, and only then could I really tell that something was up. I was minding my own business eating a bacon sandwich – I had skipped breakfast at the hotel – when he called me over and asked if he could have a word in the separate coach's room adjoining the changing area. I knew then what was coming and, in the very same room where I was to resign five years later in an emotional vacuum, he asked me if I wanted to be England captain. 'Too right,' was the essence of my response.

He added that he wanted to carry on as a player and that he was still playing well enough to hold his place on merit. I was inclined to agree but did not want to give any guarantees as I was quickly thinking what it would be like with roles reversed and him playing under me. I could see there had been a lot of emotion flowing through him and just shook his hand and told him, sincerely, that I thought he had done a great job, which he had. And that was it.

Nasser and I had always had what might be termed a complex relationship. I had a lot of respect for him in many ways and thought he was a fine player and intelligent captain who certainly brought the best out of me. My understanding of him grew as time went on when I was skipper and I experienced the job's pressures. Yet as a player under him I struggled to understand why he behaved as he often did. He would sometimes blow a fuse at people in the most foul manner and was capable of treating people such as scorers, dressing-room attendants and waiters in a very unpleasant way. I have seen him throw bags at people and when he wrote an article a few years later suggesting the England team were mollycoddled, I considered it pretty rich, considering I had never played with anyone who was so insistent that people should carry his gear. But he could be good company as well, and I enjoyed playing with him.

Despite this, I had virtually no social contact with Nasser after he left the team, although we would have had plenty to talk about and more in common.

My joy inside at this sudden appointment was fairly restrained, partly because it was a Test match day and I was quite wound up because I knew I was going to be batting later on. I was expecting that we would have to bat through two sessions to get the draw and was geared towards that. I also did not want to give anything away in the dressing room, and so kept a determined poker face. My only outlet was to ring Nichola and my dad. I sneaked out of the Edgbaston pavilion into the car park to break the news to them, and even then I was relatively matter-of-fact about it. So was Dad. 'Well done,' he said, before getting back to what he was doing. I did not expect him to go over the top, as it is not his way. When I rang him to say that I had been given the OBE following the Ashes win he replied, 'Other Buggers' Efforts, is it?' I actually suspect he was pleased, underneath, on both occasions.

I think Nasser might have let a couple of his closer mates know, and I learned afterwards that a few people in the ground, including the press box, suspected something was up during the day. The first time the more eagle-eyed could have spotted what was happening was when we went out to field on the final morning when South Africa batted again. Nasser went for everyone, snarling and effing and blinding, nailing us for any slight mistake to a degree that was unusual, even for him. I did not think too much of it. I had the feeling there might have been an element of 'This is how I started, this is how I'm going to finish', a proud determination to be true to himself until the end. It certainly made for a fairly obvious contrast to the way I had been conducting things in the short form of the game.

From the field you could see the selectors gathered in one of the upstairs lounges having a meeting, which was not the usual thing on the last day of a Test. We batted out the draw comfortably enough and Nasser could not speak in the dressing room afterwards, he was too emotional. Duncan made a speech of thanks and said that I was now going to be in charge of both teams. I looked at Alec Stewart, for some reason. Bloody Hell, I'm going to be captaining Alec now!

The appointment only really hit home that night when I went out with my old mate Anthony McGrath and we had a couple of glasses of wine. 'Bloody Hell, Maggs, I'm the England cricket captain,' I blurted out at one point. 'How on earth have you got to that position?' he asked by way of reply, and we both burst out laughing.

Everyone else had gone home for a quick break, so it was just the two of us staying over in Birmingham as we were going to head straight to Lord's ahead of the second Test that was starting on the Thursday. The next morning I had to drive down to St John's Wood, where I was going to be paraded before the media and have my photo taken in the Long Room with my cap and blazer on.

Just after hitting the road I realised that my new Jaguar – I had recently begun my sponsorship deal with them – was very low on petrol. I got to the outskirts of Birmingham but allowed the needle to go all the way down, and ended up running out of fuel about one hundred yards down a hill from the next garage. I had to ask two passers-by to help me push it up the final bit. In that unmistakable accent, one of the Brummies loudly observed, 'And to think that you're the bloody England cricket captain.'

I made it down to Lord's and had my portrait taken inside the pavilion that I loved so much. I already knew that this was going to be very different from my experience of captaining the one-dayers, not just different but far more difficult. The one-dayers were pretty straightforward because the group was one I had played with or captained at a lower level; they were young and were going to find it easy to buy into my new ideas. This was perhaps not the case for the more seasoned internationals who populated the Test team, a collection with whom I was going to have a solitary day to get through to before the start of the second game in the series. There was Darren Gough, Mark Butcher, Alec and Nasser, the last of whom could not, with the benefit of hindsight, have been in any fit mental state to play in the match. I know that I certainly would not have been able to play a Test three days after I resigned the captaincy, such is the turmoil that it throws you into.

Having had Tuesday off, we all met up on the Wednesday and, frankly, I did not have much of a clue what to say to them and how to motivate them. It was a far-from-ideal scenario in which to take over, and I did not feel I could do much more than just see how the week went, try to be myself and then work out where to go from there.

You need a decent few days away from the spotlight to attempt to communicate how you want things done but, given that there was just 24 hours before the start, there was no point in making any speeches about my plans for increased fitness work or my emphasis on players trying to enjoy themselves. Everyone develops a layer of scepticism once they have been around a while and it would not have been worth it. I had not even had the chance for a prolonged sit-down and chat with Duncan, so I limited myself to telling everyone to go out there and play.

There was also a specific problem with Darren Gough, who was weighing up whether he wanted to continue as a Test player at all, given that his knee was not getting any better. The ball was moving around a fair bit and we were bowled out within 50 overs for 173, having to go back out there fielding before tea on the first day.

Goughy was like a bear with a sore head. Within two overs of coming on he was standing at the end of his run saying that he had had enough of this and that after this match it was him over and done with. I was at mid-on and, as you can imagine, not exactly delighted to hear this within minutes of leading the team onto the field for the first time. During the evenings of that match Goughy had the odd meeting about his career, and I quickly discovered that there are few things more harmful to a team than whispers and speculation among the group about what one of their number is up to.

Also in the first half-hour Nasser, who looked as if he was having a bit of a sulk, dropped an absolute sitter that Graeme Smith presented him with in the covers. Maybe it was not so much a sulk as a reflection that he was not in a proper mental state to be playing a five-dayer at Lord's. I could not blame him. Behind the stumps Stewy was doing his best to be bubbly, while I was not quite sure what was going on with Butch. At the time I do not think he reckoned I was ever going to be a decent captain, and had the appearance of someone asking who this idiot was in charge. He may have had ambitions for the job himself and was wondering what might have been.

It quickly reinforced to me that no matter how talented your individuals are – and we had plenty of talent – if your attitudes on the pitch are not right, then you do not have a prayer. You will get completely dismantled by decent outfits if you are not united in the cause, and I could already see that there was a lot of work to be done to tighten the unit. To me being successful was, and is, largely to do with getting the 'one per cent' things right, which can add up to so much. For instance, I was always keen on people sitting on the balcony supporting their team-mates while they were batting. It is an unselfish thing to do and sends a message to the opposition that they are up against a group of blokes who are looking out for each other. I was unhappy that in this Test there were four or five of our number loitering around the dressing-room attendant's room when they should have been out watching. The old guard did not really buy into my way of thinking on this. I am not saying that it is a huge thing, but it is symptomatic of a good team, and being on the balcony is better than watching on TV or having a fag out the back.

At least there was some comic relief amid the catastrophic mauling we were getting, as Smith followed up his 179 in Birmingham with 259 while his team ploughed on to 682–6 declared. Alec had taken a blow on the head and went off with blurred vision, forcing McGrath to take the gloves. Behind my sunglasses and under my 'brimmer' (sunhat) I was crying with laughter and trying not to show it as Maggs attempted to keep to Goughy and was taking it on the chest and fumbling the ball like a circus act.

On a more serious note, I learned a lot of valuable lessons from that match, which we lost by 'only' an innings and 92 runs, thanks to us posting 417 in our second knock. Freddie made a powerful 142 and I felt this was an early start to what was a mutually beneficial relationship in which, most of the time, I pushed the right buttons with him. Fred actually averaged more than 40 with the bat when I was captain, and I believe I got the best out of him in that regard. People have asked me if there are comparisons with the Mike Brearley–Ian Botham relationship, but the answer is that I really would not know. What I am sure of, however, is that every successful England team has had its blockbuster players such as Botham, Flintoff or Pietersen. To me, part of managing them was exercising a bit of live-and-let-live. To a degree you have to accept the whole package.

Overall, my impression from that first Test as skipper was that we had to be more supportive of each other and cut out some of the cynical 'old pro' attitudes, be a bit more optimistic and try to engender more of the sense of enjoyment. Afterwards I took Nasser into the back room of the dressing area and gave him a bit of a volley before he went home. At one point he had given a rollocking to Jimmy Anderson as if he was on autopilot and forgotten his new status, and had also got involved in a brief spat with Smith. I lied to the media that I did not mind this when actually I did, but our clear-the-air meeting actually turned into a good conversation with a positive outcome. I said to Nasser that I could understand him being a bit all over the shop in this match, but that he would have to turn up next time with a better attitude, or not turn up at all. He, rightly, said to me that I needed to put my stamp on the team, and I knew that the process would be easier with better preparation before the next match.

In fact, I could completely understand some of the more experienced players quietly rolling their eyes when someone like me comes in and tells them they should be enjoying it more. They had probably heard it all before, especially those who went back to the days of great instability in the 1990s. I just wanted to give them the freedom to smile and play with instinct, and I did not even mind a bit of gallows humour in the right context.

There was no grace period or recognition of the awkward circumstances from some of the old Yorkshire curmudgeons, the usual suspects. Geoff Boycott described us as 'pathetic' and exercised his grudge against Duncan Fletcher with an unpleasant personal attack, while I had to defend myself from Ray Illingworth's immediate accusation that I was into 'captaincy by committee'. Thanks for your understanding, gentlemen.

Another part of the learning process was having to be party to unpleasant decisions about players you are close to. It was decided to drop McGrath for the next Test at Trent Bridge, which was not easy for me, and, being dispassionate about it, I was still not particularly happy with that. I felt Maggs's last two Tests had been difficult to play in and that, when you drop someone, you should always be sure that the player coming in is superior. I was not convinced that Ed Smith, whom the other selectors wanted due to his strong county form, was a better player but I went along with it against my better judgement. They were worried that McGrath struggled with the short ball, but I think it would have been better to give him a longer run.

I was looking forward to being able to put my stamp on the team and got the chance before the Trent Bridge Test, which was 10 days away. On the Tuesday before the match I sat the whole group down and went through a few of the core principles relating to how I wanted the team to be. I told them what I had told the one-day team, which was that we had to put our faith in our physical trainer, Nigel Stockill, and that whatever he said would go in terms of fitness. Your body is a tool of your trade, and I wanted us to be in better shape.

I talked of the unit, and how I wanted everyone to celebrate each other's success and not just their own. I wanted 11 captains on the field, as I felt Australia had, each in charge of their own space. I said that I wanted people to express themselves and that they should have a proper go rather than being negative. A lot of it is just common sense, but it is easy to lose sight of and it is not so easy to engender the most positive atmosphere. I am sure the youngsters lapped it up while the older ones thought, 'Who is this muppet?' All the time I was informed by my experiences of the previous winter in Australia. Also, I wanted to be cool with the older players such as Nasser, Butch or Graham Thorpe when he came back, and not make them do six laps of the outfield at the close, and told Nigel to make sure he was respectful of them. I always knew, anyway, that we would be looking to replace them in time.

The nerves really got to me before that Test, far more than at Lord's, where everything had seemed to happen in a blur

and where I had been cut a bit of slack due to the circumstances. In a way, it was not the worst thing to have been
completely hammered first time out, as the expectations of the
public and media had been lowered for a match in which there
would be fewer excuses. If you start so well, as Kevin Pietersen
did after taking over from me, then the only way is down.

Goughy had retired and I was almost relieved after the attitude he had shown at Lord's. He had been replaced by James
Kirtley as a horses-for-courses selection. Whatever I said in the
meetings, it appeared to have had the desired effect and we
were unrecognisable from the near rabble that had gone down
two weeks previously.

Nasser and Butch, two of those I had been more uneasy
about captaining, put on a superb partnership and it spoke
volumes for the former captain's character that he played so
well for his 116. If I had any concerns about Ed Smith, he
answered them pretty well with an accomplished 64. But after
working hard for an 83-run lead we were skittled for 118 in
the second innings and Nasser was kicking a few things about
in the dressing room because he thought we had blown the
game. I was trying to get across the fact that the pitch was
now very unpredictable and that chasing anything over 200
was not going to be simple, especially as at this point South
Africa had a reputation for being bottlers. Not for the first or
last time my apparent fortitude was a total act – I was petrified of going 2–0 down and getting off to what would have
been a disastrous start in my new position.

Shortly after we walked out for the fourth innings a group
of lads in the crowd started chanting, 'We all agree, Nasser is
better than Vaughany.' I thought, 'Blimey, you don't get much
of a chance around here.' About an hour later, when Kirtley
had started to rip the South Africans out, they piped up with

the 'Michael Vaughan, My Lord' chant. I suppose you could call that fickleness or passion. Fred bowled very quick from the Radcliffe Road end, which helped set things up for Kirtley, an excellent pro whose slingy action was in its element with the ball zipping around so much. He took 6–34, we won by 70 runs and I was off and running.

I soon discovered that you could never relax as England captain and leave players totally to their own devices, even though I was keen to cultivate a more relaxed atmosphere in which they would think for themselves a little more. We had moved straight on to Headingley where, before my home crowd, I was fervently hoping to build on the Nottingham success. Leading the team out at Leeds on 21 August, however, turned out to be a fairly isolated highlight of the match as a few old attitudes reared their heads.

On the second day Marcus and Butch were going well – I had got out for my fifth straight modest score since becoming captain, suggesting it was already affecting my batting – in our reply to South Africa's 342. They had the momentum, South Africa were toiling and if the light was bad it was only very marginal. The crowd were not happy and I was not ecstatic either at the Marcus-led decision to come off. It seemed to me the old pro's instinctive choice to get off whenever you were offered the light. Marcus duly got out shortly after the resumption and we had lost the impetus that they had done so well to build up. A bolder and better think-on-your-feet option would have been to stay out there.

In both innings the South Africans scored runs lower down the order and we were left chasing more than 400 to win. On the fourth evening we were in trouble at 165–5, although Butch and Freddie were unbeaten on either side of 50 at the close, and there was upbeat talk in the dressing room about possibly being able to pull off something special the next day. That night, however, I noticed that they both lingered a bit too long for comfort in the hotel bar, to an extent that I thought might be detrimental for the next day. They were not especially out of order, but it was just pushing it that bit too far. It was Butch's way to unwind with a couple of beers of an evening, and I had no problem with that at all, but Fred has never needed a second invitation to get stuck into a few and I felt there was an element of him being led astray, which was not difficult. Both were examples of players needing to tread the delicate line between having a carefree, instinctive approach to their cricket and not being unprofessional. The boundary was to be crossed on more high-profile occasions than this.

We duly lost our last five wickets for 44 runs inside the first hour next morning to complete a bitterly disappointing defeat. It was especially galling as Shaun Pollock had flown home for the birth of his child and missed the match, something we had failed to capitalise on. Afterwards I was asked in the press conference a couple of more general questions about the calibre of cricketers England was producing and I gave pretty straightforward replies. That caused an additional rumpus but I was not in the mood for caring.

Any honeymoon period was abruptly over, judging by the reaction to my comments about the mentality of the cricketers our system comes up with, something that obviously touched a raw nerve with some correspondents. According to the *Independent*, I had 'looked a broken man', having been in charge of 'a leaderless rabble of quite shaming proportion'. Steady on, I thought, we beat this lot one match ago (my second in charge) and we still might square the series. Who says we are inclined to go over the top in this country?

I stayed on at Headingley to play in what turned out to be

a cracking 45-over match against Surrey, which we lost by two runs. After my wobbly Test form it was reassuring to hit a 90 that nearly won us the game, but my mind was still on the final Test coming up at The Oval in early September. It did not augur well that we had sufficient injury problems for the squad announcement to be delayed, with Nasser found to have broken a toe at Leeds and Kirtley also struggling.

They both didn't make it, and while I was going to miss Nasser's batting I was, in all honesty, not that sad to have him away from the dressing room for the match. It was not that he had been undermining me, more that it was going to be more straightforward asserting my authority for at least one Test match without him around. I suppose there was still a shadow hanging about, which was not his fault. In any case, there was an excellent experienced substitute for him in Graham Thorpe, who was ready to return after his latest bout of personal difficulties. The match was also going to be notable for being the last in Alec Stewart's outstanding career.

It became one of the greatest Test matches in which I captained, one in which we came back in most unlikely fashion after a dreadful start that had me fearing the worst when they were 345–2 near the end of the opening day. We restricted them to 484 and then came up with some superb batting, Marcus making a quite brilliant 219 and Thorpey raising the rafters with 124 on his comeback. Having gained an unlikely lead, we bowled them out for 229, with the contrasting pair of Martin Bicknell and Steve Harmison taking four wickets apiece.

Bicknell was one of the most underrated bowlers of my era, someone who should have played more for England as he was such a good technician. I also really enjoyed having his mature presence in my team, someone who understood the game inside out and knew exactly how to set his own field. Had our bowling unit not become so established and consistent after that, and had he been that little bit younger, I would have wished for him to have won more caps under me. It would have helped him if we had not been heading for the subcontinent that autumn. As for Harmy this, for me, went down as the Test in which he and Fred really came into their own as a bit of a double act. You could tell how much they were already hitting it off as mates, and in that second innings Harmy gave a taste of what was to come that following winter, crucially getting Gary Kirsten and Jacques Kallis in consecutive overs.

Us knocking off the 110 needed was only soured by my getting out caught behind for 13, about which I was disproportionately gutted for some reason. Afterwards we all drank together in that Oval bath and toasted Stewy, following that by taking an enormous Swiss training ball onto the outfield for a game of football in the sunshine.

To come out and win a game like that at The Oval was some achievement, but perhaps even more heart-warming was the thought that you could see the makings of a real team. In Harmison and Flintoff we had two players who were that little bit special, plus a good mix of talent that was young, middle-aged and experienced in cricketing terms. Much as I liked Stewy and found him very supportive, it was probably a good time for him to go so we could bring in a younger man behind the stumps who would happily fall in with the direction we were taking.

I was able to overlook the fact that since taking over as skipper I had made only 140 runs in eight innings. Fortunately most of the media overlooked it too. After that Oval match I was reminded that everyone loves a winner and that, as ever, this is a results business. In many ways it could not have been a better set of introductory experiences – bewildered newcomer at Lord's, first-time winner at Trent Bridge, supposed villain at Headingley and leader of heroes at The Oval.

11

The Need for Change

Immediately after we lost the third Test against South Africa I chose to speak out about what I considered some of the root causes of England's failure to win consistently on the international stage. Some called me naive to do so but, ill-advised or not, I genuinely felt the subject was worth an airing. My basic argument was that there were structural faults in our domestic cricket that needed to be addressed if we were ever to get near, with any regularity, the soaring standards that Australia had been setting for many years. I pointed out that our excessive fixture list, the number of teams and lack of preparation time for matches all worked against us producing elite players. Predictably there was a backlash from those who wished to maintain the status quo in county cricket at any cost, with the admonishment that I should concentrate on trying to get my 11 men to win against South Africa rather than try to solve the deeper ills of our cricket.

At the time I was contracted to produce a column for the *Daily Mail* (I decided not to renew it when the deal ended because I felt it wrong for the England captain to be identified with one newspaper). So in my next offering I thought I would attempt to clarify my thoughts, while not backing down either. It is interesting to look back on the article that came out on 28 August 2003.

Four days on from our defeat at Headingley and it seems there is as much fallout from my subsequent comments about county cricket as from the result itself.

Aside from taking stick for losing a match which I fully accept we should have won, I have also been accused of undermining our whole domestic game by questioning its direction.

My basic argument is simply that we are playing too much cricket, and that we should reduce the number of County Championship games being played each season. Essentially, I believe that less can be more when it comes to first-class cricket in England and our ability to produce a world-beating national team.

What I wish to categorically state is that I am not in favour of diminishing county cricket, or that I lack respect for those who play it. All I want is for my fellow players to be able to perform to the top of their potential, and I do not think that is possible with the fixture list as heavy as it is. For us to lead the world there needs, in my view, to be more time set aside for players and coaches to work on skills and fitness. I do not see how this can happen when you have a situation such as that affecting Glamorgan recently when they played 21 days out of 24.

While I would not propose cutting the amount of one-day cricket, there would be huge advantages in playing just one Championship game per fortnight.

This would make it far more like Test cricket, because there would be a real hunger to succeed and the preparation could be thorough in a way similar to internationals.

If we are honest, most English professionals would admit that there have been times when they are driving to the ground barely able to remember who they are playing against, let alone having any detailed plans to win.

When my Yorkshire team-mate Anthony McGrath was called up for England duty this summer, the difference that struck him most was preparation.

It was not just all the drills we were able to do in practice, but in the way we were discussing plans to combat the opposition on the Tuesday morning before a Thursday start. That kind of thing, along with video analysis, rehab, fitness and sustained technical work, is just not possible with such a heavy domestic programme.

I admit we played badly and lacked the disciplines against South Africa at Headingley to execute the things we wanted, but the shortage of planning was not an excuse we could make.

I know some county coaches who complain that they barely get any time to properly coach as they are so busy organising logistics, such as getting from one place to another.

In fact, I have never met anyone who disagrees with the fact that we play too much, from senior officials at the ECB to humble county pros. So why don't we do something?

I do not want to see the number of counties reduced and our system will always produce a number of Test-class players because there is plenty of genuine talent out there but, nevertheless, there is a wide gap between our domestic and international cricket.

I feel every part of the game needs to look at where we are going for the overall good of the sport. This is not to hide from what happened at Headingley, for we all know our performance was substandard.

We fully intend to put that right in next week's fifth and final Test at The Oval.

And we did, but not before some more huffing and puffing from the county set. The debate at the time was a pretty hot one, with the likes of Bob Willis and Mike Atherton among those advocating change through an alliance of interested parties called the Cricket Reform Group. It strikes me as ironic that with one hand I supported having that discussion, while with the other I eventually helped kill it off for a while by being part of the effort that won the Ashes.

Whatever the rights and wrongs of my argument, my words of August 2003 clearly did not have much effect, judging by the schedule I came across five years later when playing for Yorkshire before what was to be my last Test series as captain, once more against South Africa.

How is this for a mish-mash of a fixture list in 2008, spread around the country with an incomprehensible set of different cricketing formats:

Twenty20 match on 24 June v Durham at Chester-le-Street
Twenty20 match on 26 June v Leicestershire at Headingley
Twenty20 match on 27 June v Nottinghamshire at Trent Bridge
County Championship match between 29 June and 2 July v Durham at Headingley
Friends Provident Trophy semi-final on 5 July v Essex at Chelmsford
Twenty20 Cup quarter-final on 7 July v Durham at Chester-le-Street
County Championship match from 11 July onwards v Kent at Canterbury

I did not have to play in all of these, but the question might be asked how players can fulfil their potential in any form of the game when faced with a fixture list like that? I fully under-stand that no system can be perfect, that ours is rich with tradi-tion and that it is simply impractical to rip it up and start again. I also think that standards in all forms of county cricket have definitely risen since I came into the game from a combination of greater professionalism and, yes, the introduction of the hugely controversial Kolpak players.

But I still think it could be better, and a greater appliance of science and theorising should not always be confused with progress. There is too much theory-based stuff going around and not enough actual 'doing'. My belief, as ever, is that you have to combine the best of old-school thinking with that of the new school. In one respect I was pleased to see Durham win the 2008 County Championship because Geoff Cook seems to be an old-fashioned coach running a sensible set-up. He had a good captain and a good set of senior players who he essentially let run the team. He likes a good cricket chat that is not too theory-based, does not take it so painfully seriously that it is to the detriment of all concerned, and in the end he delivered a good team who won the title using good, common-sense methods.

My belief is that the counties should play only 10 or 12 four-day games, as 16 is just too many. The basic aim has to be to allow players more time to work on their skills. This would help us produce players who can do things when we come across flat wickets, which is the environment in which England players always seem to struggle. We need guys who can come up with something different to make things happen in places such as the subcontinent.

Speaking of which, I would like us to have a look at allowing every county to play two four-day games per year in India in what is now known as pre-season around March and April. It would expose every player, not just the elite 15 who get into a national performance squad, a chance to experience those conditions and learn some of the methods required to take wickets there. It would encourage spin and real pace and the kind of skills needed at the highest level. It would be a test of the guys' characters and I am sure there must be commercial opportunities in it as well. You would find out about mediocre players, because if you don't have much in your armoury it gets completely exposed out there.

The county chairmen are the most powerful people in the game, and until that changes they are always going to look after their own interests, so I think that realistically there are always going to be 18 counties. We should remember that ours is a superior domestic system to most in the cricketing world, but we should not be satisfied with anything less than the best. In Australia they have six professional teams, compared to our 18, and although we have superiority in numbers (less than we might because of the number of foreigners), the end product is generally not as strong. If we had fewer teams, we would weed out our mediocre players, but as I say, it ain't going to happen. The aim must be to beat Australia consistently, not just on an occasional basis.

The need to have excellence built into our cricket is all the more urgent because of the nature of the general sporting culture in our country compared to the likes of Australia and South Africa. They have much more of an outdoor lifestyle and are more driven to succeed at sport and prove themselves on the world stage. If you excel in sport there, it seems you get glorified, whereas we still have a tendency to be suspicious of people who have an absolute desperation to be the best they can be, such as Nick Faldo, Jonny Wilkinson and Andy Murray. I do think it is changing for the better, and the 2008 Olympics certainly helped, but there is still some cultural resistance towards doing everything you can to win.

India is certain to produce more outstanding cricketers as the country develops and more people get access to the game. They are finally bringing 21st-century marketing techniques to the sport, and the impact the Indian Premier League makes is bound to draw in more talent further down the line.

In my view, a major opportunity was missed when it came to setting up an EPL (English Premier League) to capitalise on the boom in Twenty20 cricket. The proposal to have nine franchises for three weeks per season was an excellent one and I do not accept that it would have been to the disadvantage of the established counties, as there could have been a profit-sharing system. Sadly, the vision to implement it was lacking and fear of the unknown got in the way. The counties, who are so powerful in the running of the sport, are too scared of anything to do with franchises.

Another benefit of fewer games would be to allow more of the counties' contracted players to feature in the best of the local leagues. The professional game needs to reach out more to the grass roots of the sport and I think everyone who plays county cricket would benefit from playing four or five Saturdays per summer in the top leagues. The grass-roots aspect of the sport can easily be overlooked by people in my position, but I have not forgotten that had it not been for my dad playing for Worsley, and me coming along to watch, I would probably have ended up in another sport. One crucial area is that more of the money coming into the sport should filter down to help create excellent facilities at club level.

That is where kids and parents often enter the sport, particularly if they are not at an independent school, where cricket is usually more readily available. While there is no question that the Sky television deal has brought much-needed money into the game – and their coverage is excellent – it is a worry that some children, as well as adults, may not be watching it in the way I did as a youngster simply because they do not have access. It is absolutely essential that we have cricket talked about in playgrounds throughout the country, and much of that springs from what they have seen on television. When I was young I wanted to be David Hirst, Chris Waddle, Graham Gooch or David Gower in the playground. I just hope we are not missing out on talented kids when there are so many other sports competing for them, so we have to have decent grass-roots facilities.

When I was in Western Australia in late 2006 with the performance squad, coming back from injury, we practised at a public park cricket facility opposite the local zoo in Perth. We were messing about and all these club players started arriving in immaculate gear into the dressing rooms, which had a huge plastic board with all sorts of tactics being planned. I thought it was the WA state team, but in fact they were club players in a league side, although later they were joined by Mike Hussey, Justin Langer and Adam Gilchrist, all training alongside these league players.

I do not think the odd outing in the leagues would do international players much harm either, and the participation of county pros would raise the profile and standards among the better clubs. Again, it is what happens in Australia. Going back to the leagues would remind possibly pampered pros of how much the game means to the postman or builder, for whom it may be the highlight of the week, and how much enjoyment they get out of it. There would also be exposure to a particular type of pressure to perform, because that is what would be expected of you.

Coaching is another area that would benefit from a more streamlined and coherent schedule. At the moment the coaches seem to me to be largely managers, spending half their time organising travel arrangements. There are not enough practice hours, in which a coach should be earning his corn by helping players with their techniques and giving them ideas to improve their games. They do not have enough time to coach, and with a bit less cricket I think we would be able to find out who really are our best coaches. I see a lot of level-four coaches who are good people and good organisers and qualified up to their eyeballs – but do they have that special eye, like Duncan Fletcher, to recognise talent and temperament and make you a better player? That is how Duncan improved us as a team and I do not see enough of that expertise around the place.

Good young players need to be attached to counties, but academies cannot be a substitute for the great lessons of life and cricket that you learn playing in the leagues. Yorkshire's academy play as a team in the Yorkshire Premier League, but it would be much better if the players were individually allowed to play for clubs. As a teenager I learned so much by sitting in dressing rooms with hardened club cricketers, and not just about the game of cricket! You sit there with a 40-year-old who has been at work all week and you cannot talk or act like an idiot, as you might do with your contemporaries; you have to be able to communicate.

Becoming totally ensconced in the professional game early on also leads to players learning to work the system. In one case I came across recently a young player of some promise, by no means exceptional, who had featured in just a handful of Championship games, walked into the chief executive's office demanding a three-year contract. Otherwise, he said, he would be off to another county that were interested in him.

I also have reservations about the ECB performance squads that cater for supposedly the cream of up-and-coming players. They meet up at Loughborough and do lots of wonderful stuff which is all intricately linked to modern theory, but to me the best way to develop is to take yourself off to Australia and South Africa, stand on your own two feet and just play. I know that guys such as Strauss, Collingwood and Hoggard, who wintered with clubs in Australia and South Africa during their youth, found it absolutely invaluable. You are not mollycoddled or given everything; you have to organise yourself on and off the pitch and become self-reliant.

It is a real regret of mine that I never had a winter abroad playing club cricket, because I was always going on an Under-19 or A tour within the England set-up. There are so many players who did not come through these highly organised routes. It was interesting to see a couple of guys pulling out of performance squads at the end of 2008 because they said they wanted a 'rest'. Maybe it was more that they just wanted to get away from the mechanical grind of the system.

The issue that gets many English players' blood boiling, and that of some observers, is that of the Kolpak players, those from overseas who can play for counties by taking advantage of trade agreements. Some undoubtedly have their benefits, and I think the likes of Deon Kruis and Jacques Rudolph at Yorkshire have, for instance, been good role models in how they prepare for matches, which is in an extremely professional manner.

A major reason for their influx is the pressure the modern game puts on coaches. They are expected to deliver results very quickly, so of course the temptation is to import talent. The money is pretty good for coaching staff these days but the turnover is higher, and naturally they do not want to lose their jobs. I do not think we will be seeing too many more Doug Padgetts, who spent decades at Yorkshire and was one of my great mentors. The days of one Championship division are long gone, and now you have six-figure prizes for where you finish in the table as well as all the money that has come in with the Twenty20 competitions.

There are good livings to be made out of the game, and if a few Kolpaks can ensure survival for you rather than sticking with a promising local lad, it is understandable who they will go for. I am honestly not that sure whether I would ever have emerged from the current system of county cricket. When I was in my early twenties and averaging just over 30, would they have kept picking me, or would they have thought it better to bring in a Kolpak?

Given that the constitution of the England and Wales Cricket Board ensures we are always going to have 18 counties, I would like to see the Championship broken down into three groups of six playing 10 first-class matches a year. You could then have one official overseas player – who you could not chop and change, as is done now with bewildering regularity – and two Kolpaks, if we could get everyone to agree to it, which is probably being idealistic.

Another objective of having fewer matches is that by July players are not just thinking, 'Here we go again, where's the bus headed for now?', and instead are really up for what they are doing. No matter how deeply you love the game, it is hard to compete with the necessary intensity when you are playing too much.

None of this was tackled properly by the Schofield Report, formulated by a golf administrator, which came out after our 5–0 humbling by the Australians in 2006–07. I believe the report was largely a public-relations ploy that grew arms and legs, a knee-jerk reaction from the ECB to what was obviously a very disappointing tour. They wanted to be seen to be doing something about it, and the response was let's-form-a-committee-and-produce-a-report. A lot of the recommendations

I was not convinced about, although I did support the creation of the managing director's job, filled by Hugh Morris, who is someone I always rated highly as a bloke. His role would seem to provide a decent bridge between the national team and the Board and their interests, which was something that had been missing.

I was not, however, keen on the increased power of the chief selector as I remain a big supporter of the principle that the coach and captain should pick the team. Those two should be the main men, with the selectors acting more as scouts, and I would even go as far as to say that the captain and coach should appoint the selectors so that there is a cohesive approach.

My own participation in the report seemed to be an after-thought, as I was spoken to at the last minute, I believe because Richard Bevan of the Professional Cricketers' Association suggested that it might actually be a good idea to hear what the England captain had to say.

During the formulation of the Schofield Report one point that was repeatedly made by many interviewees was that we needed to see less cricket, and focus on quality rather than quantity. In fact, since the report came out we have seen only an increase in the amount of international cricket, which is placing even more demands on the players.

Of course, the tour that preceded it was not successful, but the previous five years had been a pretty good period for the England team in Test match cricket. Injuries were a major factor and I felt it was a real kick in the teeth for Duncan Fletcher after all the good work he had put in, and he felt very undermined by it. His soul was taken from him when he was told there was going to be a report; it really hurt him, especially as he was not part of the panel. That was very bizarre.

What has to be remembered, when putting into context the

arguments about the game so many of us care deeply about, is that it is a myth that England have ever ruled the world as a team. There have been some good patches, but we have never produced an unquestioned 'Team of the Era' as the Australians and West Indians have done. And when you think of the number of countries where cricket thrives, ours is not a widely played sport in global terms.

There are many good things about county cricket, and I genuinely believe that we have no shortage of talent to challenge the likes of Australia, South Africa and, increasingly, India. We can all agree on that. But it is a fast-moving world with shifting habits and tastes in which we can no longer even be sure of the primacy of Test cricket. A little streamlining and innovation from the 18 men who hold the real power in the English game – the county chairmen – would not go amiss.

12

Laying the Foundations

Chatsworth House seemed even more glorious than usual on 27 September 2003, the date and wonderful venue for our wedding reception after Nichola and I got married at Christ Church, Fulwood. Matt Sanderson was my best man and my Yorkshire team-mate Matthew Wood among the ushers. The weather was kind to us, we had 200 friends and family and it was just about the perfect day-nighter, going on late into the evening. Not only that, but the preparations for it had been, as I was discovering, a rare opportunity to get my mind off the all-consuming job of being England captain.

So, too, was our honeymoon in Dubai, spent lazing around on Jumeirah Beach, which we had just about enough time to slot in before heading off to Bangladesh for my first tour in charge. Even then it was not entirely possible to escape from the game, as the Indian waiters there wanted to do nothing but talk cricket. I befriended one of them and he would go and buy me the *Sun* every day from down the road and deliver it to me. Sad but true.

We flew back from the Middle East, and I knew that I would be going from the lap of luxury to a very contrasting environment with a somewhat different level of creature comforts and convenience.

This, however, I was determined to turn to our advantage, because the lack of distractions in Dhaka provided the perfect opportunity to get on with the task of imposing a new culture on the team, something that I knew would be easier when we were away as a group. From the outset I had been keen for us to improve our overall fitness, as much from the perspective of injury prevention as anything else, and this was going to be the real start of it.

Also, doing hard fitness sessions as a team was a good way to find out more about people's character and how they would react to a tougher programme than we were used to. So from our arrival in Bangladesh, where we were due to play two Tests and three one-dayers before going straight to Sri Lanka and then coming home at Christmas, we insisted on early starts in order to put the boys through a harsh regime.

After South Africa, and given the way that the last Test had gone so brilliantly in his absence, I would admit to being of a mind not to bring Nasser with us and to make a new start in that way. Duncan Fletcher saw it differently, however, and he advised that we still needed a quota of senior players before we brought more youngsters through. He was right and I was premature in my thinking, because the likes of Nasser, Butch and Graham Thorpe did a fine job for us that winter as we sought to get some winning momentum going. In hindsight I would say it takes three to six months for a captain to bed in properly and for everyone to realise how it works, which is one reason why I would have advised Kevin Pietersen to stick with it a bit longer before he resigned so soon after succeeding me.

I knew Bangladesh would be tough in many ways, even

though they were struggling to justify their position as a major Test nation, and I always thought Sri Lanka was about as hard as anywhere to visit as a cricket team, with the heat, humidity and the Murali factor. It would also be a chance for me and Duncan to really get on each other's wavelengths and spend prolonged periods of time together, which is not so straight-forward when you are flitting around the venues in England.

With the older guys I was mindful that at that stage of their careers they could not train the same as 23-year-olds, so I went out of my way to assure them that allowances would be made. What I really wanted to see was them commit to the programme in their own ways, which they did. We also did loads of fielding and catching, while in the gym the guys were pairing up to help each other through their various pain barriers.

You could feel a bit cut off in Bangladesh, and we had a welcome visit from then Somerset chairman Giles Clarke – later to be the ECB chairman – welcome in the sense that he brought with him the gift of a few very nice bottles of wine for Marcus Trescothick. He had a bit of style about him, I thought.

Bangladesh were not a total pushover, but there was a danger of reading too much into beating them. It was, nonetheless, good for my morale that I managed to get some decent runs, even if it was not against the world's greatest attack. It was important to nip in the bud suggestions that I might find the captaincy too detrimental to my personal form and maintain the respect for my batting from those now under me. Harmison took nine wickets in the first Test to re-emphasise his quality, but there were already signs that he was not going to be the easiest player to manage on tour.

He had a back niggle after the first match and when it became clear that he was going home to have his problems checked out his mood became unmistakably happier. I was not too upset when a few of the media lads picked up and wrote that we were not entirely happy with him and had told him to sit out the rest of that whole tour as a way of giving him a kick up the backside. That was one of the frustrating things about Harmy: you often felt that to get the best out of him you had to manage him so carefully. We wanted him to go to Loughborough for training and treatment when he got back, but he was not enthusiastic about it, which did not go down well either.

We won the one-dayers, which was not exactly the biggest story back home in England because our opposite numbers in rugby were on their way to winning the World Cup in Australia. We had slid even further down the agenda when we got to Sri Lanka in November because the rugby final was looming and our one-day series was pretty much washed out. I was texting the likes of Matt Dawson to wish them luck and admit how envious I was. I watched the World Cup final in the bar of our hotel in Colombo with Fred and Colly and found it inspiring. You could not help dreaming about being the person who lifted that cup and, like every red-blooded male from England, I was no different in wishing I could have been Martin Johnson that weekend as we looked on from the sodden Sri Lankan capital.

Seeing him lift that cup added to my inner drive and already I could not wait for us to have our own go at the Aussies. I think it was the first time that I properly fantasised about lifting the Ashes urn aloft.

Rugby fever was still burning strong at home as we faced our first trial-by-Murali, as far as Tests were concerned, at Galle, where there were a couple of incidents prior to the match. The day before, I went out bodysurfing with Gareth Batty in the sea just outside our hotel. It was pretty choppy with a strong undertow, and we ended up getting dragged out and were unable to swim back. We both managed to scramble onto different rocks and, unnerved, I started to wave at various people gathered around the swimming pool up at the hotel. They thought I was being friendly, when actually we needed some assistance. In the end I managed to get the attention of a lifeguard, who came out to show us the way to swim back in out of the strong currents. Slightly embarrassingly, it was written up as some sort of *Baywatch* drama, and while a bit disconcerting, it was not quite that bad, even though that stretch of coast is notoriously dangerous. According to a report on Cricinfo, I had bravely swum in to raise the alarm. Sadly I was not quite the hero.

Another strange thing happened before that game when Nasser approached me on the morning of the match. He said that he was sick and was unable to play, the kind of thing that can happen to anyone in that part of the world, so I went up to Colly and told him that he would be making his Test debut. There was a bit of a delay to the start because it was wet and we arranged a photo of the 11 players who would take the field. When he saw what was going on Nasser seemed to change his mind and said that he would be all right after all. I am sure he was genuinely ill, but I had to say to him that I could not go back to Colly and tell him that he would not now be winning his first cap. A curious episode.

As it turned out, Colly played a full part in us batting out a really gutsy draw, holding on for nearly three hours on the last day as we escaped with nine wickets down at the end. Batty and Ashley Giles also managed to frustrate them after Chris Read had fallen cheaply. It was around then that I began to get the sense that Chris was not going to be the long-term option for us behind the stumps. A decent keeper and a nice lad, for sure, who on occasions could be particularly good fun around the bar, but I just felt that he struggled with the pressure of playing for England, and Fletch was feeling the same. Maybe we could have managed him better, but it is part of leadership that you have to make harsh judgements, and we were eventually to make one about him.

Beyond that, I felt that the draw was the first real dividend for all the hard work and bonding we had done in Bangladesh. That resistance in Galle had been forged by the early mornings in Dhaka and Chittagong and evenings when we had little more to do than just hang out with each other eating ham, egg and potatoes. It is the kind of place where you have to create your own fun, such as having quiz nights and movie nights, and everyone spends most of their time in the team room. Basically, the worse the place, the easier it was to create a sense of togetherness.

After Galle we moved up to the beautiful hills of Kandy, where the second Test starting on 10 December followed a similar pattern. I made a hundred in the second innings that would stand as one of the finest of my career as, again, we had to hold out in difficult circumstances, with Read, in fairness to him, playing his part. Getting that 105 was a huge moment for me, affirmation that I could still bat really well while being burdened with the captaincy. We even looked as if we might pull off a sensational win at one point.

Nasser had returned for that match, although there were further signs that he was suffering some sort of delayed reaction to handing over the captaincy and was far from happy. In his eyes, we had been a bit too friendly with Murali off the pitch and when the great spinner came in to bat he received a volley of abuse from our former captain, calling him a cheat in pretty choice language. It was true that it was very easy to get on with Murali, a delightful character who is almost like a little kid in his enthusiasm for the game, but that is beside the point. Nasser got hauled up before match referee Clive Lloyd and it was reported that I might have been unhappy with the ex-skipper for undermining me. I was perfectly happy with him, in fact, because I always wanted players to act real and be themselves. And in being ultra-competitive and screaming abuse about Murali and his action, it was plain that Nasser was being nothing other than himself.

I really felt that, after we had held and frustrated them for those two matches, there was a chance they would fold in the decider that took place just before Christmas. We got off to a great start, but when Marcus got out just before lunch on the first day it went downhill from there and we were the ones who ended up folding, losing by an innings and 215 runs.

It was a very deflating end to the tour, but I was actually far from downhearted about what had gone on over the previous 10 weeks. We had discovered a lot about our squad, the fitness ethic had been allowed to bed in and we had competed hard in difficult circumstances that were easy to underestimate. Looking back, that tour was a platform from which we could really start to achieve things.

There was never any doubt that Harmison was going to come back in for the trip to the West Indies that had been scheduled to start in March 2004. Kick up the backside administered, we knew that everything would be suited to him in those conditions and that he would be a vital part of our armoury. Similarly, there had been some discussion about whether we would persist with some of the more experienced batsmen, but we definitely wanted the core of Butcher, Hussain and Thorpe in that environment. Once again, Duncan's judgement was to be proved right, although this time I was not disagreeing with him. It was also the first time we managed to get Andrew Strauss into the squad, and right away I could see that this was the kind of character I wanted in my team. He had been around the one-dayers in Sri Lanka and his whole demeanour just confirmed what we had first thought, that he possessed the right credentials to be a Test player of stature.

I was still concerned that this was not the case with our wicketkeeper, however, and I came to a fairly definite conclusion about him on the first day of the first Test in Jamaica. Their opener, Devon Smith, was on his way to a hundred and after lunch had repeatedly smashed us through the off side, puncturing the attacking fields I was setting. I went up to Chris Read as we walked off for tea and asked him if the ball was still doing a bit and he replied that it had done nothing all session.

What? In his view it had done nothing and he had not deemed it necessary to relay that to me at all. I thought, I have a keeper here who has been watching me set these attacking fields and he has not bothered to tell me that the ball is stuck on the straight and narrow. I always wanted my keeper to tell me everything that is going on and be my lookout man for any developments in the conditions. He has the best seat in the house and I want to hear if it is just starting to swing conventionally, or reverse-swing, or if the pitch is slowing down or flattening out, or if my angles for field placings might be just out. I can get a vision of what is going on from mid-on or mid-off, but there is no better position to read what the bowlers are doing than from behind the stumps. If a bowler is slightly dropping in speed the keeper will sense it – and I will want to know because it may be about time to take him off.

That really infuriated me, because we lost that second session, and losing one session can cost you a Test match. No matter how much the selectors were fans of his glove work, I knew then that his days in the team were numbered.

As it was, the match was neck and neck after the first innings, largely thanks to two knocks of class and not a little courage from Butch and Nasser, who delivered exactly what we wanted from them. The pitch was very quick but they soaked up everything that Fidel Edwards and Tino Best could throw at them. It was frighteningly brisk and Extras was our top scorer with 60. We sat there in the viewing area, a great atmosphere in the ground, thinking blimey, this is really proper West Indian cricket. The boys reckoned that it was some of the most rapid bowling they had ever seen and I do not think younger players would have been able to cope so well.

Harmison had arrived on the tour fitter and more determined than I had seen before, having trained with his beloved Newcastle United while at home. In the warm-ups he was on the outfield with his Swiss ball and doing press-ups and sit-ups, training with energy and professionalism as if he was Alec Stewart reincarnated. You could not help thinking that if he only did this all the time he would be an all-time great, and I suspected that he had it in him to deliver something special on that tour.

Make that sensational, as in their second innings he completely blew the West Indies away by taking 7–12 with a quite devastating display as they were all out for 47. That was when I set that umbrella cordon with eight fielders waiting for the edge, and while there was an element of making a statement, it was not, as one or two suggested, an attempt at showing off. The whole philosophy of field-setting is that you put men where you think the ball is likely to go, and I just could not see where else the ball was going to fly to. I did not work from manuals and just went with my gut instinct that, as he was bowling outswing at 95 mph, we needed eight slips.

There are few better feelings in cricket than winning a Test match away from home and we went back to the hotel to celebrate, the guys sitting around the pool bar comparing bruises from that first innings. It looked an easy victory on paper, 10 wickets, but we knew we had been in a match.

It was this series that was to see the emergence of the 'Fab Four', as they were christened, of Matthew Hoggard, Harmison, Freddie Flintoff and Simon Jones, the last getting a proper run for the first time. This was the attack that was going to drive us forward, with Ashley Giles bringing his underestimated influence to bear as well, by frustrating the batsmen over the wicket. With our Aussie bowling coach Troy Cooley supervising them, they were a great unit as they all brought something different: Hoggy with his conventional swing, Simon with his pace and reverse swing, Freddie and his amazing accuracy at pace, and Harmison with his bounce and movement. I could hardly have asked for more – well, possibly McGrath, Warne and Gillespie, who were at their peak – but I knew then that we had something to compete with that. I didn't dare to dream that injuries might allow this collection to stick together for a couple of years, but they were certainly young enough.

Jones properly announced himself with five wickets in the second innings of the second Test at Port of Spain, with victory meaning that we could head to Barbados just one draw away from ending our 36-year record of failing to win in the West Indies.

Playing a Test at Bridgetown has to be one of the best experiences possible for an England cricketer. It's a great place to visit and to play; we have loads of supporters there and the locals are still mad about the game, even if there is, sadly, no longer the mania for it that there was 20 years ago. I got to the ground at 8.30 on the first morning and the locals were doing karaoke in the stands. We had our families there, we were on the brink of a major achievement and we were playing well – it was all set. There were to be some memorable individual performances: Fred's five-for in their first innings, a beautiful hundred from Graham Thorpe in our first innings when the ball was doing plenty, and Hoggard showing he was so much more than a workhorse by getting a hat-trick in their second innings, sending the whole place nuts.

We rolled them for 94 in their second innings and knocked off the runs for the loss of two. Our hotel was at the far end of the St Lawrence Gap at the south of the island and it was a memorable journey back from the ground. We drove down the west coast and along the Gap, supporters tooting their horns and banging on the bus and cheering all the way. It was fantastic.

On the dressing-room balcony after the match, away from the euphoria surrounding us, Fletch and I had a chat on a topic that we knew was going to cause controversy. I said to Duncan, and he agreed, that it was time to give Geraint Jones a chance with the gloves and ditch Chris. I had actually wanted to do it before Bridgetown, but on the basis that you do not want to change a winning team on the verge of clinching a series we had stuck with him.

Geraint had done well in a practice match before Bridgetown and he had this great energy and attitude about him around the dressing room and out on the pitch. When I first came across him I had immediately thought that Geraint was my type of player, and it turned out that Duncan shared exactly the same feeling. Perhaps I was a bit naive and unaware of the sensitivities and protocol surrounding the dropping and picking of players on tour. I basically assumed I could have what I wanted, especially as the coach wanted it too, but this was a delicate one as Chris had a devoted supporter in selector Rod Marsh and many followers of the county game. Chairman of selectors David Graveney said there was a time when he used to get more letters about this particular issue than anything else.

We felt we were in a position of strength after going 3–0 up and basically thought, 'Right, let's just do it.' Apparently Marsh went ballistic when he found out about it back in England, but on the front line we were sure it was the right thing to do, and it was also a decision supported by a lot of players within the team. After we had announced it to the media in Antigua prior to the fourth Test that began on 10 April, I started getting phone calls from officialdom. Graveney rang me to express his concern, and I replied, 'Come on, Grav, give me a break, you know we're right.' The problem was Marsh, who did not get on at all with Duncan and with whom I communicated very little. It was hard on Chris, and certainly nothing personal, but then sport is hard. I thought he was a better bet in the one-day game, where he somehow seemed more at ease, and he was certainly a good enough finisher of an innings in that format. Fundamentally, though, I wanted one keeper for both forms of the game.

Our ecstatic mood slipped somewhat when we arrived in Antigua and found that we were being put up in an appalling hotel at Jolly Harbour. There was paint peeling everywhere and we seemed to be surrounded by shaven-headed punters who kept knocking on our doors for autographs. When we drove

into the hotel they were there with their St George's flags singing
'Barmy Army!' We knew we were not going to get too much
peace.

It was an example of how players can get really grumpy on
tour when the organisation falls below their expectations. I
would not say there was mutiny in the ranks, but the dump
we were in, with its sub-holiday-camp decor, really brought
everyone down and some players threatened to go and stay
privately. It is also another illustration to me of why you cannot
consider yourself a seasoned captain until you have done a
winter abroad. It is so much easier when you are playing at
home because you can jump in your car and get away from
everyone, whereas on tour there is an enormous caravan moving
around and you have to keep people happy. While the accommodation was certainly not up to scratch, I thought we were
probably being a little bit precious.

The Antigua match will rightly be remembered not for
Geraint's debut, but for Brian Lara's staggering unbeaten 400
in their total of 751–5. I am convinced we had him out before
he had scored, with our new keeper's first significant act in Test
cricket being to have caught him off Harmy. We all heard the
nick, but Darrell Hair was unmoved. Lara then proceeded to
humiliate us and, on the small and wonderfully atmospheric
old ground in St John's, work his way towards his total with
an astonishingly clinical display.

There was no doubt in my mind that he was taking the
mickey when it came to the way he milked Gareth Batty.
Whenever I moved a fielder for Batts, he would deliberately hit
the ball there, in fact whatever I did he would try and make
me look stupid. He was that brilliant. I found Lara easy to like
off the pitch, even if he was not suited to being a captain. I
was gobsmacked by how he batted in that innings, and even

when faced with other great knocks – such as Ricky Ponting's 156 at Old Trafford in 2005 – I never had the sense of someone being able to do things at will in the way that Lara did. I felt sorry for Batts, who was a decent cricketer and our lone front-line spinner in the absence of the injured Ashley Giles. His father, George, had coached me in Yorkshire and they were good people. Marcus and I were required to bowl 31 overs between us in that innings – we were that desperate. I scored 140 in the second innings and we ended up drawing pretty comfortably.

Rain dominated the one-day series that followed, with torrential downpours dogging us the whole time from Trinidad to Grenada. It was there that we were invited onto the yacht of Hampshire chairman Rod Bransgrove, on which Ian Botham, now Sir Ian, was staying. When all concerned had got stuck into a few beers, Beefy took to the speedboat that was attached and gave a few of the lads a go on a two-man inflatable towed behind it. It was a little like old-style Caribbean touring as it should be. Unfortunately, Ashley, who had been hoping to make his return from injury, managed to pull his groin while holding on for dear life and being flung about at the end of the rope, and he had to miss the one-dayers in St Lucia that followed. Beefy was out in the middle for Sky at the toss as I explained, with a straight face, that Ashley had suffered a little niggle in the nets and would sadly be unavailable.

We finished the tour off with an excellent win to level the series at Bridgetown, scene of the whole trip's high point, and we headed home happy. By now I was brimming with optimism and really encouraged by what was going on – how we had bonded as a team, how everything was gelling with the backroom staff and, especially, how we were bowling together as a unit. I felt so much more authoritative and in control as captain than I had done when we set off for Bangladesh at the start of the winter. Expectations could rightly be high for the summer ahead, although it was hard to believe just how much of a habit winning would become.

13
Upping the Run Rate

There was precious little time to luxuriate in what we had achieved in the West Indies with a mere 15 days separating our final one-day victory in Bridgetown from the first Test at Lord's against New Zealand on 20 May. While trying not to get ahead of ourselves, Duncan and I were already preparing for what we were going to face more than 12 months later against Australia, and there was one specific area we were focusing on: run rates.

In the West Indies we had been able to play more of the attacking cricket we wanted, and certainly more than had been possible in Sri Lanka. Yet the Australians would produce a challenge in a different league, and we saw the three-match New Zealand series as a great opportunity to start putting in place the strategies we would need for 2005.

At that stage Australia were rattling along in Test matches at around 3.6 runs per over, so if they batted a whole day they were getting well over 300, while we would get to about 270. With the strength of their bowling attack – Glenn McGrath would go for only two per over and Shane Warne at a similar rate – you could have decent days and still find yourselves well adrift. In the past there had been times when we had batted the same amount of overs as them but had still faced considerable deficits. So we saw it as crucial, if we were to have any chance of beating them, to assemble a batting order that could be aggressive and go along at a reasonable lick, even though that was bound to be far easier said than done against the world champions.

Such a brief interlude following the West Indies was never going to do our bodies many favours, and predictably mine was suffering more than most from the workload. I was aware of my right knee being sore but just presumed that it would muddle through provided I looked after it. Not for the first time I was proved wrong on that score, with my preparatory session in the Lord's nets ahead of our opening game against New Zealand sparking off a whole sequence of events with long-lasting repercussions. I was facing a young left-arm spinner from the MCC ground staff, Zac Taylor, when I went to sweep him. I slipped and landed on my right knee, causing it to lock completely. As I was to discover much further down the line, holes were starting to develop in the articular cartilage as a result of overuse and the operations I had undergone previously. 'Oh shit, it's gone' was the limit of my immediate diagnosis.

It was pretty embarrassing, being stretchered out of the Lord's nets, and I was extremely concerned, apart from being in pain. It had happened on a few occasions now, and every time the muscles around the knee seemed to go into shock. For a week I could hardly move the leg – and by the time I got my mobility back much water had flowed under the bridge.

Perhaps things happen for a reason. Andrew Strauss was brought in to open in my place and on his home ground made 112 in his maiden Test innings and 83 in the second before he was run out. His partner, Nasser, had a hand in that but then redeemed himself with a memorable hundred that won us the game. He ran off at Lord's waving his bat and decided that there could be no better way to end what had been an outstanding career, going out on such a high.

Strauss's success did not surprise me. I tended to make fairly quick judgements on players largely based on how they acted in the dressing room, and from the outset I had a really positive feeling about him. His self-assurance told you he was going to be able to cope, irrespective of his helpful knowledge of the Lord's slope.

By now I was back in Yorkshire having treatment on my knee because I was desperate to play in the second Test and, had Nasser not bowed out, it would have left us with major selection problems. Fletch and I had already broached the subject of how much longer it would be right to have him in the team. We had the feeling that he would not go on beyond that summer, but with Strauss's emergence his exit was perfect timing in all sorts of ways.

What disappointed me in the aftermath of Nasser's retirement was that there were issues with the ECB about paying up his central contract. I thought it disgraceful after the great service he had given to the English game that there would be quibbles about it, especially as his last act was to help the team by removing an awkward dilemma. At first they were only going to pay him up until the end of May, and it took some intervention from the Professional Cricketers' Association to get him paid up in full. I thought it was a disappointing reflection on how the players were still seen by their employers.

Slowly, we were heading towards a situation of not having any players who had been scarred by previous defeats against Australia. I did not really want any coming under that category

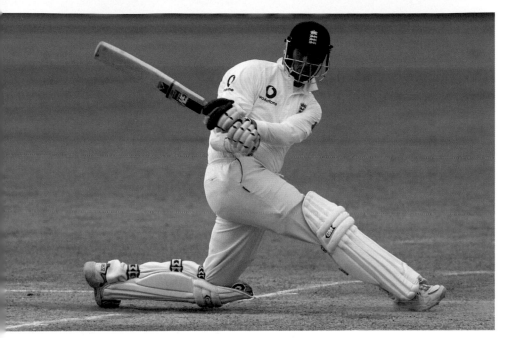

arcus Trescothick, such a masterful player of spin, sweeps for six against Sri Lanka at Old fford in 2002.

finest moment (as a bowler), getting the great Sachin Tendulkar out at Trent Bridge in 2.

Hit on the shoulder by Jason Gillespie at Adelaide in 2002 en route to 177. I later discover
it was broken.

I thought the best way to tackle Glenn McGrath on the Australia tour of 2002–03 was to
take him on.

Left: Brett Lee, with the Fremantle Doctor behind him, bowled like the wind in the 2002 Perth Test.

Above: Nasser Hussain, flanked by Matthew Hoggard, feels the strain as he drives us on to a consolation victory at the Sydney Cricket Ground in 2003.

Below: Winning the triangular series final against South Africa at Lord's in 2003 was a dream start to my one-day captaincy career.

I was so proud to marry Nichola at Fulwood Parish Church at the end of the 2003 season.

The new England captain is pictured in the Long Room at Lord's before the 2nd Test
v South Africa in 2003.

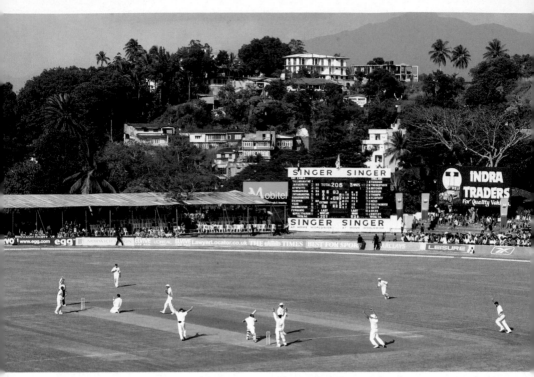

Kandy, a beautiful venue for a sometimes bad-tempered 2nd Test v Sri Lanka in December 2003.

The 'Fab Four' of (l–r) Matthew Hoggard, Steve Harmison, Andrew Flintoff and Simon Jones together against the West Indies in Trinidad in 2004.

knee injury in the nets at Lord's in 2004 was
spark off a wide-ranging sequence of events and
nch the England career of Andrew Strauss.

I rated New Zealand's Stephen Fleming
as arguably the best captain that I came
up against.

er the 2nd Test against New Zealand in 2004 I could celebrate both a series victory and the
th of our daughter Talulla Grace here with Andrew Flintoff *(left)* and Marcus Trescothick.

A congratulatory pat from Freddie after making my second century of the match at Lord's against the West Indies in 2004.

playing in the 2005 Ashes, although we could probably have accommodated one, possibly Graham Thorpe.

Headingley against New Zealand was a cracking Test, but not one in my case that stands out for anything spectacular on the field (I made 13 batting at number four). Nichola was expecting our first child and being there was something I intended to do if at all possible. After rain had ruined the first day, the Kiwis had got to 291–5 late on in the second when Phil Neale, the England manager, took a call to say that things were happening and Duncan told me to go. I would not have gone if I had been batting or if the game had been at a real crisis point, but there was an hour of play left, which I considered just about missable in the circumstances.

As I sped out of the car park I was ordered to slow down by a steward – only at Headingley! – and then my mental block about avoiding petrol stations whenever possible meant that my fuel was so low I had to stop for a fill-up on the way to Sheffield. I had the nozzle in my hand when Nichola's friend rang to tell me that it was all kicking off and that I needed to get there as soon as possible. Fortunately they had saved a parking spot for me right outside the door so that I could rush in and make it with five minutes to spare to see Talulla Grace born.

Strangely, my brief disappearance seemed to spark something of a national debate on radio phone-in programmes and in some newspapers about whether it was right or not to attend the birth. I could not have cared less what they were saying.

We won at Leeds and then repeated the dose at Trent Bridge, where Chris Cairns was making his Test farewell. Ashley came good with bat and ball after taking more than his share of criticism and Thorpey hit a gem of a century as we won by four wickets chasing 283. It was a good series win as the Kiwis were a very competitive side who had pushed us hard. They were one bowler short and had batted again like a team who are more instinctively comfortable in one-day cricket, but you had to admire them for producing a tough side from limited resources. I always thought that if New Zealand had an inherent weakness it was that they were likely to have a mad hour at some point when you could take four or five wickets, through poor shot selection or an over-aggressive intent.

By now we could really see the Ashes side formulating. I envisaged Simon Jones coming in for Martin Saggers, who had played against the Kiwis, and appearing on the radar were Ian Bell and Kevin Pietersen, who was coming close to qualifying as an England player. Until you saw Kevin at the highest level you could not be sure, but every report I was getting was that he was going to be pretty special.

The most heartening thing overall was that we were winning tough games and were coming through to claim victory from difficult positions – New Zealand had made 386, 409 and 384 in their three first innings in that series. Twice we had to chase down very challenging totals in the fourth innings and on both occasions we had been up to it.

Our one-day form slumped following that, partly because of injuries – Fred's loss to ankle problems was particularly hard to make up for – and losing important tosses, and partly because of our inability to get it right in the first 15 overs. We suffered the ignominy of leaving it to New Zealand and the West Indies to contest the triangular series final at Lord's, with memories of the Test wins rapidly diminishing.

A personal worry was that my own form had been dwindling, so it was time to call for the batting guru, Fletcher, to try and help me sort myself out. In one-day cricket I still struggled to get the same rhythmic movement as I did in Test cricket.

He came up to the New Rover club in Leeds and spent three days in the nets working with me while bowlers from the Yorkshire academy supplied the ammunition. This was Fletch in his element, really getting down to the finer details of batting and making crucial tweaks to your alignment, balance, the way you allow the weight to come through your feet, getting my trigger movements going. He was brilliant at pointing out subtle adjustments without doing anything too radical.

I loved the few intensive sessions that I had with Duncan. Because I knew we had worked so hard on ironing things out, and because I had such faith in what he was telling me, I would arrive back with a warm glow knowing I had done everything possible to prepare. That was a very nice feeling to have when it was mixed in with playing at Lord's, where I had such a sense of well-being anyway. I never enjoyed batting at number four and waiting to go in, but despite being in that position in the first of what were four Tests against the West Indies, starting on 22 July, I still had a lovely calm about me.

Rob Key made a double hundred while I got a century in both innings as, for the first time since I had become England captain, we actually declared in a Test match. Now, Duncan never really liked declaring – maybe it was the southern African in him that made him want to nail the game every time and make sure we could not lose – but I could see rain coming and we were nearly 480 ahead. If a side can get that chasing in a fourth innings then good luck to them. I wanted to make sure we had the time to win the game, but Duncan was still not entirely happy. It was another instance of him being much more risk-averse than I was. Ashley Giles took five wickets and it turned out to be win number four of the summer.

It gave me great pleasure that Ashley, such a good friend to whom I occasionally served as agony aunt, was having such a splendid season, and he took another five wickets in the fourth innings at Edgbaston, where it spun a mile. Win number five was achieved, and we were now having to become accustomed to a new kind of pressure, not one generally associated with the England cricket team – the expectation that we would win.

When you are losing, the pressure is very different. Everything gets analysed to the most intricate degree and people read things into non-existent situations trying to find a reason why it has all gone pear-shaped. When you are winning, they tend to sit back and want to be entertained, and we were starting to get into this uncharted territory. I could hardly complain about it as there is always pressure at this level, but I was watching closely among the lads to see how they were reacting.

There were no signs of any adverse effect on Fred, whom I was using in short bursts to protect his ankle. I saw no harm before the third Test at Old Trafford in talking him up as arguably the best cricketer in the world at the time. Nor did there appear to be any complications in the heads of the rest of the team as we overturned a deficit of 65 runs from the first innings to chase down 230 and win by seven wickets.

There was an easy comparison to make with where we had been 12 months ago. Back then we were going to south London on the back of a torrent of criticism to try and save the series against South Africa – now we were travelling down trying to complete a 7–0 summer. It so happened that the team we put out at The Oval on 19 August very much resembled the XI that would play in four out of five Ashes Tests the following summer. Thorpe had broken a finger at Old Trafford, while Butch was continuing to suffer a succession of different minor injuries. This meant that Ian Bell came in for his debut, and the only two changes that would be made between that XI and next summer was Pietersen for Rob Key and Simon Jones for Jimmy Anderson.

You could see it all converging. Bell made 70 in the first innings and looked a fine player right from the start, although he was still very immature. Had he matured quicker after making his debut then I am sure the upward trajectory of his career with England would have been considerably sharper. For some reason he still seemed one of the younger players in the team even when he had acquired plenty of experience, which was why I was staggered a few years later when Peter Moores started talking of him as a potential captain. I am dead against assuming that just because someone has been in the team for a long time, they should automatically get a turn at being skipper. I do not see any reason why, if someone appears a born captain, they should not be given a try only shortly after coming into the team.

Lara was at it again in that match, deliberately making me a look a complete prat with my field placings, so unbelievably talented that he could hit it wherever he wanted. During his 79 I would put in three slips and two gullies and he would still be able to guide the ball between them. Then I would set a 7–2 off-side field and he would walk across his stumps and flick it through the on side. I would put mid-off wide to try and cater for bowling in the fifth-stump channel and he would manoeuvre the ball straight down the ground with his wrists.

But our superiority was such by now that even his genius was not enough to stop us. Harmison's developing love affair with The Oval was blooming and he took nine wickets, relishing the zip and bounce. He would love to play every match at Old Trafford or at Surrey's headquarters – you can almost see the spring coming into his step when he turns up at the ground.

So this was a whitewash and we celebrated accordingly,

although there was hardly a chance to do so as our incredible
schedule, stretching all the way back to Bangladesh, meant that
we were now faced with playing a three-match limited-over
series against India at the beginning of September, and then the
ICC Trophy, which we were hosting despite summer rapidly
turning into autumn.

It was time to turn my attention towards one-day cricket and
to try and tackle the enormous disparity between my batting
in the two forms of the game. The first match against India
saw me get a duck in an easy victory, which was hardly the
way to celebrate joining the 17-strong club of England players
who had featured in both 50 Tests and 50 one-day internationals. I was managing an average of 45.5 in Tests but 23.52
in 50-over cricket, perhaps indicative of different priorities I
was subconsciously assigning to the two formats.

There was no question that it was about time I addressed
that imbalance, and over the course of the next five months I
was to enjoy my best spell with the bat in the limited-over
game, averaging more than 45. That mirrored the fortunes of
the team as a whole, as our more settled unit started to look
as if we might be beginning to crack it. We had a lot of confidence from what we had achieved in the Tests over the summer,
and beat a formidable India side 2–1. The ultimate measure of
just how we had under-achieved at limited-over cricket as a
nation was the simple fact that we had never won a significant
ICC event, and now, on our home soil, we looked ready to do
it.

Yet again, though, Zimbabwe was proving to be an emotive
issue, with our planned four-match tour there en route to South
Africa later in the autumn already arousing strong feelings from
within and outside the sport. Because of the extraordinarily
crammed schedule, and Zimbabwe's weakness, we were

planning to leave several of the senior players at home for it, irrespective of the politics. The Ashes was looming, we seemed to have been playing non-stop and South Africa was going to be very demanding, so it made sense for us to go to Harare with a weakened team. This was the backdrop while we were trying to win the rather unloved ICC Trophy, and in the end Trescothick, Harmison and Flintoff were left out. Apart from anything, we knew that the last two would have been kicking up a fuss about going.

As for Tres, we already knew that the less touring he did, the better it would be for him in the long run. He was never good at the start of tours because he loved a routine, and when you arrive in a country the first week is less structured than the rest of the trip, which becomes a constant cycle of playing, travelling and sleeping. He would take a week to get into things and would not sleep especially well when there was not enough structured activity to occupy his mind, so this was a good opportunity for him to rest up.

After some negotiations, it was decided that everyone else bar those three should go. It was a condition of the three 'big guns' being left out that I would lead the trip, and although I was not doing somersaults of delight at the prospect I agreed. David Morgan, chairman of the England and Wales Cricket Board, was particularly keen for us to go to Zimbabwe.

So we sat down with Harmy on the Saturday morning of our Trophy match against Sri Lanka at Southampton and said that we understood his need to have a rest, and that he could stay at home. We added that we would appreciate it if he could help in keeping the whole decision low-profile so as not to inflame sentiments any further for those of us having to make the trip. Duncan and myself were uneasy about going as it was, and the whole argument really did not need heating up any more. I assumed we had agreement on that and he said it was fine, but then we opened the *Mail on Sunday* the following morning to see him announcing in his regular column that he was not going and that he would not have gone even if requested. The management already felt in a difficult position, so you can imagine how that went down.

The ICC Trophy had a group format before semi-finals and a final, and it looked as if we were going to need to beat Sri Lanka at the Rose Bowl in order to make the last four, where Australia were waiting for us. I was desperate for us to win that Southampton game, more than anything because it would give me a chance to see how the lads reacted to playing against Australia. It was a rare opportunity at a peculiar time of year – we were now into the latter half of September – and I did not want us to miss it. A semi-final was important enough in itself, but playing Ricky Ponting's team was different from playing anyone else and a few pointers were bound to emerge from the perspective of facing them nine months down the line.

The question I most wanted answering was: could we still play this aggressive, in-your-face cricket that we had been trying to develop since the start of the year when confronted with so many outstanding players in one team? You can do it and talk a good game against the other sides, but sometimes against Australia the approach had been very difficult to put into practice, such was the aura about them.

Fred got a dazzling hundred and we duly beat Sri Lanka with ease in a rain-affected match. I immediately made a little speech in the dressing room, saying we had now got what we wanted and that we had to look forward to it and play without fear. I did not mind, on this particular occasion, trying to build the Edgbaston game up as much as possible.

As it turned out, we played with exceptional poise in what

I came to regard as a match of quiet significance. It was by now 21 September and the ground was far from full, as I suspect the public did not quite understand the competition we were playing in or why we were playing it at that time of year, and most people were at work or school anyway. But the atmosphere was still fairly charged, despite the weather and the empty spaces at a ground where we usually enjoyed massive support. You could feel that the 10,000 or so who did turn up were extremely committed, another reminder that playing Australia was incomparable.

They batted first and we used Harmison and Fred in the middle of their innings to stifle their expected charge, with Harmy roughing up Andrew Symonds to such an extent that he panicked and I ran him out for nought. We made things uncomfortable for them from the start and they noticeably did not enjoy that awkward type of bowling in mid-innings. Eventually we had restricted them to 259, a certain part-time Yorkshire off-spinner taking 2–42 off his 10 overs.

Marcus and I got us off to a great start and Strauss carried us over the line to what became a relatively comfortable six-wicket win with an innings that further indicated his mental toughness. Winning the man-of-the-match award for my 86 topped out a great day and we had a good night out in Birmingham. I could sense that the win had flicked a bit of a switch among some of the lads – an encouraging recognition of what might be possible if we stood up to Australia and expressed ourselves.

We saw a few of the Australian boys when we were out on the town that night and there was a bit of a confrontation between Symonds and Harmison. Something might have been said in drink, and it did not take much for Symonds to be wound up, while Harmy is not one to be underestimated either.

This was all part of why our Durham colleague was often a fascinating and challenging person to manage. He is the nicest lad in the world in most ways and a gentle giant, but there is a fiery side to him as well. When the pressure is on he has a fairly well-honed defensive mechanism which makes him quite awkward. His response to pressure is sometimes to be quite lethargic and cynical and to talk the game and himself down. I often found his earthy sense of humour quite amusing, but you also had to be careful that it did not act as a drag on others.

I thought we had quite a good one-day system going then, and apart from anything our fielding was pretty sharp as well. It was now 25 September and I felt sure that our final act of a vintage summer was going to be, at long last, sealing victory in a major one-day tournament on our home soil. The West Indies were the opponents at The Oval, an unpredictable side but very beatable providing we approached it in the right way. Perhaps subconsciously we thought Australia had been our final, and the endless arguments about Zimbabwe were also proving a distraction, probably to me more than the rest of the players.

We did not play our best, but we still should have won after having them 147–8 chasing our total of 217. We just could not prise apart their veteran keeper Courtney Browne and Ian Bradshaw, who both played incredibly well despite the fact that the match finished in near darkness. It was a memorable climax and we would have beaten them, had Fred not been refused a stone-dead appeal for lbw against Browne. I was distraught at that defeat and that particular decision, although we got a few that went our way the following summer that more than made up for it. That is how cricket is, although you do not always feel that way at the time.

It was a dark and cloudy day, entirely matching my mood by the end of it. The fact that I was completely shattered did not much help either, but somewhere amid the fuzz of fatigue and disappointment I knew we were getting close to being a very good side in one-day cricket. My optimism was also buoyed by the knowledge that Kevin Pietersen would be coming into the team, although at the time I saw him primarily as a one-day player, with the jury still out when it came to his potential in Tests.

I had already marked out Ian Bell, rather than Pietersen, as someone I wanted to play in the Ashes ahead of either Mark Butcher or Graham Thorpe. In fact, there was a lot of talk in the selection meetings for the winter parties – made all the more complicated by the Zimbabwe situation – about whether we should retain Butcher for South Africa, but it was narrowly felt that he did not deserve to be jettisoned after his summer injury problems. I had also argued for Essex's James Foster to be called in as second wicketkeeper, but was voted down by the Chris Read fan club.

We had been going at it since February and I was fit to drop. In that period we had amassed a record of 10 Test wins and one draw, plus had a brush with one-day glory that included a win over Australia. I knew that it would take only a few weeks away from it all for my enthusiasm to be rekindled for a winter pregnant with possibilities.

14

The Final Pieces

It is fair enough that people expect a lot of you as a professional cricketer, let alone as England captain, but I think people have to be realistic about the limits of our life experience. I knew enough to understand that going to Zimbabwe was not a great thing to do in the eyes of many and that it was an issue that struck a raw nerve in our country. However, you are getting into something of a moral maze when entering an issue such as this, and making complex ethical judgements is not what we are trained to do.

There are things that go on in all the countries that play cricket that are probably not that savoury, and certainly beyond the limits of my understanding and knowledge. It was never that I did not care about, or was oblivious to, what had gone on in Zimbabwe, but I did not think it was right that sportsmen whose young lives had been focused on succeeding in our profession should have to take profound stances on their own. So it would not be true to say that I was getting on the plane to Southern Africa in November 2004 with a tortured conscience.

Our first stop was to be the cricketing backwater of Windhoek in Namibia, and it was interesting to go somewhere off the beaten track. In fact, I really enjoyed our stay there as it took me back to going on an England schoolboys trip to Zimbabwe in happier days for that country, or as a youngster at Yorkshire going to South Africa for pre-season. Namibia was the kind of place where we could all knuckle down together, train, have games of football, play golf and enjoy the odd barbecue alongside the business of playing cricket. They were very pleased to see us and could not do enough to make our stay pleasant, even though there was quite a bit of rain about. They were so keen for our games to go ahead that they brought in a helicopter to try and dry the outfield.

It was our first trip with Kevin Pietersen on board, and of all the fresh faces he was the one I was most keen to look at. If I am honest, I was not immediately struck by his quality in practice, thinking that he looked a decent enough player but that his technique might be vulnerable at the highest level. I could not see that an unbelievably good player was developing at that stage, although I had been reasonably impressed with him in a couple of county outings against Notts. He had stood at backward point and chirped me a bit, and I thought he had some potential, but no idea just how much.

Namibia were not a bad side, but we beat them and everything seemed pretty calm ahead of us going into Zimbabwe. I had lulled myself into a false sense of security, thinking that the arguments were over, that we were going to travel to Harare and Bulawayo, get the matches over and done with, and then move on quickly and leave the whole wretched issue behind us.

But then the day before departure word came through that the Zimbabwe government was going to ban the majority of our media, including the BBC, from entering the country to cover the cricket. This immediately sparked off frantic diplomatic activity among the administrators, which continued as we set off from Windhoek for Harare via Johannesburg. We were a young team, so I knew I now had to take a leading role, particularly as the whole subject was so difficult for Duncan, given his family links there.

This development had completely changed my view of the trip, because it was now ceasing to be a normal tour conducted under normal conditions. Any trip an England team makes is covered by the media because ours is primarily an entertainment business, and if there was to be no coverage, or very restricted coverage, then that made it completely different from other tours and was a deal-breaker as far I was concerned. You could no longer argue that the visit was about cricket and not about politics.

I told our manager, Phil Neale, that I would not be leading the team to Zimbabwe under these circumstances, and with the support of Duncan I also informed David Morgan and John Carr of the ECB that this was our position. The decision was made to break our onward journey at Johannesburg, where we had to change planes, and to retire to an airport hotel while the media matter was sorted out. Phil played an absolute blinder in getting everyone's bags off the aircraft, including those of the pressmen, who on this occasion literally did not know whether they were coming or going.

So off we went to the hotel, and while shuttle diplomacy went on we spent the next day staging a head-tennis tournament at the hotel, which was followed by a team drink-up. There were more than a few shades of Cape Town 18 months previously as we had team meetings and twiddled our thumbs while officialdom tried to sort the mess out. It did not help that Morgan declined to travel back to Johannesburg for the discussions, sending just Carr. With Duncan feeling unable to get involved due to family considerations, a lot of the burden for making decisions fell upon myself and Richard Bevan of the PCA. Interestingly, Richard was getting clear messages from senior officials at the International Cricket Council that now was the time to make a stance against the people who ran Zimbabwe cricket. For a brief time, it really looked as if the whole thing would be abandoned, but when the authorities in Harare performed their unprecedented U-turn and let all the media in, there was little alternative but to go.

When we got there it was calm enough and the Meikles hotel seemed very normal, apart from the obvious security. It was not hard to spot the government security-services people sitting around in the lobby in plain clothes trying to act as if they were ordinary citizens. I loved Zimbabwe and its hospitable people and had always had a great time there on previous visits. While far from a disaster area, it was sad to see how it was discernibly more run down than before, with the roads obviously in a worse state. Duncan lamented how much less clean the streets were than they used to be.

Harare Sports Club was still the beautiful ground I always remembered and we worked pretty hard in training, keeping a low profile off the pitch while the journalists went about their business unhindered. We had a bit of a sticky run chase in the first of our four matches on 28 November, with KP, on his England debut, seeing us home with an unbeaten 27. The running of the sport in Zimbabwe had slid into a chaotic state and they were a much weaker team than they had been in the World Cup, with most of the white players having retired. We thrashed them in the other three games, trying a few new combinations but not learning a huge amount. One of the more bizarre occurrences when we were there was when I was told by the ICC to remove a logo from my bat because it was too big, even though it had been approved previously as being the right size. That told you a bit about their sense of priorities. By the end,

I was pleased just to get out of there and move on to the main tour in South Africa.

The Zimbabwe trip had taken it out of everybody and I was a little concerned about how we were all going to gel once we got to Johannesburg, as there would be two distinct groups: those who had been on the road for nearly four weeks already and those freshly arrived. My fears were well-founded as there was a slightly frosty air around the place, mainly between Duncan and the duo of Flintoff and Harmison. Fred was there with his family, and had joined Harmy in saying publicly that he would not have gone to Zimbabwe even if he had been asked. Duncan was never especially great at hiding his feelings or forgetting things that had upset him, and he had felt let down by them going public, believing that they should have kept that opinion to themselves for the sake of the others once they had been told they were rested.

It was not a great start to what was going to be a hard tour, although there were no obvious arguments among the players themselves. Not everyone seemed happy, particularly Trescothick and Butcher, and we had a terrible warm-up game in Potchef-stroom, where we got hammered by seven wickets. While the game was going on I was sitting on the balcony watching with Tres when he suddenly turned to me and said he was really fearful he was going to lose his place in the team. I said, 'What are you on about? You're probably our best player.' He said how guilty he was about not having been in Zimbabwe and I told him that it was not a problem and that the plan had always been to rest him.

There just seemed to be a lack of positive atmosphere around the camp, and so after the match I called a team meeting back at the hotel. I said that we had to pull together more other-wise we were going to get beaten up in the forthcoming series.

There was definitely some intangible problem with half of the squad having come from Zimbabwe and half not, possibly stemming from insecurities, which only backed up my belief that ideally you wanted the same team in both forms of the game as much as possible.

Another issue was the demeanour of Duncan, who I thought had probably found the whole business of going to Zimbabwe tougher than he was letting on. To me he was definitely feeling the pressure of trying to deliver in his adopted country, where he had made his name as a coach. By now he had deservedly built up quite a reputation on the international stage (which had not been the case on the last South African tour) and I am sure he wanted to show people what his team could do and what he had done for us. He never seemed to settle over that whole tour, and the players sensed this. Later on in the trip, he had a blast at a few of the players who arrived to prepare for the one-dayers while the Tests were still going on, saying they were partying too much and distracting those still engaged in the Test series.

So in Potchefstroom I demanded that anyone who had any problems should come to me, and that we should show an all-round improvement in team unity and purpose. It was not that we had the luxury of several preparatory games these days, and the only ones we had played were the Oppenheimer one-dayer and the match in this grim outpost of Afrikanerdom. Butch, who was never himself on that trip even before he got injured, was definitely one of those who could not get his head around warm-up matches.

All in all, I was fairly pessimistic about the outcome as we headed to the first Test in Port Elizabeth just before Christmas. Fortunately the South Africans may have been even more disunited than we were, and they helped us by picking a curious

XI that excluded wicketkeeper Mark Boucher, a very thorny opponent, in order to up their quota of ethnic players.

At the time I was still surprised that we won that Test, although Strauss made a good hundred in the land of his birth and Butch, despite appearing out of sorts, made 79 as we scored 425 in the first innings. Looking back, the crucial thing was our bowling attack and the reuniting of our deadly quintet of Hoggard, Harmison, Flintoff, Giles and Simon Jones. Fred bowled especially quickly, while Simon took 4–39 as they collapsed in their second innings and enabled us to get off to a winning start that I was most grateful for.

I considered the result 'one against the head', although there were plenty of occasions when this team would surprise me. Even though sometimes I did not feel the atmosphere was that great off the pitch, when it came to the games we would summon up a bulldog spirit that would pull us through. The happier surprises outnumbered the times when I was expecting us to do well and was left disappointed.

Christmas was in Durban again, and on Boxing Day my worst fears about our overall situation seemed to materialise. South Africa had strengthened their team for the second Test and we were bowled out for just 139 and then conceded a near 200-run lead, only for the same spirit to kick in without warning to such an extent that we nearly ended up winning. We were almost perversely good for the last three days, making 570 in the second innings, with Tres, Strauss and Thorpe all making hundreds, and then having them eight down before bad light stopped us finishing them off, despite us staging a sit-in on the outfield. A little more luck with the ball and we would have won it anyway.

A triumphant 2004 concluded with us in Cape Town, going out to a waterside restaurant where, overall, there was plenty to celebrate as we looked back. We had gone through the year unbeaten in Tests with a 11–2–0 record and there was every reason to feel cheery about the 12 months to come. I was not, however, over-optimistic about the immediate future and the prestigious match at beautiful Newlands, which had again attracted a massive amount of support from home. Whether our level of performance was to do with getting caught up in the festive atmosphere or not was irrelevant, I just felt we were still not clicking as a unit.

Butch had injured his wrist and was to miss the Newlands Test. I said to Fletch that I thought this was probably the end of his Test career, irrespective of whether he was able to recover quickly or not (it turned out to be a long-term injury). I just felt that with the way we were developing the team, and with half an eye as ever on the forthcoming Ashes, this was probably the right time to get a fresher face in the batting line-up. I actually rated Butch very highly as a player, and in many ways he was great to have on tour because he is a likeable and creative guy whose talents clearly extended beyond cricket, including his highly skilled guitar playing. He was bright, too, and his banter was always of a pretty high order. The fact that he is a multi-dimensional character was often commented upon, but in pure cricketing terms I thought he was one of the most gifted batsmen I played alongside, especially against pace. He played the short ball as well as anyone I saw, ducking and weaving, and certainly never lacked courage.

I was conscious, however, of the team's overall make-up and felt that Butch, Harmison and Flintoff all together in the same team might be a bit much. There was an element of being too-cool-for-school about this illustrious trio, and while having two of them on board was perfectly manageable, three of that personality type could be a bit of a crowd. I did not mind them being slightly partial to the sauce, either, but I have always thought you have to be careful about the amount of maverick tendency in one team.

None of them were mad on team meetings, and I do not think Butch, in particular, was at all keen on some of the things we were making the players do. He never showed a huge amount of interest in talk about strategies, the technical stuff about whether the plan against so-and-so should be to aim for the top of off stump, or fourth stump halfway up or fourth stump hip high, for example. He would probably rather everyone aimed at the top of off and be done with it.

We lost an important toss and played badly at Newlands, where nobody got a fifty and Harmy continued to struggle with the ball. The result was a 196-run defeat and so, not for the first time on this tour, I decided to call a clear-the-air team meeting when we got back to the hotel. I wanted people to be honest with each other about the reasons why we were not hitting our straps. I said to them that I still thought there was an element of hangover from the Zimbabwe trip and the fact that half of us had been there and half of us had not. Several players had their say and I demanded that we should finally draw a line under that whole issue. This time it seemed to do the trick.

There was a perceptible increase in our energy when we got to Johannesburg for the fourth Test starting on 13 January with the series poised at 1–1 and the South Africans sensible enough to have finally recalled Boucher. It turned out to be one of the most memorable Tests I have played in for reasons ranging from spats with officialdom to brilliant individual perform-ances.

This was where I became aggravated with both match referee Clive Lloyd and my opposite number, Graeme Smith, with whom relations had not been especially cordial. There was a lot of rain about initially, and we were still batting late into the second day, with us in total command thanks to yet another hundred from Strauss and decent contributions from myself and Rob Key. We were going well when the umpires put a stop to play because they said the fielders could not see the ball properly.

Cricket tends to be a bit squeamish about the light issue as a whole and I felt this was utterly ridiculous, making my feelings clear to the former Lancashire and West Indies legend. We were particularly unimpressed with him because he did not appear very alert. At a hearing with Lloyd after play Smith gave evidence against me, leading us to nickname him 'The Witness' when he came in to bat. He had already got up my nose by calling me what I thought was 'Queer' when I had come in to bat – not the most mature thing I had ever heard, to put it mildly. A few years later, when we became more friendly and he had gained my respect, he explained that it was actually the name of some TV character in South Africa.

The backdrop to all this was the simple fact that England–South Africa matches are always pretty fraught and competitive. One reason I was so pumped up for this particular match was the knowledge that we had to compete in this kind of series if we were to have a launchpad for the Ashes. It was really full on, and excellent preparation for what lay ahead. I declared on 411 at the wrong time, just before the sun began to shine, and Herschelle Gibbs came out to smash us for 161 as they got an eight-run lead.

I can honestly say I did not care whether we lost or drew this match and therefore the series, I just wanted to have every chance of winning it. So before we went out for the second innings I gave the instruction that we were to go all out for victory, and that the batsmen should not hang around. We made 332–9 at just over four runs an over, with Marcus making a quite magnificent 180, probably the best knock I ever saw him play for us, and one that broke the game open. Not for the only time in our partnership, Duncan was not entirely happy with my declaration. Sometimes with Fletch it was a case of you could take the boy out of Southern Africa, but not the Southern African out of the boy.

He would give you that look that told you he was not best pleased, but then he knew I was more of a punter than he was, and Nasser Hussain for that matter. Duncan had not been particularly happy when I had declared on 570–7 in Durban, either. I always valued his input, but when I thought the time was right I would just walk out onto the balcony and do my traffic-policeman impression, calling the boys in. My philosophy was that England teams were always so up and down that when the chance of a win presented itself you should always go for it if at all possible. The fluctuating nature of our form was never more evident than on that tour.

I pulled them in at the Wanderers on this occasion and Duncan was fretting good and proper because Harmy was struggling with injury, Ashley was barely able to bowl and Jimmy Anderson, who had come in for Simon Jones, was struggling to find form. He had lost his rhythm completely, as it turned out, so it was going to be all down to Fred and Hoggard. Not that asking South Africa to score 325 in around 65 overs was particularly revolutionary anyway, but I wanted to give them a sniff. As it was, Hoggy produced a performance with the ball to match that of Marcus with the bat, a superb display of swing bowling that filleted their entire middle order and gave him figures of 7–61. We won by 77 runs with 8.3 overs left and partied in appropriate style that night at our Sandton hotel. Some have described that shopping and hotel complex in northern Johannesburg as a five-star prison, but it certainly did not feel like it that night. Jailhouse Rock, maybe.

The final Test on 21 January was back at the scene of my first major contribution for England, the notorious Hansie Cronje declaration match five years previously at Centurion. South Africa, as is their wont, were slightly negative in that match when they could have pressured us into having to last out a longer final innings of a game which, as in 2000, fell victim to the rain. As it was, they gave themselves only 41 overs to bowl us out to level the series, and thank heavens for that. We were 20–3 at one point and my unbeaten 26 was unquestionably one of the most important little nuggets of my career. As captain you get a huge amount of pleasure walking off at the end and that was a particularly satisfying feeling, departing that peculiarly charmless ground in Pretoria. Typically, we could not cruise to a simple draw and had to add some drama to the proceedings – it was an arse-nipper, as we say in the trade.

I was delighted to have won that series and kept the momentum going as we headed into the summer of 2005, because there was no way the early tourists Bangladesh were going to beat us as we prepared for Australia in the coming months. We had beaten South Africa despite not being quite right as a team, and it had all been down to individuals standing up to be counted at crucial times. The fine contributions from the likes of Strauss, Trescothick and Flintoff were not going to be enough against Australia; I knew we were really going to have to play more as a unit. The whole trip from Namibia onwards had been much tougher than it looked and I still felt we had never really recovered from the fact that half of us had arrived from Zimbabwe and the other half from home.

I knew that we would be better at home and there would not be the issue of Duncan having to prove himself in South Africa, which I felt had contributed to a deflated atmosphere a lot of the time. I always thought that to be seen as genuine contenders to beat Australia we needed a win that winter, and that much had been achieved.

In South Africa there remained the seven-match one-day series to be played, which was to be all about one man – Kevin Pietersen. I was at the crease when he came out to bat at the Wanderers in his first match, a ground that lends itself to the feeling of gladiators in the Colosseum. I stood there watching this lad with a racoon hairstyle walking out to a deafening cacophony of boos and thought, 'Now we're going to see what this boy is made of.' In fact, even at that very minute I was thinking of the Ashes, because this was going to be such a good pointer to what his temperament was really like beneath the extrovert you saw on the surface. He was clearly nervous, but you could tell as he made an unbeaten 22 in a Duckworth-Lewis situation that he had plenty of that quality Fletch delicately termed 'dogfuck'.

He loved the occasion and the scrap and in his second game made 108 not out in Bloemfontein, the heartland of Afrikanerdom where they have never been that well disposed to our green and pleasant land. I still thought he had technical frailties and he looked vulnerable outside off stump when the ball swung away. About the only form of defence he had was attack, although he quickly balanced his game when he became established with England.

But I had seen enough. After that first hundred I turned to Fletch and said, 'We have got to get this lad in the Ashes team.'

I knew there was a chance it could backfire spectacularly, because at the time he was going through a phase when he would get on a run of noughts or make a succession of big scores; he looked a bit all or nothing. I saw him as the kind of free spirit who would really help take the battle to the likes of Shane Warne and Glenn McGrath. It certainly did not bother me that he was a Flash Harry off the pitch at that stage, our very own king of bling.

What I did not want was a team of clones and I thought that, with the spine of the team that we had, we could cope with this sort of maverick. The question I was wondering about most was how he and Flintoff were going to be together, and that was to prove an ongoing issue. It is bound to be when you have two players who love the limelight and being at the centre of the action. Kevin would openly admit that he loved the lights, camera, action while, whatever he says, Fred is not averse to having his name up in neon either. Because Kevin was going to come in late before the Ashes we would have to make sure that he would fit in with what was going on and not upset the apple cart.

He went on to make three hundreds and a 75, and we were all dazzled by his stroke play in the face of hostile crowds that he eventually won round by his sheer brilliance. This was another example of why the appliance of science can only go so far in cricket, and sport in general. There was no formula, management psychobabble, stats or amount of training anyone could produce to provide the inner motivation that drove Kevin on during those matches. I am sure that if those games had taken place somewhere other than South Africa, he would not have been quite so sensational.

You can talk all you like in team meetings, but the single most important thing is that the player has the ability to motivate himself from within. That is what separates people. KP in South Africa was an extreme case, but more mundanely I always like to think of that little fellow inside you, ticking away all the time, every day demanding that you become that little bit better than you were before. For the challenge we were about to face, I was adamant that we were going to need 11 self-starters.

15

On Captaincy

Every job has tricks of the trade that you acquire as you go along, the best job in the world included. I used to employ one of my favourite little tactics at the toss, which I would always walk out to in my blazer and brimmer. Part of the ritual is that when the two captains meet on the outfield they swap team sheets, but I would never look at the opposition team sheet as soon as it was handed to me, instead just crumpling it up and putting it straight into my pocket. It was a bit of psychology and I wanted to send the message that 'I'm not interested in your team and whoever you've got in it.' I used to like to check whether my opposite number had a good old look at our final XI, but I would put on this front of not being interested – even if I was desperate to know whether someone like Glenn McGrath was playing!

Being a cricket captain involves so much more than just wearing an armband. So what are you? It might be said that the job involves being, in no particular order, a diplomat, strategist, spokesman, babysitter, actor, selector and disciplinarian.

First and foremost, you have to have the respect of those you are leading as a player. I was fortunate in that when I got the England captaincy I had just had the best year of my career as a batsman, so that bought me a lot of kudos among my team-mates, particularly the younger ones who saw me as the leader of their brigade. To be a leader you have to possess a natural manner, and it is vital to be yourself. That means the way you act cannot change too significantly, because there is nothing worse than someone trying to fundamentally alter their personality the moment they are appointed skipper. You would get found out straight away.

I felt I had always had a decent relationship with my peers in whatever teams I had played in, which was a good base to start from. I would go so far as to say that the actual captaincy on the pitch is the smallest thing you have to worry about when appointing a captain, because that comes from experience. To play for England in the first place, you need to have a pretty fair idea of the game's tactics anyway, and you only learn the finer points by going out there and doing the job under pressure. You learn the most from the mistakes that you make. I call it learning from doing.

Your tactical moves such as bowling changes and field placements, your plans against certain batters – that all comes from experience. The more you do it, and the more situations you come across, the more you log in your head so that you can remember what worked and what did not work when it arises again.

So, after having the basic level of respect, I would say the next thing you need is to be able to speak clearly to a group of people and relate to them properly. Man-management is absolutely key, particularly as cricket is probably a sport unlike any other in terms of the sheer amount of time you spend with one another. What stood me in good stead by the time I took over England's captaincy was the richness of the experiences I had already had in the game.

I had been through the county ranks at Yorkshire, one of the harder schools, been on England A and Under-19 tours, experienced the troughs and the highs. I had been a bad lad and a good lad, drunk my share of drinks, chased after a few women when I was younger and seen how doing the wrong things can affect your preparation and performance. I had played averagely when I first came into the England team and not quite delivered, and then I had learned how to deliver to the extent that I was rated the number one batsman in the world. So my journey had been wide and varied, and I could relate to most types of cricketers because I had seen and studied them all.

You have to talk the same language as the older guys who have been around and acquired some world-weariness, as well as the 20-year-old who is fresh into things at this level. They all need to feel wanted. Then you have to relate to the large coaching staffs that are now the norm in modern cricket, as I believe they need managing as well.

Dealing with the media is a massive part of being the England cricket captain, and understanding how they work is absolutely vital. I was forever inquiring of the ECB media liaison people how they saw things, and would seek views from a few of the press and broadcast guys that I was friendlier with. Andrew Walpole, our long-standing communications man, was always an excellent sounding board, while Mike Dickson of the *Daily Mail* once advised me that trying to control the media was like trying to control the weather.

So if you had a shopping list of attributes for the perfect cricket captain, I would say you need respect from the other players, to be a good enough player yourself to hold your place on merit, an ability to communicate with and manage the players, coaching staff and the media, and an acute understanding of the tactics and strategies of the game. Not much to ask, really.

But probably above all these things, what you really need is luck. When Napoleon was asked who he preferred as generals, courageous ones or tactically brilliant ones, he replied that he wanted, above all, lucky ones. I am happy to admit that I had my share of luck, particularly in the 2005 Ashes. Glenn McGrath's ankle; being able to bat first in the last four games, which I felt was absolutely crucial; a lack of injuries meaning we used only 12 players over the series; the rain and bad light at The Oval. We were probably due some luck against the Australians at that time and it came. At the end of my captaincy, on the other hand, I had a strong feeling that, apart from my falling energy levels, my luck had run out.

I had a lot of respect for Nasser Hussain, admired his many virtues and enjoyed playing under him, but I learned a few lessons from how he was with the players. Fundamental to my thinking about the England captaincy is that it is about relieving pressure, while I thought Nasser was too prone to do the opposite and put pressure on individuals. In county cricket you see so many players who can turn it on beautifully in that environment, and they look as if they are loving playing for their team. Then they are picked for England and they suddenly look scared and timid.

My philosophy was that anyone playing for England was already having to cope with quite enough pressure that they placed upon themselves, so therefore it was essential to minimise that. I had studied the Australians and one of the things about them was that they always looked to simply enjoy the game of cricket and all it entails. Naturally it is easier when you are a high-class team, but they just seemed to love what they were doing. A lot of our senior players, on the other hand, never looked as if they enjoyed it hugely, and sometimes it was as if there was an element of viewing playing for England as a job.

Another of my principles is that if you are taking it too seriously, it is impossible to be at your instinctive best and let your talent flow.

The more you can take yourself back to your youth, and remember that state of mind as a 12- or 14-year-old when you played the game just for the love of it, then so much the better. I wanted to try and instil that, but it was pretty difficult with the old school of players who had played under Nasser. I cannot ever remember him saying, 'Enjoy it.' At the end of his tenure he was so overcome with seriousness that he seemed to struggle to understand how anyone could actually enjoy the game of cricket, although eventually I could see how he reached that point. Tactically he was good, and management-wise he was sound, at least with the older players, and he spoke well to the team unit.

But I always felt he could have made more runs if he had been able to let himself go a bit more, because to me he had no shortage of natural talent. I think part of it with him was that he was most comfortable as the underdog and loved it when he was backed into a corner, hence his tendency to excel when we were in trouble and do less well when we were in a strong position. He loved to talk the opposition up because that would bring the best out of himself, whereas my way was to talk ourselves up and try not to be too preoccupied with who were playing against.

Obviously you would need to discuss strategies against certain opposition players, but against Australia, for example, I would try and emphasise that they were human, with the same body parts as everyone else. I had noticed in the 2002–03 series that the senior players in our team seemed to be in awe of the Haydens, Waughs and Pontings, as if they were superhuman. I got fed up with hearing that McGrath was a genius who could land it on a postage stamp. I could understand it because they had been beaten up by them so often that it had left them scarred. That is why, in the lead-up to the 2005 Ashes, I wanted a fresh set of players who would look as if they were enjoying the battle, even if at times they were not. Just picking some new faces sent a powerful message.

I always tried, if I was doing a team talk, to put myself in the players' shoes and think what I, in their position, would want to hear from the captain. I did not invent the on-field huddle – as far as I know, James Whitaker when he was at Leicestershire can claim that distinction in our sport – but I did introduce it into the England set-up. The main reason was that there were so many support staff around that it was about the only time you could get the players on their own. I could give them my message, just me and the players, before we set about the task. It could vary from a kick up the backside to just basic encouragement and a few reminders. I also liked the fact that you could ask other players to make the address in our private little circle, and that if you thought someone felt insecure or needed more responsibility, they could give that final address.

When I was given the job I said that I wanted 10 other captains. I had felt with England teams that Nasser had been left isolated at times in the captaincy, although it was partly his doing because he was not very approachable. So at any given moment I might walk past one of the fielders and ask what he thought we should be doing tactically, to make sure they had their eye on the ball. I would always try and go with their suggestion to make them feel wanted and part of the decision-making process. I never viewed this as captaincy-by-committee; I just wanted others to keep thinking. In their heyday the Australians always struck me as a group who seemed to be debating the game as they went along and I wanted us to be more like that. I was one of those players, by the way, who did not exactly come up with a stack of ideas when I first got into the team.

I probably took on board the advice of team-mates less as I got more used to the job, but at our best we worked like clockwork with everyone knowing pretty much exactly what they should be doing. That said, cricket is a very individual sport wrapped up in a team format, and at the rarefied level of the international game each player requires different man-management. This was an aspect I paid a lot of attention to, and if we take as an example the Ashes-winning side, they were all very different in how they needed handling at the time:

Marcus Trescothick – He occasionally needed 'bigging up' in terms of his self-belief and you would not want to be critical of him at all, but he was the ultimate professional when it came to practice, so there was no need to keep an eye on him in that respect.

Andrew Strauss – Needed no managing at all. Knew exactly what he was doing and was never intimidated by a situation.

Ian Bell – Quite young at the time and so I felt he was a bit vulnerable. You would try and lift his confidence and remind him what a good young player he was.

Kevin Pietersen – A free spirit who needed telling that he should just react to the situation. When he first came into the side I did not think he had much defence, therefore it was essential that he played to his strength and kept attacking. His defence is much better these days.

Andrew Flintoff – The hardest to captain because he was such a genius on the pitch but away from it he has this knack of upsetting people because he can be lazy. There is also a fun element to him off the pitch (particularly in the evenings), but then I never wanted a team of clones. Often it is the most naturally talented players who cannot stand the modern way of meetings and constant technical talk, so I tried to limit that side for the likes of him and KP and allow them just to play and express themselves. We never wanted the team meetings to go on too long for that reason.

Geraint Jones – A dream to captain and manage. You need people you can trust completely and he was one of those. His thought processes on the pitch were excellent and he came up with some great ideas for the bowlers. Towards the end he lost his confidence and had taken so much criticism it was bound to get to him. A great lad.

Ashley Giles – Very interesting to manage, even more so because we were very close mates. I would manage him in different ways, sometimes telling him to pull his finger out and other times offering reassurance. We would spend many a pre-match day at Starbucks or their equivalent around the world, talking about life. There were times when he said he was shot away and could get quite emotional, so you needed to maintain his spirits. Before the Edgbaston Test in 2005, when he had taken so much stick following the first Test at Lord's, he was very low. The way we celebrated with him when he got Ricky Ponting out in that match showed what a strong unit we were and how much Ashley meant to us.

Matthew Hoggard – I used to bollock him all the time. I considered him the shop-floor man, doing the hard and dirty work, with the other bowlers occupying the plush offices. If ever he got too big for his boots and tried to bowl jaffas, I would forcibly remind him from mid-off that he needed to get back to the shop floor. He could be stroppy and awkward and would have his low moments on tour. But he was great to have in the team – I absolutely loved Hoggy.

Simon Jones – Another interesting one. He was often unsure of his fitness and you could guarantee that one or two days before every game he would pull up with something or other. He has so much skill and ability, but somewhere I suspected he had a fear of playing. I liked him and he had that price-less X factor – he was someone who could make things happen.

Steve Harmison – He could be a tough guy to manage on tour, because he often did not want to be there. Harmy was fine out on the field and he loved to bowl. He was very keen on long spells, so much so that he might sulk for an over after he was taken off, even if you could see he had been tiring. He was not great in practice, but I thought generally the best way to get the most from his abundant natural ability was to encourage him.

As a captain what you ideally want in a team is the right mix of players, and that was a crucial ingredient of our Ashes success. We were a team that, in the most genuine sense of the word, had 'character', and I loved the mix we had of the Freddies and Harmys with the Strausses and Geraints. In a perfect world you would want about seven dependable and predictable characters, and then around them you could have the flair players such as Freddie – and that was pretty much what we had. You need those who give energy, and providing you have enough of them, you can absorb those who at times might flatten some of the fizz in the squad.

Modern thinking seems to frown on any kind of cynicism or gallows humour within the team unit, and it can obviously be negative if you have too much. But I always thought cynical, British-style jokes about the rain or how a Test against Australia might only last three days were pretty harmless. At times there was something to be said for those who were inclined to prick the balloon. If you have everybody spouting positive talk and Peter Moores-style management gobbledygook, I do not think that is healthy.

I had other old-fashioned ideas as well. I did not like laziness or anyone wearing the wrong kit and I had a particular aversion to lateness, which was drummed into me from my early Yorkshire days.

To me the make-up of the back-room team was also essential to functioning at your best as an international captain, and we had a great mix of characters amongst them as well. For instance, there was our video analyst, Tim Boon, who was very strait-laced and cricket mad, talking about the game non-stop, and then you had assistant coach Matthew Maynard, who loved a fag and a pint and an old-fashioned cricket chat. He was good on the game but was also great at relieving the pressure of being around the England squad, talking complete crap about anything other than cricket when necessary. Someone like Darren Gough was always worth his weight in gold within any squad because he constantly made people laugh and relieved pressure. The one-liner is a great asset, and Freddie used to come out with some classics when he waited to bat, because his way of letting out nervous energy was to talk a lot and often take the mickey out of himself.

The one time I always tried to act very cool was at the toss, even if my hands were shaking a bit before those calls, which you knew could be crucial. There is a lot of pressure in making the right call if you win it, because that can shape the whole game, and there were times when I would be in two minds and not unhappy about losing it. Generally, the decision-making process after winning the toss was something I enjoyed, because at heart I am a bit of a punter. I do not mind having the odd bet and I have heard it said that the best captains have a slight gambling streak within them, which I would not disagree with.

There is one view in cricket that if you win the toss in a Test then 80 per cent of the time you should bat first, and the other 20 per cent of the time you should think about it for a moment – and then bat first. I do not go along with this, although if the opposition possess a Shane Warne or Muttiah Muralitharan, then there would need to be very compelling reasons not to have first go with the bat, because they are even more lethal on wearing pitches. Sometimes it can be viewed as negative, batting second, but that is not necessarily so. In fact, during my time with England the character of wickets changed considerably. Increasingly, they would get better to bat on as the match progressed, the best zip and carry being seen in the first two and a half days. The number of records getting broken in the fourth innings has to a certain extent been testament to that. But, basically, if you put a side in, it has to be with the expectation that you will be batting by midway through the second morning at the latest.

When it comes to field placings, you often have to go with your instinct and make a decisive judgement, knowing that if you leave something an over too late, or even just one ball too late, you can miss a huge opportunity. Perhaps it is a bit like investing in stocks and shares – you have to be able to call the top and bottom of the markets. That said, the stories that once went around that I spoke to businesspeople for advice about captaincy were codswallop. I know people in business and like talking to them, but their world does not have much in common with the intricacies of cricket. I did seek advice soon after being appointed, however, from among others Mike Atherton, who in Soho's Groucho Club one night gave me the sound advice that I would have to get rid of the old guard and inject more vibrancy into the team.

But when you are out in the middle you are on your own in many respects, and the buck ultimately stops with you. From the start of play captaincy is a non-stop process, constantly assembling your thoughts and trading things off in your mind and thinking of certain tactics against certain batsmen. For instance, when Adam Gilchrist was in the opposition, I would always be trying to make sure that Freddie had plenty left in the tank for when he came in. Gilchrist was a phenomenally good player, and one of my most satisfying captaincy episodes was the way we handled him in the 2005 Ashes.

Especially pleasing was at Old Trafford in the third Test, where we packed the gully area in a way I had not done before, knowing he was not in great form and that his bread-and-butter shot was slashing the ball square on the off side or just behind square. I brought Ian Bell up 10 yards and just afterwards Gilly hit it straight to him. That is what happens when things are running for you, but there are other times when you think you might have hatched the smartest plan in the world and it just does not work.

In any match you are constantly looking five overs ahead, but I would say that the really good captains are looking games ahead, or even whole series ahead. At my best, in the two years leading into that Ashes, Duncan Fletcher and I were always planning a long way down the line, actually having a vision of players who would be dropping out of the team in the long-term building process, such as Alec Stewart, Graham Thorpe, Nasser Hussain and Mark Butcher. Our overall vision was that we needed a young fresh team to beat Australia, so all the time we were thinking about who was on their way out as much as who was on their way in. Happily, a lot of it was done through natural wastage, with players either getting injured or choosing to retire.

So there needs to be a balance between the short term and the long term, all the time with clear goals in mind. Fifty-over cricket is all about winning the World Cup while, whatever people say about other series, Test cricket for us is all about beating Australia. In England that is what everybody wants you to deliver.

Captaincy took its toll on me in all sorts of different ways, but the most cricket-specific impact it had was on my batting, and my one regret is that I didn't bat more consistently as skipper. Before getting the job I was very much a free spirit and played mostly on instinct, but after being appointed I knew I would have to change my mental approach because there was so much to think about. Up until the England job cropped up, I would think about my batting for part of the day and then be able to switch off easily. Then suddenly you are thinking about other players, about the team and about your own performance as the captain. The result was that it affected my concentration as a batsman, because when I was actually at the crease I was not in the bubble the way I used to be and became more afraid of failure. Cricket just became too important towards the end of my stint and I had lost my early sense of joy. I could not get myself in that mental zone more often and I am still not sure what the answer is.

I have been very lucky to play under, and against, some fine captains. As I have mentioned, I personally enjoyed playing under Nasser and I learned a lot from what I considered to be his mistakes, such as talking the opposition up too much and his handling of younger players, whom I thought he was inclined to make too fearful. But he had a clear idea of what he was doing and led by example when backs were against the wall. He tended to be safety-first, but then sometimes he did not have the bowlers to be much else. A good hand of bowlers helps enormously in making you look a terrific captain.

At Yorkshire I liked David Byas. A basic, old-school captain with a complete lack of bullshit that I respected. Adam Hollioake was excellent when I went on the A tour to Australia under him. He was much more about doing than talking, really instinctive, and he cultivated a sense of enjoyment among his players, trying to make sure they relished the pressure moments. When I first came into the Yorkshire team Martyn Moxon was great to me.

Of the international captains I came up against Stephen Fleming stands out. I liked his calm demeanour; he was very cool and refused to over-complicate things. Like most good captains he was an excellent communicator and a really good reader of where the game was going. I am sure if he had captained a team with the talent of Australia he would have been pretty much invincible. I played with him a bit at Yorkshire in the season I was made England captain and we compared notes about the ex-players who did not think we would be tough enough for the job, in his case people such as Martin Crowe, in mine Ray Illingworth. He always told me simply not to listen and do it my way.

Steve Waugh had some brilliant performers in his charge, but I still learned a lot from him. The biggest single thing was that he never allowed a batsman a comfortable moment, and certainly I never felt able to relax at any time, even when I was in that rich vein of form in 2002–03. There was never that easy over before the lunch or tea break because he would always do something different, such as put himself on to bowl medium-pace bouncers at you. I thought Rahul Dravid was a decent captain, although I am not sure he entirely enjoyed it. An impressive man as well.

South Africa's Graeme Smith was someone I had my ups and downs with, although by the end I held a high opinion of him. From a captain's point of view, apart from an in-form Brian Lara, I found him about the hardest batsman in the world to set a field to and stop scoring because of the way he can work the ball through the on side. As a fellow skipper I came to very much admire the way he dealt with the particularly difficult off-field issues that are unique to South Africa and the politics of their game.

I have the utmost respect for Ricky Ponting, although I do think some of his decisions during that 2005 Ashes were very debatable. Nasser got slaughtered for the decision to put the Australians in at Brisbane in late 2002 but Ponting's choice to stick us in at Edgbaston was even more of a shocker. Perhaps he got a bit complacent at times that summer, and since then he has definitely improved in his tactical thinking. I am not sure Lara ever really bought in to being captain; he was just such a great player that it seemed to be more about him than the team.

An oversized ego is definitely not what you need as a captain. Apart from it perhaps stopping you understanding other human beings, in pure cricketing terms you have to accept that there are periods when others have the upper hand and negative fields need setting, as you should just 'sit in the game'. At the same time, you cannot let your self-esteem be hurt too badly when the ball flies through the gaps – there is only a certain amount you can do, because it's the batsman who hits the ball.

I have been approached since stepping down as captain to do some 'workshops' – one of those modern concepts that seem to be all the rage in cricket – about how to do the job, but to be honest I am sceptical about the value of trying to distil the essence of captaincy as part of some coaching qualification. I think that good captains tend to be born, not made, and there is no manual you can produce to do the demands of the job justice.

16

The Run-up to the Ashes

What was one major reason for our success in the 2005 Ashes? The fact that we did nothing. By this, I am referring to the period after the one-dayers in South Africa, which saw us able to come back and relax, enjoying a proper break before the start of what was sure to be the most demanding summer. The ECB have not always got this aspect of scheduling right, but the planners were spot on in allowing us time to get away from cricket and properly recharge before the season was upon us.

Having got back from South Africa in mid-February I was not required to play for Yorkshire until 6 May. Yorkshire and I often would have liked to have seen more of each other, but I needed the break and this was an example of the central-contracts system doing me a favour. About the only thing I did in my duties as captain was an appearance for Test sponsors npower at Earls Court in early March, where I reaffirmed our intention to play aggressive cricket in the forthcoming series, and also warned that there might be the odd disappointed player as we formulated the team. However, there is no such thing as a day off in your mind when you are England captain and, even when just spending time with the family, I would wake up in the morning thinking how we were going to configure the XI to take on the Australians.

My main preoccupation was getting Kevin Pietersen in the team, as it looked as if Mark Butcher's long-term wrist injury was going to free up a spot for Ian Bell. We had two Tests coming up against Bangladesh, which would be a formality, and the big question surrounded Graham Thorpe, for whom two more appearances would add up to 100 Test caps.

His back had been causing him quite a few problems and he was now making no secret of it. Although he was a player for whom I had huge respect, my mind was made up that, on balance, I did not want any players who were carrying too much baggage from previous Ashes series and that the team needed a fresh look about it. I would have wanted to him to get the 100 caps his career deserved, but there could be no room for sentimentality. My main concern was that, even though Bangladesh were on a different cricketing planet from Australia, Kevin should be in the team to face them so we could all get the feel of playing together ahead of the summer's main business. I did not want anyone making their debut in the Ashes.

So before the series began, I forced myself to have the awkward conversation that was necessary with the Surrey left-hander. Deep down I was really not sure how desperate he was to face the Australians this time around, especially with a deteriorating back condition and the 100 caps having been gained by then. We had also learned that he was due to take up a coaching position with New South Wales at the end of the season.

It was after we arrived at Lord's for preparations ahead of the first Bangladesh Test that I decided to broach this difficult subject. As we walked across the outfield I said, 'If you think you're struggling to make it through this whole summer then I would rather you pulled out of these two games as well.' He later wrote that I was naive for thinking that those last two caps were not important to him. Of course I recognised that, but there was the not insignificant consideration in all this of giving ourselves the best chance to try and beat Australia.

In the end I decided to back off and not make a stand, partly because of my awareness that Thorpey was hardly a bad option for the Ashes anyway, given his proven quality. So Pietersen had to sit out a series which really did not tell us a great deal about a great deal. We hammered Bangladesh twice as Bell got his first Test hundred, which would have been a boost for him, however devalued this particular currency was. The bowlers got a few overs in their legs and took a few wickets, but that was about it.

I struggle to see how Test cricket is ever going to catch on in Bangladesh, now that there are much greater rewards available for their better players in Twenty20 competitions. I am afraid that we will see Test cricket reduced to a formidable hard core, and I am not even sure how important it will continue to be in Pakistan – with all their domestic security issues – or in Sri Lanka, whose commitment to it might also wane.

I was under no illusions that it was the one-day matches that followed, and not the Tests against Bangladesh, that were going to be the important preparation for the Ashes. This included the Twenty20 match at the Rose Bowl on 13 June, which was to be our first encounter with Australia of the summer. At the time the ultra-short format was not, remember, approached with the seriousness that it is now, but if the tourists reckoned that we were going to be taking this lightly, then we intended to give them a shock.

We had also discovered an invaluable source of information about the Australians from an Englishman working in Australia, which we were keen to tap into just prior to that match. I had asked him six months previously to compile a dossier on the players we were coming up against. The thing I was most interested to know about was what type of characters their players were. It was easy enough for us to get in video footage and dissect them technically, but what I wanted was an insight into, for instance, what made them tick as a group, if there were any cliques that we did not know about, any personality clashes or the like.

He came back with some very interesting information, for which we were grateful. He gave us plenty of stuff about pure technique, but also gave us fascinating pointers. A picture began to emerge from what we learnt from him and other sources suggesting, among other things, that Matthew Hayden liked to play the bully but did not like being got at, and that Shane Warne was not popular among a lot of the other senior players, though he had some of the younger ones such as Michael Clarke on his side. I had assumed that they were a pretty watertight unit, so it was reassuring to know from someone who was familiar with them that they were human like the rest of us, and that they had the same divisions as most teams. The difference with them in this regard was that they won so regularly, and that always has the effect of covering up any differences in the ranks. My immediate thought was that if we could just beat them a couple of times, the fault lines might start to open up.

I was also keen to send out the signal to our public that this England team would be different. We were going to have a real go, and that even if we ended up losing, it was not because we had lacked the courage or belief to properly take them on. The night before the Twenty20 game I spoke to this effect, but over the previous month we had already managed to get all the players thinking along these lines anyway, so my talk was nothing new. It should also be stressed that you can only adopt this attitude if you have the players to carry it off, particularly the bowling attack. I knew by now that we had the essentials: good variety in our bowling, batting talent high up the order and, with Ashley Giles at number eight, the potential to make runs down the order.

One thing I wanted from these one-dayers was confirmation that my instincts about Pietersen were right, and more than anyone I wanted to see how he would react to taking on the best team in the world. I wanted to see that swagger, especially with more reports reaching us that Thorpey was having back trouble. The Bell-Pietersen-Thorpe issue was looking far more clear-cut to us than the great debate in the media about batting positions might have led people to believe.

From the start of that match in Southampton you sensed an atmosphere around the ground that was slightly different. We carted their bowling around and then shot them out for 79 to win by exactly 100 runs. Goughy aggressively bounced Andrew Symonds and we made life as uncomfortable for them as possible. Of course, they could dismiss the whole match as a bit of a lark and they did, but I felt there was a little bit of complacency about them – hardly surprising, perhaps, given their crushing results in recent series.

Obviously, you could not get too carried away with a match like this, but it did create exactly the kind of buzz that we wanted. It was already noticeable to me that when we had played them in 2002–03 there had been very little talk among the lads of us having the capability to spring an upset. It was more 'Hayden does this, McGrath does that.' Now it was discernible that around the dressing room we were talking up our chances of beating them, and I always saw that as the first step to winning.

The weekend that followed saw the start of the NatWest triangular series and was more significant for many reasons. The most important development of all was that any doubts about whether Pietersen should be in the Test team completely evaporated. First Australia lost to Bangladesh in Cardiff, where it emerged that Symonds had been out drinking late and was dropped from the team. Then their bus turned up late at Bristol, where we were playing them the following day, and we beat them by three wickets before a feverish crowd.

Steve Harmison took 5–33, Paul Collingwood took a miracle catch to dismiss Hayden and Kevin smashed 91 off 65 balls to take us home, particularly punishing Jason Gillespie. Saatchi & Saatchi could not have come up with a better advertisement for bringing him into the Ashes side. As I watched from the dressing room a succession of players came up to me. 'Vaughany, we've got to play this guy, he's a freak' was one I recall. They were pushing against an open door by now.

Our next encounter with the Aussies was a 57-run defeat at Chester-le-Street, which I missed as a precaution with a slightly sore hamstring. Then came a rain-ruined match at Edgbaston on 28 June best remembered for the confrontation between Hayden and Simon Jones. Simon had fielded a ball off his own bowling and hurled it back in the direction of the stumps but was way off-beam, hitting the broad-shouldered Australian opener in the chest. In the verbal confrontation that followed, several of our players were notably quick to join in and support the bowler.

Now, it was definitely a poor throw, and while I honestly

do not know whether our fiery Welshman meant to do it or not, I do know he was not acting under specific orders. What we had tried to engender among the players, however, was a general recognition that if things got heated in the middle we would back each other up – unlike what had so clearly happened during the previous Ashes series with Andy Caddick. I did not want the Australians seeing us holding back as they had then, because it sends out totally the wrong message.

More premeditated where Hayden was concerned was the tunnel of children holding Union Jack flags that greeted the tourists' openers when they came out to bat. This had been coordinated by Colin Gibson and David Clarke of the ECB, and it had the desired effect of annoying Hayden, who started walking outside the 'guard of honour'. It was a sign that we were getting under his skin, albeit in a less physical way than Simon had done. A bruise is just a bruise, but judging by Hayden's follow-up comments in the press, Jones had certainly got to him.

Our bowling attack in this one-day series was the same as in the Ashes, except for Gough being in for Matthew Hoggard. They were regularly knocking over the Australian batsmen for low scores and now had the experience of bowling as a unit against the world champions. The fact that the limited-over series came before the Tests was another example of good planning. It was less necessary before the 2009 series because, as Andrew Strauss said, the Aussies didn't have quite the same aura that needed to be experienced by the younger players.

A very evenly contested triangular series – ignoring Bangladesh – finished with a thrilling tie at Lord's. They had us 33–5 chasing 196, but in another show of our resolve we managed to get level with them. Unlike what happened before previous Ashes series, the Australians were not getting into the habit of battering us.

That left three more one-dayers against Australia, this time in a straight series. Who said the structure of the international calendar can be hard to follow? The first of these was at Headingley on 7 July, where we had a pre-match team meeting that was one of the more remarkable in my time. Without warning, Marcus Trescothick put his hand up and announced to everyone that he was seriously struggling against Glenn McGrath, that he did not feel he knew which end of the bat he was holding against him, and that he would appreciate any help anyone could offer. I could sense one or two of the lads thinking at first, 'You weak dick, just get on with it,' but I personally thought it was one of the bravest things Tres could do. Once his unusually frank admission had sunk in, you could feel this massive goodwill towards him in the room. The next day when he walked out to bat every single member of the squad was out on the balcony to cheer his every stroke against McGrath, even the false ones.

His confession and the advice and encouragement he received obviously worked, because he made 104 not out that day. It goes to show that whatever level of cricket you are playing, from club thirds to international, self-doubt is a natural common denominator, and maybe it is a lesson to everyone that if you are open enough to admit these things and get them off your chest it can work wonders. I scored 55 and we beat them by nine wickets, by now feeding off the energy from a crowd who were coming to enjoy the unexpected spectacle of their team standing toe-to-toe with the Aussies and getting the better of them. Aside from its bearing on the forthcoming series, we were again looking like a decent one-day outfit.

But not so fast, and it was only three days later that Ricky Ponting and co began to show that they were not world champions by accident. They came to Lord's and beat us pretty comfortably by seven wickets, although I was not that distressed, because there were pluses such as Fred getting a very fluent 87, becoming the latest of our batsmen to make a good score against them.

I was more worried by what happened in the final game at The Oval, where they gave us a good and proper stuffing. Kevin again shone with a 74, but our 228 was chased down in a fairly humiliating 34.5 overs. There were a few concerning developments, such as Adam Gilchrist smashing our bowling out of sight, especially Harmy. Gough got hit for 37 runs in four overs, but while that was the match which suggested to me his days as a front-line one-day bowler were finished, it was less relevant to the Ashes. Gillespie, who had looked a reduced bowler prior to this, took some terrible stick from the crowd by dropping me and then came back impressively to take 3–44 and look more like his old self.

Suddenly this beating Australia business was not seeming quite such a walk in the park, although when I reflected on it the following day I still thought we had a lot to take away from these opening skirmishes. They had finished the stronger, but honours were just about even over the series, in which our bowlers had all taken wickets and our batsmen had familiarised themselves with getting runs against their bowlers. My main emotion was that I was by now fed up with playing one-day cricket and that I could not wait to get my whites on again.

There were now eight days left before the first Test and I was keen that they should be managed properly. Duncan and I formally relayed to David Graveney that we wanted Pietersen in ahead of Thorpe, and it was decided to announce the team unusually early, a full week ahead of the match. We wanted to put a quick end to any speculation and make sure there was one less thing to worry about. Chris Tremlett was in the twelve, but not in contention for the XI, barring injury.

So these were the men for the job, a group of players whose oldest member was Ashley Giles at 32. In line with the principle that Duncan and I had long established between ourselves, there was no long-term 'scarring' from defeats by the world champions. If nothing else, we were going to have the exuberance of youth on our side and there was, hopefully, going to be some shock of the new. This England was going to present Australia with a different challenge.

Having tied this up, I was keen to escape for a few days before spending the following six weeks in the blistering spotlight. So I went with the family down to Devon to stay with our friends David and Sheila Jacobs. David worked in the sports gear business and for some reason we have developed a tradition of going out for dinner on every Thursday night of a Lord's Test, to somewhere quite nice such as the Ivy or Langan's. He has seen all my centuries at the ground over the years.

Peaceful as our stay was, and however convivial the company, it was impossible to shut off thoughts about what was coming up. In fact, part of me was petrified by the prospect of what was going to happen, because our recent performances had raised national expectation to such a pitch. I knew we were capable of doing something special, but going into a series with this level of anticipation was pretty alien territory.

I was worried about the immediate build-up to Lord's and thoughts were starting to crowd in. How we were all going to react, whether we would pick up any late injuries, even how I was going to act when I walked out for the toss with Ponting.

As it turned out, our immediate preparations started off with a fundamental mistake: we met up at our hotel in Marylebone on the Sunday, which was too early. We had changed hotels, staying at the Landmark rather than the Regent's Park Marriott, and while the Landmark is a delightful place to stay, and walkable to Lord's, it felt a bit too prim and proper for a bunch of lads like us. On the Monday we had a fascinating talk from the polar explorer Alan Chambers. I felt we probably should have done that a month previously for it to have much effect, although throughout the series we did make references to the 'Iceman' when the going got tough.

Three days' practice might have been a bit excessive, because the media interest was at a level I had never come across before. Around the hotel everyone wanted to know us, the public constantly wanted to take our pictures and it all added to the enormous buzz of nervous energy that was about.

We did individual practice on the Monday, and I was keen just to have my own private net to work on technical aspects at my own pace. We had Tuesday morning off and I went for coffee with my regular latte partners Strauss, Trescothick and Giles, with whom I would enjoy putting the world to rights. Then it was up to the ground for some of Nancy's food, which was always one of the best things about playing at Lord's. We practised on Tuesday afternoon, and while two days out from a Test would always be the hardest session, this one had an intensity all of its own. Wednesday tends to be much lighter and all about doing what it was right for you as an individual before the whole team draws together in the evening.

For the skipper, Wednesday is rather more arduous, and I had to slip off quickly from fielding practice to tell a huge assembly of media how we were going tackle the match. As ever, it was a case of trying to walk the line between talking

ourselves up, keeping expectations realistic and not giving too
much away – the usual game. As was customary before the
first Test of a series, there was then a captains' meeting with
the series referee, in this case former Sri Lanka player Ranjan
Madugalle.

It was there that Ricky brought up the concept he had at
the time that batsmen should take the fielders' word for it when
it came to marginal catches on the ground, rather than refer
them to TV replays. He put this to me, but I declined. 'Sorry,
mate, we are just going to stick with the system we know,' I
said. There was nothing personal or fractious about it, and I
did not have especially strong feelings on the matter either way.
What I did not want, though, was to let him feel he could
dictate things under any circumstances, and if it wound him
up a little then all the better.

I did not really know him at the time and it remained that
way. I had massive respect for him as a batsman, but you are
never quite sure what someone is like as a captain until you
are up against him. My intelligence about Ricky, gleaned from
the likes of Mark Nicholas and Darren Lehmann, was that he
was a tough competitor and highly respected by his team. There
was also a suggestion that he had a fuse on him that was
capable of blowing. In fact, Ponting was hardly unique among
Australian cricketers in this way, as I had always found them
to be a pretty combustible breed just under the surface, even
the phlegmatic Lehmann. There was always quite an edge to
them and – don't get me wrong – that was one of the many
things I admired about the Australians.

As Strauss liked to stay in his room on a Wednesday afternoon, Giles was my regular Starbucks buddy at this stage of
the week with Tres coming along sometimes, too. So we went
for more coffee, a bit of a chat and a look round the shops.

When we played the early-season Lord's Test, there would invariably be a big football match to watch the night before the game, but not when it is high summer. I actually would have appreciated that distraction from the huge build-up of nerves.

The night before the first match in Australia on our 2002–03 tour my stomach was physically aching with anxiety, and I thought it was different from any other sensation I had known. That sickness was starting to come back now and I needed to suppress it for the team meeting early in the evening. We went through how we were going to bowl to their batsmen, in some cases accompanied by videos. For instance, we had footage of Hayden struggling against the ball swinging back into him, and of Gilchrist having problems against bowlers coming round the wicket to him and playing on.

There was a bit of guidance about field placings, although these can change so much depending on the situation. I was conscious of the need not to overdo it. My basic message was that we were good enough now to trust our own games, good enough to compete against them. There was a reminder that we had not played especially well as a team against South Africa, but had still possessed sufficient individual talent to win the series. I tried to emphasise that it was the process that was the important thing, and if we got that right the result would look after itself. Most of all, this was the time of our lives, and we should try to enjoy it.

The rituals continued on the morning of the match. One of mine was the constant struggle not to forget my blazer; many was the time Phil Neale would have to rush back to the hotel to pick it up. By now I was taking it with me as a reminder when I went down to breakfast, where I would invariably be joined by Tres. He would always disappear back to his room for a while after breakfast and then take me and Strauss to the ground in his car. There was an eerie quietness about us as we ate that morning, and I could tell this because I was aware of hearing the muzak being played in the restaurant.

Up at the ground, first the batters would go over to the nets for a hit and then we would meet up as a team. We always liked to do our fielding warm-ups at the top end of Lord's, but John Buchanan had got there very early and put his cones down on our territory, like some German putting his towel on the sun-lounger, so we had to warm up at the bottom. I was impressed by that from Buchanan – smart work, I thought.

There was plenty of cloud cover when I walked out for the toss, and I was unsure what to do. When there is cloud like that around you get some movement and zip, but then you do not want to be batting second against a team that has Shane Warne in it. I did my usual trick of not looking at the team sheet when it was handed to me. By the time the coin went up I was leaning towards batting first, but I was not the unhappiest man when Ponting called correctly and announced they would have a bat.

Two years and 26 Tests had gone by since I had been made captain and this was what it was all about. There was no going back now.

17

Golden Summer

To walk through the Long Room at Lord's on the opening day of any Test is a priceless experience, but on 21 July 2005 it was something else altogether. Your journey is usually accompanied by polite applause and encouragement, but this time there was a sort of throaty growl, with the normally strait-laced members urging us on with a passion I had never come across before. Then as we jogged down the steps onto the field there was a football-style roar before we gathered together for the huddle.

I could tell the boys were already in a state of high excitement, so there was no need for any stirring last words, in fact if anything I was trying to calm them down. There was no great oratory from me; I just told them to control the ball out of their hand and to have a go. Whatever we do in this series, I said, let's have a really good go at them.

Steve Harmison's first over at Justin Langer was electrifying. You could see their openers were pumped up and so was Harmy, who came in like an express train and clattered Langer on the helmet with his second ball. Ricky Ponting also got hit when he came in and much was made of the fact that we supposedly failed to approach him and inquire if he was OK or not. In fact, a couple of us did move to do that and there was certainly no preplanned scheme to ignore any injuries to the batsmen. It actually became clear with barely perceptible body language that he did not want to be helped, and that is why we did not crowd around.

What was a tactic, however, was to fling the ball in to our keeper every time we fielded the ball. A couple of times I got the ball and threw it back in very close to the batsmen, and I think they reckoned I was doing it deliberately. I was not, but when I saw that it was winding them up I made sure that we continued with it. I had no intention of hitting them but was keen to show intent in the field. If they wanted to blame anyone for it then it should have been Darren Lehmann, who at Yorkshire had drummed into us that banging it in to the keeper made a team look like a strong unit with energy. There are no stats for how you act in the field and how athletic you look, but I always considered it a major factor towards winning games of cricket.

It was an astonishing day that ended with us 92–7 after we had dismissed them for 190. They had scored at nearly five per over and probably got a few more than they should have done after we had them in serious trouble. I thought it augured well, however, as most of our plans for their batsmen seemed to be working. Matthew Hoggard had got Hayden out by swinging it back into him after he had planted that big foot down the wicket; Ponting likes a push outside off stump early on and we had him caught in the slips; Gilchrist was caught by the wicket-keeper off Fred coming round the wicket. They had come out with guns blazing and clearly felt the force of the occasion.

We had enjoyed the cloud cover and dismissed them in 40 overs, and when we were back in the pavilion the sun started to come out. I thought all my Christmases had come at once – they are all back in the hutch and now the sun is shining and the wicket will flatten out! I anticipated getting a decent lead, but Glenn McGrath was to intervene with another brilliant display at one of his favourite grounds. He hit an area outside the right-hander's off stump that made him almost unplayable, getting the ball to nip back and keep a little low. He was always lethal from the pavilion end, and this time he absolutely knocked the stuffing out of us.

We were all out for 155 and I thought it was more a case of McGrath bowling brilliantly than us choking. Brett Lee had bowled at the speed of sound and put the frighteners on our tail, but at least Kevin Pietersen had justified our faith in him with a fifty on his debut. We went on to lose after they got away from us in their second innings and then bowled us out for under 200 again.

I was much more worried about our batting and their bowling than the other way round. Of obvious concern was the fact that their two titans could hardly have got off to a better start, McGrath taking nine wickets and Shane Warne six. I had been bowled twice and it was not just me who would require some running repairs before the second Test. On balance, though, I was not as despondent as I fully expected the media to be after all the build-up. There were some comforting aspects to reason with: we had taken 20 wickets, none of their batsmen had made a hundred, Flintoff already looked as if he had a couple of their numbers and Harmison had put the wind up them. Pietersen had made a pair of fifties.

In truth, I was merely clinging to these things. I told the team that they should go and get away from cricket before the next two games, which were back-to-back, and tried to talk us up. In private, I had left Lord's feeling drained and fairly depressed. There were nine days to go before we would have the chance of another go, and I knew that the general reaction to this result would be that this was the same-old-England, which was understandable enough. If I am honest, a large part of me thought what everyone else was thinking. I went home and tried, unsuccessfully, to relax by spending time with the family, having a few rounds of golf and turning my phone off. I also had another private batting session in Leeds with Duncan Fletcher, the benefits of which were bound to show sooner or later.

Given the scale of the media interest in the series, I was keen that we should try and rise above the hype, which is a more difficult exercise than it sounds. Before Lord's Hoggard had given an interview in which he had accused the Australians of 'bigging themselves up', which ran contrary to our policy of trying not to get involved in any verbal tit-for-tat in the media. It was not as if there was insufficient pressure anyway.

Some of the most vicious criticism was directed at Ashley Giles, with former Zimbabwe captain Dave Houghton asserting that we were effectively a 10-man team with him in it. Nonsense, of course, but these things were liable to get to Ashley and he had a dart back in a newspaper column. Knowing Ashley as I did, I was worried about his state of mind, and when we arrived at Edgbaston on the following Monday ahead of the second Test he had this haggard, drained look about him, as if he had really been going through it. I sat him down and told him that he had to forget about it and try to put a sheet over it in his mind. He needed reminding of the futility of getting involved in these things and of how much we all rated him and wanted to support him. He was someone who always liked to talk things through and he seemed more at ease by the end of our chat.

On the Wednesday morning we had a team meeting in the committee room at Edgbaston, where I told the players that I did not care about Lord's and did not want to hear about it.

I knew that our chances in the whole series might well hinge on what happened on the first morning in Birmingham and wanted to instil that message. I said that all I wanted us to focus on was coming out fighting in that first session and that if we were batting we simply had to go out and attack. We had looked timid at Lord's with the bat and there could be no repeat of that. It would have been tempting to go through a detailed analysis of what had happened in the first Test, but I thought the best pressure-relieving strategy was simply to say: give it a whack. I was also feeling brighter through the knowledge that Edgbaston was a ground which tended to bring out the best in us and where we enjoyed passionate support.

The next day, 4 August, we were all lying on the outfield doing our stretching exercises when I heard a commotion on the other side of the ground, which seemed to spread around the terraces. I looked over and saw McGrath lying on the ground, and then a golf buggy came over and he was lifted onto it. We later found out he had trodden on a ball and damaged his ankle. Nothing serious, we hoped. Was I filled with strong feelings of compassion for my fellow man? In all honesty, no. I quickly thought of those nine wickets at Lord's and what it would look like if you took him out of their attack.

When I walked out for the toss I was yearning to win it so much it hurt. I saw the wicket – it looked nice and placid – there was a bit of cloud, no McGrath, and I was desperate for us to have first go. When Ponting won my heart sank into the turf, because frankly I just could not see us winning batting second against Warne. Then Ricky announced that he was going to have a bowl. I could not believe my ears and almost had to stop myself saying, 'You sure, mate?' Is he getting complacent? Has he seen something in this track that I haven't? I was not about to question him.

If the first day at Lord's was extraordinary then this was not far off. Tres and Strauss batted exactly to order, and by the end of it we had cracked 407 at more than five per over. A key innings in the context of the series was Fred's 68, a quite horrible knock during which nothing seemed to come off the middle. Somehow he survived and had his little bit of luck that seemed to kick-start him for the rest of the summer. I was in the car park afterwards and Geoffrey Boycott came up to me: 'Not a bad day, but it don't win you Test matches batting like that,' he said. 'We'll see,' I replied.

The first ball of the second over in their innings was the one that provided one of my most satisfying captaincy moments of all. I had a gut instinct that Hayden was feeling uneasy on the drive, so I pulled Strauss out of third slip and put him at extra cover for Hoggard, and sure enough Hayden drove it straight to him in the air. It is the kind of hunch that can make you look more of a genius than you actually are, but I had been convinced it was worth trying. We kept with that field to him – an extra cover in catching position, mid-off very deep, mid-on unusually straight and midwicket also straight. We were saying to him that we were not going to give him scoring opportunities down the ground, and if he wanted to take us on, fair enough. I think it got to him somewhat.

We got a lead of 99, but in fairness to Ponting it was just like the days of Steve Waugh: you simply could not relax for a single ball against Australia. They reduced us to 131–9 and at that point I thought the Ashes were gone. It was the 51-run stand for the last wicket between Fred and Simon Jones that was the single most important partnership of the summer, the difference between giving them a defendable target of 282 and something that they would surely have overhauled. The significance of those 23 balls that Simon held out for, while

Fred carted it around at the other end, can hardly be over-stated.

The best over I ever saw in international cricket was the one Fred bowled on the Saturday afternoon to stop their second innings in its tracks. Coming in with ferocious pace, first he got Langer to play on and then he produced vicious in-swing at Ponting, before getting two to move away and find his edge. The fevered atmosphere and Fred's brilliance almost sucked the breath out of me.

It is one of the lesser known facts about that series that I used Hoggard quite sparingly throughout, and over the five matches he actually bowled only 132 overs, but he had the priceless ability of picking up wickets, and this time he got Damien Martyn to chip it to midwicket. Another slice of genius was Harmison's disguised slower ball that dismissed Michael Clarke, which came in the extra half-hour that I had asked for. By the close they were on 175–8 with the match seemingly won. A lot of the wives and girlfriends – this was in the days before infamous WAGS became part of the English language, incidentally – were in town and quite a few of us went for a meal.

There was an air of celebration and I, for one, thought that we had won it, which was complacent of me. On Sunday morning the dressing room had a real vibrancy to it as we anticipated moving to 1–1 in the series. The ball had been reverse-swinging the night before, Flintoff was bowling as if he was heaven-sent, and I thought that there was no way Warne, Lee and Michael Kasprowicz would be able to cope. I was just assuming that within 20 minutes we would be back in the pavilion and debating what we do before moving on to Manchester. The crowd obviously felt the same, judging by the almost party atmosphere that greeted us when we walked out.

Everyone in Birmingham had committed the cardinal sin of underestimating Australia, for whom Warne came out flailing while Lee displayed surprisingly good technique. I was starting to get slightly edgy by the time Fred induced the great leg-spinner to hit his wicket, with 60 still needed. Time to relax again, with the arrival of their one genuine tail-ender, the genial Kasprowicz. However, when he started to hang around and have a go and they got to within 40 I started to think it was getting a bit tight for comfort.

Then they got to within 20, and while I was now seriously alarmed I also noticed how their approach was changing. At first they'd been happy-go-lucky, but as the reality of possible victory was growing, they were becoming more cautious and holding far more conversations. I think that if they had carried on trying to smash it they would probably have got over the line, but thankfully they started to become more sensible. As the game reached its agonising climax, I started to try and square the emotions in my head. There was the gut-wrenching prospect of us losing a huge match from a winning position, and I was trying to balance that with the thought that we had competed well with a fantastic Australian side, and that we had ultimately been undone by the genius of Warne taking six wickets in our second innings.

When Simon Jones dropped Kasprowicz at third man with 15 runs needed I started making the serious mental readjustment to us having blown it. Now I was just focusing on taking the game on as long as I could, in the hope that a mistake would be made or someone could conjure up a bit of magic. You're only one ball away, I kept telling myself. So I kept the sweepers out on the boundary because it was clear that the fours were really hurting us. They'd got to within two when Harmy bounced Kasprowicz, he fended it off and Billy Bowden,

God bless his crooked finger, judged him to have gloved it to Geraint, who took a catch that was harder than it looked.

People remarked how calm I had seemed in the frenzied climax to that run chase in what many recall as among the best Tests ever played, and surprisingly it was true – I did have this feeling of inner peace. I loved it when I was captaining and games got tight, because I grew up as a cricket fan and I enjoyed the feeling of being out there making the decisions. I always felt more in control when I was captaining rather than batting, and had much less fear of failure. Having said that, it would have been inhuman not to have felt the surge of joy and relief when Bowden poked his dodgy digit into the air.

I took two life lessons from this match, things I thought I already knew but which obviously needed reinforcing. The first was never, ever to underestimate Australia. The second, which occurred to me as I watched the last pair's increasingly frequent committee meetings, was that if you allow victory to happen then it probably will, but if you start thinking about it too much you create your own obstacles.

The dressing rooms at Edgbaston are next to each other, and Warne and Gilchrist came in to have a drink. I liked getting to know the opposition in this way, although at Lord's we were so sickened by defeat that there had been no post-match fraternisation. I thought they were good lads. We had a bit of a pub crawl down Broad Street that night, having made a false start with our mini celebrations the night before. All I had really asked for in this series was that we would go into the fourth match with it all still to play for and that was now guaranteed to happen. We were competing in a way that England teams had not competed against Australia for many years.

They say that you should smell the roses along the way, but it is not easy when you are caught up in the maelstrom of hype and excitement that we had created. When we checked into the Worsley Marriott hotel it scarcely crossed my mind that we were almost within a boundary throw of where I had first seen cricket played, and where my mother's side of the family have a long lineage. Twenty years after lobbing that ball over the bowling green to the amusement of my dad and his mates, I was back again.

My message to the team was that this was the time of our lives and that we had to keep riding the wave of goodwill towards us in the country that had built up since the previous Sunday. Word was also reaching us again that there were divisions in their team, that cliques had developed and that Warne in particular was a man apart from the others. McGrath was struggling to recover from his ankle, and many were writing him off for this match, though I was not so sure.

For all my exhortations to the lads to enjoy it, I certainly did not feel like that inside. The mask was on again and the day before the match Fletch and I were walking onto the outfield when I decided to unburden myself: 'I keep on telling them to enjoy it, but I'm finding this pressure very tough, I'm not enjoying it all,' I told him. 'Don't worry, I feel a bit the same way,' he said, and we had a laugh about it. 'Just try and enjoy this match,' he said. After the immediate euphoria of Edgbaston had worn off, it was bothering me that I was yet to make a score in this series and I was desperate. Even Fletch's private tuition did not seem to have paid off. 'Just react to the ball; you're doing the right thing,' he said.

A problem shared is a problem halved, I always think, and I felt better after that. Another thing that improved my state of mind was meeting our mascot at the toss, five-year-old Connor Shaw, who had undergone three major heart operations. He was such a refreshing and innocent presence and his cheerfulness in the face of real adversity put a silly old game of cricket into perspective, which was just what I needed.

The pitch was a beauty, I won the toss, and there was no hesitation about batting. When Tres was out it was Warne's 600th Test wicket, and from the other end I could tell that it gave their whole team a lift. I had gone out there resolving just to play on instinct and started off OK, but was dropped by Gilchrist and, even though he did not seem fully fit, the infernal McGrath was still good enough to bowl me on 41. Fortunately, to hysterical cheers around Old Trafford, it was a no-ball. It was when I got past 50 that everything began to flow, and I was transported back to 2002–03 when I was flaying them around Australia. McGrath did get me out, but only as catcher off Simon Katich, of all people. By then I had made 166 in 215 balls, part of our overall 444 that was made at nearly four runs per over. Bell, who had also failed to contribute much up to that point, showed that he had some toughness to match his talent by hitting 59.

I felt that, although we ended up with a draw by falling just one wicket short of dismissing them on the last day, this was our best performance of those five Tests. We were level with or better than them in every session bar one, when Warne got after us with the bat and made 90. There were fine individual performances littered everywhere, the most visible being Simon Jones's six wickets in their first innings and Strauss's brave century in the second, after Brett Lee had nearly ripped his ear off with a bumper. There were important lesser contributions such as Ashley bowling at his best in their first innings and a cameo from Geraint Jones in our second. Geraint made 27 in 12 balls as we chased our declaration, his little knock indicative of how he batted entirely for the team, not caring about his average or getting out, and having a pure slog when asked.

We scored at 4.5 runs an over before declaring that innings, setting up a final day which began with an almighty crush around Old Trafford as people converged from all over the country trying to get in. As I drove into the ground I assumed there was a bomb scare, while Fred needed a police escort, the traffic was so bad. I was sure we were going to win, although this time I had not made the mistake of underestimating the resolve of our opponents. Ponting was absolutely magnificent that day in making 156, one of the best knocks I saw and a captain's innings if ever there was one.

Unfortunately Simon Jones had to go off with cramp, which hurt us as we tried to dislodge the likes of Lee at the end. Getting these tail-enders out was like trying to pull chewing gum out of your hair. With his reverse swing I think we might have knocked them over, but you could not fault the Australians' resolve. Again they went like the clappers in another phenomenally quick-scoring game, rattling along at not much short of four an over when they surely could not have expected to reach the 423 we had set them.

There was a crushing sense of deflation as we failed to winkle out one of Lee or McGrath for the last wicket, but my spirits soon lifted when I looked over to their balcony at the end. They were jumping up and down as if they had won the World Cup, so while we were still on the pitch I called together the team, who were absolutely spent. 'Just have a look at their balcony and memorise it,' I told them. 'For the first time ever we can see an Australian team celebrating the draw. Log that away, and remember that if we keep playing like this we are going to win the Ashes.'

It was a fantastic game. We had boxed them into a corner and pummelled away, but still we could not put them down, which was to their enormous credit. That was a mark of the team they were: there were cracks in their unity, their middle order was not firing, a key bowler was short of fitness, we had had a bit of luck and we were playing out of our skins. And still it was only 1–1.

We now had a much-needed break, although that did not mean there was any ceasefire in terms of psychological shots being fired. Warne was trying to ratchet things up, saying that some individuals in our team were not performing, which even by his usual standard of spurious wind-ups was total crap. I arrived at Trent Bridge and had never been so deluged with media requests. All the interviewers were asking what Fred was like as a person, and some were investing me with almost mystical powers as captain. I was finding Karl Morris, a sports psychologist I knew through his work in golf, a useful man when it came to putting the whole whirl into perspective.

All was well in our camp, although on the Tuesday before the fourth Test Simon Jones was to come up to me with perhaps the most bizarre observation I had ever heard. 'I don't think I should play here, I don't bowl well at Trent Bridge,' he said. 'I've got a niggle and don't think I should play.' I told him that he most definitely would be playing and that he would be fine. Maybe that was all he wanted to hear.

The opposition had worries of their own and had dropped Gillespie, while McGrath was out, having felt the after-effects of coming back too soon at Old Trafford. So their line-up now had Kasprowicz back in alongside Shaun Tait, the frighteningly quick but somewhat raw paceman. I knew that if we could bat first and make runs they would be in severe difficulties, given the way our attack was performing.

On 25 August, I won the toss, the pitch looked good and for the third match in succession we posted over 400, Fred and Geraint's sixth-wicket stand of 177 being the centrepiece of our first-innings 477. Again we rattled along, scoring at 3.87 runs per over. Mind you, when they replied in making just 218 they went along at 4.43. That was what made the whole series so watchable: it was non-stop entertainment.

There had been some rain delays on Friday, and on Saturday morning Simon Jones, the man who could not bowl well at Trent Bridge, took 5–44 as they fell a long way short of our total. When we got them nine down I called the bowlers together and asked if they thought they had enough energy to allow me to make them follow on. I have never been a pace bowler, so I was going to leave it to them. They all said yes, though Simon was not there because he was collecting his sweater. So I asked him separately, 'Can I enforce the follow-on?' He said yes, and was in such form that I gave him the new ball, only for him to walk off with an injured ankle after four overs.

That had absolutely not been factored in to my plans, as it now placed a huge burden on the others to stop Australia setting us an awkward total to chase. As ever, I was conscious of Warne being in their ranks and of what he can do in the latter stages of the game and knew that anything vaguely defendable would present quite a challenge.

Once again we helped our cause by covering the small details, such as having a fielder like Gary Pratt ready to do twelfth-man duty. We had used Gary before as he was often not in the Durham first team and would often be available – he was a familiar face for us and we all knew what he could do. He was famously to run out Ponting, who lost it as he walked off and saw Duncan smiling on the balcony, but I really could not see what he had to complain about. I could not see the difference between us using Gary and them having Brad Hodge, a fine fielder and Lancashire player familiar with Old Trafford, on the pitch for such a long time in the previous Test. I had had particular reason to notice his presence, as he had taken an excellent catch down at fine leg in the second innings to dismiss me.

Whatever, it was another example of us having right royally got under their skin, which was all to the good. Another area of supposed controversy was the number of times our lads were going off the field to take comfort breaks, which was suggested to be a deliberate tactic to get massages or advice. It is true we did go off a lot and the reason was officially explained away as being because we were concentrating on making sure we were properly hydrated. This was true enough, but I reckon the real cause for our lads needing the loo so often was that they were so nervous.

It did amuse me that this was getting to the Australians, and because of that we were hardly likely to order the boys to keep it in. Their annoyance was another pointer to their general state of mind. When Ricky shouted at Duncan I knew we had him where we wanted him. Not that this was a particularly fractious series with any more sledging than normal. Hayden would chunter away and Warney was chirping as usual from slip. I would give it the proverbial dead bat most of the time. 'Warney, I know you're not a united team, don't pretend,' I said to him once.

Our reduced attack stuck to it manfully, restricting the target to 129, potentially awkward but in my mind too small for us to embarrass ourselves. But us being England, and them being Australia, it was somehow never going to be that straightforward. Throughout my time I always thought that was why England were a good team to watch – you could never be sure what we were going to do next.

At 32–0 the game looked over, and again at 57–2 we were back into calm territory, but both times they got a couple of quick wickets. It became one of those occasions when I found it hard to watch, and after the fourth wicket went down I walked to one of the rooms upstairs in the pavilion, where Phil Neale was doing some logistics and travel arrangements for future fixtures. At times like that I would try to lose myself in some mundane task just to kill some minutes, helpless as I was to do anything after getting out in the eighth over. At 103–4, however, with KP and Fred going OK we were, yet again, looking as if we were cruising before Lee and Warne, much to their credit, again refused to let the match die. Everyone was flapping in the dressing room, with plenty of anxious laps being walked as 14 were needed with Ashley and Hoggy now at the crease. Ashley was nervous and Duncan, brilliant at these times, had reassured him by telling him this was a fight-or-flight situation, and that he was programmed to fight. Hoggy was sent out with the instruction to block Warne and look for his runs off Lee, who was bound to give him something to score off if he hung around.

As at Edgbaston, I feared we had screwed it up, and I was feeling sickened that Warne had got me for nought. The Aussies just kept fighting, but our numbers eight and nine showed immense character – that word again – to get us over the line. With four runs to go everyone gathered on the balcony, and when Ashley flicked the final two runs all hell broke loose. I hugged our physio Kirk Russell and, rather embarrassingly, toppled over the wooden bench.

My immediate thought was that, as we now could not lose the Ashes, the minimum we could achieve was already a massive improvement on our recent history against Australia. Another heady night of celebration followed – the ability to have a good night out after winning was one thing you did know you would get with England. That evening we went out to the Living Room in Nottingham, where it was brought home to me how big this whole thing was getting. As cricketers, even England cricketers, you hardly expect to be treated like the Beatles – at least outside India – but this time we were absolutely mobbed. Everyone wanted to talk or have a picture, and the bar manager had to put us in a cordoned-off area at the back with bouncers to fend off the eager fans, who were flocking in.

It was a taster for what was to come in the 10 days preceding the final match at The Oval. Everywhere I went people were wanting to talk about the Ashes, shaking my hand, begging us to finish off the job – grannies, grandpas, everybody. We were plastered all over the media and the recognition had shot to a whole new level. Even my family were getting besieged for interviews, but we decided to bin any requests. I would never deny that I enjoyed the flattering aspects of the fame the job brought, but this was now at a level which made me feel a little uncomfortable. I am sure Fred was getting it more than me.

The big debate prior to The Oval was who should replace Simon as, despite him trying everything including sitting in an oxygen chamber, it was fairly clear his ankle would not recover in time. We were always leaning towards Paul Collingwood over James Anderson, even though it might be seen as a defensive move. Colly offered so much to the team and I knew that with his fundamental toughness he would not be overawed by the experience. Not that I think Jimmy would have been, but we felt Colly was the better bet for these circumstances. Fred and Harmy were consulted about being part of a four-man attack and they did not object.

What I used to do when faced by a dilemma over which players to pick was to physically write down different team sheets, so that I could study them separately. Sometimes I would hold them up alongside each other to see which looked the better. And when I did that on this occasion I thought we looked a little more solid with Colly in at seven.

There were no special preparations for this match – we were not going to repeat the mistake before the first game of the series, which now seemed a lifetime ago. I perhaps had too much time to think between the last two Tests, and my overriding feeling was that this was going to be my one and only chance to win the Ashes, certainly as skipper. Australia is such a difficult place to go to and win and I was aware that they would have much the same team next time. There was no prospect of us having a mystery spinner there, which I considered essential as the ball would not reverse so much Down Under, as had crucially been the case for us in this series. This was a once-in-a-lifetime opportunity for us to make history.

The hype was in overdrive, with the ECB understandably trying to capitalise on this enormous boost for the game. On the Tuesday Colly and I got paparazzied as we sat outside a coffee shop, with the accompanying headline that this was the very moment I had told him he was in the team. He knew already, as it happened. Faxes arrived from the Queen and the Prime Minister wishing us well. When I did the press conference, the media representatives were virtually hanging from the rafters, it was such a crush.

I was scared that we might crumble under the enormous weight of expectation and kept the message simple again the night before the match: let's go for it and try to enjoy this possibly life-changing stage of our careers. I do not suppose Ricky Ponting was particularly relishing any thought of defeat either, knowing the kind of questions he would have to answer in the event.

I woke up on the morning of the first day feeling perfectly

relaxed – although there was little reason to be. I had never known a cricket ground so full for the toss when I walked out with Ponting half an hour earlier than usual at 10 a.m., it now being 8 September and allowances being made for the time of year. The pitch looked great and I was ecstatic to have won the call of the coin again. We had a real chance, I thought, to make 500 and bat them out of the game, and that seemed a realistic prospect considering what had happened in the previous three Tests.

As it was, we fell short of 400 for the first time since Lord's, which I considered a huge opportunity missed. There was another massive effort from Strauss to make 129, but it was Fred who batted with most assurance, looking as if he was going to get a big one before the restored McGrath found his edge on 72. Was 373 going to be enough? I thought that it probably would, given that there might be time lost in the game, but on this ground I would have wanted 450.

My prayers seemed to be answered when play was called off for bad light after tea on the Friday, much to the delight of the crowd. That was another novelty in this match – the paying punters, apart from those from Australia, showing their delight at the prospect of not having any cricket to watch. We were also helped by the relatively pedestrian pace of Hayden's batting, and at times he looked as if he was more interested in getting a score to save his career rather than level the series. After the way he had been so dismissive of us in the previous series it was continually gratifying to see him struggling with his gloves, his stance. At Trent Bridge Hoggard seemed to have him on toast and he was being reminded of what a humbling game this can be.

We had gone along at 3.53 runs per over, and now they were progressing at 3.43, which was going to make winning the game difficult for them. While they eventually got 367 off 107.1 overs, I felt that they would have had more chance of getting the win if we had bowled them out for 280 in quicker time. It was with a mixture of astonishment and delight that, on the Saturday afternoon, I realised that they were accepting the offer of the light to finish the day early on 277–2. Play had already started half an hour late due to a wet outfield. It was another of those 'Are you sure, mate?' moments, as when we had been put into bat at Edgbaston. What were they thinking of? I could not get off the field quick enough.

One explanation could be that Fred's bowling was spooking them, because he was on fire. On Sunday morning, he bowled magnificently, unchanged during a session that we knew was going to be absolutely crucial. After his first eight overs I thought it was worth asking whether he was tired and he just brushed me off, leaving me very quickly to come to the conclusion that if it ain't broke, don't fix it. One thing that this team was very good at was sensing instinctively when the important phases of a match were upon them, and applying themselves accordingly. It was as if Fred knew that if we could come out on top in that phase then we were nearly home and dry, and that he could be a central figure in beating a team that was the world-beater in its era. He did not disappoint.

That spell of bowling got us right back into the game and we even managed a six-run lead. There were now four-and-a-bit sessions between us and the Ashes, and with every run scored and over that passed, the balance would tilt in our favour. All around the ground our supporters were putting up umbrellas as if they were doing some kind of ancient rain dance, while one or two Australians were waving yellow cardboard suns.

With the light marginal, Ponting brought Warne into the

attack almost straight away – a smart enough move regardless of the conditions. Not only was he at his most lethal in this situation, it was also going to plant in our head what was going to come our way on the final day. The policy reaped rewards when we lost Strauss to a close catch by the wicket, bringing myself in. We went off soon afterwards and then held out for another spell before the gloom closed in again. I sat in the pavilion enjoying the bad light – you could never know how exciting staring at the covers could be. At the same time I was thinking that, with Michael Clarke on at the other end, there might have been a few easy pickings around and that we could have been pulling further ahead. On balance, though, I was happier to be off than on.

Most of the crowd had gone home by the time play was abandoned shortly after six. We were 40 runs ahead, with nine wickets in hand and 98 more overs possible, in theory at least. We were in control of our own destiny.

That night I went out with five other players and our respective partners for supper at Pizza Express, on the other side of Tower Bridge from our hotel in the city. There was Marcus Trescothick, Paul Collingwood, Andrew Strauss, Ashley Giles and Matthew Hoggard, and the atmosphere was pretty buoyant following that masterful Flintoff performance with the ball, which had got us right back in it. The following day, we would have to bat for probably 60 or 70 overs and the Ashes would be ours.

There were no signs of collective nerves that evening, not on the surface at least, and the atmosphere was very congenial. Everyone in the restaurant was coming up and wishing us well. I smiled weakly at them but was completely drained, spent mentally, and I would have been delighted for the whole thing to have been rained off there and then – sod any glorious final day.

Back at the hotel, I could hardly sleep and kept getting up and peeping through the curtains to see if any clouds had arrived, which we had been told was a possibility. I drifted off now and again, until at 6.30 I finally got up to find that it was, disappointingly, a beautiful morning.

I had no appetite for breakfast but forced some down before getting a lift to The Oval with Colly. I was worried about the idea of a victory parade being made public, knowing that it would stir up the Australians even more than they were already guaranteed to be. That was one of my thoughts as I sat in the passenger seat being driven along the Embankment and over Vauxhall Bridge against the rush-hour traffic. I never liked driving to the ground on match days; I always liked to sit there and contemplate what lay ahead. This time it all felt a bit surreal. I was thinking that within 12 hours I could be lifting the urn – and I could not get that out of my head, trying and failing not to get ahead of myself. In pure cricketing terms, to have to bat out the last day on an excellent wicket at The Oval to win the Ashes was all that you could ever ask for.

On arrival I could sense that the team were very excited, with even more nervous chat and banter than usual. I already felt that this was going to be far from easy and I could not stop wondering what would happen if Warne got a hat-trick, or Glenn McGrath got a hat-trick, which of course he nearly did. They had such great bowlers that it was possible they could still bowl us out in a session if everything went their way. What would it be like if they launched a run chase? Would I be able to keep the composure I had maintained during the series?

Yet when I put my kit on and went out to practise, I had an unbelievably fluent net for some reason, feeling supremely confident about my own batting. We had a team gathering by the nets and I told them that today was a day when we had to play attacking cricket. We had said at the start of the series that the way to beat Australia was to take them on and be positive at all times. We had to stay true to that on our final day. If anyone was thinking about batting out for the draw, we would get found out. Everyone agreed.

Even at nets, before 9.30 a.m., the ground was absolutely packed. Again I was thinking we were only a few hours from glory and I was trying to stop myself envisaging the stage they would bring onto the outfield for the presentation, and thinking about what I would say during the interviews. Don't get ahead of yourself, don't start thinking about making sure you are humble in victory and thanking all the right people.

When the bell tolled, Tres and I walked out and I felt in incredibly good nick. I hit McGrath for a couple of cover drives, then cut him and crunched Brett Lee for a couple of boundaries, and I was starting to think this really was going to be a fairy tale, me smashing a hundred to seal the Ashes. Then the old man McGrath bowled me a decent nut and Gilchrist took a flying one-handed catch. I walked off to be replaced by Ian Bell – good luck, Belly, I said – and before my first pad was off I heard the roar that meant that he had gone straight away and that we were 67–3.

In went Kevin Pietersen. The first ball was a bouncer that hit him on the shoulder and this time I literally jumped off the bench to look at the television. My first instinct was that he was out, but luckily Billy Bowden made the right decision under pressure. Tres was now facing Warne going around the wicket and it was spinning ridiculously. Usually he was really composed against the slow stuff and a brilliant player of even the best spinners, but this time he just did not look comfortable. He

was one of those guys who, when he was batting well, made
the dressing room a very calm place, but he was struggling and
that made me very unnerved. So much so that I went out of
the dressing room to the relative quiet of the canteen over-
looking Harleyford Road to sit down and do some logistical
planning of our Pakistan tour with Medha Laud, who was
responsible for such things at the England and Wales Cricket
Board.

I did not even watch the telly, just hoping that I would not
hear any of those sickening roars that signalled a wicket. I
know people might think that, as captain, I should have been
on the balcony with Duncan, but by that stage, with what I
had gone through, I was just desperate for an excuse not to
be out there for a while. Then Tres got out to Warne, and I
started to think we were going to lose and that I really had
to be there. Brett Lee was bowling the quickest spell of the
series from the pavilion end and peppering KP, who looked to
me to be unsure whether to attack or defend. Freddie went in,
and all the while Colly was so nervous that he was actually
lying down in the dressing room, almost in the foetal position,
staring up at the monitor. Duncan was on the balcony wearing
his Oakley sunglasses, trying not to look as if he was cacking
himself.

In pressure situations many people, even tough characters,
act in an abnormal way, so we had Colly lying on the floor
and Ashley walking round and round the dressing room, doing
about 500 laps. We got to lunch with Fred out and Colly in
on 127–5. Kev had been absolutely battered by Lee, hit on the
shoulder, nicking one over the slips, being dropped by Warne
on 15, and top-edging to fine leg. He came in and admitted
that he was in two minds whether to twist or stick. I told him
straight: please just attack, because if you last for an hour we

will have taken the game away from them. He asked what to do if Lee bounced him some more. Take him on, hook him, I replied. Go with your instincts and talent.

I had been trying to tell myself that this was going to be a good day, whatever happened, because over five Tests we had really taken it to one of the greatest teams ever. There was no shame in drawing a five-match series with this lot. Deep down I knew I was kidding myself – today was potentially the mother of all sickeners.

They went back out and Colly grimly hung in there for the most crucial 10 he will ever make, but Warne got him after 72 minutes' resistance and Geraint Jones followed him quickly. All the time, I was in the dressing room, fiddling with my kit, packing and unpacking for no reason whatsoever. Thankfully KP was now flailing away brilliantly and had got hold of Lee. My heart soared each time he hooked him, and with every ball it was tipping our way. Some people thought we were safe once Ashley had survived a few overs, but it was only shortly before tea, when we were 250 ahead, that a wave of relaxation finally washed over me.

The crowd were going nuts. They were singing 'Jerusalem' and you could hear the popping of champagne corks in the boxes, although the guys waiting to go in still looked nervous. As Giles and KP's partnership built, the talk began about how we were going to celebrate. A really sweet memory for me is how much everyone enjoyed each other's success. When Ashley got his fifty the balcony erupted, particularly because of the abuse he had had to deal with early in the series. We all knew what a key player he was for us. As for Pietersen, you could hardly overstate the significance of his innings.

This was now totally surreal, cricket's gradual rhythms meaning that the magnitude of the events was slowly unfolding in front of us. Our innings ended with us 341 ahead and the light starting to fade. No doubt the last thing Matthew Hayden and Justin Langer wanted to do was go out and bat for a handful of overs. I gathered the lads together and told them how proud of themselves they should be. I asked them to make sure they enjoyed the moment, as it might not come around again. However many minutes we are out there, I said, make sure they are the best of your career, because you know what it took to get to this place. I knew they would bask in it; this was a proper team that fundamentally enjoyed playing the game and celebrating the good times.

The final act itself – the umpires removing the bails – was anticlimactic in the extreme, but who cared? I held up the urn, and then felt the excruciating pain of champagne going straight into my eyes. Bloody hell, this is agony, I thought, as I tried to smile. I ordered all the backroom staff to join the lap of honour, even though it took wild horses to drag Duncan out there.

Fantastic. Camera crews everywhere, the crowd going nuts. Randomly, I saw Chris Evans in the stands, going berserk. I wished that lap could have gone on for ever, but there were duties to attend to. Strangely, I gave a very flat press conference, as if allowing my emotions a temporary lull. TV, then radio, and I could not wait to get back into the dressing room.

I had my whites on for a long time, and as we had naturally decided to ditch our cars, a bus had been laid on to take us back to our hotel by London Bridge. En route it was like that final scene in *The Italian Job*: it was rocking, almost literally. We were singing rugby songs, stupid ditties. Even Fletch, the old man, was singing.

Outside the Grange hotel it was packed, with security having to forge a path for us to get off the bus. Quickly upstairs to get the disco kit on, and to say hello to the other halves. I had one in the bar and then went off to a club and drank champagne for a couple of hours. Sloshed. I spilled some champagne down the front of my shirt and got paparazzied – it looked as if I had chundered.

I got back to the hotel at about 3.30 a.m. and Freddie and his crowd were still in the bar, completely smashed, so I had a couple more. I went upstairs for a few hours' kip and came back down at about 7.30 a.m. to sign hundreds of shirts. Freddie was still going. A few more TV interviews, and the day of the victory parade was beginning.

18

After the Lord Mayor's Show

One of the things I recall of the night that followed the sealing of the Ashes win – and time has not made the memory of that evening any sharper – was Nichola laughing and saying to me, 'You're going to get on that bus and there might not be anybody there.' I reckoned she could be right, as the thought of central London coming to a standstill for a few cricketers seemed a bit ridiculous.

This was quickly dispelled, however, when we left the hotel for our first appointment of the day at the Lord Mayor's offices. There were drinks on offer there, which we took, and for many of us that was a bit like pulling into a petrol station when the gauge is showing almost full. From there we walked onto the bus, which was crammed with our families, a few ECB officials, photographers and some members of the broadcast media. It was quite surreal, and it was obvious that the British public were not going to stand us up on our victory parade. Outside the Mayor's office it was absolutely packed, with people hanging out of windows, standing on bus shelters, even some people climbing up trees.

The journey took about an hour, and although it was good fun, it seemed longer than that. I was in a daze, gripped by a strange mixture of hangover and adrenalin, with this extraordinary scene unfolding in front of us. My arm had waved so much it had nearly fallen off before we reached Trafalgar Square for a celebration rally with a bit of a sing-song. Could so many people really have been touched by this? Although I have come to question whether the whole exercise turned out to be a wise thing to do or not, I certainly did not reflect upon it at the time. And given the state we were in, we just went with the flow.

From Trafalgar Square we went to 10 Downing Street, it now being about 24 hours since my stomach had been churning so badly I had not been able to watch at The Oval. We were ushered into the garden and quickly discovered that there were no drinks there. So we asked whether they were meant to be running a dry ship, and an assistant disappeared and came back with some lukewarm wine. This was fairly undrinkable so we collared Tony Blair's son, Euan, who helpfully took himself upstairs to his dad's private kitchen, from where he brought back some properly chilled wine and beers. Various urban myths have grown up about that day, about whether someone secretly irrigated the garden at Number 10 or threw up on the bus, but I honestly do not know.

I was present, however, when Tony Blair came out onto his doorstep to ask, jokingly, what we and our accompanying photographers were doing there. 'They've come to take your picture, you knob,' said Hoggard. The drink, combined with traditional Yorkshire subtlety, might have been talking by this stage. Then it was on to Lord's for a final picture and yet more drinks in the Long Room.

I had had enough of everything by now and just wanted to get home. I went back to the hotel and tried to venture out again with Colly and Ashley, but I was emotionally and physically drained, too knackered to enjoy it. I longed to get in the car and drive back to my home comforts.

The following weeks were still fairly mad. The commercial talk about our new market values started almost immediately, a special stamp was being brought out with me on it – heaven forbid – and media requests were flooding in by the day. As were literally hundreds of letters, which I particularly enjoyed. In truth I basked in it all and the sense of achievement, but at the same time I just wanted to chill out and be me.

For all the delight, there was an element of fear as well. I realised that my life had abruptly changed and I had gone from being the normal bloke who was primarily a sportsman to something of a celebrity who everyone wanted to know. For all that I liked a degree of notoriety through what I had done in sport, I was less enamoured of everyone wanting to know everything about me. I was given the freedom of Sheffield, which I considered a real honour, and about 10,000 people turned up outside the Town Hall for the presentation, which was incredible. And so it went on in the fallow period before we were due to set off for Pakistan in late October.

All the while there was a creeping concern in the back of my mind about the state of my right knee. I had been struggling with it in the latter half of the Ashes series and quietly had a couple of cortisone injections to make sure I could get through everything. So while luxuriating in our new status I was also doing painful rehab work to make sure I would be ready for Pakistan, unaware that this activity would become such a fixture in my life for more than the next 12 months.

Between the Ashes and Pakistan the ICC were staging their latest brainwave, a Test match and one-day series between the champion nation, still Australia, and a Rest of the World all-star team. I had been overlooked as skipper for the Test in

Sydney and, incredibly to me, Duncan Fletcher had not been selected as part of the all-stars' coaching team, which smacked of vengeful ICC politics. I received a late invitation to play in the Test when there was the odd withdrawal, but Duncan and I agreed I should give it a miss, which was unquestionably the right thing to do.

Fred was picked for both formats while Kevin Pietersen was in the limited-over XI and Harmy deservedly made it into the international Test side. The whole concept was flawed as it was the wrong time of year, the select team was undercooked and they duly got hammered, so I did not feel I had missed out on anything, a view which Fred and Harmy seemed to support when they reported back.

A recurring theme in the media interviews was how the whole Ashes experience might affect us. I had written about KP, for example, 'As long as we can keep him grounded and he doesn't get too carried away with his celebrity lifestyle this young man can be one of the best.' I was asked about it again at the airport press conference on 25 October prior to our departure for Pakistan. I made all the right noises but underneath I was worried about the effects of what we had been through.

In some ways Pakistan could not have been a better place to go, a tough tour about as far away from distractions and the bright lights as cricket can take you. But there was a lot of adjusting to do as our lives had changed since we met up a day too early back in July as a group of likely lads at the Landmark hotel in Marylebone ahead of the first Ashes Test. Many of us were now pretty mainstream 'personalities' who had either been offered new commercial opportunities or enhanced versions of what we had already. It had been widely reported that KP was dating the model Caprice, which added to the new-found sense of flamboyancy around the team.

In all professional sports teams there is talk about money, but I quickly noticed more discussion than usual about the commercial deals among us. This was only natural to a degree, and I do not suppose I was immune to it myself. I suspected the team was going to be harder to manage, and one aspect of it was that individual sponsorships were now at such a level that players would focus on them rather than on what they had to do for the team's collective backers.

Although the bus ride to Trafalgar Square had been a great experience, it was perhaps all a bit too much, and whoever gets offered it next time should give it a miss, as happened in 2009. There had also been, since The Oval, a nagging sense that, for me at least, it might never get as good as this again. In some ways, if you could pick your timing, this would all have happened to me at 33 or 34 and I would have been happy to sign off there and then.

But I had enough experience to realise that in sport fairy-tale endings are rare, and when we met up there was a buzz just from being back among the group with whom I had shared so much. The tour got off to a reasonable enough start and, in any case, it was not hard to appreciate what an incredibly fortunate lot in life ours was when Ashley Giles, Marcus Trescothick, Matthew Hoggard and I visited child victims of the Kashmir earthquake at a hospital in Islamabad.

I was not bothered by our batsmen getting low scores in our opening match and we picked a strong side for our final warm-up match at Bagh-e-Jinnah, the picturesque park ground in Lahore. When the knee suddenly locked while I was running between the wickets with Strauss I was reasonably relaxed about it. This was the sort of pain I had occasionally experienced when walking down the stairs at home and similar to that in the nets at Lord's before the New Zealand Test that had given

Straussy his opportunity. I had been back for the next Test after that and rather assumed that would be the case again. I certainly had no idea what it was the start of.

There seemed little chance that I would be ready for the first Test at Multan on 12 November, and I duly pulled out to leave unofficial vice-captain Marcus in charge. Tres was not quite right in himself because his father-in-law had suffered severe head injuries in a domestic accident, and a large part of him evidently wanted to go home. It was all the more remarkable, therefore, that in the circumstances he batted so brilliantly to set us up for a victory in my absence, a win that would have been ours had we made the 198 needed to win on the last day.

We played well in that match but threw it all away on the final morning to go down to a 22-run defeat which, in the recent history of English cricket, may come to be seen as a very significant result. Watching, I got a sense that we were in trouble, and my worst fears came true. If we had won that game, we would have opened up the divisions that are always simmering in a Pakistan team, and they would probably have over-reacted by making huge changes to their side. We could well have gone on to win that series and have been seen to have taken all the Ashes hullabaloo in our stride. While I had a certain amount of fear about the reaction to beating Australia, I was also excited by the fact that we were a young team who could stay together and get better over time.

Then we went on to the second part of what must be one of the great non-glamour combinations in international sport – from Multan to Faisalabad. It may be some time before they open a branch of the Hard Rock Café in either place. As had happened in the New Zealand series the previous year, I was able to come straight back into the team, but this time the knee still did not feel right. I was starting to worry about the future

and it was distracting me from the present. At Faisalabad I
failed in both innings of a drawn match most remembered for
a soft drinks gas canister blowing up by the side of the pitch,
making a deafening sound like, I can only imagine, a car bomb
going off. In the shock that ensued Shahid Afridi craftily took
the chance to dig his studs into the wicket on a length, skul-
duggery which was cleverly spotted by Sky's cameramen.

The bizarre behaviour of the opposition was one of the few
things I found interesting about playing Test cricket in Pakistan,
which always seemed slow-paced and attritional. This match,
in which Pietersen had batted beautifully, was a tame draw
and we were still in the series as we headed for (relatively)
more cosmopolitan Lahore for the third Test on 29 November.
I did some one-on-one work with Duncan after that and it
paid dividends as I moved up to open in place of Strauss, who
had gone home to be at the birth of his first child. Ignoring
the soreness in my knee, I was out sweeping on 58 and we
took some flak for playing that particular shot too much as a
team.

They made a massive 636–8 and it looked to be dribbling
out into one of those boring Pakistan Test matches until
Shoaib Akhtar suddenly ripped us out on the last afternoon,
bowling at the speed of light and then completely stuffing
me with a slower ball. Shoaib was the epitome of Pakistan's
mercurial brilliance, but I was very disappointed that we had
not shown more fight. It was not that the guys were not
trying or were not training or netting with intent, I felt we
had just lost, intangibly, that little bit of competitive edge.
Another factor was worrying about how people back home
might be viewing us. In short, too much thought was
crowding into the process.

My knee was really bad in that match and I knew then that

something was going to have to be done. I flew home before the limited-over series and three days later was under the knife. It was the third operation on my right knee since turning professional (the others had been as an 18-year-old, and then prior to the 2002–03 Ashes tour) and the intention was to tidy up little flaps around the cartilage. With the benefit of hindsight, the ECB should have taken additional advice and I should not have gone to India at all in the New Year, but instead have focused everything on being ready to get back in time for the following winter's Ashes.

Every cloud has a silver lining, and being back in England for the operation meant I was able to be home for the birth of Archie, our second child. The day after the operation, which took place on 8 December, I was dreadfully sick at home through the after-effects of whatever they had knocked me out with. But Nichola had gone into labour and I was going to have to drive her into Sheffield, despite the sickness and the pain in my knee making me feel like passing out.

When we got there the nurses knew I was struggling, so they put me on a bed and I promptly fell asleep. Nichola had lined up a friend to support her in my expected absence, and five minutes before she actually gave birth I was woken up to be present for the big moment. As Nichola remarked, there was still enough Ashes fever about for the nurses to have been fussing more over me than over her as she went through the latter stages of labour.

As I embarked on the rehab work my knee started to feel better, and we had a great day out at Buckingham Palace, picking up our OBEs and MBEs before our departure for India in mid-February.

Within a few days of getting there, however, I knew there were problems. Whatever you do in the gym or in training, nothing ever quite simulates being out in the middle for proper practice and I could feel from our first warm-up match at the Brabourne Stadium in Mumbai that I was just not right. On this occasion the locking sensation was different and it was accompanied by searing pain.

We had gone up to Baroda for our final warm-up before the first Test and I was grimacing in our first net session after arriving. I could not even think about coming down the wicket to the spinner or trying to sweep the ball. I turned to Fletcher and said, 'I'm knackered here, this thing still isn't sorted out.' I was not the only one in our party having problems, as it turned out, although the difficulties being encountered by Marcus were of a very different nature.

I was always aware that he was not a good traveller, and it had already been clear to me in Pakistan, earlier in the winter, that he was finding the whole situation of not going home very stressful when his father-in-law suffered his accident. In Baroda he had the room next to me and in the middle of the night I was awoken by some thudding. 'What were you up to last night?' I asked the following morning. 'I was having a bat,' he said. 'Did you make any?' was my flippant reply.

In fact, it was not that unusual to hear one of us batsmen practising in front of the mirror at funny times of day or night, so even then I was not unduly perturbed about Marcus's plight. Besides, I had worries of my own as I was fairly sure my tour was coming to a premature end. It was with that likelihood in mind that we had a meeting in my room to discuss possible strategies and selection for the Test tour, and Marcus seemed just about OK.

But in the couple of days leading into the match it became apparent that Tres was really not himself, and we were to discover later that our doctor, Peter Gregory, was spending a lot of time with him. It got as far as Marcus and I having a chat and me telling him that if he felt this way then he needed to go home and get himself right – I was the last person to whom he had to show how loyal to the cause he was, and I knew he would not leave a tour without good reason.

Meanwhile, it was in Baroda that the doubts really started setting in about the management of my knee condition and the effectiveness of the communication between the coaching and medical people. I had a cortisone injection on the first morning of that match versus the Board President's XI and Dr Gregory told me I was OK to play. By now I had developed an amateur working knowledge of these situations and protested that I was never able to take the field within 48 hours of the injections, as they always needed time to settle down. Shortly afterwards Fletch came up and asked what number I thought I should bat, two or three. 'I can't play, I've just had a cortisone in my knee and it will take time to work,' I told the surprised-looking coach. 'Oh shit,' he replied, having been in the dark about this.

Although we were still unsure of Marcus's exact state of mind, he had been picked to play in the match and had not objected to doing so. I only became really worried about him at breakfast on the third morning, when he appeared hyper-active and panicky, and was very pale.

After play resumed he actually batted quite nicely, although it transpired that it was all on autopilot. When he got out in that second innings he came back into the dressing room and burst into tears before running out into the viewing area, which was in full sight of the public. Fletch told him quite sharply to get back inside. Maybe because of his relatively tough upbringing Duncan was slightly unsure what to make of what happened to Marcus, but then we all were. Initially, there were even some immature comments from some of the younger lads about him going doolally before the seriousness of what was going on sank in.

I went back to the hotel at the close of play and, alone among the players, was allowed to see him. He was in a bad way and clearly needed to go home. For entirely different, physical reasons I knew the same thing applied to me. It was a deeply unhappy day. I had a feeling then that it would be a long time before the names Vaughan and Trescothick appeared together on a team sheet, although I never thought that we had already played our last game alongside each other for England.

I waited around on the remote chance that there might be a substantial improvement in my own situation and even went up to Nagpur, where the first Test was taking place. Alastair Cook had arrived as my possible replacement and immediately looked as if he was going to fit in. It was not a great shock, therefore, that he made a hundred on his debut.

I knew that my tour was over, and to make matters worse Simon Jones badly hurt his knee in the nets. Three Ashes winners lifted out of a tour within less than a week – it must have been some sort of record. Fred was given the captaincy, the thought being that he would act as a galvanising force on a trip that was falling to pieces, and in the circumstances he did a terrific job.

It was 27 February when I finally went home, and after arriving back I was given something called an ultrasound-guided injection into the knee. I was extremely worried when it appeared to have had a negligible effect, adding to my anxieties about where the whole process was heading. It turned out that there was simply too much damage inside the knee for injections to be of use any more.

Before I had the supposed 'clean-up' operation in December

after coming home from Pakistan I had been told about something called microfracture surgery. Our medical people said it could be a solution, but that it was a career-threatening procedure and would likely mean that I would be out for a year. That would see me missing the return Ashes in 2006–07 and I did not want to countenance that. If I had my time again I would have done it straight away, but as ever hindsight is perfect vision.

I was starting to become quite frustrated with the mix of official advice I was getting, so put my faith in what Yorkshire suggested. It was decided that we would do six weeks of intensive rehab work to build the muscles up around the knee and then see where we were. This kind of work was, and is, hell. That feeling of Groundhog Day can set in so badly in these circumstances that you get fed up with seeing the walls of the gym, so I would go to different places to go through my routine of exercises.

Sometimes it would be Sheffield, sometimes Headingley, sometimes a David Lloyd club, sometimes the house of former England and Yorkshire physio Wayne Morton. Anything to get a change of scenery. There were days when it would feel better, days when it would be worse. On 19 April I managed a net with Yorkshire's first team, indoors at Trent Bridge where they were playing, but I knew it was still not great.

I was extremely grateful for the support of Wayne, and contrastingly fed up with comments from the likes of Boycott about visiting this specialist and that in the United States. On 29 May the wretched knee felt sufficiently better for me to play in a C&G Trophy game against Scotland at Headingley, and it went OK, with me making 67 at a run a ball.

That led to three Championship games with Yorkshire that I went into more with hope than expectation. Again I did OK, and hit the ball sweetly during an innings of 99 against Middlesex at Southgate. A few of the cricket correspondents turned up to watch and when I spoke to them they seemed more encouraged than me. However it looked, I knew I had made those runs literally on one leg, as I could barely twist or turn. Knowing that I still had a decent eye and a straight bat was not much compensation for the underlying knowledge that the problem was still far from over.

I was willing to try anything, and after discussing it further with Nichola, she sought out a contact of hers in the NHS in Sheffield who put me in touch with a specialist in Southampton, Neil Thomas, reckoned to be one of the leading experts on knees in Europe.

Without telling England, I drove down to the south coast with Yorkshire physio Scott McAllister to listen to Dr Thomas's opinions about the various options open to us. He talked about having a fake cartilage put in, but his favoured option was to go for the microfracture surgery. He was also not as pessimistic about the amount of recovery time as I had first been told, nor did he think that it was career-threatening. If it went well and I did the right things, it might be only six months before I was back.

I came away knowing this was the probably the best option and wishing I could have turned the clock back. But Yorkshire had another match immediately afterwards against Sussex at Arundel, and I said to Scott that we would see if things improved, and if not then I would go under the knife again. I remember the home team's Mushtaq Ahmed coming up and suggesting that I just carry on and hobble around at mid-off and skipper and bat a bit, but the fact that I could not do everything I wanted when batting or in the field was driving me to distraction. When the pain forced me to sit out some of

...ley Giles, always a popular team member, celebrates taking the wicket of Dwayne Bravo.

...ve Harmison, Rob Key and Andrew Flintoff celebrate our 7–0 summer of 2004 at ...e Oval.

Andrew Strauss's brilliant start to his Test career continued with a hundred against South Africa in 2004.

On safari in South Africa: (*l–r*) Gareth Batty, Darren Gough, Kevin Pietersen, myself and Geraint Jones.

... made fitness a priority after taking over the captaincy.

A sadly all-too-familiar sight: Glenn McGrath takes another wicket in the first Test of 2005 at Lord's.

Freddie gets Justin Langer at Edgbaston. Ricky Ponting also fell in the best over I eve saw.

Eureka! Steve Harmison dismisses Michael Kasprowicz as defeat stares us in the face at Edgbaston.

ns at last in the 2005 Ashes: driving to the boundary at Old Trafford during an innings
166.

stitute Gary Pratt runs out Ricky Ponting at Trent Bridge. He was not happy with
ncan Fletcher's reaction.

Left: Ashley Giles and Matthew Hoggard guided us to victory in the nerve-jangling climax to the 4th Test.

Below: Kevin Pietersen hits out The Oval, watched by Adam Gilchrist and Matthew Hayden

Duncan and I were a good double act, and the Ashes win of 2005 came after two years'
planning.

I wanted the backroom staff to join in the team pictures of our Ashes triumph.

In the garden of 10 Downing St with Tony Blair, just about making sense.

Receiving our honours from the Queen at Buckingham Palace.

the fielding later in that match I decided something had to be done. 'Scott, I'm having it done,' I said.

So we had a 'summit' meeting at Headingley two days later with Wayne, Scott and England Test physio Kirk Russell. I had long known Wayne and had a lot of faith in him. I told him that I would put myself in his hands, that he would choose the surgeon and that afterwards I wanted him to do the rehab work with me. I wanted one person to take the responsibility of getting me back playing again rather than being passed about between England and Yorkshire. My message to him was that if I never came back, I wanted to know that he and I had done everything possible to make it happen.

We went up to see the surgeon, Nick London, in Harrogate, and he told me that the worst-case scenario was that I would never play again. So what? Anything was better than limping around, but the knowledge that I was going to miss the Ashes hit me like a freight train. Why the hell had I not had this done in December or January? That would have then given me the extra incentive to get back for the Ashes. I was, frankly, scared because apart from anything else it is quite a big operation.

Knowing that I was going to miss Australia partly made me wonder what the point of the whole thing was anyway, and the thought of being on crutches for three months did not fill me with joy either. There was also a degree of bemusement that, despite being on a central contract with the ECB, there had needed to be a large element of do-it-yourself in plotting the way ahead.

The operation took place on 3 July, and as I had experienced before, you feel very positive afterwards for a few days. Then there is the slump as reality kicks in, but the feeling was more level this time because, even on crutches, the knee somehow felt as if it was moving in a different way. It might have been purely psychological but it was something to cling to. Somehow it all seemed to be in sync with the rest of my leg, although there was still a long and painful road ahead, painful in more ways than I expected.

19

Looking On

In the whole process of getting myself back into the England cricket team – which was to take well over a year in the end – the three months that followed the microfracture surgery were the worst. Not only was there all the uncertainty of what the future held, but there were practical problems galore from not being allowed to put any weight through the right leg.

I could not even drive for the first two months, which made me feel somewhat helpless, and had to be ferried to my sessions with Wayne, who would get me swimming every day. I have never much liked swimming, but he was brilliant in that he understood how goal-oriented I am, and would constantly set me challenges and targets. I respond well to those, and if they do not exist I am likely to lapse into being brain-dead. When I started working with him I was barely capable of doing a few lengths of front crawl and he told me that within three months I had to try and swim a mile non-stop. No chance, I told him. Yet I started to improve and got there in the end.

Seeing the guys play against Sri Lanka and Pakistan that summer was a pretty trying experience. I did not want to go to the grounds, fearing that I would feel like a spare part and only get in the way. There was very little contact with Duncan Fletcher at the time as I kept my distance and Andrew Strauss felt his way into the job, as Fred was also absent by now with injury. The nearest I got to top-class sport was spending a couple of days at Hoylake for the Open golf.

It was great seeing the family and spending time with new arrival Archie, although I was hardly able to help Nichola out, given my indisposition. I became very frustrated at the time and quite depressed, having to snap out of feeling that I was some kind of bad parent because I was sitting about all the time. Becoming a father is a big thing for anyone, but when you are a cricketer and living such a strange and often selfish life it can be even more of a culture shock. With all the uncertainty about the future, no cricket, no mobility and not being much use at home, I was wondering where I fitted into the grand scheme of things.

The things that seep into your mind can be alarming, and sometimes irrational. What am I going to do in later life? What is ever going to replace the soaring highs I experienced at a relatively young age? Are my knees going to be so bad that I won't be able to kick a ball around with my son?

There were a couple of times when I felt tearful at home, but it is not really my way to show much emotion, so I bottled it up most of the time, all the self-pity and insecurity. Only a year previously I had been in the midst of winning what some considered the greatest Test series of all time, with the stratospheric high that had brought. Since then there had been the trip to Pakistan and constant false starts and worries with my body and my cricket, culminating in an operation I bitterly wished I had gone for six months earlier.

What I had to look forward to were the sessions with Wayne, and they were purgatory most of the time. Every time I entered Wayne's world he was my training partner, opposition and taskmaster rolled into one. There was swimming, the treadmill, walking up hills, rowing challenges, mountain-biking and cycling to Leeds United's training ground, where former England cricket trainer Dean Riddle worked and the then manager Kevin Blackwell kindly allowed us to use their facilities. I continued to do occasional work with Dean, who is great at what he does, when he moved to Sheffield United, of all places.

The work with Wayne sounds almost like fun looking back, but it did not always feel that way at the time. Gradually we could do more and more, and by early September I was starting to get a buzz from it in the knowledge that one day this was going to let me play cricket again. On 10 September I felt able to tell the media that I was optimistic that I would be able to fly to Australia at some point that winter. In the back of my mind, partly as a motivational thing, I was not entirely ruling out being able to play some part in the Ashes.

At this time we were moving house to Derbyshire, with all that entails. Our own house sale fell through three times, and I probably got more agitated about it than I normally would. They do, after all, say that moving home is about the most stressful thing that occurs in life after divorce or bereavement.

I was pretty focused on myself and what I had to be doing, but had noticed that Strauss had started to perform a decent job as England captain, including in the famous forfeited Test against Pakistan at The Oval. After a horrible start in the one-dayers against Sri Lanka, when the bowlers were getting carted everywhere, he looked a natural in the job. As he learned, not much time goes by without some kind of major incident occurring when you are England captain, and he seemed to handle all the madness of that Oval match with aplomb.

Darrell Hair was at the centre of that whole affair, and whatever you think of that incident, I have to say he was one of the umpires I encountered over my career that I rated highly. The Oval episode, and the ICC later going along with the wishes of the Pakistanis to change the official result to a draw, even though they had refused to carry on, was part of a drift towards undermining the authority of umpires that remains worrying for the game.

The use of technology has been a long-running debate in cricket, and in the West Indies series of 2009 we saw the new referrals system in action, which was another development taking the human aspect away from the game. Frankly, I just got bored waiting around for the decisions, and I am sure there were less committed cricket-watchers than me who would have switched channels and looked at something else.

Basically, the only extension of technology I would like to see is the TV umpire being able to judge no-balls, thus making life easier for the man out in the middle, and using the 'mat' that runs from wicket to wicket on-screen to see whether a ball has pitched in line or not. Otherwise, just leave it to the umpires and accept that it is a character-building experience when you get out to a stinker, and that it will probably even itself out in the end. The only alternative is to go the whole hog and use blanket technology and reduce the umpire to the status of clothes peg and hat stand, which I think would be wrong.

Another innovation I would like to see brought in is a daily rotation system in Tests in which the third umpire is properly used, meaning that each man has to do only two sessions in a day out in the middle. I am sure fatigue is behind some of the terrible decisions that you see from some of the weaker umpires, who are used as part of an unofficial quota system from different countries. I would also like to see just the best 12 umpires in the world used, regardless of their race or nationality.

In England the standard is pretty good, although a few of the umpires you encounter in county cricket are a little bitter and cynical. The better ones have a balance between authority and understanding of the players. Australia's Simon Taufel is about the best I have come across and I like his work ethic, whereby he keeps fit and turns up at practice the day before. Neil Mallender is another good one and Rudi Koertzen has an excellent manner about him, even though his decision-making in the 2009 Ashes was far from perfect. Darrell Hair was a stickler for the rules but never afraid to make a decision, and I would put him near the top of my list.

Another thing I had noticed from afar that summer was that after two Tests the selectors had got their way and put Chris Read back in as wicketkeeper, and I knew that Duncan would not be happy about that. It annoyed me that they had gone over the head of the skipper and coach, the selectors seemingly emboldened by the fact that my alliance with Fletch had been temporarily broken.

The big issue at the time was whether Fred or Strauss should be made captain for the Ashes, as realistically, whatever my daydreams, I was not going to be on the plane flying out to Australia for the start of the tour. Fred, who was still out of the team and recuperating from ankle surgery, had made it clear that he still wanted the position, and felt that after the excellent job he had done in India he deserved to lead the team. David Graveney seemed to have assured him that the job was on hold for him, but it was a tricky and messy situation all round, because Strauss had clearly enhanced his reputation while being stand-in for a stand-in.

I had no direct input to the decision, but I am not sure when it came down to it that Straussy at that stage really wanted to be skipper of a potentially disgruntled Flintoff. Fred had made his ambitions clear and I think that is what swung it for Duncan, who was given the casting vote. Graveney was for Fred and Geoff Miller was for Strauss, so it was Fletch who had to make the final decision.

It was no great surprise when, in mid-September, Fred was duly confirmed as Ashes captain because the media had already flagged it up extensively. Perhaps because there was an air of predictability about it, the debate then seemed to extend out to whether he should not just be given it full-time. There was an element of why are we waiting for Vaughan? I had been around long enough to understand these things and had no wish to be seen as a distraction, so in early October I rang Graveney and offered to stand down altogether in order to clean up the whole situation.

I thought it might help everyone concerned, and although I had no wish to relinquish something so dear to me, it would allow me to concentrate everything on just becoming an England player again. Graveney's response? A firm 'No thanks.'

So I was obviously still reckoned to have a future in the corridors of power, even though all through the period of my summer absence I had had no involvement in selectorial decisions, apart from being the occasional informal sounding board. I did not know if I would ever play again, let alone be captain, so I did not think it would be right for me to have a say.

However, when Fred was appointed I was immediately aware that this was not necessarily the dream scenario. I knew the relationship between him and Duncan was fragile at best, so my instinct was that they might need some sort of link between them. That was a major reason why I thought I could be very useful to have around, at least some of the time during the Ashes tour, and it was a view shared by Steve Bull, the team's sports psychologist.

My knee was getting better all the time and I was now pretty confident that my comeback was going to be a reality, and so with the seasons changing it clearly made more sense for me to continue my rehab in Australia, out of the English winter.

By now my movement was so good that I was looking forward to being out in the middle again. The general idea was for me primarily to be with the 'shadow' performance squad that was going out there, but for me specifically the first stop would be Brisbane ahead of the start of the first Test on 23 November.

I had good reason to go to Brisbane. My mate Darren Lehmann had invited me to do a corporate event there, and Fred had invited me to have a chat with him two days before the first Test, just to see if I could give him a few pointers, and I was happy to be of assistance if he wanted. I also needed to have a catch-up with our physio Kirk Russell about my physical progress.

I knew this was a potentially delicate situation and that with all the hype around the series people were likely to read things into situations that did not exist. I was very anxious, therefore, not to be seen with the players or to be perceived as getting in the way or somehow trying to muscle in on the squad.

I became aware, however, that this was indeed believed to be the case in some quarters and there were mentions of it in the media. That was completely wide of the mark, and my intention was only to do what was right for the team. There was no sense of me feeling proprietorial about the England side and I did not want it to look that way, but some in the media were jumping to their own conclusions. Unusually for me, because I thought I had developed a fairly thick skin, I found this very hurtful.

I wanted to make myself scarce and was due to fly out to join up with the performance boys in Perth on the afternoon of the opening day of the first Test at the Gabba. My intention was to briefly sit with Graveney in the stands in the morning, well out of the way, before going off to the airport. My flight was delayed for a few hours, however, and I was disappointed because I was champing at the bit to do some serious practice again and start playing matches. Also, I wanted to be out of Brisbane and away from the Test squad.

I was sitting there with Graveney when I was asked by our media liaison man, Andrew Walpole, to do an interview with Sky. I went up to their box and on the way back I was walking near the dressing room and saw Phil Neale, who invited me in. I felt very uncomfortable, even though most of the boys were out in the field. In the back room I spoke to a few of the non-playing squad members, but there was no way I wanted to be seen in the viewing gallery. I was quickly out of there and quite happy to disappear to the other side of Australia, and it had nothing to do with the fact that we were getting heavily beaten in the opener.

I now regret turning up at Brisbane, not because it was the wrong thing to do but because of the way it was portrayed and interpreted in some places. That affected me a surprising amount, and I was more than frustrated that some of the media seemed to be quick to get on my case about it. Perhaps they were not able to appreciate this, but I had been through an enormous amount to get close to a comeback, and apart from anything I just wanted a taste of that Test match atmosphere to give me one last motivational push over the final yards. At least that bit was worth it. But wanting to cast some kind of shadow over the team? No chance.

Over in Perth I carried on working my backside off, buoyed by the fact that I was slowly returning to full fitness. The performance group was basically a squad that mirrored the Test group, with the intention that if any of them got injured there would be a replacement on tap, acclimatised and ready to step in. My hope was that if the improvement kept coming and I scored runs, I would be up for consideration along with everyone else if the situation arose.

This camp was my first real experience of working with Peter Moores, who was then in charge of the academy at Loughborough. At the time I was impressed by him, and I have no doubt that this was the sort of role at which he excelled. He had a lot of energy and enthusiasm, with some decent training ideas, and was good with the younger players.

The third Test was to be in Perth, and by the time the full England team got there things were going badly wrong. From a seemingly indomitable position in the second match at Adelaide we had lost the game, getting rolled over on the last day by Shane Warne and then being unable to stop them knocking the runs off. It was a crushing defeat that met with a huge reaction both back at home and among the travelling supporters and media. When these things happen, reasons are inevitably sought and molehills tend to become mountains, so I feared that there were going to be more false interpretations of my presence in Australia.

The knee was still not perfect, but the full range of movement was coming back when I took part in a match at Hale School following the Adelaide debacle. A couple of journos wasted no time, turning up at the ground in the hope of a chat, but, even though I got on fine with them both, I was not in the mood for it. I had had enough of talking about injuries and could see no point in commenting on a Test defeat that I knew had really hurt the players.

I did not watch much of that Adelaide match because we were training most of the time during the day, and could not have made much informed comment anyway. Aside from anything, I hated losing to Australia and was upset we were two down and heading for inevitable series defeat.

What I did privately think about the Adelaide debacle was that Monty Panesar should have been brought into the team, his omission having attracted a huge amount of comment. I respected the decision to leave him out in favour of Ashley Giles at Brisbane, a less spin-friendly ground, because I thought it was ballsy. The easy thing to do would have been to bring in Monty to public acclaim, but Duncan would not have been swayed by fear of public reaction. That was Brisbane, but at Adelaide, where it was more likely to turn, you needed your best spinner.

It became clear that Duncan had been of the same view, wanting to pick Monty, although we had not discussed it, and he was obviously getting fed up with defending the team and himself and holding the party line. Defeats like this are many times worse for an England team in Australia because of the massive levels of scrutiny and interest, and the fact that their media are constantly looking for any excuse to hammer you.

When the England party got to Perth and I had contact with a few of the lads, you could tell they had just been on the wrong end of a severe mauling. Fletch did not appear in the best of spirits and some of the thinking was clearly becoming a bit muddled, which was where I came in. There was a two-day match against Western Australia scheduled at the WACA, one of those nondescript affairs between Test matches that rarely achieved anything, and understandably some of the England players needed a rest. As we were a bit short of bodies, I was asked if I would play – and I emphasise that it was me that was asked, rather than me doing the asking.

All this succeeded in doing was putting the focus back on me being in Australia, which perhaps I should have seen coming. I was just delighted to be involved again and wearing the shirt after all I had been through, but what I did not enjoy was the intense spotlight on my presence in the team. I spent the first day fielding, and then what made it worse was the slightly farcical situation on the second day when we were batting. I was due in at number six but then started to get pushed down the order, and in the end did not come out to bat at all, as we closed on five down with Sajid Mahmood promoted ahead of me.

While it was good to have had a whole day in the field, and I could understand preferring to give Test players a knock, the whole thing seemed to be badly thought through. One report described my presence as 'supernatural', and it was turning into the issue I had been desperate to avoid. Inevitably the media wanted to speak to me afterwards, and were annoyed when I was denied to them. The idea was not to blow up my reappearance in the team any more than necessary, although it turned out to be the wrong judgement. I should have just said how I was pleased to get an unexpected chance to turn out for a harmless warm-up match and so on and been done with it.

Fred seemed quite pleased to see me and to enjoy chatting with someone who could sympathise more than most with what he was feeling. I actually felt for the whole team, because when that Australian team were as rampant as they were then, and fired up by the memories of 2005, they were simply an unstoppable force. You get beaten, you have to explain yourself, you start taking it all personally – it was a spiral that I fully understood.

The ECB looked after me well on that trip. I had a flat by the beach in Perth, and Nichola and the children came out to join me before Christmas. After the Perth Test match – which ended with us handing the urn back despite a rearguard action from Alastair Cook and Ian Bell – the performance squad was broken up and those staying on for the one-dayers were invited to Melbourne while the others went home.

Three days before Christmas it was announced that I was in

the one-day squad and I agreed to do my bit in the daily media conference. I still did not know if I would be restored as captain for the limited-over matches, and was keen to skate around the subject for fear that it would undermine Fred for the final two Tests. I did my best to explain my presence but it was all in the context of this being a tour that was going drastically wrong, and inevitably people were searching for reasons why. The reasons were actually simple enough: we had lost more than our fair share of key players for various reasons (the likes of myself, Trescothick and Simon Jones) and Australia were still very much at their peak. Everybody knew that they were going to slip from their pedestal at some point – Shane Warne's retirement announcement shortly afterwards would be a major factor – but any cracks had not yet appeared. They were a better team than us, plain and simple, and there was not a great deal Fred could do about it.

The one good thing about not being part of the Boxing Day team was that I could enjoy a proper Christmas without the holding back that usually goes on. That set me apart from the team, and I was going to make damn sure during the Boxing Day Test that nobody could accuse me of getting in the way. While the Test side were playing in the newly refurbished vastness of the MCG, and toiling badly, I was out in the nets with the likes of Stuart Broad and Chris Tremlett going through my one-day routines. It had got to the point where I was finding the talk of me being a distraction a distraction myself, and it was not helping me in the nets. I absolutely hated this whole issue.

It was an unnerving experience, still being the official England captain and yet feeling so uneasy being around the team. I hardly watched a ball of that Melbourne Test, and although my gear was kept in the changing room at the MCG, I made sure I only went in there when the lads were out fielding. And when I did enter I just sneaked in to grab my stuff or deposit it, nothing more. I have never felt more apart before or since, and it should not have had to be like that, but when things are going belly-up a thousand reasons for what is occurring are created.

This was the case when we headed up to Sydney just before New Year to prepare for the final Test. On New Year's Eve some of the players went out with Fred on a boat, while others went to a party laid on by the ECB by the water's edge. I was not aware of there being any particular splits in this team, or of the divides being any greater than is normal when a team are under huge pressure and taking a real beating, as had happened again in Melbourne. But of course the fact that we were not all together on the last night of the year was seen as symptomatic of a group that was disunited.

Personally, I had never been so pleased to see the back of one year and the dawning of a new one. If 2005 had been off the scale in one way, then 2006 had plenty made up for it. Never before had I meant it so much when I toasted the arrival of 2007.

While the Sydney Test was played out we stayed at apartments near the casino and I trained with the one-day incomers, including Paul Nixon. I suspect we had a more enjoyable week than the Test boys, who were going down to a 5–0 drubbing to Australia in Australia, about the worst experience you can have as an England cricketer.

Despite the explainable circumstances of defeat, the ECB decided that they needed to be seen to be doing something decisive about the direction of our whole game, and so announced an inquiry, which became the Schofield Report. It smacked of being a public-relations gimmick at the time and I never really changed my mind on that. In Test terms, we had beaten Australia in 2005, drawn with India away and the following summer beaten Pakistan at home. Now a weakened side had been hammered by one of the best teams in the history of the sport. A World Cup was fast approaching. After all he had achieved since 2000, was it any surprise that Fletcher felt so slighted by the perceived need to have an inquiry into recent history?

In a room at the Sydney casino, the day after our whitewash was completed, it was formally announced that I would be resuming the captaincy. I was very pleased to see one chapter of my life coming to an end and a new one beginning.

20

Revolving Doors

It might appear that it was something of a nightmare returning to take over a team that had just been kicked around from one end of Australia to another. The start of 2007 was not a great time to come back in some ways, because there was an element of shell shock around after the Ashes, but it was not the worst either, because we could start afresh and clear the guys' minds after the drubbing they had just received.

A new leader was probably just what a team in that position needed, although in truth this particular captain was still not 100 per cent fit. I just wanted to get out there and play, and while those who had been hammered were likely to be in poor shape between their ears, I did not realise quite how badly they had been affected. No team loses 5–0 in a major Test series without a few cracks appearing, and there were certainly a few fault lines opening up in this one.

Duncan was feeling the heat and beginning to react to what the media wanted him to do rather than doing things his own way, which had always been such a strength of his. The Fletch I had known was really strong and single-minded in making his decisions, and one of the first things I noticed was that he was now being affected by media pressure. An unusual situation, although very understandable given what had happened. I would like to think he was pleased to have me back on board.

I thought it would be a useful exercise to sit down one-on-one with each player at the start of the triangular tournament against Australia and New Zealand, because after a year out of the captaincy it was important to reassert myself, and the colour began to come back to Duncan's cheeks as we talked the Ashes through. He is a proud man and hated to lose so much.

The first match was a Twenty20 international on 9 January, and it was a case of different format, same result. We got hammered by 77 runs – cue more ridicule – but it was great just to run out with the team and I even managed 27 in 21 balls.

One of the few good things for us in that match was a spirited cameo from Paul Nixon, whose inclusion in the squad I had quietly lobbied for, and whose selection had met with much scepticism. I just felt we needed a bit of character injecting, and that he fitted the bill. He was already 36 years old but he never failed to create a buzz and we needed that bit of 'Badgerness' about us (Nixon was always known for being mad as a badger). He would make us laugh on the field – something that clearly had not happened for a while – and he wound some of his team-mates up as well, but a few of them probably needed that. Nico would go around repeating 'I'm living the dream!' and shout it out as we ran onto the field. It was a risk picking him, particularly with his age, but it was one worth taking because we could not have got any worse. I am glad that by the end of the World Cup he had repaid our faith.

He created a lot of healthy banter off the pitch as well, which was also needed. It was difficult to control the players because they had been beaten up so badly in the Tests and it was a stiff examination of my rusty man-management skills. I did not want to come back in and act all headmasterly, and maybe I think

I went too much the other way by encouraging them to enjoy themselves. Looking back, it arguably resulted in too much partying among the team over a period of weeks, for the only time in my captaincy, as I tried to foster a spirit of enjoyment while keeping everyone on the right side of the professional line. We definitely went overboard around the time we went to Adelaide later that month and reached what was to be our nadir.

By then, halfway through what was an interminably drawn-out triangular format, we were all over the place. I had got injured again, pulling a hamstring in Hobart, and at the beautiful Adelaide Oval we went down heavily first to New Zealand and then, three days later on 26 January, to Australia. They chased down our feeble 110 for the loss of one wicket in just 24.3 overs before the lights even had to be turned on. With unfortunate timing it happened on Australia Day, that festival of no-holds-barred patriotism, and Duncan felt compelled to issue an apology to our fans.

We perhaps drowned our sorrows too much while we were in Adelaide, but by this point I felt the lads generally needed some refreshment in all senses. I basically opened up my captain's suite at the hotel as a kind of free bar to the touring party, and you have to say it worked out as within two weeks we were on our way to the finals of the Commonwealth Bank series.

In Adelaide we always went to a particular bar on the corner and then back to the Hyatt hotel, which was pretty vibrant, and we were all staying on the same floor so the fun would continue up there some evenings. In those two weeks encompassing Adelaide and afterwards we were probably not, in the obvious sense, the most professional England outfit I have ever been involved with, and yet the results started to come.

We were like a throwback to the 1970s, and we just about managed to keep it away from Duncan, although I should think he suspected.

Who says sport is an exact science? I have never believed in curfews and I think you have to leave it to individuals to work out for themselves what is the best way for them to prepare. If that involves a glass of wine before a match I do not have a problem with it, within reason. If players cannot behave like adults, you will find out soon enough anyway.

Having said that, I would not recommend going to the extremes that Fred reached when we got to Sydney with a place in the triangular final still within our grasp. It was this incident, and the warning that came with it, that caused a particularly dim view to be taken when he was found to have been out so late during the World Cup in St Lucia, the notorious 'Fredalo' incident.

On this occasion in Sydney, Fred had been out with Ian Botham until late into the wee hours and it was clearly affecting his performance at fielding practice once the sun had come up. I was not directly involved, because I was injured again and watching things unfold from the physio's bench inside the SCG pavilion, but you could tell Fred was having problems with his coordination during the drills. In fact, he could not even throw the ball 30 yards back to the thrower, and he was taking hits on the chest from the odd ball that was flying off the edge.

Duncan came into the pavilion and told me that he had to do something this time because Fred was captain again in my latest injury-enforced absence and it was just not on. He and Duncan were at the end of the road with each other anyway around this period, so he called Freddie in and gave him a major slap on the wrist. Without wanting to lose my sense of humour about it, I agreed with the coach that he could not let it pass as the other players had all noticed the state he was in and were giggling about it.

Meanwhile my own frustrations were continuing, and it was in the course of my comeback game in Brisbane on 6 February that I felt my hamstring get tight and go again. But we were on an upward curve by now and, despite my golden duck, my team-mates produced a fine performance to beat the Kiwis by 14 runs and secure our place in the final.

Before Brisbane Paul Collingwood had come to us in a poor state of mind. He had had a decent Ashes series but was starting to find playing in Australia that peculiar form of torture that visiting cricketers will tell you about. He said he could not buy a run, so for a bit of a laugh I said to him and Strauss, 'Why don't you try one of those pink handles?' Matthew Hayden was using one to support a breast cancer charity and, although we were not connected to any official campaign, I thought it was worth trying anything different. Maybe it was just coincidence, but in that match Colly went on to get 106 and Strauss 55. I always thought pink suited them.

It was a superb effort and Fletch wanted to give me a big hug when I walked back into the dressing room after what was my valedictory match in that series. Inside, though, I was finding it hard to celebrate because I thought it was probably the end of my one-day career. I was heading home and feared that I was going to miss the World Cup.

In my absence the lads went on to complete a magnificent comeback by winning the CB series under Fred's captaincy. They did not even need a third match to win the best-of-three finals. After that whole topsy-turvy month you would have to conclude that, no, sport at the highest level is not necessarily an exact science.

An injection into my hamstring when I got back to England seemed to do the trick and a week before our scheduled departure I was declared fit for the World Cup.

The feeling I had when we assembled at Gatwick at the beginning of March was that I honestly thought we could do something big. I knew our first match against New Zealand was going to be an important one, and thought that if we could get some momentum going we were good enough to thrive in what was yet another long, drawn-out format. My personal confidence, though, was deflated by all the questions about my leadership and my one-day record as a whole, which had hardly been bolstered by the 43 runs scored over the three ODIs I managed in Australia.

Nonetheless, I was pretty happy with our warm-up camp in St Vincent, where we beat a Bermuda team whose defining player was a portly spinner called Dwayne Leverock, who was actually quite useful. We had a lovely hotel on the beach looking out to Young Island about 500 metres away and most mornings all the lads would swim over there around the moored yachts. We would practise hard, play football with the locals on the beach and in the evenings we would sit outside playing poker. This was cricketing life in the Caribbean as it should be.

But I was soon getting worried about Duncan's frame of mind, the lift he had eventually experienced in Australia having evaporated. During the first week Darren Gough, who had been disappointed to be left out of the squad, did a question-and-answer public appearance back in England in which he was critical of Fletch, and what he said made it into the media. It was fairly standard fare from Goughy – who had never been in contention to make the trip, despite press speculation – and he is rarely short of an opinion. For some reason, his words really got to Duncan and he called me to his room to talk about it. He was getting very agitated and spoke to the ECB about the possibilities of disciplining Darren.

I texted Goughy, who replied that he had just said it to get a reaction, but Fletch would not let it rest. If things like that can get to you, it shows you are at the top end of your stress levels. Duncan is a great one-day coach and it had been very frustrating to him that he had not managed to achieve with England as much in the shorter form of the game as he had done in the Test arena.

He wanted to prove himself, but at the back of our minds we knew this was going to be difficult, with Steve Harmison having quit three months beforehand and Marcus Trescothick, the best opening batsman alongside Graham Gooch that England has ever had in one-day cricket, out of the picture. That had disrupted our preparations enormously and he was irreplaceable.

Neither I nor Ed Joyce was the style of player who could smack it over the top, but we felt we had to play to our strengths as we saw them. There was talk of Mal Loye coming in, but for me he was not the right character for the team. He had talent but I felt there was a certain insecurity about him as a player and I thought we needed more stability.

We travelled over to St Lucia in reasonable enough spirits and prepared to face New Zealand on 16 March in the crucial opener that would provide the winner with immediate impetus to reach the semi-finals. The Kiwis were a very good one-day outfit, well drilled, with everyone knowing their roles under an outstanding captain in Stephen Fleming.

We batted first after losing an important toss and, despite getting them 19–3 in their reply to our 209–7, a fine knock from Scott Styris on an improving wicket for batting saw them

home with 11 overs to spare. It was not the end of the World
Cup, but what happened that evening became far more notorious and was ultimately to prove far more destructive than
our drinking exploits in the triangular series a few months
before.

As I know to my cost, this was the Friday night the word
'Fredalo' entered the English language after some of our players
stayed out far too late, despite us having a match against Canada
on the Sunday. The common factor was probably that it
involved the guys who were disappointed by their performances
in the match, the likes of Ian Bell, Liam Plunkett, Nixon, James
Anderson, Jon Lewis (who did not actually play) and, of course,
Freddie.

It would have been OK by me to have just one or two beers
down the road to unwind, but it is easy to get sucked into a
night out in that environment where there's quite a holiday
buzz and others are having a good time. My own evening was
desperately boring. I went to the Chinese restaurant across the
road from the hotel for an early meal and, afterwards, I was
in the hotel lobby when a few of them were discussing nipping
out. I was reading the climbing book *Touching the Void* and
was really into it, so just wanted to go up to my room for an
early night and read some more.

The next morning I went downstairs and Reg Dickason, our
Australian security man, was in the breakfast room. 'Vaughany,
we've got a bit of shit on here, mate,' he said, 'Fred's been out
in the water.' This did not sound too alarming, until he added,
'At the wrong time of the evening – and the press have got
hold of it.'

My first thought was that Fred had already pushed the limits
in Australia. 'Any others?' I asked Reg, who told me that 'quite
a few' had been out late. This really was the last thing we

needed to be dealing with, our superstar player and a few cohorts having too many ales in front of the public with another game coming up tomorrow.

It was a very difficult morning. Fletch decided that we would grab the whole squad and get them all in the same room to write down on a board what time they had come in before the assembled company. Fred looked rough and was very apologetic. There was dead quiet and a frosty atmosphere in that room, with all those out after midnight having to walk up to the front and scrawl what time they had got back.

When Jeremy Snape, the Leicestershire captain and qualified psychologist who had been brought in to help with that side of things, walked up to the front I thought, 'This will go down well.' Bowling coach Kevin Shine had also stayed out, ironically about the only time he had had a night out all winter. I knew something had to be done in the case of Fred, and it was pretty clear that we were going to have to drop him to make a point. We sat him down in the afternoon to tell him he would not be considered for the next match. He was not happy, and you would not expect him to be.

I knew there was going to be a delayed reaction to all this as far as the team was concerned, long after the alcohol had gone through the players' systems. I actually thought Fred would cope with it OK; it was the younger players I was more concerned about, as they were not as used to all the focus and attention.

Mentally they would not be as tough as Freddie. He told me he had not been on a pedalo and I have no reason to doubt him. He later admitted to the media, gravely, that 'water was involved'. I still feel it was the right decision to suspend him, but the look on the younger players' faces told you they would struggle to cope with the longer-term fallout.

Fortunately Canada were not strong enough to take advantage of our disarray and we then regrouped to beat Kenya the following weekend, although the victory was probably hairier than it should have been. I had always thought that for us to do well in the World Cup everything would have to go our way, and it was already clear that was not going to be the case.

Our problems were nothing compared with what had happened in Jamaica, where the Pakistan coach and former England player, Bob Woolmer, had been found dead, initially sparking off a frenzy of speculation. We were all shocked and saddened, and only the previous week I had enjoyed a long chat with him in the swimming pool in Montego Bay before the World Cup opening ceremony. Bob loved to discuss his theories on the game and had a real passion for it. I always got the impression he would have liked to have got involved with England if that had been possible.

It had been a very difficult week and I think that was what really pushed Duncan to the edge. Immediately after the press conference that followed the Kenya match, we had a falling-out over a media story so trivial I cannot even remember what it was. It came up in conversation and he just said, 'I never read the press.' I replied that I had seen the cuttings being put under his door and that I was sure he did read them at times. 'Are you accusing me of being a liar?' he shot back. I just thought, 'Jeez, this is getting tough,' and walked off.

If you hear players saying they do not read the press, you can be pretty sure they are stretching the truth. Certainly we have a look at headlines, and if you do not read any further it is still likely that a mate will tell you what has been written. In England it is hard to keep clear of it; in dressing rooms there will always be someone asking, 'Did you hear what so-and-so wrote about you?' It is easier to avoid when you are abroad, although the advent of laptops, texting and the internet makes the temptation great even then.

My uncharacteristic mini-spat with Duncan showed the tension around the camp. We went to Guyana after that to prepare for a match against Ireland, and there was plenty on my mind as we took the twin-prop over to the South American mainland.

There is not a lot to do in Georgetown and in the one major hotel there you are cheek-by-jowl with the other teams. I always hated being in the same hotel as other teams. Although I have friends in all the other countries, there is always the awkwardness at breakfast about how sociable you should be with them, or whether you should be cool and tough. The South Africans were there for two and half weeks; it must have been tedious in the extreme.

We had a horrible match against Ireland but, thanks to Colly getting us out of the mire, managed to win a hiding-to-nothing encounter with a degree of difficulty. The spirit around the team was not as good as it might be, and from a personal point of view my form was at an all-time low. I just did not know whether to stick or twist, to try and manoeuvre the ball or to say sod it, and try to just whack it.

The ridiculous format meant that the next stop on our Caribbean odyssey was Antigua, where we should have beaten Sri Lanka on 4 April. If we had won that day I think we would have got through to the semi-finals, and beating the Sri Lankans ought not to have been beyond us after getting them out for 235. Ravi Bopara, who I think has a special talent, played an unbelievable knock and with Paul Nixon so nearly got us over the line.

We needed two off the last ball but Dilhara Fernando stopped his run-up just before delivery in order to see how Ravi was going to set himself up for the shot, and when he finally did deliver the ball he bowled him. Not in the spirit of the game, perhaps, but it definitely put Ravi off and I could not help admiring what a smart move it was from Fernando. Earlier there had been a five-ball over that none of the officials had spotted – that was the kind of tournament it was turning out to be.

Next up was Australia – again at the soulless new ground they had built in the middle of the island of Antigua, which was to prove unfit for play in the 2009 Test series – and it was another game we had a decent chance in. A measure of how badly wrong they had got the organisation of the tournament was that the stadium was far from full, and it had nothing of the character of the wonderful Recreation Ground in the capital, St John's.

Pietersen and Bell batted beautifully to put on 140 and we should have posted more than our 247, which they were to overtake with 16 balls and seven wickets to spare. My latest meagre contribution was five, and the only thing that stands out for me was the speed generated by Shaun Tait, who bowled me. He has the quickest first ball I ever faced; his first over was always very tricky until you got used to the sheer pace.

Our performance against Sri Lanka had given us a bit of a lift and Freddie was showing that he was mentally strong enough to perform despite the flak he had received for what went on in St Lucia. Also, the format that the International Cricket Council had dreamed up in their infinite wisdom meant that we were somehow still in with a chance of making the semi-finals as we headed to Barbados, provided we could beat Bangladesh and South Africa.

This thought was managing to sustain us, plus the knowledge that life can never be too bad when you are on an island I enjoy so much that I own a property there. Bangladesh was another ugly win, but thanks to Collingwood and Nixon steadying us, we got past their total of 143. An indicator of my state of mind had come in their innings when I dropped my opposite number Habibul Bashar at mid-on. Even by the standards of a fielding career punctuated by some poor spillages, this was a complete dolly. After shelling it and swearing my head off, I picked the ball up in sheer anger and hurled it at Nixon and, to my amazement, found that Bashar had got into a mix-up with his partner and was run out. It was quite funny, but it showed how distracted I was. I knew we were not clicking as a team and that I was not playing well, and just had a feeling that the team was not quite at ease with itself.

I was trying to give out all the positive vibes that I could, but deep down I knew that at the end of the World Cup it would be the right time to go, at least from one-day cricket. I was being asked about it and stubbornly refusing to admit it, driven by the inner fighter in the hope that I would get a hundred and would be away. I had batted very negatively against Bangladesh for my 30, and far too many things from outside were affecting me, such as little comments in the dressing room or in the media. I could sense there was a lot of talk back home about how bad it all was.

When you are in a strong frame of mind that kind of thing is just water off a duck's back, but I had started agreeing with the critics. I still, to this day, think that I should have become a very good one-day player, but in that format of the game I could never switch my mind completely to the business of batting; I always had other things going on in my head, particularly when I was captain.

Still, by having won the matches we were expected to win, we became the team that this format would not let die, no matter how average we were. We faced South Africa knowing that victory would, remarkably, get us into the last four. I was desperately trying to think how we could add anything to the players' preparation and that was when I bumped into Sir Steve Redgrave in the lobby of our hotel, where he was on holiday with his family. So I asked him if he had a spare half-hour to give an address to the players. Being the very decent bloke that he is, he agreed. He just spoke off the cuff about the pressures of sport and preparation for the big moments and I considered it very useful, although I thought that one or two players did not pay sufficient attention, which was pretty disappointing.

In the end even the great Olympian could not save us. We won the toss, considered to be a good one to call correctly at Bridgetown, but could only post 154, with Andrew Hall taking 5–18. To make matters worse, they came out and smashed it everywhere, to win by nine wickets with more than 30 overs to spare. Graeme Smith hit an unbeaten 89 and not for the last time, as it would turn out, he was at the crease to put a major full stop in my career.

We were deservedly booed off by our supporters – it was a horrible sound. I had always tried not to give too much away to the players and stay level, but for the first time they would have looked at me in the dressing room and known that I was really struggling. I just stood in a daze, wondering what I was doing there. As captain I was already questioning the decisions I was taking and also as a batsman I was asking myself if I should be in the team – that is the hardest question a captain can ask himself. I got back to the hotel and, after telling Nichola that I felt I ought to resign, got straight on the phone to my manager, Neil Fairbrother, to seek his advice.

Guided by him, I decided not to do anything in haste and, besides, there was a 'dead' match against the West Indies still to play. The next afternoon about 5 p.m. I had a call from Duncan, inviting me down to the outdoor bar by the Hilton's swimming pool. I sat down and, in a very matter-of-fact way, he told me that he was stepping down, that the journey that had begun in the autumn of 1999 – coinciding with my first senior England trip – and had taken in so much on the way was at an end.

And then almost instantly, for the first time on the whole trip, we found ourselves relaxing with each other. We had a few rum and cokes and sat for an hour and a half just talking, having quite a few giggles and going over everything that had happened since we had been there. On the one hand, we were finally considering how trivial cricket is in the grand scheme of things, but on the other, when talking about the future he was still passionate about the team going on and being successful. It always struck me with Duncan just how genuine his passion was for the England team, despite him being Zimbabwean.

I think he would have liked to carry on, in many ways. We had a Test series coming up against India and he had never beaten them, so he felt it was unfinished business there. Ultimately, I think it was the way he took umbrage at the media coverage that got him down, I think criticism really got to him. One of the things you have to do as England captain or coach is to try and understand how the media works, and for some reason Duncan could never quite get his head around it, or reach an accommodation. I actually found the media side of things quite interesting, and up until my last six months in the job could accept pretty much anything. Maybe it just gets to you in the end, as it did with Duncan.

He was a bit upset as well in some ways as we watched the sun going down, but I felt it was the right decision on his part. He had done a fantastic job, but it was time for a new direction. I told him that, as far as one-day cricket went, I also wanted to go, but he said he wanted me to continue and that I still had a chance of becoming a really good one-day player.

Such was my respect for Duncan that it did sow doubt in

my mind, and there was also the aspect that I knew that if the one-day job was gone, the Test job would follow as, whatever I said in public, I always believed that having just one captain of England was best.

The next day we were training in the morning when, out of the blue, three-quarters of the way through nets, he suddenly called everyone together and told them that the West Indies match would be his last in the job. There was deathly silence and I spoke on behalf of the players, thanking him for everything he had done, and I burst into tears. There were three or four others among us doing the same and Fletch was unusually emotional, he was very touched by the reaction. Despite what happened at the World Cup, we all appreciated what he had done for us, and apart from that there had been some close friendships formed.

It was a surreal five minutes because afterwards everyone made their way to these mini-marquees where all our gear was in the shade and started packing up in silence. Three or four minutes later Fletch announced, 'Come on, we're still practising!' and we went back for another 20 minutes, although it was the worst netting I ever saw as an England player, because everyone was so distracted.

We went on to play the West Indies on 21 April and, somehow predictably, I went out there and hammered a fluent 79 in 68 balls as we chased down their 300 with a ball to spare. I felt so relaxed and finally I really did think, sod it, I'm going to have a go. I even fielded like a gazelle. I wish I could have brought that mentality to my one-day batting throughout my career, but I could not. It turned out to be my last ODI for England, although most will remember it for being Brian Lara's farewell appearance. Had the game actually mattered, it might have been considered a World Cup classic.

As I was walking towards the media conference afterwards Pat Murphy of the BBC came up to me and, off-air, asked if I was going to resign. On this occasion I just said to him 'Why don't you **** off,' and walked on, which as England captain I probably should not have done.

At that stage I knew in my mind I had to go, although Colly came up to me the following day and told me that this World Cup had not been my fault, that there was nothing I could have done about it with the personnel available. I told him I thought it was time I disappeared from the one-day scene. There was no way, however, that I was going to be making an announcement, and apart from anything I did not wish to detract from the significance of Duncan's departure. Considering what he had done, apart from this crushingly disappointing winter, he was receiving a lot of appreciation – and he deserved it.

Duncan was a figure of giant stature within the whole England set-up, someone it was going to be mighty difficult to replace. Yet no sooner had he gone than Peter Moores was promoted from running the Loughborough academy, without so much as a 'situation vacant' ad being placed anywhere. By the standards of English cricket, the revolving door had spun with remarkable speed.

21

Feeling the Pressure

Talk about a culture shock. Less than a week after getting back home, and merely a day after the farcical end to the World Cup that saw Australia beat Sri Lanka in the light-affected final at Bridgetown, I was playing for Yorkshire in the distinctly chillier environment of Edinburgh in the Friends Provident Trophy. Instead of moping around at home, I thought the best thing was to get right back into it and get my own game in order, so it was pretty much straight onto the Yorkshire bus heading north, and it was great to see my county team-mates again. Martyn Moxon, someone for whom I had the utmost respect and who had taught me a lot about the game, was back in charge at Headingley, so it was good to be working with him.

Inevitably there was plenty of criticism waiting for me on my return and people saying that I should surrender the captaincy, but from somewhere I found a new lease of life and energy. Peter Moores came to see me when we got back to Leeds to have a chat about all that had happened in the winter and he seemed to have bags of enthusiasm. He told me how he envisaged things working, which would be a bit different from how it had been before.

Duncan always thought that the skipper should be the boss, running the side while he was there in a consultative role to advise and guide. Peter saw himself more as the overall manager, with the captain looking after things just on the pitch. At the time I was not at all alarmed, in fact I thought maybe this was just what I needed. The all-encompassing role of the captaincy as it had worked with Duncan was becoming quite hard and if Peter wanted to take some of that on, it could work well. I had heard a lot about him, our paths had briefly crossed and I was quite excited to meet him. I always think change can provide a short-term boost, although in the longer term there has to be quality underpinning it if those benefits are to continue.

I left the meeting feeling quite energised and thinking maybe I did want to carry on as one-day captain after all. Maybe it was all the nonsense you have to put up with as captain that was holding me back, all the thinking about everybody else and their development, and if I just focused on my one-day batting then the runs would come. It all seemed pretty simple. I was going to be freed up to smash the bowling around as if there was no tomorrow.

But the flak kept coming from all quarters as the inquest into our winter dragged on. I was prepared to accept most of it, although I remember being outraged when I heard Dominic Cork demanding that I be sacked as one-day captain. About two weeks later, I was thinking that he might have had a point after all.

A few days after the Scotland match I went down to Southampton to play in a Championship game against Hampshire and made a decent 72 in the first innings before getting hit on the finger in the second by Stuart Clark, the Aussie who had given my colleagues so many problems over the winter.

The break meant that I was ruled out of my scheduled Test

comeback at Lord's against the West Indies, despite trying desperately to make it, an effort which included spending time in an oxygen chamber and using magnets for 10 hours a day to try and heal the break. Andrew Strauss took over the captaincy – the match was drawn – and I went down there for a few days to observe and get a feel for how Peter worked and acquaint myself with the new set-up.

While I was there, I went over to the media centre and did an interview on Sky. I came across all bullish and said that, despite being written off, it was up to me to prove the doubters wrong and that I would come good in the one-dayers. I remember walking out of there and thinking to myself, 'I don't believe what I have just told them. I have just given an inter-view convincing them that I still want to play one-day cricket for England, but in my own mind, I don't!'

So there was still confusion in my head, and my finger was probably still not properly ready for the second Test on my home ground, due to begin on 25 May. Yet I was so desperate to play and found myself hitting the ball quite well in the nets, and despite all the questions about what right I had to come straight back into the team after missing Lord's, I felt curiously fresh and calm approaching it. My reasoning was that we had lost our last Test series 5–0 and drawn the first match of this one in which the number three, Owais Shah, had failed to make a decent score. So it just seemed like a no-brainer to me and, although I am no magician, I thought we looked like a team that needed its leader back.

The media really drove me on that week; I was aching to prove them wrong. Fletch's term 'dogfuck', which referred to the animalistic feeling he believed existed somewhere inside every decent player, must have been at work. I was so committed and focused, feeling as if they had backed me into a corner, having convinced myself that, rightly or wrongly, now that Duncan had gone, they wanted another scalp. Broadly speaking, I liked a lot of the people I knew who worked in the media, but the constant swipes were now annoying me, and I felt as if they were pretending they had some intimate knowledge of how my mind was working. Perhaps I was annoying them too, with the occasional reference to myself in the third person that had unconsciously slipped into my language. It probably came across as arrogant, but I think it was down to me desperately trying to prove myself after all I had been through with the knee in the previous 18 months. This kind of thing really was not the style of Michael Vaughan . . . sorry, myself.

Joking apart, there was a slight siege mentality setting in. A few suggestions were made that I believed I was some José Mourinho-type character who reckoned himself to be 'The Special One', which really wound me up because he was not someone I recognised in myself. But I managed to stick to my basic philosophy of dealing with the press, radio and television, which was always to try and be nice. I go back to the movie *Road House* from my young Yorkshire days, which tells of a bouncer working in a bar where fights are always breaking out and all these chairs and tables are flying around. The main character used to go around saying 'You've got to be nice', and I used to constantly remind myself of that. I was always trying to avoid showing that I had been riled – forever wearing my mask.

Finally, blessedly, more than 18 months after holding that imitation urn above my head on that glorious September afternoon at The Oval, I was ready to lead England out in a Test match again. When it came to the toss I was a complete nervous wreck. I was physically shaking when I was flipping the coin, far worse than in the Ashes. I just felt that I had to deliver. My finger was not 100 per cent, I had barely a played a match in the longer format of the game since 2005, and I was thinking that my hand might not hold up, my knee could give way and my hamstring could go again at any time. I felt there were all these rifles loaded and pointing at me.

Yet curiously, from the moment I won the toss, chose to make the West Indies field and did a quick interview in the middle, I felt great again. I went back to the dressing room, put my kit on and sat on the balcony. It is strangely positioned at Headingley, right next to the box where the scribes sit, and despite the proximity of those who had been winding me up I felt supremely cool. The ground looked like a full house and I thought to myself that all these people are here to watch me today; it was weird. It sounds conceited but I occasionally got this feeling, especially at Lord's, and I received a huge ovation when I walked out to bat in the ninth over, even better than what had usually greeted me in Leeds.

I did not start that well, but when I was under pressure I would try to use a mental technique that involved giving myself a mark out of 10 for how I had played each ball. It helps you stay in the present and not get ahead of yourself, as every ball becomes a game of its own. In the 18 overs before lunch, which I went into unbeaten on 25, I assessed myself on every delivery. When I was playing at my best I would find myself in my own cocoon, cut off from the crowd and all the chirping around me. For the first 15 balls that morning I was giving myself three or four out of 10 because my feet were not moving, but after that my self-imposed marks began to go up, and that innings between 50 and 100 was about as fluent as I can play.

The shot that brought up my 16th Test century, an edge through the slips, was not the prettiest, but reaching three figures – marked by KP giving me a massive bear hug that squeezed the breath from me – was perhaps the greatest feeling I have ever had on a cricket field, including the Ashes. I had thought my career was over and had come into the game severely under the cosh – and as a Yorkshire player at Headingley it made everything all the more special. I had felt it had been the hardest possible examination of my whole psyche, and I had come through.

Nonetheless, I was furious with myself when, on 103, I hit it sweet as a nut straight to Runako Morton at deep midwicket off Jerome Taylor. This was quickly replaced with a feeling of great satisfaction as I basked in the ovation, and when I got back in the dressing room I thought, 'How the bloody hell did I do that?' I was also happy that my surgeon, Nick London, had been there to watch.

After taking my kit off I went out to the viewing area and there were all the morning's papers lying around, which I had studiously avoided reading earlier in the day. Now I had a look at a few and thought, 'Thank God I didn't read that,' as there was some fairly brutal stuff about me inside the previews. I am sure that if I had read them I would have been going out to bat thinking, 'Why did they say that?' I am at my best when there is quiet in my head, the kind of peaceful mindset that batsmen such as Pakistan's Mohammad Yousuf seem to have. There is a tranquillity about him at the wicket that I tried to capture myself.

A brilliant double ton from KP and eight wickets from Ryan Sidebottom saw the match end in a colossal innings and 283-run victory over the West Indies. For the first time in two years I had the chance to answer some positive questions when I spoke to the media afterwards. It seemed that from the start of the rehab work on my knee I had been fielding nothing but negative inquiries, so it was a joy to be able to be so genuinely positive again. It added up to one of the most satisfying weeks of my career.

The elation I felt at Headingley, however, was soon to dissipate.

In the days after the match the ECB asked me to do an interview with Donald McRae of the *Guardian* about my comeback, looking forward and looking back, I presumed. I did not think a great deal of it at the time, afterwards reckoning I had played a reasonably straight bat to most of the questions, as I usually did, and trying not to tell any complete porkies. We had talked about the World Cup and I had been pretty honest about my own failings with the bat and, of course, the interview covered the subject of Fred's boozy night out.

No harm done, I thought, but that was before I was presented with the finished product just two days ahead of the third Test at Old Trafford.

'VAUGHAN SAYS FLINTOFF RUINED WORLD CUP,' ran the headline, with the introduction: 'Michael Vaughan has blamed Andrew Flintoff for destroying England's team spirit and contributing to a disastrous World Cup campaign in the Caribbean.'

Among the things it quoted me saying were: 'You have to be honest: the "Fredalo" incident did affect the team. It did affect morale.'

I was shocked when James Avery, one of our media staff, alerted me to it because I had been mindful to avoid controversy and thought that what I had said about the Fred incident was pretty much a statement of the obvious. What I was absolutely not trying to do was to pinpoint my long-time colleague as the reason why we had not achieved what we should have done. He had done more than anyone to help me regain the Ashes and I was indebted to him for that. Yet you could hardly say in all honesty that his night out in St Lucia had been a help, and I felt the fallout from it had naturally affected the younger players. All fairly self-evident.

To make matters worse, Fred had undergone ankle surgery the previous week and now we were playing at his home ground. The timing was abysmal, and this was a real low for me because it was looking as if, as England captain, I was putting the boot into one of my star players, which would never have been my intention. Maybe I had been naive, but I believed that what I had said had been blown up out of all proportion. Jim Cumbes, Lancashire's chief executive, came out and described me as 'despicable', which added unhelpful fuel to the fire.

It really killed me because I had always tried not to criticise individuals, but then I made matters worse because I specifically denied using the word 'Fredalo', when it was clearly audible on the interview tape, as the paper later gloated. There were several reasons why I denied it. First, I genuinely thought I had avoided the term, and then there was the awareness of the damage that had been done. I had just made a triumphant return at Headingley and was desperate to put all the negative stuff away for the sake of myself and the team, including Fred. Although he had fairly broad shoulders and was used to being in the news, he really did not need all this at the time.

I went to do a press conference on the Wednesday, where I defended myself and had a bit of a dip at McRae. I regret it now, as I should have just apologised for any misunderstanding and allowed things to move on. Denying I had said it was a type of defence mechanism, and it was indicative that my state of mind was still fragile. I tried to ring Fred and tell him how sorry I was, but I could not get hold of him. The next day there were stories that I had had a 'peace lunch' with Fred at Old Trafford, but this was not true. We share the same business manager, Neil 'Harvey' Fairbrother, and the two of us went to his office just outside Manchester. I sat down in Harve's office and when Fred came in, he left us to it in an atmosphere that was frosty and awkward.

Fred felt I had let him down and I could understand that, but I explained that I felt that I had been stuffed a bit by the article, which was not truly representative of what I had said overall. He would have known the feeling. Fred and I had been through a lot together, and while he had done some things that I did not always agree with, I could never, ever fault the effort he gave me on the field and I was grateful to him for that. I considered it one of my real achievements as captain that, under my leadership, his runs per wicket had gone down by more than four and that his batting average had gone from 32 to 40. I hated the fact that some of the public would be thinking that I had left Freddie to be hung out to dry, and again it made me question whether it was time for me to hand the job over.

Fred rang me later in the day to tell me not to worry and in an interview described the incident as a 'storm in a teacup', which was good of him. Relatively late on in my captaincy career I had learned a lesson and thereafter I became even more cautious in interviews.

So much for the euphoria of Headingley. Once again I was a nervous wreck before the Old Trafford match on 7 June; not only was I a little anxious about how I would be received, but the team could also have been affected by the distraction, and I was responsible for it. I was disappointed in myself and again wondering if I was the right man to lead the team. Nasser Hussain had walked past me that morning and asked casually how I was. 'Oh yeah, it's great this England captaincy,' I laughed, sort of.

I won the toss, we batted first and when I walked out to

replace the dismissed Andrew Strauss I was booed by some sections of the crowd. It hurt, particularly because with my odd trans-Pennine heritage I had always had a fantastic reception at Old Trafford as much as Headingley. I knew they would have read this stuff about what I supposedly thought on the subject of Freddie and it was not a nice feeling getting jeered on one of your home patches.

Fortunately the match went well enough from a team and personal point of view. Alastair Cook made a really solid hundred and Monty Panesar again showed his love for the extra bounce in Peter Marron's superb Old Trafford track by taking 10 wickets in the game. I got a couple of 40s and we won by 60 runs, but still my head was not quite right. I found that Leeds had taken a lot out of me, and so had all the hullabaloo leading into the Test.

On the penultimate night of the game I asked to see Peter and Geoff Miller in the coach's room at Old Trafford and told them that, after all the confusion, I really did want to stand down as one-day captain. We were playing back-to-back Tests to finish the series, so I did not want to announce it until after the final game coming up at Durham because it would spark off another load of off-field intrigue, but I had made my mind up. They would have a week to sort out what would happen when it became public.

I told them I thought I had reached the end of the road with one-day cricket and that I could not see myself going to the next World Cup. I also said that if they felt they wanted to bring someone in to do the Test job as well, then I would understand and step aside altogether. I wanted to carry on, but I made it clear that if the split captaincy had a chance of working – which I doubted – then it would have to be someone I could have a good relationship with.

There were insinuations that I had jumped before being pushed but that was not the case. I felt it was the right thing for the team and we needed to make a few fundamental changes in our one-day cricket, and that included getting a new, energised leader, and someone who would be there for the next World Cup.

It had been a proper Test match with real intensity, a far better contest than at Headingley, and the Windies had pushed us, especially Shivnarine Chanderpaul, who was brilliantly dogged that series. The win was completed the next day and in wrapping up the series 2–0 I had edged ahead of Peter May in becoming England's most successful captain with 21 victories in 35 Tests. It was Peter Moores' first series win as coach and we all duly celebrated in harmony.

Up at Durham, largely thanks to Chanderpaul again, the West Indies would not lie down entirely in the third Test, but we still managed to beat them by seven wickets and it was great to see Colly get a Test hundred on his home ground. In the final session of the last day the two of us were together at the crease to overhaul our target of 110, me just missing out on an unbeaten fifty. Colly was someone who had been much on my mind over those five days.

The previous evening I had publicly announced that I was stepping down as one-day captain, because they wanted to unveil my replacement immediately after the match before the squad met up. They had asked me who I thought would be the best person to take it on. There were not many candidates, to tell the truth. Strauss inevitably came under discussion but it was felt that there would always be the doubt over whether he was actually good enough in the short form of the game to warrant a place. I always thought he would make an excellent England captain but the one downside was his ability in

50- and 20-over cricket, which was why it took him so long to get the job.

At the time it was felt that KP was not ready, so they went for Colly, who I was, personally, both happy with and happy for. Since he had first come into the team we had always hit it off and, as one of my best friends in the game, I knew exactly where I would stand with him. The dreaded split captaincy had arrived, but I was unperturbed.

The Test series against the West Indies had taken it out of me, what with not having played much longer-form cricket going into the summer and the extreme focus of the media on seemingly my every move. My head was starting to bang a bit, so I was happy to melt into the background, watch Colly from afar, take some time off and play for Yorkshire. My time with them included a Roses match, which you would never describe as relaxing, but by the time the three-match Test series against India was approaching I felt pretty refreshed.

The one-day internationals against the West Indies had ended in a 2–1 defeat, with Chris Gayle having given us a bit of a battering in his inimitable way. I never liked to see England lose and I was certainly not watching my team-mates and hoping for a defeat, but realistically it did make it a bit easier for me coming back into the dressing room for my first series as Test captain only. I was aware, given the tendency we have in this country to go overboard about everything, that if we had smashed them there would have been more column inches speculating about whether it was time to dispense with me altogether.

I still feared that the split captaincy would not work in the long term, but I genuinely believed that it was a good way to introduce an overall captain into the job, giving him a chance to get a feel for all it entailed while being under a little less scrutiny. I would love to have had a little more time as one-day captain with Nasser in the Test job before taking over the whole thing.

So Colly was happy to go back to the ranks for the India Test series, and when we met up ahead of the Lord's Test starting on 19 July I asked him if he was comfortable with me coming straight back into the position. I am sure I did not have the kind of feelings that Nasser referred to when he came back into the England dressing room in 2003 after sitting out the one-day series that preceded our Tests against South Africa. It helps that my ego is not that large – which is not to say that excessive ego was one of Nasser's shortcomings – and I was quite ready to be philosophical about the whole process anyway.

My personal fondness for Colly helped, and I thought that if he was starting to do a brilliant job I would be happy to step aside regardless, as my time was bound to be up at some point. I did feel part of my role was to give him an insight into what it would be like as Test captain, were he to take over both positions.

There was a real energy about us at this time, due to the youthful look of the team and a relatively inexperienced attack in particular. There was no Flintoff, no Harmison and no Hoggard, and there were a lot of questions about how we were going to fare against India's high-quality batting. Our bowling line-up was Chris Tremlett making his debut, Jimmy Anderson, Ryan Sidebottom, Monty and Colly.

It was a very refreshing side to lead out and our cricket was full of buzz and aggression. My personal liking for Lord's did not yield a century this time, but I made 79 in the first innings and Straussy fell just short of a hundred. Jimmy and Ryan were outstanding in their first innings and then KP got a fine 134 in the second dig to put us in command. We should have won on the last day but the rain intervened, and we would have been victorious irrespective of that had not Steve Bucknor failed to give out their last man, Sreesanth, when he was stone lbw.

Tremlett showed some promise and I thought we were really finding a pool of players here. They were great to work with, there were no complications off the field and I found it very fulfilling. I was very much in control of my own game, my confidence was back and I left there reckoning we had a good chance of upsetting Rahul Dravid's team in the series.

There was still some flak thrown in my direction, however, this time concerning the over rate, a problem for all captains that some people underestimate. I had been trying to manipulate the field more than usual, based on the fact that when you are up against good batsmen on a good wicket you are not going to take wickets by just setting standard fields. We knew they were susceptible to the short ball and to away-swingers, so I was trying to cover all that. Lord's is, in any case, a hard place to get through your overs quickly. It takes a long time for the batsmen to come in and out because of the distance from the dressing rooms to the wicket. Also, the sightscreen at the pavilion end is not great, so there is always some messing around with that.

There were nonsensical suggestions that I was somehow showing off in my field placings, but at the time I felt secure enough to ignore the criticism. At the same time, I was beginning to feel there was an 'open season' feel to all the flak I was getting and that I could not do a great deal right in some people's eyes.

Lord's was, however, a pretty calm encounter with our Indian visitors compared with what was going to transpire in the Trent Bridge match immediately afterwards.

We arrived in Nottingham with the wicket absolutely sodden and thought we wouldn't play at all on the first day, but they brought the boundary in and we managed to get going at three o'clock. We lost the toss and they automatically put us in to face a ball that was doing everything. We scraped our way to just short of 200 and, with the wicket predictably much improved upon drying out, India managed a 283-run first-innings lead.

But I was feeling good and in the second innings produced what was commented on as being among my most fluent hundreds for England before being out for 124. The ball was swinging everywhere and I was right on top of my game, my technique surviving a thorough examination. When I was batting with Collingwood we actually managed to draw level with seven wickets still left, and I said to him we just need to get a lead of 170 here and, with the pitch deteriorating, we could give them a really proper game.

The match had by now taken on a very aggressive edge, largely due to what became known as Jellybeangate, some aggressive chirping and the antics of their excitable young fast bowler Sreesanth, which all require some explanation.

Sreesanth had bowled a no-ball from way in front of the crease to Collingwood around the wicket, and a nasty beamer to KP as well. My team were not choirboys but his language, and that of Zaheer Khan, was pretty excessive, basically just constant swearing, not even proper or amusing abuse. Sreesanth had lost control of his emotions and also barged me as he walked past, which I thought was pathetic. As for the beamer, I just hope he did not intend it. I have never been a fast bowler, but those who are tell me that to bowl a beamer like the one he sent down at Kevin is almost impossible to do without it being deliberate. He has enough talent not to have to cross the line, but will do just about anything to unsettle you if you are playing well against him, as I was at the time.

I like aggression on the pitch and was more or less impervious to it when directed against me, but there has to be a degree of mutual respect. In my time playing against India I noticed that there was a general deterioration in the respect that they showed to the opposition, mostly among the younger players. Harbhajan Singh, for example, came out and said Ricky Ponting was not a great captain and just lucky to have had great players under him. I thought that was pretty disrespectful to one of the great batsmen of the modern game. The senior Indian players such as Dravid and Tendulkar were a class act and absolutely fine, playing it hard but fair.

The Indians had, it turned out, taken huge umbrage at the discovery of a jellybean on the crease when Zaheer came out to bat with his usual swagger. Now, I can honestly say that I was off the pitch at the time, but I know that some of the lads eat sweets during the match and if someone leaves a jellybean on the floor, is that really a hanging offence? Against the West Indies a jelly baby had fallen out of someone's pocket when Marlon Samuels came in. He just said, 'Cheers, lads,' and picked it up and ate it, which I thought was the appropriate response.

Zaheer, who is a fine bowler and had a great match at Nottingham, said that the jellybean incident had spurred him on to take his nine wickets in the Test. Obviously not a man who takes a great deal of motivating, then. The whole thing got blown out of proportion and we were labelled an immature side, with a gobby wicketkeeper in Matt Prior. Like most keepers he likes to chirp, and particular offence seemed to be taken at something the stump microphone had picked up about him claiming to have a Porsche. It was suggested he was boasting when it had really been nothing of the sort. What happened was that the series sponsors, npower, had earlier in the match sent a magnum of champagne to the dressing room because the mike had picked up Prior mentioning them in some context and it had got on air. There then developed this joke among us that if we talked around the stumps about some product or other we might get one of the items sent to us. Hence Prior mentioned Porsche, Colly started banging on about Sony plasma-screen TVs and Cooky listed his favourite beers.

Pretty harmless stuff all round, I would maintain, and I think the Indians used the jellybean incident to try and distract attention from the behaviour of Sreesanth, which really was out of order. I also thought it was indicative that we are getting a bit silly in this country when everyone is obsessing about a jelly-bean. Maybe it was reflective of our culture's increasing love for the trivial in general. We fought hard in that game before suffering a collapse against some very good bowling. The margin of defeat was seven wickets but some of the dispro-portionate media coverage made that seem almost incidental. It was not as if we had abused Zaheer's race or something.

If I mention the media from time to time, it is not because I had any real hang-ups about the press and broadcasters, and not because I fail to appreciate that coverage of the sport is an essential part of making the cricket world go round. It is because I think the public possibly underestimates the effect that the coverage and commentary has on the England team, which is why understanding the media is such an important part of the captain's role. We were a young side in that match, and as much as we may try to insist in macho fashion that nothing bothers us and that we ignore criticism, my experience was that England teams, rightly or wrongly, always get affected by the sort of thing that happened at Trent Bridge. Duncan felt the same, which was one reason he was so sensitive about what was said in the papers and on air. On this occasion it was all because of . . . a jellybean!

Much of the negative press flowed from that and when we turned up at The Oval for the third Test starting on 9 August I sensed that there was a danger the publicity would blunt our aggressive edge. Throughout the series we had been getting stuck into India and having a go, or as Mooresy would say, a 'red-hot go'. I feared that aspect would be diminished, so we sat the players down and said that we just cannot allow these things to affect us, and that we must continue to be ourselves. If that requires a siege mentality, then so be it. I actually felt we were always at our best when we had a bit of the under-siege paranoia.

Unfortunately, we were timid on what was a very flat pitch and once the Indians had piled on 664 that was the series gone. Strangely, Anil Kumble, who I had a lot respect for, was their only century-maker on what was his last Test appearance in England. They left themselves a day and half a session in which to bowl us out and I was quite pleased that we managed to hang on for a draw with relative ease. There were none of the distractions that had accompanied the Trent Bridge match, but then we had had a little bit of the sting drawn from us.

Losing our six-year unbeaten home run in Tests was disappointing, but I had always thought that this series would be tough for us from the start, with all the changes we were making and the bowling being weakened. There were also some encouraging things to cling on to for the future. Jimmy Anderson was maturing and we had rediscovered Ryan Sidebottom, who caused Tendulkar real problems every time he came to the crease. Tremlett was a revelation in that series and he almost reminded me of Harmy in his pomp. Like Harmy, Tremlett is slightly enigmatic. Potentially he has everything, but there seems to be something in him that stops him reacting positively. He suffers quite a few niggling injuries and I think there might even be some sort of general fear of playing, but in this series I really thought we had found someone who could push Harmison into keeping his standards high all the time. That is exactly what you want in any squad, and I always believed Steve needed someone behind him to make him fear that he might not get picked next week. When he has had that little bit of anxiety he has usually come back stronger.

So all was far from doom and gloom, and there was no anticipation on my part that the really good times as England captain were soon to run out.

22

There May be
Trouble Ahead

Proof that my batting was back in full working order came at the end of the summer in 2007 when I was selected for the ICC's World Test Team of the Year. The experts' decision was, I suppose, recognition for the fact that I had made 546 runs at 54.60 during the summer. I had been overlooked for the captaincy of the ill-fated World XI that was selected to play Australia in late 2005 after I had led us to the Ashes victory, Graeme Smith being preferred instead. I had long since given up trying to follow the logic of the ICC on most things, but this was a very nice accolade and maybe better late than never. I still have the (unused) cap for the 2007 World Team hanging up in the kitchen.

Following the 1–0 Test series defeat, I had again retreated to Yorkshire and watched as Collingwood led England to an excellent 4–3 victory over India in the one-day series. I was pleased for the lads and particularly for him. This split-captaincy arrangement seemed to be getting off to a reasonable start and although the inaugural Twenty20 World Championships in South Africa in September were not quite such a success for England, they were followed by a winning one-day series in Sri Lanka prior to the three Tests. Winning in any type of cricket in Sri Lanka is not easy, so the guys deserved all the credit they received.

In all, it meant that I was away from the England set-up proper for around three months ahead of the three-Test series in December, and perhaps I was never again to be as comfortable a part of it as I had been before. I played a bit for Yorkshire, did a lot of work on my knee and had the pleasure of playing in the Dunhill Links golf championship at St Andrews, which was something I enjoyed enormously.

As far as the Test squad went, there had been talk of Mark Ramprakash coming back, and voices on the selection panel felt there might have been an argument for restoring him. I could not see that as a feasible option as it always struck me that, for all Ramprakash's brilliance in first-class cricket, something just does not click with him mentally on the international stage. I recalled playing with him in Auckland in 2002 and how, after getting out, he had just sat there in the dressing room for about two hours with his pads still on, not moving or saying a thing. 'Are you going back out there for another go?' I wondered. I just felt that he was prone to try too hard at this level and that if things did not go right he could be an unsettling influence on others. My philosophy was that it was essential to have individuals who could cope with the pressure in Test cricket when things go against you, as they often do. In the 18 months leading up to the victorious Ashes we had it absolutely spot on with the type of characters we had assembled.

Back in late 2003, when we were last in Sri Lanka, we had lost 1–0, but, looking back, I had felt that it was the first building block in the campaign to beat the Australians, purely because we had been able to identify characters who could fight. I was hoping that, four years later, the same sort of building blocks could be put in place as we looked forward to the 2009 Ashes, in which I fully intended to be captain.

There was something of a rude awakening for me, however, when I made a promotional appearance for npower in Sheffield not long before I was due to depart on the 2007 visit to Sri Lanka. I did a few interviews and all the inquiries I was getting were about whether, in light of the success in the recent one-dayers, I still thought I should be captain. I reckoned I had done a decent enough job in the summer and now, just because Colly had won a few games, I was wondering if my authority was going to be questioned every time we had some success in the shorter form of the game.

That triggered more negative thoughts in my mind and I drove home thinking that maybe Colly should take over from me as Test captain. You try not to think about these things, but in reality is it is quite hard not to. Insecurity was seeping back in, and it was on the plane going to Colombo on 16 November that I started writing my therapeutic 'diary'.

Peter Moores crops up in it regularly, such were the frustrations our relationship sometimes caused me. I should say that there were plenty of things I admired in him – such as his energy and drive, thoroughness and positive outlook. I did not think he was a bad guy but unfortunately there was not a great chemistry between us.

Contrastingly, I had had such a close relationship with Fletcher that I felt I could almost tell him anything. I did not have the same vibe with Peter, and as we had now been working together for nearly six months I sensed I never would. I know these things take time to develop, and he was perfectly entitled to have his vision about how things should be. But I felt that I wanted the team to go in one direction, with many of the guys we had used before, and he wanted to go in a fresh direction, with a brand new set of players. I was convinced that men who had enjoyed positive experiences with England before were the type we needed.

A lot of the players on the Sri Lanka tour were either new young players I was delighted with or ones I had seen before and not necessarily fancied. I went along with picking them because they deserved a chance, but I was not accustomed to having this number of lads around that I was unsure about. That added to my emerging insecurity, and so I felt I had to have some kind of confessional outlet, hence my little note-book, into which I would pour out my thoughts.

I wrote in my diary:

Do what I do. That's all that matters. Process looks after goals. Work on my balance alignment. Stance must be back on my heels. Stay upright and tall with a strong core. Quiet mindset. Let's-see-what-happens attitude. Work very hard on the basics. Lots of close underarm throws. Talk positively about the captaincy job. Play the ball inside my bubble. Play it under my nose. Don't worry about the end result, just let it happen. Enjoy the decision-making. Don't take myself too seriously in batting and captaincy. Enjoy the challenge. Train as if it's a match situation. Keep my head in the now and don't think too far ahead. These are all the things I do well when I am at my best.

Clearly it was in that period of my absence that there was a real shift in the whole running of the team, and when I re-entered the England environment I could feel the change. Maybe it was like someone who has been away on a long work trip returning home to find that the running of the household was different from when they left.

When I arrived in Sri Lanka I was basically told straight

away about all the new team directives: this is how we are
going to motivate ourselves, this is how we are going to warm
up, this is how we are going to warm down, this is how we
are going to conduct team meetings. Peter did ask what I reckoned about it all, and my reaction was to say that we already
had a formula that had brought pretty good results when we
were not weakened by injuries.

A few things had happened before the tour that had made
me a bit worried about how it was all going to work out.
Andrew Strauss was a player I loved having around, but he
had been showing signs of staleness and it was felt that he
would be best served by a break from the game while we were
in Sri Lanka. I agreed that this was probably in his best interests – that has subsequently proved to be the case – but a by-
product of going along with that decision was that I knew I
was probably going to have to give up my position batting at
number three.

I had batted there all summer and felt really comfortable
because it gives you that little bit of extra time to clear your
head of captaincy thoughts after walking off the field, rather
than rushing straight off and sticking your pads on to open. I
was not very good at instantly forgetting about what I had
been doing on the field, which bowling changes I had got right
or wrong, and being able to stop analysing the general state of
the match. So much so that I never even liked batting at number
one, because I appreciated the possible extra over you might
get from being at number two. Part of me thought opening
might be a good thing, but deep down I knew I should have
been stronger and insisted that my rightful place was number
three.

I could now get a sense of how Nasser may have felt when
he came back into the dressing room after his one-day resig-

nation in 2003. Certainly this immediately felt different from when I had come back in after my colleagues had lost to the West Indies in those three one-dayers. Now, there was a big buzz after what they had achieved in the limited-over series, and understandably so, because it was a superb outcome. The Sri Lankans had not had Murali, but then we had not had Freddie either, and there was no arguing with the result. I could sense a fizz about the lads and there were quite a lot of new personnel I was not familiar with. Fletch and I had been very big on having the right characters around the team, from the players to the support staff, to the point where we were pretty blinkered about it. I did not know whether some of these guys would have passed our test.

Certainly there could be no complaints about any lack of physical work ethic with Peter in charge, indeed it seemed that all he wanted was work, work, work and train, train, train. It showed how much things had moved on from the autumn of 2003 when we went to Bangladesh and I insisted that we should all get in better shape. Peter liked everyone to use this positive language, which was fine – provided you are naturally that type of person. On the other hand, I think it is counter-productive and tiring if you are not the type to be perpetually upbeat, and there are plenty in cricket who are not.

Personally, I was inclined to the view that this constant positive-think was all American-style bullshit, the sort of thing you read in management manuals. In leadership positions you need people who are natural and who stay on the level whether you win, lose or draw. The most important thing was to adopt the right tone at the right time as the situation demanded. Sometimes it might be a rollocking, sometimes upbeat, some-times a bit of a joke might not go amiss. A few of the players and backroom staff seemed to be talking in this forced manner, and I just wanted them to be themselves and be the naturally jovial types that they by and large were. I began to feel pretty uncomfortable with all the lingo and the constant meetings that were being arranged.

I am all in favour of positive attitudes but when it comes to planning to win a cricket match there is only so much you can do. Ultimately it is about picking 11 players and going out there and playing and taking it as it comes. There is a limit to how much analysis and preparation you can do. I remember having a conversation with Peter at The Oval in which he was excitedly stating all these things we were going to do, how there was this transition in our performances from Good to Great, and I was thinking, 'Steady on, we're going a bit fast here.' You only become great by playing consistently well for a couple of years; it is all about delivering your skills over a long period.

There were two and a half weeks' worth of preparation before the first Test on 1 December, which had been switched to the beautiful mountain city of Kandy to allow the new ground in Galle, rebuilt after the Tsunami, more time to be prepared. For whatever reason, I just did not feel in any kind of form. My physical batting technique does not change much, and for me it is all about what is going on between my ears. Negative thoughts were abounding and my preferred method of just reacting in my own bubble to the ball from the other end was proving hard to capture. I was still a little unnerved by all the hype around the one-day team at the time, and questioning whether I should be the captain after their success.

More and more changes from the way Fletch and I had run things were starting to emerge. In my absence Peter had got rid of the player management committee on tour that had been a long-time fixture and which I had always considered worked well. It would consist of three or four senior-ish guys who would control the way the squad was run in terms of things such as travel arrangements, clothing rules, how we would prepare for matches and dealing with outside commitments. The players had enjoyed ownership of what we were doing and now, all of a sudden, that had been taken out of our control.

Selection had been very much between me, Duncan and David Graveney, which would allow us, the people on the ground so to speak, to make decisive choices and get on with things. Some in the game thought we had too much power and now, thanks to the report compiled by a golf administrator, there were new rules and some of the power had shifted back to the selection panel. Whereas before with Duncan I would be able to say I want so-and-so in the team and he would nearly always say OK, now I would say the same thing to Peter and he would tell me he would take it to the selectors.

I did not resent this too much, and was not against change in principle, but I felt that many of these alterations were brought in purely to get rid of the old regime rather than replace it with something improved. I think in some ways Peter felt he had to do things differently, because by the end of Duncan's coaching reign quite a few of the players had negative things to say about some of the things he did. Some of them probably felt that Duncan had not managed them well towards the end of his tenure, not speaking to them in the right fashion or not speaking to them at all.

For me that was more to do with Fletch being stressed to the eyeballs towards the end, but prior to that his methods had been amazingly effective, overall, when we were not crippled by injuries. I think a few of the players might have had short memories on this.

After arriving in Kandy I had another session with my private confessional diary:

> I must get over the anxiety I am feeling towards myself and the game. Thinking too much about what will happen in the future. How long will I captain for? What will happen when I don't score runs? What will I do after cricket? Do I still want all this? Am I liking the new regime? I am worried about what everybody is saying about the captaincy. I will update after the Test. My state of mind must improve. I think it can now I have written down these things.

We came within 20 minutes of saving that first Test, which we had begun well by dismissing Sri Lanka for 188. Kumar Sangakkara undid us with a brilliant 152 in their second innings to set us a target of 350 for victory. We never really got close but, as he did in the first innings, Ian Bell produced another fine knock and with Matt Prior there it looked as if we would survive – before Murali abruptly ended our resistance.

The second Test in Colombo on 9 December petered out into a high-scoring draw, and I appeared to have cleared my mind sufficiently to be able to make a decent contribution with 148 runs across the two innings.

Mahela Jayawardene, who had been immovable in making 195 in their first innings, criticised us afterwards, saying that when we batted we should have done more than score 258–5 on the first day. It is all very well saying you have to be more positive against Murali, but when he has two men on the sweep there are very few boundary options against him. I think Mahela was a bit disrespectful in what he said and that, as a captain, he should have understood that we were a slightly transitional team missing a few regulars and that we were short of a few

'X-factor' players such as Freddie. Maybe we had got up his nose a bit, which is all very well, but it obviously had not worked as we just could not get him out.

During the second Test I started to give myself marks – I am wondering if I was going a bit loop-the-loop here – on various aspects at the end of each day's play: enjoyment, captaincy, batting, anxiety, positive mindset, energy levels. On day three of that Test I wrote:

> I must stop being too harsh on myself, I am obviously starting to listen to too much of what everyone else is saying.

On day four, however, my mood had changed:

> The captaincy is starting to get my anxiety levels up. I feel frustrated about the state of the game and our own players, especially Monty. Be patient and more supportive of Monty. He is under as much pressure as me.

As much as I love Monty and think he is a genuine talent, he is a really hard guy to captain. You basically have to do everything for him in terms of his thought processes. He does not have a natural way of saying, 'Right, skip, I'm going to go round the wicket and deliver this kind of over and I want this kind of field.' On a pitch like the one in Sri Lanka you want your senior spinner to have his own thoughts. I was thinking, 'Come on, Monty, you've got to deliver here for us.' I was getting too anxious about my position and so desperately wanted to win that I was making excuses and blaming other people rather than looking at myself honestly.

At the end of the game I went back to the diary:

I must realise that being stressed is all part of my position. I had a good game. Stay like this and results will follow. A good team night out.

It was a good night, but something happened that showed my personal stress levels were above normal. We had a karaoke session downstairs at the Hilton in Colombo. A few of the media came in, among them Dean Wilson, cricket correspondent of the *Mirror*, and I did not have a problem with that. But he got out a camera and started to film the players singing and I got very annoyed. I grabbed him and took him outside and told him you cannot take pictures of the lads when they are out relaxing. I thought him a decent bloke and I am sure he meant no harm by it and, while you do not want pictures taken on a night like that, it was an over-reaction from me. Another indication that I was more uptight than I should have been.

Down we went to Galle and the new stadium that had risen from the appalling human disaster of the Tsunami. It was raining all the time when we got there, so there was not much else to do but have a fret in my diary.

Struggling to focus. Boredom is creeping in as there is nothing to do at the hotel and there is no practice. I must stop being critical and irritable about little things that I cannot control.

One thing my diary did show me was that I was still passionate about the team and our performances, including myself doing well. If I was complaining, it was because I just wanted the perfect set-up for everybody to operate within. My relationship with Peter was actually going OK at this point and we had a good chat in Galle. I think he realised for the first time that we were quite an immature team. We had missed Strauss, as much as for what he offered inside the dressing room as on the pitch. That whole aspect often gets overlooked and I could hardly put enough importance on having guys around with maturity, making good decisions about themselves and going about their business in an exemplary way. The value that Strauss brought was much the same as those players who had come in for criticism, such as Ashley Giles and Geraint Jones, now also out of the team as well. For me they were bankers, the spine of the team who brought overall stability through their character. You look at that great Australian outfit and they had a whole raft of top senior pros such as Gilchrist, Hayden and Langer. If you have those pillars you can throw in around them the talented players who are mercurial and a bit less predictable.

After a rain-curtailed first day of the Galle Test on 18 December, when we won the toss and put them in and then did not get the bowling quite right in favourable conditions, I recorded:

> Felt very stressed and anxious all day. Even as I am writing this I feel desperate for success as player and captain and very uptight. Must just enjoy the game and stay in the now. Work hard before the game and then let the game take its natural course. Remember to do what I do best, support the players and don't expect too much of them or myself. Relax and play – this won't last for ever.

After day two, which they ended on 384–6 with the infuriatingly brilliant Jayawardene 149 not out, I was particularly in need of literary release:

I'm beginning to question whether I am really the right man to captain. My head is constantly aching. Thinking all the time about the bowlers. We aren't looking threatening. Monty is really starting to irritate me with his lack of cricket knowledge. Boys looking lost in the field, never streetwise, always need telling things. Keep smiling, stop feeling sorry for myself. There is nothing more I could have done. Getting 20 wickets looks a long way off in these conditions. Desperately in need of a bowler who can take batsmen out of their comfort zone, i.e. Murali, Warne, Shoaib, Tait. Someone who can unsettle the batsmen on these placid pitches. Harmy does it to a degree but only when the ball is moving laterally.

At this time I was having regular half-hour massages around my neck and head to try and dissolve the tension. Obviously things did not improve when we were bowled out for 81 in 31 overs on the third day, causing further recourse to my confessional chamber:

Mentally I was weak, fearing the good ball. The short ball, the pitch, the opposition.

At one stage on that day Giles Clarke, chairman of the ECB, had left his executive box to walk around the boundary while we were fielding. He turned to me and made a gesture lifting both arms, as if telling me that we had to raise our standards. 'Don't be a tit,' I thought. Did he not think we were trying? Back to the diary:

This is what my day has brought me to, trying to think of the team I would like to start the first Test in New Zealand [in the New Year]: Strauss, Cook, Vaughan, KP, Bell, Colly, gloveman, Broad, Sidebottom, Harmison, Monty. Once again the Sri

Lankans have proved that you need really tough characters to succeed and compete. Once the going gets tough, fragile players go missing. Mind is wandering in the field. Need to start identifying tough players with immense character like we did with Strauss, Colly and Geraint etc. Must make sure I stay upright in my stance at all times and keep my front leg away from off stump, this allows my bat to come through. Focus is the key, relaxation and self-belief.

As a captain one of the hardest things is that after a day's play you go back to your room and constantly think about all the decisions you have made. One of my issues is that I always want everything to be perfect. The trouble is, I am not. All through my captaincy, even when we had rounded off a convincing victory, I would get frustrated that we had not won more easily, that a 200-run victory had not been by an innings. I would go back to my room and beat myself up. After day four of the last Test against Sri Lanka I wrote:

Must get home and assess where I am at. We need three senior or strong characters to join the team and carry it on, otherwise mentally I could be struggling. 2008 should be a great year for me if I stay focused and relaxed and don't allow any external things to get in my mind. I have made a great comeback in 2007 and there is plenty more to come if I stay relaxed and be what I am. Not too serious, focused but not anal. Looking forward to the challenges, i.e. batting on iffy wickets, facing bumpers, captaincy, travelling, realistic, enjoyment, not over-analytical.

At the end of the Test, which ended with us batting out a draw, I invited Mark Garaway, our video analyst, and Mark Saxby, the masseur, to my room. They were backroom staff from the old regime and I always felt very comfortable using them as a sounding board. We had lost back-to-back Test series for the first time in my career as captain and I was feeling pretty low.

> Got Garrers in my room along with Sax, they were the only ones I thought I could trust. I talked to them about standing down and they told me to get home and enjoy Christmas and reconsider.

It was good advice, better than anything I was going to get from the chairman of the board. Before the Test he had invited six or eight journalists to dinner and given an interview telling them that he had some ideas for individual bonuses, saying it had come from me. However he said it, the line that appeared in the media just before the match was that Vaughan wants individual bonuses for hundreds and five-wicket hauls. I addressed this in my little black book:

> What a load of bollocks. I have never heard of something so stupid.

It was everything I disagreed with in terms of team sport. I was extremely grateful, however, for a big banner that the Barmy Army had unfurled on the last day, saying 'MICHAEL VAUGHAN, ENGLAND'S GREATEST CAPTAIN, WE'LL SUPPORT YOU EVER MORE'. That really lifted me and, as we headed home, I was more philosophical than I had been when journeying back from the World Cup. Unlike in the Caribbean, I did not feel we could have done a great deal more, and had we survived those remaining overs in Kandy, we would have come out with a drawn series. I do not care what Jayawardene might have said, that would have been a great effort.

We actually had a pretty jovial drive back to Colombo by bus before the northerners and southerners went their separate ways, as there were different flights back to Manchester and London. Peter and I had quite a good chat and agreed we needed to bring Strauss back in to add a bit of seniority to the place. I got back home to the village, our finished new home, and had a good Christmas with the family.

It helped that, in personal terms, 2007 had gone well with the bat, and I had made a return to the game that I had often thought was not possible. At the back of my mind was the concern that the selection process was moving away from where it had been. Marcus Trescothick, Strauss and Colly probably would not have played for England if everything had been based on stats in county cricket – something Moores was keen on – but Fletch had spotted the character in them to deliver at the highest level. I was worried we were going back to a more scientific reliance on figures, but around the table for Christmas lunch all that could wait a while.

23

Changing of the Guard

What was to prove my last year as England skipper could not have started in more serene fashion. Nichola and I took the family skiing in La Plagne in France in early January 2008 and watched the kids try it out, which was hugely enjoyable. I was not allowed to do the downhill stuff myself, but I tried a bit of cross-country on those impossibly narrow skis before discovering it was far too difficult. So I walked around, took the gondolas up to the top of the mountain, did some reading – it was all fairly blissful.

However, it was not long before cricket politics began swirling around in my head again and the England captaincy intruded on my winter idyll. After a few weeks of speculation David Graveney had lost his job as chairman of selectors following 11 years' service in the post. He was to be replaced by his now promoted fellow selector Geoff Miller, but it was all news to me as I had been completely unaware of the process going on. It led to more insecurities and the year's first entry in the diary while up on the slopes.

I had no contact at all from the ECB regarding Grav's position. Was not once asked what my relationship was like with

Grav. I was surprised not to get a call until after the decision
was made. I believe Giles Clarke had made his mind up to get
rid of him. Should work well with Geoff but I always have a
doubt about a vice captain or an assistant going to the boss's
job. The only concern is the new role of the chairman [of selec-
tors] since the Schofield Report. Some of his interviews suggest
he will have much more power. Quotes about team discipline,
ICL [Indian Cricket League], Ashes '05, never heard Grav
mentioned in team discipline matters, that was always left to
the management. ICL comments look like objectives from the
ECB. Giles Clarke continues to concern me. £30 million invested
into our game, £14 million into floodlights at all county
grounds. Don't see how lights at grounds is going to improve
our cricket at all.

I had basically liked working with Graveney. When I took
over as captain I did have concerns that some of my conversations with him would somehow find their way into the
media. I was fond of the saying 'loose lips sink ships'. But
over time I forged a great working relationship with both
him and Duncan Fletcher, whose relationship in turn with
Grav was always quite frosty. Apart from my first tour, when
perhaps a couple of guys were picked when I might have
gone with younger ones, generally he was understanding of
our position, so I hardly had cause to complain about him.
I had got used to having things more or less the way I wanted
them and Grav was always very supportive. What he was
especially good at was communicating to the media the
messages that we wanted to get across to a wider audience.
So it was a big disappointment to me when he left, and I
thought he was made a bit of a scapegoat. Some people who
had sat on the Schofield Report, such as Nasser Hussain,

were not mad on Graveney and maybe felt this was the opportunity to get rid of him.

Nasser had had a bit of bother with Grav, and Duncan had made it known to Nasser while coach that he was not getting on with the selectors' chairman either. But I was never asked, even though I thought that the captain and chief selector's relationship was absolutely crucial to the team's well-being. Peter Moores also seemed to have a good relationship with Grav, so I think he could have continued. Again, I think change is often a good thing, but this looked like change for change's sake. I could not necessarily see what Geoff was going to bring that David did not.

I always exercised care in my dealings with Grav and Miller. One of my strategies was that I would make excuses not to speak to them when they were physically present at cricket grounds. The reason was that if they were at a ground, they were almost bound to spend quite a lot of time in the press box, and that if you told them something it would often filter through to the media. If we spoke on the phone, I would always ask them where they were before I got into a serious conversation. I am not saying they would hand over highly sensitive information, but there was a danger that the odd thing might slip.

At this time I was still looking very much at a long-term future with England, at least as a player but probably not as captain. I said as much when I visited an npower promotion in Sheffield in early February, looking ahead to playing not just in the Ashes of 2009 but also the series that would take place in Australia 18 months after that.

It was with this upbeat ambition that I set off for New Zealand to join my colleagues, who were not managing to emulate the one-day success they had enjoyed in Sri Lanka earlier in the winter. Word had begun to reach me on the grapevine that the players were being treated slightly different from before, a bit more like schoolchildren. The word was that they were constantly being told what to do and when to do it to an over-the-top degree, which ran contrary to all my thinking.

Before I arrived the squad had been particularly demoralised by an episode that immediately followed the thrilling fourth one-day international at Napier on 20 February. The match had ended in a tie, with the Kiwis equalling our total of 340 in what the pundits would call a pulsating encounter. Having traipsed off the pitch after giving it their all, the players were then ordered by Peter to do a full training session, either there and then or early next morning before their departure to the next venue. The idea, apparently, was to show that we were somehow harder than the opposition. Our guys reluctantly decided to do the session immediately, just to get it out of the way. This sort of token display showed a fundamental lack of understanding of international sport – and to nobody's surprise it turned out the Kiwis had looked on and found it highly amusing and not intimidating in the slightest.

I always believed that if players do not know how to prepare themselves before they get to England level, they have not had the right upbringing in the county game, or they do not have the right character to deliver anyway. You cannot just spoon-feed players all the time; you have to give them some respon-sibility to make their own decisions.

This was the beginning of Peter and me really seeing things from different angles. With Duncan there had generally been agreement on the same players, just liking the look of some of them or having a feeling that we did not fancy others. Our views always seemed to coincide, for example in the contentious case of Chris Read. Fletch always found it difficult to relate to, and to coach, the guys he felt were never going to be a big part of his team. He tended to put all his energies into the men he thought were going to be big players for him and that was probably one of his weaknesses – communication with the lesser guys. But his shrewdness about cricketers' technique and character was such that it outweighed anything else.

By contrast, there were now concerns in some corners of the camp that Peter was considering making Ian Bell vice-captain in the one-dayers. Talented player though he was, I could not see any kind of leadership skills in Belly at the time, and nor could others who had been around a bit. It added to my doubts about Peter's overall judgement.

When I got to New Zealand and met up with the lads, it was clear that there was a lot of irritation with the way they were being treated. It was becoming apparent, for example, that having a day off to recharge the batteries – an essential part of successful long cricket tours – was regarded as a criminal offence. This was not an especially happy ship and that was reflected not only in the 3–1 defeat in the one-dayers, but also in the performance we put in during the first Test on 5 March. We were pretty dreadful in going down by 189 runs to a spirited Kiwi side, who made 470 in the first innings. We responded with 348, and on a turgid third day we managed just 199 runs in 93 overs. The fielding was also poor, but when we got them all out for 177 in the second innings it might have been possible to overhaul the target of 300. Instead we were dismissed for a dismal 110, and Belly scored nearly half of those runs.

'With the talent we have, to get bowled out for 110 isn't acceptable,' I said when I had to front up to the press afterwards. 'We hold our hands up and admit that we have not played a good game at all.' No mask needed on that occasion.

This came after the series defeats against India and Sri Lanka and the media piled in. Meanwhile, I was writing my own secret match report in the diary, although doubtless without the same elegance as the professional scribes:

> The team is starting to get irritated by the new management regime. Being told what to do and treated like schoolkids. I was also concerned about the captaincy and the way Peter sees the captaincy situation. Peter loves talking and having the last word.
>
> Athers [Mike Atherton] did an interview with me before the Test. He asked a lot of questions about the relationship [between me and Peter]. We lost the game badly, the team were lacking firepower in the bowling department. Harmison has been struggling for a while with his accuracy and pace. Mentally he doesn't seem strong enough either, looks like he's struggling with his confidence levels. Hoggard is really down on his pace in a three-man bowling attack. He was always a threat when he had Harmison and Flintoff and A.N. Other seamer with him. Hoggy was a great workhorse in that kind of bowling unit. Gut feeling told me after the first innings that whatever happened in the game we had to replace those two. Lost badly, so it looks like we are making scapegoats out of them, certainly Hoggy.

We moved swiftly on to Wellington where the second Test was beginning just three days later. We had decided to bring in Jimmy Anderson and Stuart Broad for our two established, Ashes-winning opening bowlers. It was a big decision but I knew it had to be made. You get an instinct for when there has to be change and it was agreed that these two were lacklustre and low in confidence, so it was the right time to bring in two younger lads to try and give us the impetus and energy we were lacking.

One of my most unpleasant responsibilities was to tell players that they were dropped. I walked over to Hoggy in the viewing area the day before the game and I said, 'Hoggy mate, you're going to be left out.' He just went, 'Right, cheers.' And that was it. 'Have you anything to ask me?' I inquired. 'No.' He walked off and I knew he was absolutely gutted. So was I, because I was close to him and he had given me absolutely everything when he played, getting the most out of his ability. He played a huge part in the Ashes and used the new ball brilliantly. It was not pleasant, and the fact that I was the one who had to break the news reinforced my belief that, on tour, selection should be down to captain and coach. I opened up to the diary:

Telling Hoggy was hard, as I know he always gave everything. Harmy knew it was coming. We have James Whitaker [selector] with us for three weeks. I believe it is a 'look good' exercise because of the Schofield Report. Me and Pete pick the team, and I have to tell the players I am not sure what he is doing here.

The Schofield Report had ordered that a selector should always be on tour and I had never been on a trip before when the captain and coach were not officially picking the team. When we had the player management committee, we used to get opinions from others about who should be picked for a particular match and then go away and make the decision. We never even used to ring home; we were trusted to make those decisions, which I thought was the right way. If you got those decisions wrong over a period of time then you would lose your job. And even with a selector on tour, it still ended up being my job to go and tell a guy who had given me everything for five years that he was dropped.

Peter and I were actually relatively fine with each other after the Hamilton defeat. I think he was relieved that I had come to the conclusion that it was right to drop Harmy. Before the series I do not think Peter was keen on picking him but I felt that he deserved a chance; we had brought him on tour and it looked as if he was doing all right. But he did not deliver. When I mentioned to Peter that I thought we should drop Harmy his eyes physically lit up, no doubt seeing it as progress towards getting a new set of players in.

Another big selection decision on that tour was whether I should carry on opening or whether we should have Strauss back in the team in his favourite spot. I wanted him back in and opening, while Peter was keen on bringing Owais Shah in, although he also wanted Strauss, but not as opener. I was a bit weak on this, and at the start agreed to go along with being opener alongside Alastair Cook, despite not being happy with it.

I went into that second Test at Wellington knowing that if we lost it I would have to resign, and at 136–5 in the first innings it was looking pretty perilous before Tim Ambrose made an excellent 102, supported by Colly, to get us to 342. Then Jimmy Anderson took 5–73 to dismiss them for 198, but still there were underlying tensions shown up by something that happened after the third day's play had ended.

We decided to warm down by having a game of football on the outfield. Everyone agreed that we should play, but then Jimmy went over on his ankle. We feared that if he did not play the next day we were going to get lynched when it came out in public, particularly after his first-innings heroics. What concerned me was the finger-pointing going on at our fitness trainer Mark Spivey, with the insinuation that he was going to be in deep shit for allowing us to play. In fact, the game had been a universal decision and it was wrong that he was automatically getting the blame. Luckily Jimmy was just about OK and we got away with it.

Our fielding was again not as good as it might have been in that match, but we still won it by a not entirely resounding 126 runs, with Ryan Sidebottom taking five wickets in their second innings. It was a great feeling to have won again after a barren run of seven Tests and this was a team young enough to be able to look forward. Nonetheless, my satisfaction was far from unreserved, as demonstrated in another private match report:

> It was exciting to captain a good young team and this is a group that could take us forward. I am still not sure how my relationship is with Peter Moores. I'm not completely trusting him. An article has appeared in the *Sun* saying that Owais Shah is not happy and I'm not sure where that has come from. Somebody has told them I don't like him, which is wrong in personal terms. There is a difference between not liking someone and not fancying his temperament at the highest level.
>
> I am finding Peter goes over things again and again rather than just getting to the point earlier and moving on. He continues to talk round in circles. Maybe it is the pressures of being coach of England. Or maybe this is what he is normally like. The batsmen are not playing their natural-instinct games and I'm starting to think it's because of the constant analysis and picking. It's very like Yorkshire at the start of my career, talking about the product rather than how to do it. Averages, stats, they just happen; the process is more important.

After winning in Wellington we had a great celebration. We had won early on the fifth morning and it happened to be St Patrick's Day, so an appropriate few glasses of Guinness were taken. There was an element of relief for me all round because I knew I had so much riding on that match.

We arrived in Napier and I was quickly back into tension mode as we began the build-up to the final Test, which started on 22 March. A pointer to my state of mind came just before the game when I had a bit of pop at John Etheridge of the *Sun*, a journalist I had known a long time and got along fine with. He had written the story quoting sources close to the England team suggesting I did not get along with Owais and I confronted him about it, quite aggressively, in the lobby of our hotel. I walked away thinking why on earth did I bother getting involved with that? I should be focusing on the match. I went upstairs to my room and outlined my private fears.

My head is filled with negative shit. What if I snick another one? What will happen if I get another low score? It's affecting my balance. No confidence in batting order. My head feels heavy and stressed. Should I go if we lose? How am I going to score runs? Blaming the environment rather than controlling what I do. Same as Sri Lanka. Must change this quickly or it is going to end. Deep down I don't want it to. Must work harder on own mentality and not get clouded and worked up by other issues. It will be better at home and there are still five days and the chance of a series win to go.

The key is for me to control my emotions. Don't get worried if other people are not doing their job properly. Remember how I felt in my comeback against the West Indies. Determined, focused, nervous, that's normal. Quiet mind, calm, very patient, excited and confident. Must keep telling myself what a good player I am and keep saying 'Be Lucky!'

The run-up to Napier had been one of the worst weeks in my captaincy career. There was a lot riding on the match and there were certain things going on around the camp that were just not professional, which added to all the stress. It even spread to the wives and girlfriends, who were out there with us. For the second match in succession I was going into the game knowing that defeat would probably mean enforced resignation.

I felt myself becoming increasingly defensive in my own team environment, and the turmoil I felt inside was reflected in my match performance. At the end of the first day we were a very average-ish 240–7 from 94.2 overs after winning the toss. I was out lbw for 2 in the fourth over to the young pace bowler Tim Southee. I got back to my room that night and felt very emotional. I also turned to the diary:

> My head is spinning, I played the worst shot of my Test career. The pressure in my head is unrelenting. I need some serious help. It is time to make some big decisions. Peter and me just does not work.

One of the issues between Peter and myself was that we were too similar in some ways. A reason I had gelled so well with Fletch was that his thinking tended to be on the safe side while I was always much more let's-have-a-go, instinctively making decisions and living with the consequences. Duncan liked to ask other people, get some views, weigh them up and debate them, while I would just say, 'Let's go with it.' Peter was bolder, a bit like me. Also, I always felt that as I was the captain leading the men out onto the field I wanted control. I still think that the England captain should have ultimate control, but Peter wanted to be in charge from the sidelines. There was an element of the perfectionist about us both. When you are winning it swims along fine, because you do not really mind anything that happens provided the results are right. When we were losing, I wanted to be the one to get us out of it in my own way, while Peter wanted to throw around instructions as well.

What I found is that he wanted to do everyone's jobs for them. So he would come to me and say, 'You are going to tell them this in the huddle, aren't you?' Duncan would never have done that; he would trust me to get on with it. I wanted to be trusted. Peter would explain the whole game scenario sometimes as if I did not understand it. He would continually quote from psychology books, or Mike Atherton's or Sir Clive Woodward's autobiography, or somebody's else's book, and I would end up thinking, 'Give me something I haven't heard before.'

I was always grateful for the support and professionalism of my team-mates and perhaps never more so than around that time. KP was in superb form and hit 129 to take us to 253 in the first innings of that match and then Ryan Sidebottom produced a brilliant spell to reduce them from 103–1 to 168 all out, finishing the innings with 7–47. Then in our second innings Strauss really proved his worth with 177 that, with another Ian Bell hundred, allowed me to declare at 467–7 and set them a whopping 553 in the fourth innings. They got to within 121 runs of it, Monty taking six and their score flattered by a late burst from Southee, a young cricketer of great promise.

My own batting contribution was just two and four, indicative of my mindset, but I was pleased overall because we had fought hard and were a young transitional team that had under-gone some key changes. It was our first away Test series win since South Africa in early 2005, and while New Zealand were not of that calibre, winning away from home is never easy and the Kiwis had some very aggressive batters. I had known that with the likes of McCullum and Oram in their ranks they were going to have a dash and if they stayed out there for 90 overs they were going to post decent totals. It was Fleming's last series and as one of the great Test captains he had really wanted to go out with a win.

It was a considerable achievement to come back and claim the series, yet on that last day as we were trying to get them out I was thinking to myself that I was really not enjoying the experience at all. I was not enjoying the system I was working in, not enjoying being captain any more. Behind the glasses and under the brim of my sunhat I was just feeling miserable. I was not myself around others, and the decision-making process had become a bind. I was actually, at certain points, allowing other players to make the decisions, which was not me at all. I was always pretty forthright in what I thought, but I was letting things take their course too much. I was declining.

It had been a really strange time. A few of the players who had been around a while saw not all was right with me and certainly some of the backroom staff did. When we won the game I had a weird emotion that I did not want to celebrate. We had just won a Test series in New Zealand and, whereas in the past I would have jumped about and made a speech in the dressing room, this time I felt very low. Peter liked to hand out these big cigars when we won. It always seemed a bit forced to me and I just did not want one. I went and sat outside instead, before going to talk to the press.

In the media I had a pop at the fact that some people had

thought the wives being around was a bad thing, as they thought had been the case in Australia on the last Ashes tour. To me that was always trivia, and although there had been a few issues on this trip, it was generally complete rubbish. When Jessica is around, for example, KP always seems to get a hundred. The more she was on tour the better, as far as I was concerned. Afterwards I went and sat outside again with a couple of the lads. I had not even made an end-of-series address to the team as a whole. I just did not feel myself.

The night before the final day of that match a few people had come to my room, guys like Colly and our masseur Mark Saxby, because I think they could sense that I might make some impulsive statement about my future after the Test. They were telling me to carry on and that I should just get home and move on.

On the night of the victory we all went out on a boat, which turned out to be quite good fun, and then, back on dry land, we went to a bar where the Barmy Army were, to thank them for their support. There was a lot of singing and my mood had lifted considerably.

The next morning I felt pretty low again and that was when, before the flight home, I went to see Hugh Morris with my concerns about myself and the coach. Peter and I had talked during the Napier Test about the future, during which my impression that he would like a younger captain was reinforced. We talked about my place in the batting order and I said that I was going to go home and think about a few things. When I spoke to Hugh I said that maybe I was the one at fault and it would be better to have a change because Peter and I were not on the same wavelength. We ended the meeting with me saying, as I had done to Peter, that I was going to get home and think about a few things and that I would speak to him in about 10 days.

Time for another personal report before we began the long journey back to the northern hemisphere:

I feel that Peter has been a little bit disrespectful to the old regime. He believes the Schofield Report and has listened to it too much. He wants to change everything including personnel. On this trip I get the feeling he would like a young captain that he can control and brainwash. I have been reading Justin Langer's book and that has convinced me that I have to come back fighting. I feel a bit better since I have told a few people that I was struggling mentally. I've been thinking far too far ahead about things. Peter's constant talk about stats and averages makes me feel uncomfortable. You sense that if you have three bad knocks your time is up. I don't think that's the case but it's the sense I'm getting – if you are not averaging x.

He wants everyone in the team to write down 100 things that could improve the standard of the team????? His style seems out of a book and not very natural. I haven't been on level 4 [the coaching course] but it seems that all coaches off those kind of courses are very clone-like. Colly, Tres, me, Strauss, Simon Jones would never have played for England in the current set-up. I just don't think we would have averaged enough to get selected. It's going to be interesting to see how Hugh deals with the scenario. He appointed Peter without really sending out the job worldwide to see who applied. He came straight from Loughborough. At the time I thought it was a great move, just what we needed, with a young English coach coming through the system. Maybe I was a bit naive.

Under my captaincy, I felt proud that we were a very professional, driven team, but also one that was at its best when we were instinctive and enjoyed ourselves. Not perfect, obviously, but close to a good combination of what I called new-school and old-school. Touring a great country like New Zealand and winning a Test series ought to be something that cricketers look back on as the time of their lives, but myself and others felt this trip had been a joyless experience. It seemed to me that during the one-day series Peter had somewhat overwhelmed and hampered Colly, who was still pretty new in the job, and not allowed him just to be captain and develop into a leader. He had not given him the confidence to lead the team in the direction he wanted.

The journey home after winning an away series was usually time for satisfied reflection and excited contemplation of what was to come in the new summer. Instead, I felt flat, and the journey north seemed to drag on even longer than ever.

24

Twenty20 Vision

When I got back from New Zealand I decided to go and seek the advice of trusted people close to me who I thought could help steer me and my troubled mind in the right direction. Neil Fairbrother, sports psychologist Karl Morris and the former Professional Cricketers' Association chief executive Richard Bevan, who had moved on to football's League Managers Association, all got a call or a visit.

I spoke to Hugh Morris further about my concerns, but already I had the mental uplift of realising that captaining England – and doubtless coaching them – is easier for everyone concerned when you are at home, because you have the luxury between matches to go off and do your own thing. It is amazing how liberating simple things like getting into your own car and having your own space can be. On tour you just see the management or your fellow players from dawn to dusk, whether it is in the breakfast room or the dressing room. My diary reminds me that for some reason it really started to bug me around this time that I had never been asked which grounds I thought would be best to play the Ashes on in 2009. They had gone for Cardiff rather than Old Trafford, which seemed incredibly short-termist to me, regardless of how much money the ECB had been offered by various Welsh authorities. When it came to Ashes venues, I really thought I was qualified to speak.

What I needed to do was focus more on how I was going to be part of that Ashes battle in 2009, which was already being so eagerly anticipated. Our battles with Australia have now been elevated in the public consciousness to such a level that it sometimes seems they are all people want to talk about in cricket. The thing that required my focus more than anything else was my batting, but my mind was in a pretty fragile state.

On 16 April I decided to play in Yorkshire's season curtain-raiser against the Leeds/Bradford university side. It was suitably freezing and while the students acquitted themselves well, it was an appalling match from a personal point of view. I got a six-ball duck in the first innings and two off 23 deliveries in the second, my only scoring shot of the whole game being an edge through the slips. I was suffering real anxieties and felt battered and beaten, my confidence in playing the ball had gone and I had lost all trust in myself to make the right decision.

I was practising very hard at Yorkshire and hitting the ball sweetly in the nets, but as soon as I got out to the middle something did not feel right. I tried to have a laugh with my team-mates about failing against the university side and dismissed it as me not being 'up' for it enough after playing Test cricket. But inside I knew it was bad, because I had been perfectly motivated to tackle the undergraduates.

The negative thoughts were crowding in on me, so I had a sit-down with Karl and we went through a few processes. We felt that my problems were not just to do with the normal cycles of playing sport but also with general mental stress levels. Unbeknown to the ECB, I also spoke with Nichola's father, Ray Shannon, who works in London coaching businessmen and top executives in lifestyle issues. I had always got on well with him and I said, 'Listen, I'm just nowhere near where I should be here, I need some help.' When I went down to see him he felt

I was in a similar state to some of those he was used to dealing with in high-stress jobs from other walks of life. We wrote down a lot of things I had been feeling and went back over the various experiences I had gone through in the previous few years. Ray actually thought I was at the relatively low end of stress cases, but we came to the conclusion that so much had been going on in my head that I was hitting a kind of brick wall.

Many of the factors seemed to stem from the aftermath of the 2005 Ashes, where a massive high had been followed by a deep-reaching low. In no particular order, they included my public visibility changing massively; the press's perception of me fluctuating with all the glory and then the injury; all the sponsors' requests needing to be met; leading the team and worrying what the team thought of me; the effort of getting fit again; the coach situation; worrying about the backroom team and their future; what to do with the money I had made. It had been an incredible ride, but clearly it had really sapped me.

We also looked at what had happened away from cricket and at my home life, which had involved getting to grips with raising a young family and the upheaval of buying a new home on which we had undertaken major renovation works. Every day you wake up and there are 10 builders around the place. You wonder when it is going to end. I had never realised, either, not just how wonderful having children would be, but how time-consuming it is. I used to play and come home, lie on the sofa, turn the TV on or read a book and basically chill out without having much worry about anybody else. That was now gone and I was coming home to two very lovely but quite demanding children, so the time to relax completely had also vanished.

This is not to say that I was anything but a very lucky man compared to most people, but the analysis made me realise just how hectic life had become. What it came down to was that I needed to relax more because I have a tendency to take myself quite seriously. I think a lot of people would regard me as pretty laid-back and fun-loving, but there is another side of me that is very much the perfectionist and if things do not go right I chip away at myself. When I meet people I often see the weakness in them before I see the strength, it is as if I have to find the weakness to see if I think they are strong or not. That is the way I am. It was always very important to me when judging a player to be able to see their strengths quickly.

Perhaps my personal debacle against the students was a blessing in disguise because, despite not getting any big early-season scores for Yorkshire, I quickly felt more calm and controlled inside after seeking Ray's help.

At this time there was one issue dominating cricket's landscape: the inexorable rise of Twenty20. The Indian Premier League was just about to make its debut amid much hype, while the ill-fated arrangement with Sir Allen Stanford and his millions was being negotiated. It troubled me sufficiently in the spring of 2008 to record more thoughts in my trusty confidant, the notebook:

Test and four-day cricket has become the least important game to the players. Test cricket will be tested to the max over the next two years because of the influx of Twenty20 competitions and the amount of money the players can earn for a three-hour contest rather than a five-day contest. In the future it could cause problems around the dressing rooms because you are going to have guys travelling the world playing five-day games mentally taxing themselves over the longer format and earning x and then guys coming in and out earning more. I was a bit sceptical about the IPL to start with, but now having seen it, it looks very exciting and something all players will want to be a part of. A very dangerous time for Test cricket, especially as the Indians are involved and they are the powerhouse of cricket. If they are backing Twenty20 it will be a success.

ECB 'sources' are telling the media that I was a part of the negotiations for Stanford and that I was not happy with getting no money. That is absolute bullshit.

I was never part of the negotiations, although I was an active member of the Professional Cricketers' Association. I was apprehensive about players earning a million dollars in one three-hour game, and all my reservations about Stanford proved to be justified. It was suggested in some parts of the media – apparently fed by the ECB spin merchants – that Andrew Strauss and I were just trying to make sure we got part of the Stanford action, which was rubbish. I was more concerned that a young player who had not done the hard yards compared to other players, i.e. working hard through the county system and getting established at international level, might suddenly get a million dollars and it could adversely affect the game and the players themselves.

Whatever else was going on in the sport, I had arrived in London NW8 for the start of another series against New Zealand – incredibly, we were playing them virtually non-stop for five months; how brilliant was that for scheduling? – in a pretty good frame of mind. Lord's is one of those places that make me feel good just by walking through the gates; I was a long way removed from the generation of England players who used to almost dread playing there. Just being inside the pavilion was a boost to my confidence because of my record at the place, and when you walked into the dressing room there were the honours boards to remind you of the place's history. On that middle Monday in May it was reassuring to see that I had already made five hundreds at headquarters. I loved practising there, the food is good, everything about it is comfortable.

On the first night I did a Vodafone function, which was being hosted by Mark Nicholas. We got on well and I think he could sense that some media pressure had been building around me, and when he asked me in private how I was I told him, in all conviction, that I was going to get a hundred in this match. I did not know why but I could just sense it. I had this vision of myself waving my bat to all corners of the ground and it stayed with me in the build-up to the match. You get that sometimes, while the opposite can also happen: you walk in and think, 'Ooh-er, I don't like the look of this.' There was also the boost of having moved back to my favourite position of number three to allow Straussy to open.

The rain ruined the match as a contest, and Jacob Oram saw to it that we could not force a win on the final day. It was a strange game for me in that I did not get to bat until the Sunday. I was still prone to get too tense, and by Saturday night, when I was next man in, I was imploring myself to relax. I felt incredibly nervous before going out to bat on the Sunday morning, and tried to reason with the situation: 'Look, you like it here, and even if this is going to be the last innings you ever play for England, just go out there and enjoy it.'

On this occasion it worked and there was a great release when I made my sixth Lord's hundred. I did not even celebrate it that much, certainly not as much as the time 12 months previously when I had also marked the first Test of the summer with a ton. Whatever my fondness for the ground, it was frustrating that I could never make a big hundred there, and after half a dozen of them my highest score at Lord's remained 120. This was not the prettiest of the collection, in fact the first 60 runs were fairly scratchy, but that was where I was at with my batting at the time. Still, I nonetheless felt I had answered some of the pre-match speculation about my position with 106, and in my 13 Tests since coming back I had now managed nearly 1,000 runs at 43.

The talk at the time was about 'cosiness' in the England camp, with too much security for places, but I did not feel I had seen or heard of anyone batting in the county game who had done enough to warrant someone else being dropped. I wanted Collingwood in the team, because even though he had not scored many lately, he offered so much to the set-up and was also one-day captain. You have to have energy-givers in any sports team, particularly in cricket, because you spend such long periods with each other, and Colly is one of those. In fact, I always thought consistency of selection was an indication that results were going OK – you don't get much consistency when a team is losing all the time.

So after the draw at Lord's it was on to another big game at Manchester on 23 May, which we won by six wickets despite putting in a pretty average performance. Ross Taylor helped them to 381 and then we collapsed from 111–1 to 202 all out. This led to another example of what put me at odds with the management regime, and again it was down to my sense that too many things were being done that seemed to have come out of a manual.

Typical of our different outlooks was that, after our poor first-innings show with the bat, Peter got the batsmen out on the balcony for a meeting to discuss how we were going to go about improving things. I just felt batting was a very individual business and that it was simply that we had to get more out of ourselves as individuals. You are out there on your own when you are batting, and I would have wanted the guys to look inside themselves and ask how they could find more in their own performance.

I would maintain that it was individual resolve that helped us chase down 294 in the fourth innings after Monty had yet again shown his love for Old Trafford by taking 6–37 and dismissing them for 114 second time around. On the other hand, Peter might argue it was that meeting. In fact, it may have been down to something more simple – a gamble based on the advice of Old Trafford's wily groundsman Pete Marron.

It was a wearing Manchester pitch and, after we finished day three on 76–1, I spoke to Pete (Marron) and asked what he thought. He suggested the heavy roller, which might deaden the wicket and help us reach our target. On the other hand there was also the risk that it could get completely raked up and make life more difficult for us. In the end I decided to throw the dice. The zip in the pitch disappeared and Daniel Vettori, who had been so dangerous in the first innings with the fizz that he was getting, was now hitting the strip and finding that the ball was dying. Having looked doomed after that first innings, we won by six wickets. Monty had got us back into it – how he would love to carry that wicket around with him (and would have loved to have it available to bowl on, with Steve Harmison, in the 2009 Ashes). Strauss made a superb hundred in the second innings, yet another example of the durable character that I valued so highly.

New Zealand were not the greatest team, but this was still a fine victory given the trouble we had got ourselves in. After our first innings I had half-expected all my anxieties to come

flooding back in, but instead they never did and I was confident we were going to wrap up another series.

Two nights before the next Test match, at Trent Bridge on
5 June, ECB chief executive David Collier rang me at the hotel
to discuss the emerging issue of the matches the board were
lining up against Sir Allen Stanford's XI. I was fed up with
talking about it, and annoyed at the insinuations that I wanted
some share of the money without necessarily playing, which
were completely untrue. I had discussed with colleagues the
possibility that young players might turn their backs on the
longer form of the game to chase the bucks in the shorter form.
Collier told me that the deal with Stanford had to be signed
the next day or the whole thing would be off – they were clearly
desperate to do the deal. The Professional Cricketers'
Association needed to endorse the agreement, with the impli-
cation that it would all be our fault if it did not come off.

As one-day skipper Colly was also being consulted although,
like me, he was trying to focus on the upcoming Test. I just
said that as far as I was concerned he could sign it. I was not
going to be the one who stood in the way of my colleagues
making a fortune. Also, if I had kicked up a stink I was worried
that the Board would brief against me again, saying that I had
stopped the deal going through. Collier hardly ever spoke to
me as captain, which I thought strange, considering the huge
importance of the national team to the English game's well-
being as a whole. The players ended up signing the Stanford
deal – the ECB run the game and really there was little option.
A side letter from the players' lawyers Harbottle & Lewis stating
the concerns of the team was sent when the contracts were
signed.

We played really well in that Test, KP hitting 115 in our first
innings and then Jimmy Anderson further justifying the decision

to prefer him to Hoggy or Harmy by taking 7–43 as we routed them for 123. Sidebottom finished them off with 6–67 to give us the win by an innings and nine runs. It is an indication of my recently repaired state of mind that around this period I did not feel any urge to purge myself with random scribblings in my notebook. I felt we were progressing pretty nicely as a team, and we would still hopefully have Freddie to come back and strengthen us.

As a unit we were bubbling and there had been none of the pressure that was so easy to sense around the second Test, though Andy Flower, the assistant coach, showed tension a bit more than I expected and would walk around the dressing room and kick the odd thing. I thought Peter and I were getting on better, but I had always expected that to be the case in England. I would not have to spend six weeks' worth of breakfasts with him and could get away from the coaching regime and its relentless grind. At any meal situation I preferred to sit with my mates rather than get bombarded with intensity.

Our end-of-series celebration was a relatively sober affair, partly because I think all our attentions were switching to the forthcoming encounters with South Africa. (It might also have been that we were sick of the sight of New Zealand, and doubtless vice versa.) I always felt that for the big teams like South Africa we needed our big guns and it was not going to be enough having Colly as our fifth bowler. This was another difference between Peter and me – I was instinctively in favour of five-man bowling attacks and he felt more comfortable with four. I personally believe you can only have four bowlers when you have someone truly special – a Warne, Murali or Mushtaq (who was at Sussex with Peter) – someone who can be guaranteed to hold an end for long periods. My concern was that your seamers can get burned out on days one and two. As it turned out, selection shenanigans were to mark my final phase as England captain.

During the one-day internationals I went off to have a dabble at Twenty20 cricket with Yorkshire. I wanted to have a go at it, excited at the prospect of trying something new. I also thought I needed to keep playing because, given too much time to think, I might allow the negativity of earlier in the year to seep back in. The strange thing was that, having gone into the Twenty20s thinking I would just give it a bit of a blast, I started to take it a bit too seriously and put pressure on myself again.

It was partly down to nothing more than there being big crowds and wanting to impress them like everyone else. Apart from being pleased to see my Yorkshire mates again, I was always fascinated to see what the mood was like in a county dressing room. My colleagues were very, very switched on for this because there was potentially plenty at stake and it was impressive what a focused environment the dressing room was. We played a great game at Old Trafford against Lancashire on 20 June, where it felt like an international. It can only be a good thing, the younger ones playing in that kind of atmosphere. The skill levels were high, the pressure real and the fields were inventive. It is hard to argue that it is anything other than a great spectacle, and it could take over the cricket world if we are not careful.

I also studied the county cricket schedule around that time and it confirmed my fears about how little preparation time there was for one-day skills to be honed. We had fun, Goughy was captain and playing under him was interesting. Once, when he was training for *Strictly Come Dancing*, he put this DVD on in the dressing room during a match and we all started practising his routines with him.

I rated Goughy as a captain. He liked to listen to ideas and came up with a pretty good system, which is the key to winning these games. We would have Hoggy and Tim Bresnan with the new ball, Adil Rashid would spin it and Goughy himself would always bowl the last four from one end. When batting, the top three would try to gun it, Anthony McGrath and Jacques Rudolph would bat normally, then six to eight would try and hit the sixes. Realistically, we did not have quite enough six-hitters to win the competition, because it is the team with the largest number of them that usually triumphs.

While the Twenty20 domestic competition was unfolding, my international colleagues were not having it all their own way against New Zealand in the one-dayers, the final part of our ludicrous home-and-away marathon against them. The boys were slipping to a 3–1 defeat and from afar it looked as if there were a few strange selections. Cricket's ever-buzzing grapevine was telling me that the ship was not entirely happy.

Although I was not directly involved, this still had the effect of irritating me because as captain I had always been used to getting pretty much the team I wanted and expressing myself in decision-making. That was not happening with my mate Colly at the reins. I was baffled about Phil 'Colonel' Mustard being dropped as keeper and Tim Ambrose being inserted down the order when he just did not look that type of player. I thought Mustard deserved another chance and, although I thought he had ability, I was unsure about Luke Wright, another Sussex player, opening at this level in English conditions. I am not sure that Mustard was the new regime's cup of tea as he was, perhaps, not the most ultra-professional player, but I reckoned he had talent and some bottle.

Back in the county game, I was being reminded of how bizarre the mid-summer calendar can be. We had qualified for the

Above: The start of a long and painful road: wrenching a knee during the warm-up match in Lahore.

Right: Visiting net practice during the Pakistan series in 2006, with (*l–r*) Kirk Russell, Steve Bull and Duncan Fletcher.

I have always enjoyed playing the Dunhill Links Championship. Pictured here with Darren Clarke, Lee Westwood and Chubby Chandler.

Our last match at the 2007 World Cup was my final one-day international and Brian Lara's farewell for the West Indies.

Monty Panesar dismisses Dwayne Bravo at Old Trafford, his favourite ground.

Ryan Sidebottom had a second coming in his England career.

Alastair Cook offers congratulations after we beat the West Indies in 2007 to put my captaincy win record ahead of Peter May's.

Chatting to David Graveney at Kandy in Sri Lanka in late 2007 before his reign as chief selector came to an end.

Conversation with Peter Moores and Steve Harmison in Wellington. We were to drop the latter the following day.

practice with my close mate Paul Collingwood at Hamilton.

e look at the big screen at Trent Bridge for the third umpire's decision on Brendon
cCullum in 2008.

Left: Archie and Talulla Vaughan on the outfield at Trent Bridge after winning th series against New Zealand.

Below left: A lap of honour after what turned out to be my final series win.

Below right: Golf at Woburr This is now the only way yo are likely to see me in sporti action.

...esignation. Not a great feeling knowing you are about to blub on national television.

...nowing his temperament, the success ...Stuart Broad in the deciding Test v ...ustralia in 2009 did not surprise me.

Andrew Strauss led brilliantly with the bat and as captain in the final Test.

Able to relax with Jonathan Davies and Darren Gough during the first Ashes Test at Cardif

Artballing involves creating contemporary art by hitting cricket balls onto canvas. I really enjoy it and it helps raise money for prostate cancer charities. This painting is titled 'Monday 12th September 2005'.

Twenty20 quarter-final and then went back to four-day cricket from Monday to Thursday at Headingley, before having the Friends Provident Trophy semi-final at Chelmsford on the Saturday, 5 July. I played the four-day match against Durham but sat out the last session because I felt a bit of a strain in my leg. I needed to rest over the weekend before meeting up with the Test squad on Monday to prepare for South Africa.

Some people at Yorkshire were unhappy I was missing the semi-final, though coach Martyn Moxon understood that to travel down south on the Friday before a Test the following Friday with a slight niggle was not the best preparation. I was also aware that I was still not committed properly to 50-over cricket and to a certain extent had put it to bed in my mind. In any case, neither Martyn nor I was convinced how much of an asset I would be. I had just made a decent 72 against Steve Harmison at Headingley in the County Championship game and felt in a good state of mind for the Test match.

There was a local hoo-ha and Yorkshire's chief executive, Stewart Regan, started causing ructions about it. He came over to the dressing room demanding to know why I was not travelling to Chelmsford and I told him, 'Listen, mate, you have got to start understanding me a bit better.' I always felt very committed to Yorkshire, but as England captain, compromises inevitably had to be made, and I am not sure he could ever quite get that. The big Test series of the summer was coming up and, apologies if it sounds selfish, but I had to focus all my energy on that.

In that match against Durham I was able to have a really good look at Harmison as he bowled an excellent 12-over spell at me, and for the first time in a while I thought he was getting back towards his best. He was bowling pretty straight and achieving some decent gas, so I resolved that I would try and get him back into the England squad. In fact, he did not make it when the squad was announced for the first South Africa Test on 10 July, and in truth it would have been very hard to drop Broad, who I rated extremely highly as a bloke and a cricketer. Ditto Jimmy Anderson and Ryan Sidebottom after what they had done so far in 2008. As Fred was out, this time with a side strain, Colly was going to be the fifth bowler behind Monty. I went along with the selection as the other bowlers deserved their places, but deep down I was still holding to my big-guns-for-big-teams theory, and I knew we would have to go back to Harmison.

I arrived at Lord's and although that gave me something of the usual uplift, I was aware that my mood was not as stable as it might be. Any failure at the crease had been severely knocking my confidence, while if I had a good net or a half-decent innings it was soaring to an unreal level. In the first innings of the Test I got an absolutely beauty from Dale Steyn that knocked my off peg out and while, rationally, I knew it was just one of those things, it hit me pretty hard.

On the Monday before the Test I had done a presentation in front of the players to try and get some goals established and to pass on my experience of playing South Africa. The gist of it was that the South Africans always talk a very positive language and come out with big statements, but that they often do not match their words with actions. Basically, I did not consider them as tough as they thought they were. I emphasised the fact that if we could win the first couple of sessions, then they would go into their shells a bit, which was what had happened in the recent past. Graeme Smith and Jacques Kallis looked to be their mainstays in the batting, and in the bowling Morne Morkel was not quite the big, aggressive South African that he looked. I knew from spending a bit of time with him during his brief spell at Yorkshire that he was a nice, gentle giant. My secret fear for the series was that we would not get 20 wickets.

With the Lord's pitch flatter than ever, we got 593, despite my 'failure', thanks to a massive stand of 286 between Belly and KP. We made them follow on after getting them out for 247, but then we just could not remove them in the second innings, with Graeme Smith, Neil McKenzie and Hashim Amla all getting hundreds. I was moving the field around, changing the bowling and trying everything to make things happen, but they stubbornly refused to budge, and this had quite a profound effect. I thought, 'This is really getting to me,' and I could feel myself becoming unusually anxious and uptight as they comfortably held out for a draw with seven wickets still intact.

It convinced me that we needed Harmison and Fred back as soon as possible in a five-man attack. The last day was considered deadly dull by a lot of people and unfavourable comparisons were being made between Test cricket and the shorter form of the game. It was our sixth draw in a row at Lord's and the engraver for those honours boards for hundreds scored there must have been finding more and more employment. Some of the spectators were not happy, but we had tried our best on a lifeless strip.

My concern was that the bowlers would be tired as we headed north for a Friday start at Headingley, unaware of just how much of an issue the make-up of our attack would become.

25

The Decision to Go

What turned out to be my penultimate Test as captain was preceded by a few of the strangest days I ever had in the job. Many will remember that Headingley match starting on 18 July for the inclusion of Darren Pattinson, the Grimsby-born Australian fast-medium bowler and sometime roofer, who was playing for Nottinghamshire and approaching his 29th birthday. We had announced that Freddie was finally ready to come back in and I had said that he would be batting at seven, but there were so many injuries floating around in the build-up to the game that I could not get my preferred final XI sorted out in my head.

Chris Tremlett was in the squad but I now wanted Harmison back, as our Durham Ashes winner was looking so potent in the County Championship. Again it seemed to me that there was a concerted attempt to make us look as if we were going forward for the sake of it by persisting with Chris, when in my view Harmy was ready for a recall. I always thought a fit and firing Harmison – admittedly not always adjectives that applied to him – was worth his place. Ryan Sidebottom was a bit sore after Lord's, but in the showers the day before the match he said he would be fine to play so I did not have a worry about him. Jimmy Anderson, however, was going for a precautionary scan on his back, which was feeling a bit stiff. So there were numerous dilemmas around and if there was one thing I found unsettling the day before a Test, it was not knowing the team.

In the immediate build-up to a Test you want clear messages going out to everybody, and absolutely the last thing you need on the morning of the first day is any confusion. But on that Thursday afternoon (it was a Friday start) the picture was unclear and the phone calls were flying around. Peter Moores brought up the name of this guy Pattinson, who had been mentioned when discussing the team for the Twenty20 international against New Zealand and a little bit in conjunction with the summer's one-dayers. I said that, knowing Headingley, we needed someone who could get it up there and swing the ball because in the first two days the conditions would be green. We had Broad and Flintoff to hit the deck, Sidebottom or Anderson to swing it and we needed one more bowler on standby to pitch it up and swing it.

We went through other names. I thought of Simon Jones and was told he was not fit, although Simon was sending text messages saying he was. (Apparently he really was not, so that was a bit disappointing.) Kabir Ali got a name check but I was not sure he was quick enough for this level. So it came back to Pattinson and I said I had only faced him for three balls in a Twenty20 match, and that if he is the next best pitch-it-up swing bowler, then let's go for it. I would still have preferred Harmison, but remember that Pattinson got the call without me thinking that he would actually play.

On the Friday morning at breakfast Darren walked in and introduced himself. I felt a bit sorry for him because he had had no preparation whatsoever, but with Jimmy fit it did not look as if he would be needed anyway. After getting up to the ground Ryan went to the indoor school for a quick bowl and came out, around 9.45 a.m., to announce that he would not be fit due to a back spasm. That threw a spanner in the works, because I had told Colly the night before that, assuming Sidebottom was fit, he would be left out, but that if he made a late withdrawal then Colly would be in. It was my mistake telling him that too early and perhaps I should have waited, but I wanted to keep him in the picture. My gut feeling at 9.45, however, was that we needed five bowlers, as Fred was coming back from injury and the others were probably still feeling the effects of our marathon in the field at Lord's a few days before. Given my lack of confidence in Tremlett, my instinct was to go with Pattinson, and I had to go back and announce the side with barely an hour to the start.

Leaving it this late is always highly unsatisfactory, as it sows confusion among the guys, and especially so in this case as Colly was such a popular member of the team. Also, it did not look good because Tremlett was in the squad originally. It was reported that picking Pattinson was a major problem for me, but in the end I cannot, in all honesty, say it was. Understandably, a great deal was made of it by the media, fuelled partly by the small detail that Darren was not really English at all.

The more frustrating part to me was that I felt that Geoff Miller went missing for those few days and was not being the voice of selection when we needed him to be. He just seemed to disappear, and I was left at the end of the game being quoted about all the confusion. Apparently, I was caught by the stump microphone during the middle of the match making an adverse comment about the selectors being too fond of relying on statistics. While I do not specifically remember that, it is entirely possible that I did indeed come out with something along those lines. I actually thought Darren did pretty well, as it happens. What stuffed us all out of sight was his dad coming out and saying that he was a fair-dinkum Aussie, something that was not very helpful to anyone, his son included. I felt for him because the whole thing must have been fairly surreal, and you could hardly blame him for wanting a taste of Test cricket.

The first day of that match was as eventful as the last two days at Lord's had been dull. In the morning AB de Villiers claimed to have caught Strauss at third slip, which was clearly not the case when viewed on TV. We had a bit of a ding-dong about it at lunchtime when a few of us asked him if he thought we were playing one-hand-one-bounce. Mickey Arthur, their coach, blew it out of proportion later by saying we had had a big pop at AB, which I did not think was the case. Later in the day, when we had them three down and in a bit of bother, I dived forward at mid-off to take what I thought was a perfectly legitimate catch from Hashim Amla. He got reprieved after starting to walk off and then being told to stay out in the middle by team-mates. In the game, we all know that TV always shows these catches to be less out than they actually are, some-thing to do with the camera angle and magnification technique, but I knew it had gone straight in.

The Amla incident came at a crucial time. I have always been a great believer that you create your own luck, and this was adding to the sense that mine was running out. Maybe it was weak, but I was feeling that I was losing big tosses and that things were just not going my way. I had enjoyed my fair share of good fortune in my captaincy career, but now things were not happening as they should, in field placings, for example. At times, I had thought I had a magic touch in bowling changes and field placements and now it seemed that whenever I moved a slip out of the cordon, the ball would automatically fly through the gap. At least that was what I was telling myself.

I went back to my diary for the first time in a while to look back on the day's play:

> When I am bad is when my mentality is bad. I felt very stressed. My head was very tight. Worried about making a score. Can already hear people criticising my failures before I have even batted. Can already hear and see people saying 'God, he's done it again, maybe he shouldn't be in the team.'

In that series I experienced what must be the worst feeling for a batsman. It sounds awful, but when I was out I actually felt happy to be off the pitch and out of the firing line. I was sitting in the dressing room feeling pleased to be back in the shed. That is a very lonely feeling, when you just have no sense of confidence at all. I felt very isolated that night in the Leeds Marriott, wondering if I had lost the ability to play international cricket. All the targets and goals I had set myself – it was very important for me to have things to aim at – had become a blur. I became scared of setting targets because I knew I would be very hard on myself for not reaching them. And the most frustrating thing was that I could not understand how all this had come about.

Painfully, de Villiers's 174 was the central plank for their 522 in response to our first-innings 203 all out. It was the exact anniversary of Bob Willis famously bowling out Australia in the great 1981 Test, but there was no other connection as far as England's performance was concerned. We ultimately struggled to make them bat again despite some impressive fight from Broad, and they won by 10 wickets on the fourth day. I went in to see the press, annoyed that I had to be the first person to come out and discuss all the complications surrounding the final XI. I was pretty honest on this occasion and referred to the confused selection. 'We didn't feel as much of a unit this week, and I have a plain belief that you have got to be a unit in Test cricket,' I told the media.

The next day, after the headlines had reported me having a go about selection, I had a call from Geoff saying that he wanted to come and see me. At the same time the selectors, who now included my great mate Ashley Giles, had an emergency meeting at Loughborough. I was not entirely convinced whether Geoff could see what it takes to be a high-class Test player in this era, although he could spot talent, which is not quite the same thing. Geoff came to my house and told me that I had to explain my comments. To which I replied, 'Well, why don't you explain your lack of comment?' Geoff told me he had endured a torrid four days and been stressed with it all, but I had to point out it was part of our job. James Whitaker had apparently been very upset with some of my quotes, and that wound me up because James never does press conferences and does not have to stand in front of a phalanx of media and explain himself. Of course I made mistakes in my public utterances, but I did so many press conferences it was unavoidable occasionally. But the meeting with Geoff was amicable enough in the end, and we parted agreeing that we would try not to make any more mistakes and get on with winning the last two Tests.

That night I told Nichola that whatever happened in those next two games, even if we won them, I was going to quit. When you are in a stressed frame of mind it feels as if every phone call is a battle, and although I knew I still had so much to be thankful for, the aggravation levels meant I had had my fill of being the England captain. It was time for a new approach and a new leader. While our relationship had improved on the whole, Peter and I were still not matching up brilliantly, although I could see his virtues and that, just possibly, he might work well with someone else. With my style of leadership it was not working and so a change would be for the best.

It had all been starting to take its toll on how I was at home. We would have friends round and it was as if I felt detached. I was worried I was coming across as some kind of weirdo. I would be playing with the children and occasionally be miles away, thinking about whether I had made the right field change at a certain point, or working out whether a certain player would be best for us to pick. This was not unusual, but it felt more extreme now. I felt like a zombie inside, and all I wanted to do was sit down and retreat inside myself, even when the children were around – 'Can you not just give me five minutes?' Then I would beat myself up for being a less-than-perfect dad. When I walked down the street I was thinking, 'Can they see how much I'm struggling here?' I was starting to hate the game, and the appetite for battling and fighting that had served me well had left me. At the same time, I was training as hard as I had ever done, but it felt empty. I became a bit uncomfortable around people I did not know well, so anyone unfamiliar probably found me rather distant because I had stopped trusting outsiders.

The next day (Wednesday) the team was picked for the third Test to start at Edgbaston on the Thursday of the following week, 30 July, and we agreed that Harmison should come back in, with Tremlett and Pattinson out. The word was that it was going to be a turning pitch, on which Monty would bowl a lot of overs. The team was sorted, or so I thought. On the Thursday I went down to play in a sponsors' golf event at Wentworth and on the way back I spent 45 minutes talking to Peter on the phone. The team was being announced the next day but he was now trying to convince me that Harmy should not come in after all. He was worried about how he would fit into the new set-up, and while I could see his point in a way, I still thought he was preferable to Tremlett. I had nothing against Chris, but could never see him being a world-beater, while we all knew what Harmison could do when things were right for him.

I could still see Harmison, for example, doing major damage in a future Ashes series and made that point. He said he would take my thoughts to the selectors. A few minutes later Collingwood rang me from the Durham team bus that was heading to the Twenty20 final in Southampton. 'How are you?' I asked. Colly replied that he had received the phone call from Geoff Miller and that he was back in for Edgbaston. Oh great. I wondered if Harmison had received a call. Colly asked him and he confirmed that, yes, he had been told that he was back in the squad.

So I rang Peter back to ask why we had been discussing all this when Harmy had already been told he was back for Birmingham. There had been a complete lack of communication; Geoff had apparently thought he might as well get on with telling them so had already broken the news. It had been a good 45 minutes for Vodafone's profits but a bit of a waste for me at a time when I was trying to switch off. I turned round to Craig Sackfield, who worked for my management company and was driving at the time, and snapped, 'This is what I am dealing with here!' Our whole set-up did not feel a cohesive unit, rather like the situation I had referred to at Headingley.

I was undoubtedly getting over-sensitive at this point and it was as much my fault as Peter's that I was getting so tetchy. It had reached ridiculous levels by the time we arrived at Edgbaston for my last few days in, supposedly, the best job in the world. After the first night in Birmingham I went down to the breakfast room at the hotel and saw that the coach was already in there. I decided that I just could not face sitting with him and getting straight into intense cricket talk, so I went out to the reception and pretended that I was discussing something to do with my bill – until a couple of the lads came out of the lift who I wanted to sit next to and I went in with them.

One factor involved was that I thought there were so many coaches around it did not feel like a team at all. I was sure it was breeding a lack of self-reliance and a feeling that if, as a player, you were struggling, you would have someone on hand to call for help rather than trying to help yourself. Coaches can be crutches. When we were good I felt that there were just 11 players and Duncan Fletcher as coach, with some support in the background. Apart from Peter, we now had Ottis Gibson (bowling coach), Richard Halsall (fielding) and Andy Flower (batting), who I thought were all very good people with great knowledge, but it just seemed too many in the dressing room along with all the others. Sometimes we even had two people around just to deal with the media.

My issues were soon put into perspective when, two days ahead of the game, Colly and I paid a visit to the military hospital in Birmingham where soldiers who have been injured fighting in places like Afghanistan are sent. It was a huge eye-opener, meeting these guys with limbs missing, shrapnel inside them, with bandages all over their bodies. One guy had been in a truck that had been blown up and he showed us the DVD of it actually happening. It was staggering. Some of the stories were terrifying, yet they spoke as if what had happened to them was almost funny. Some of them were desperate to go back there.

It showed how utterly trivial our exploits on a cricket field were, and it served as another reminder to be very grateful for what I had and to be determined to go out to do my best.

There was still a problem, though, with my confidence as captain, and the fact that I knew I was stepping down – still nobody knew except Nichola – was affecting me. I spoke to the players before the match, but whereas I used to feel that their ears would prick up when I opened my mouth, I now thought they were switching off a little. There are only so many times a group can listen to the same voice.

For the final XI at Edgbaston we brought Collingwood back in and left Harmison out. I wanted Harmison back around the squad in preparation for The Oval, where I was sure he would play, but on this occasion having four bowlers plus Colly felt more comfortable because we were sure Monty was going to bowl a stack of overs. Anyway, despite loading the batting we did not get as many as we should in being bowled out for 231.

I got a first-baller and was given out caught behind despite not having hit it, and as I walked off I thought that it must be happening for a reason. In reply they made 314, which included, late on the second day, a magnificent spell of ferocious fast bowling from Fred to Kallis that was reminiscent of his heroics against Ricky Ponting at the same ground three years previously. Ironically, for me of the wounded knee, I was to finish off their innings by sprinting and diving like a gazelle to catch Mark Boucher in the covers.

That second evening I travelled back to the hotel with Colly, who had made only four more than I had in the first innings. I knew he had not been especially enjoying his job as one-day captain. 'You're struggling, aren't you,' he said. So I finally told him I was going to go at the end of the series. He said, 'Don't do that, because I'm going to go as well.' I burst out laughing. I thought, 'Wow, this is going to create some waves – a double resignation.' It spoke volumes of the state of Colly's communications with Moores that he went straight to Hugh Morris to give him the news, bypassing the man he had been working with as coach.

I actually thought it would work out for the best and mean we could go back to what I always believed was the most satisfactory arrangement – one captain for both teams. Colly was at a very low ebb with his batting and his general level of confidence, so I asked him just to go out there in the second innings and have a dash – try and hit fours and have a real go. Even if you fail, it cannot be worse than it is now. 'You and me, we'll go out together and have a little fun,' I said.

I scored 17 off 18 balls with four fours and I thought I was up and away before Amla took a fine catch at short cover to get rid of me. Colly took me at my word and formed a wonderful partnership with KP of 115 in 23 overs. They really dominated for a while and it was the kind of authority you loved to see as a captain. I hated it when the opposition took it to us, so I loved the Pietersens and Flintoffs who could go out there and really club them. I thought KP and Colly were taking the game away on this occasion, only for Kev to get out on 94 trying to hit Paul Harris for six. There was a little bit of a kerfuffle in the dressing room, asking why did he do that, but I did not think we could complain too much – you get the whole package with KP. Colly made 135, and I thought my captaincy career was going to last one more match because we were going to win.

The target was 281 and, given the South Africans' tag as chokers and the match's significance, it looked relatively steep for a fourth innings. They got off to a decent start but then Freddie got Neil McKenzie and Kallis lbw and they were quickly 93–4. The match situation was looking good as we approached tea, and I was thinking we were going to take this down to the wire at The Oval, where we have a great record against South Africa. I thought it would turn out to be an unbelievable series win and I would sign off with a fairy-tale victory.

I had reckoned without Graeme Smith, the man whose colossal innings had seen off Nasser Hussain in his last Test and was now about to dispense the same dose to me. He had been a right pain in my opening Test in charge five years ago as well, making a double hundred, and here he was again, on his way to a towering unbeaten 154. What had changed since then was my opinion of him. I thought he had matured considerably and I had come to admire the way he dealt with all the unique off-field issues in South African cricket.

We still had a decent chance when Colly caught de Villiers to make them 171–5, and you wonder what might have happened before that, had Monty and Tim Ambrose appealed properly when Smith looked to have given a catch to our gloveman off his finger. There had also been a decent lbw shout, but now he was in with Boucher, another pain in our backsides over the years, and there was nothing we could do to halt their advance.

In my desperation I kept throwing the ball to Freddie, and Monty bowled with skill for not much reward because Smith was playing him so well. There was the odd possible chance but the little things that used to go my way were stubbornly refusing to. I took all these as signs that my decision to go was the right one, plus the fact that my great friend Collingwood was going too.

And then Smith hit that ball past me when I was fielding at mid-on, to take them within 20 runs of victory. I knew it was all over. I was about to walk back to the pavilion for the last time as England captain.

*

It was the following afternoon, after I had made my resignation announcement at Loughborough and was enjoying the barbecue at home with a few friends and family, that KP rang to say that he had been offered the job as England captain. He asked what my future plans were, and I told him that at that point I simply did not know. One thing I made clear was that he needed to sit down with Peter and work out exactly where the boundaries were on management issues and on who had the final say on preparing the team.

A few days later I went back to my diary to unburden myself again:

I feel very relieved and glad it's over. What's next, TV, business, playing for Yorkshire? Playing for England? I didn't want the players seeing me in a bad way or changed from what I have been like the last five years. It was a sad day for English cricket that on my last day against South Africa I saw Jonathan Trott celebrating with South Africa, when the week before he had been our twelfth man at Headingley. I was going into the press conference and I saw him patting them on the back. It hit home what English cricket has become like. KP has got five bowlers for his first Test, which is what he wanted, that's a good start.

I was hung-over from the Saturday night and hid it very well at the press conference. Cried all morning. Very emotional. Not because I wasn't sure but because I was relieved it was ending. Hundreds of letters of support, texts from all over the world. Did not once think about the future. Just happy to be home with all those pressures having been relieved. On the Monday [day after] bought all the papers for the first time in years. Athers and Nass wrote brilliant articles, still very happy.

On Tuesday a day out with Archie, and Peter rings to ask about paper reports about a so-called rift between me and him. They do not miss a trick! I have to be very careful as I may want to get back in the team.

This was the first time since I'd taken over that I didn't have to spend at least some part of each day either ringing someone from the team or watching something on TV to do with who we might play. Nor was I sitting down and worrying about some situation that might or might not unfold. This is what had been building up inside me all the time and the only way I could get rid of it was to tell someone about it. I believe there are so many cricketers who get similar stress issues but bottle it up inside, and then over time it builds into something they cannot control. Maybe that is what happened with my friend Marcus. I had reached the stage where I had to get out and find some help in controlling these stress levels.

But for now the only thing on the agenda was a trip to a nice hotel on the Algarve with Nichola, where I happened to bump into Austin Healey, who let it slip he had been picked to go on *Strictly Come Dancing*. It was a pleasant enough few days but I knew that I was just not right in myself. The final South Africa Test was going on at The Oval and I had a bizarre inner conflict of wanting to check the score but at the same time switching channels when the sports bit of *Sky News* came on in our room. I found interviews with players hard to watch because I was so aware of how they were putting on an act. If anyone did well I would text them, I could not help myself.

Upon getting home I spoke again to Nichola's father Ray, who sent me to see a homeopath he knows named Simon Tapler, who is based in London.

I was initially very sceptical about seeing a homeopath;

I thought he might be a witch doctor and that probably all I needed was a bit of time out. But when I spoke to him I found it very refreshing, discussing real-life things in a non-cricket context. We went through everything from my injuries to my posture, which was not great. My knee issues, back issues, dealing with moving homes, kids, doing up the house, all these things were adding and creating this tightness in my head.

We also spoke about diet, about cutting down my heavy consumption of coffee and tea because my blood-sugar levels were going up and down all over the place, and cutting out dairy products because he feels it damages your joints. Every day I used to drink about five lattes and loads of milkshakes, plus eat a chocolate bar or two. So they all had to go. I had been told this by people around the England set-up, but to be honest I had ignored it because I did not think it was that important.

Within a few days of cutting out the caffeine I had horrendous headaches. He also sent me away with a couple of herbal remedies, and something did the trick because quickly it seemed to take away a lot of the fuzziness I felt in my head.

But then I made the mistake of trying to get back playing for Yorkshire again too soon. I felt I had to show people that I could come back and play among the rank and file. The team were in a relegation battle and that made me want to play more. I only gave myself two and a half weeks between resigning and playing again at Scarborough, having not had much practice. I thought I would be OK because I usually played best when supposedly fresh, but when I arrived at the ground on the first morning I knew I should not have been there. My mind was not on it and I did not play well, finding myself really irritated by some of the supporters who did not have a clue what I was going through. Then again, they did not have access to my diary:

> More remedies. Getting better. It's almost as if I am scared of anyone getting to know me. Maybe I'm more of a loner than I think I am. Feel as if I always want to sleep, always tired. All the criticism from the Ashes 2006–07. Should I be there or I should I be at home? All the critics, I started to believe them. I had lost confidence, and I made safe decisions. I believed them when they said I had lost it. My best days are behind me. All summer I have struggled to stay positive and questioned myself. Am I good enough? Why should I continue? That's it, I'm finished. I don't need this any more, it would be easier to finish. Negativity and self-doubt have flooded my mind for a while.

There were loads of stories coming out about my future, whether I was going to leave Yorkshire, become a commentator, quit cricket altogether, but none of it had come from me. A woman came up to me just before I went out to bat and asked me if I was about to sign for Hampshire. For some reason that really wound me up and my stress levels, which had been pretty good, suddenly started to go through the roof again.

Playing for Yorkshire is never relaxing, as it is about as near as you can get to playing for England because the support is so fanatical and there is so much history and tradition. Boycott was stirring things up, having a go at Martyn Moxon and at me, asking why I was not scoring runs. Usually with things like that I would just laugh, just as I would when I got stick fielding on the boundary, but it was really irritating me this time. I had three games in all at Scarborough and while I felt I had a bit of rhythm in my batting, my brain was wandering. Rather than being focused on the job of delivering runs, I was thinking about having a bit of fun with my mates and playing in the casino at night.

I did not really start to feel right until I decided that it would be best for me to rule myself out of England's looming tour of India. I had gone to Loughborough for a fitness session and spoken to Mooresy, who told me not to worry too much about putting a score on the board. That was good to hear and I thought maybe he had changed his philosophy. But it was actually during the game against Somerset when Tres was there that it all became clear. He obviously knew a thing or two about stress levels and asked me how I was. I said I thought I needed a break. He told me that it would be the best decision of my life to take three months completely out of the game. He could see that I did not have that spark and the only way to get it back would be to get away completely.

So I told the selectors that, while I did not know whether I would be picked anyway, probably the best course of action would be for me not to be considered. I had been given a central contract by this time, the awarding of which had not really bothered me either way. It guarantees you a bit of money, but not a place in the team. Strauss had been in a similar position 12 months previously when he did not get picked for Sri Lanka. Central contracts for me have always been a bit of a confusing issue, because they hand out 12 and that is nowhere near enough; it creates too many problems. I think the decision to give me one had been driven by KP because I had the sense that Geoff and Peter probably did not want me to have it. I would like to think that Kev reckoned I would have something to offer in 2009.

I was still feeling introspective and in need of putting my thoughts down:

It was only when I had a break that I started to think about the good times. It was on the break when all the good feelings of success – the feeling of receiving that ovation at Lord's, of winning and celebrating in the dressing room and being congratulated in the street, grabbing the headlines, waking up with a hangover the next morning – all the good dreams came back. I knew I had to get back out there and have a go. Visualisation is a weird but very powerful action. I would see myself scoring runs before it happened and vice versa, seeing myself fail at the worst times. In 2008 I saw a lot of the failures in my dreams. The skill is to release the good dreams. When I'm in this state I blame everything around me, pitch, bat, coach, players, captaincy. It's a pure lack of focus, but why did it happen?

When I'm good I have precise practice, clear thoughts, very calm, I'm not interested in what everyone else writes or says. People are there to watch me, even in practice. When bad I'm very stressed, head feels tight, agitated. Anything irritates me. Can already hear people criticising my failure. Sometimes I have to be out of the firing line. When I'm in a real good focus my target is clear but I'm not anal. If I set myself small targets the big ones will look after themselves.

My anxiety moments of the summer: waiting to bat against New Zealand I got more nervous than I ever have, and playing the Unis at Headingley. Yorkshire games at the end of the season. Just before any public speaking or press interviews. Speaking to anyone official face to face.

For now that was all behind me, and I had something unusual to look forward to: a first uninterrupted winter at home in 11 years.

26

Last Chances

The first stop of my winter was an October trip to Barbados for some much-needed rest and recuperation with family and friends at the place we have there. Yet even in the Caribbean out of season there was the presence of English cricket, its people and its politics. For this was the Sir Allen Stanford week, which would climax with my recent colleagues in the England squad getting the chance to top up their bank balances to the tune of $1 million each if they could beat the West Indies in a one-off match of Twenty20 cricket in Antigua.

I saw a few of the players in Barbados as they passed through on their way to the much-anticipated Stanford date. Paul Collingwood, Steve Harmison, Stuart Broad, Ryan Sidebottom and Luke Wright had all chosen to come out and get themselves acclimatised and do some training for a few days to clear away the cobwebs after a post-season break. Ottis Gibson, England's bowling coach, put the bowlers through their paces and everyone I came across seemed in pretty good spirits. They were looking forward to the game, although you could tell already that this was not going to be just any old game of cricket.

All along, I had had my suspicions about why someone would want to throw millions of dollars at players for a three-hour appearance. The time-honoured saying comes to mind:

If something sounds too good to be true, then it probably is. Through my connections with Barbados I had got to know a few people who worked in the government and a couple of my Bajan friends had already told me some interesting things about Stanford. They suggested that he was not entirely welcome on their island and that there had been issues about him buying property there. His image in the Caribbean was not quite as rosy as it appeared to those who had been so keen to jump on his lucrative bandwagon in England. I informally relayed these thoughts to a couple of people at the ECB although, in fairness, it was too late to sound any alarm bells by then, as the deal had been done. It would not have taken too much investigation, however, to discover the reservations of some well-placed people in the Caribbean about our game's wealthy new backer.

As I watched the bizarre week unfold from Barbados it looked a decent enough spectacle, although I was not in touch with all the stuff that was being written and said in the media back home in the build-up. It became obvious that strong opinions were being expressed by those actually there that the whole thing was pretty sordid and unsightly. When I heard what the reaction had been, I quickly knew that this would confuse the players.

On the night England played we went to a party with some Bajans we know, and they had put up a big screen for everyone to watch. The locals were as gobsmacked as we were about the prospect of a few big swings earning the players a million bucks each, probably more than we were. It was clear from the start that a lot of our lads just weren't comfortable playing the game. They did not look right and were not fully committed to the whole concept, probably because of the flak that was flying around back home, exacerbated by such things as Stanford coming into the dressing room and his much-publicised flirting with other halves. Pretty harmless, but it all helped fuel the fires of controversy surrounding the event. Any cricketer who plays the game for a living would be envious of having the chance to make that kind of money. Personally, I would have pulled out all the stops to win it, but something was not right and you could see that from afar.

Kevin Pietersen's captaincy had started off with a great win against South Africa and it seemed as if he could not put a foot wrong, but even now there was word that early cracks were opening up in the relationship with Peter Moores. I always knew his chances of success as skipper would depend on whether or not he could make the relationship with Moores work, and you had to have your doubts because of their past difficulties and the fact that it had not started off from a very positive beginning. There is really no alternative but to try to establish a very tight pairing in this situation, as Nasser Hussain and I had done with Duncan Fletcher and, you could quickly see, Andrew Strauss did with Andy Flower.

Kevin and his coach did not even look comfortable in their body language when they were talking together on TV, as if they were doing so only because they had to. The Stanford game was always going to be a big early test, not just because of the peculiar circumstances but because there was a massive entourage with the England party. It seemed as if everybody's friends and extended family were there, making it that much harder to manage and united leadership all the more necessary. I reckon Kevin must have felt he was being dragged from pillar to post, especially as there were also meetings going on about the forthcoming tour of India. History shows that his team got thrashed in what was to be a one-off match and, like most other people, I looked on with a sense of bemusement.

After the Stanford debacle both KP and Paul Collingwood came over to Barbados on their way home. Owing to problems with flights, not everyone could get out together and the rest of the team were staying on in the Caribbean for a few days before going to India via London. Leaving them behind did not necessarily look the smartest move by the captain at the time, and it does not with hindsight either. It is always better to fly back as a team. Anyway, we had lunch together before they headed back to England while the others were left at a hotel which, apparently, was not much to their liking.

All that sitting around and going to the beach, meanwhile, seemed to be doing me good, because I was starting to get itchy feet about wanting to play cricket again. At the end of the season with Yorkshire I had completely lost my zest for the game, but now I was getting visions in my head of all the good moments. Whereas before all I could think about were my failures, now I was beginning to think in terms of making some more big scores and having another serious shot at my international career. So I rang Hugh Morris at the ECB and asked if there was any chance of me being included with the England Lions training squad that was going to India in November for a four-week training camp with a couple of games thrown in. My thinking was that this could be a springboard back into the full squad for the tour of the Caribbean that was beginning in late January of 2009.

A three-week holiday is a long one for me because essentially I like to be busy. I loved the first week, but by the second week I was desperate to do things and had started going to the gym every day, and by the third I was really starting to plan my comeback.

*

My cricketing appetite having been restored, I travelled out to Bangalore in November, but went via Delhi, where I had been booked to talk at a conference about leadership. India's Rahul Dravid was also there and so, to my surprise, was Tony Blair. I spent a bit of time with him and found him very likeable. He told me that when he was Prime Minister somebody always wrote his speeches for him but now he was doing them himself, which I thought impressive.

My hotel room was on the same floor as his and when I went up there this man introduced himself to me as 'Tony Blair's tailor'. At that moment Blair came out of his room and I asked, 'Tony, is this man really your tailor?' and he confirmed that he was, and that he was wearing one of his creations. After a quick inspection I thought I would have some of that, and as he had his fabrics laid out in the ex-PM's room I had a quick fitting done before I gave him £250 for a couple of suits that eventually arrived in England, and which have served me well.

When I got to Bangalore it was to find they were putting us up in rooms which are actually part of the M. Chinnaswamy cricket stadium, and there was a day-night match going on between the full England team and India. I ventured out into the stands, but got mobbed by Indian fans, so I was taken into a private box where Andrew Strauss was watching. It is strange to think that he was only out there on the Lions trip warming up for the Test tour, so shortly before he became captain in both forms of the game.

I went back to my room and, even though I was shattered, I could not sleep because of the noise from outside. The room was basic, the bed was damp, the shower only worked when it felt like it, but it was the sort of back-to-basics environment that was probably just what I needed.

We fell into a routine in Bangalore of decent practice, hitting loads of balls and going to the gym. We got to 26 November and I was lying on my bed after lunch watching the BBC international news when an item came up about something happening in Mumbai. It soon became apparent that this was not the small incident that was initially reported and I lay there glued to the TV for about the next seven hours as the horror unfolded.

We were due to go to a training camp just outside Mumbai the following week and it was obvious that was going to be a problem in every way imaginable. The most chilling thing was that all these terrorist outrages were starting to feel very close to home if you were a cricketer – and this was still three months before the attack on the Sri Lankans in Lahore.

If you think of the hotels England teams have stayed at over recent years, quite a few of them have been blown up. The Pearl Continental hotel in Peshawar, the Marriott in Islamabad, the Sheraton in Karachi – they have all been attacked. And now the Taj in Mumbai, a place we all knew so well – and in my case loved – and where we had spent many an enjoyable week. You could not help thinking about the coffee shop, the bar, the restaurant where you sat on cushions, the main reception and lobby. These were all locations I was so familiar with and I could visualise what was going on there with frightening clarity.

It was decided for us that the Lions would not be going back, which was regrettable, although I felt that it was the right thing to do. At the time I did not really think about whether it would affect my chances of making it into the full squad for the tour to the West Indies, but by asking to go with the Lions I had at least shown I was serious about getting my place back. I did not think they would look too closely at my stats with Yorkshire from the end of the season, when my mind clearly was not in it, and might take a gamble. I also knew Kevin was keen to have me back in the set-up, even though my eventual omission was not one of the causes of the trouble that followed, as was wrongly suggested at the time.

It turned out that the trip to India being aborted might have hurt me after all, because they chose not to take a chance on me for the Caribbean. I was not that disappointed, however. I quite fancied a proper pre-season with Yorkshire, which I thought might be best for me in the long run. That was why I turned down going with the Lions to New Zealand in March, a decision which seemed to be justified when Tim Bresnan and Graham Onions were the two newcomers picked for the early-season West Indies Tests. Neither had made the visit to play the Kiwis, so you wondered how relevant the whole trip was. This was nonetheless dressed up as evidence of England not being a closed shop.

Coming back from India had the major advantage of allowing me to be around for the build-up to Christmas, which is something you are denied as a touring England player, and it was especially nice to see the children at this time. One thing I really did not miss were the meetings that were taking place among the players when they moved to Abu Dhabi to discuss whether the tour of India should resume. It was the right decision to go back and complete it, but being in a room with 15 lads trying to come to a conclusion was something I had been through enough with the Zimbabwe issue, enough to last a lifetime.

It was at this point that I came up with the idea of doing my Artballing project, after watching Martina Navratilova in the jungle in the *I'm a Celebrity* . . . show, when she was talking about how she had done something similar with tennis balls. It involves creating contemporary art by hitting cricket balls onto canvas and is something that I really enjoyed, while it has also helped raise money for prostate cancer charities.

So Christmas was great, although it was around this time that a different type of jungle drums were starting to beat – about how badly the relationship between Kevin and Peter had started to deteriorate. I was not surprised, and in any case quite a few of the guys in the media had been hinting at problems. It was clearly a fairly open secret.

When you are losing, it opens up fault lines in relationships only if they are there in the first place. Kevin is a proud man who would have wanted to do things largely his own way and Peter, with things going wrong, would not have wanted to see it as solely his responsibility. I went skiing in the New Year and it all seemed to kick off with news of an official meeting to discuss the issue having come out, which acted as a trigger for the whole thing to blow up very publicly.

I really enjoyed the holiday, and for a couple of hours managed to do a bit of downhill myself, even though it was forbidden under the terms of my central contract. A bit naughty, but no harm done. My winter idyll was being interrupted, however, with calls and texts from my erstwhile colleagues about the Moores–KP situation. Kevin himself texted me, saying he was going to resign.

Nobody had been sure how it was going to work out with Kevin, and not for nothing was it said to be a gamble at the time of his appointment. I felt sorry for him, because he was thrown some very difficult situations early on in his reign. I got a call from ECB chairman Giles Clarke asking me to try and get in touch with Kev, because he was reluctant to speak to anyone at the Board. I suggested to KP that he really had to explain himself to both his employers and the public and make sure that he got his point across. It was not my issue, so I was otherwise reluctant to get involved.

No sooner had we got back from skiing than I began pre-season training with Yorkshire on dark January nights, running up some of the steep roads in Headingley. On occasions we would run into students in fancy dress going for their nights out – it took me back to my very earliest years as a profes-sional with the county. There were some useful sessions with the bowling machine and Martyn Moxon, and some fun away from the cricket too. I was invited to two rugby internationals over in Dublin with some Irish friends. Croke Park was some-thing else, a fantastic place for sport.

It was great having plenty of time at home, but I was really enjoying the cricket and ambitious to get my place back. The body felt good as well, including the knee, and I did not feel as if it was going to get in the way of my hopes of winning more caps. I was doing all the necessary stuff in the gym to build up the muscles to protect it and the running was no problem whatsoever. It was only to become painful in the summer when there was sustained twisting and turning on it – when executing shots like the pull and running between the wickets.

My ambition was being kindled by watching the tour of the West Indies, although it was not the most thrilling series ever, largely thanks to the kind of wickets that were prepared. It was great to see the teams in Antigua eventually playing back where they should always have been, at the wonderful Recreation Ground in St John's. The new stadium they had built in the middle of the island was dreadful, completely open and lacking in atmosphere, even when we were playing Australia there in the World Cup. I am sure the players and spectators were delighted to return to the Rec, and it threw up the best match of the trip. As a viewer watching in the kitchen at home, it seemed ludicrous the amount of time it took when they were trialling the TV referrals. As a player, it was an interesting perspective to gain, and whatever system they eventually decide upon, it has to be something that does not stop the flow of the game like that, or people will switch off.

Being back with my Yorkshire colleagues was good, in fact the spirit between us was too good sometimes, it could be argued. I think the best teams tend to operate with a bit of edge and bite and I am not sure we had that. Our immediate goal was a pre-season 50-over tournament in Abu Dhabi in early March. My campaign could hardly have got off to a better start in our first match there against Surrey, which I placed a fair amount of importance on as I wanted to make a statement of intent. I went out and scored 115 and people made some pleasing observations about how sweetly I was hitting the ball, saying I was looking as sharp as ever. The impression was re-inforced when I made a fluent 40 in our second match against Middlesex. We went to the races in Dubai, played a little golf and practised hard; it was a good trip all round.

All the time, my main goal was to make the team for the first Test at Lord's against the West Indies on 6 May. There is always a bush telegraph about these things and the message I was getting was that I just needed to show a bit of form in order to get back in, and that pure statistics would not be the only thing that counted. The team was losing the Test series over in the West Indies and, at number three, Owais Shah had not really taken the chance offered to him.

There seemed to be quite a good opportunity emerging and I was further encouraged when I got a call from selectors' chairman Geoff Miller asking if I would captain MCC against the champion county in the traditional curtain-raiser on 9 April. What you might call the real pre-season had begun, with outdoor nets at Headingley and the ball moving all over the place. I wanted to play at Lord's but, as I explained, not as captain. I thought it would send out all sorts of confusing messages about me wanting to be skipper and that some would be only too keen to misconstrue it. I thought it much better that Rob Key should be given the job, because my days as a skipper were most definitely behind me unless in an emergency.

The match was a damp squib played in your worst idea of early-April weather, and I only had one knock, making 12 on a green seamer. That made our first Championship game against Durham up at Riverside on 22 April even more important. They were bound to put out a strong attack and I knew that if I could get any kind of decent score then it would open up the chances of playing against the West Indies, and with it the chance of a whole new chapter in my career.

We went up there three days beforehand for a Friends Provident Trophy match and I made a very nice 43. The weather was good, and I approached the Championship game on the following Wednesday with the intensity that I would a Test match. They batted and when my turn came I went out and instantly felt in superb nick at the crease on what was a good pitch. I moved to 24 without any problem, hitting several boundaries and beginning to think that it was going to work out just the way I wanted. But Steve Harmison was bowling at real pace and got one to rear up nastily at me. I saw it was not there to hit and moved my hand away at the last second, thumping it against the grille of my helmet. A narrow escape, I thought, only to look up in horror and see that the umpire, former England spinner Nick Cook, had raised his finger in response to Phil Mustard's appeal. I could see why he thought he had heard a nick, but really I did not need this.

As second-innings runs do not count as much, I knew that had been my big chance, and when I got back to the dressing room I could only contemplate the truism that you have to take your opportunities when they present themselves. I also knew that with the way Miller selected teams he would not want to take a chance on me without some strong evidence of form to back it up. He would know that there would be awkward questions from the media about bringing me back if there was not a big score to throw back at them. The 20 I made in the second innings to help see things through to a draw was not enough, and in my heart of hearts I knew it.

27

Time to Declare

Being on Yorkshire duty meant having to get used to the ever-shuffling nature of the county fixture list, which is confusing enough for players, let alone the paying public. The day after our Championship match against Durham we were up against Sussex in the Friends Provident Trophy and my decent form was confirmed when I made a free-flowing 82. I could hardly have been playing better.

So I was in good spirits the next day when I travelled down to the National Academy at Loughborough to have my first one-on-one chat with Andy Flower, him having now got the job of head coach on a full-time basis and me being a centrally contracted player. There was the odd medical test done and a personal assessment, and I was impressed by what I found in Flower. No doubt the impression was aided by his telling me that he wanted me in his team, on the proviso that I could get a few runs on the board, but regardless of that, I was pleased that England seemed to have a mature and worldly coach steering them.

The following morning was the start of our second Championship game, against Worcestershire at Headingley, and there was plenty of rain about. I was sitting in the café at the ground waiting for it to stop when the phone rang, with Andrew Strauss on the other end. They were announcing the squad the next day for the approaching Test against the West Indies at Lord's and he was calling to give me the bad news that I had not made it, although he qualified that by saying that he still wanted me in the team to face Australia. He said they were going with Ravi Bopara, and I felt an immediate sense of deflation because I already knew how the two-Test series against an under-motivated collection of Caribbean tourists in the early English summer was likely to work out.

Ravi was sure to get runs against that kind of challenge, or lack of it, and I had always thought that, barring injury, whoever was in possession for the curtain-raiser would be in for the Ashes, because they were unlikely to fail against Chris Gayle and his men in those circumstances. I said to Straussy, 'I've been in your position myself and I know how hard these calls are, but you and I both know that people are not going to fail against the Windies.' His reply was that it was a long summer, which of course was correct, but I pointed out that I could not realistically see them bringing in a 34-year-old as the supposed saviour if they went 1–0 down. On the other hand, if they were 1–0 up they would not be looking to bring me in anyway, so maybe this would be the right time for me just to remove myself from the picture altogether and retire.

It was a momentary reaction amid my disappointment, and I soon started to try and rationalise things, telling myself that you never know with injuries, and that it was worth hanging in there and trying to post some hundreds. Nonetheless, it was a real blow, because I was 100 per cent confident that I would have made the runs against the Windies to put my Test career back on track.

I felt so flat after that phone call that I did not actually want to play the game against Worcestershire, which was a weird sensation. It was freezing cold, there was nobody in the stands to watch and everything was being taken away from me – particularly the vision of walking down the steps to bat again for England that had been keeping me going.

That night I stayed in one of the on-site hotel rooms at Headingley, and in the morning became vaguely aware of the phone ringing. I half slept through it, and when I woke up I found that the missed phone call was from Geoff Miller, and that the time he had called was 6.30 a.m. Now, as the father of young children, I am perfectly used to early starts, but this was a match day and I really could have done without the chairman's dawn alarm call. And I had been told by Straussy the previous day anyway.

It was a horrible game, one of the least enjoyable I can remember in my time in the sport. I nicked behind off Ashley Noffke to be out for five and then watched as we racked up an enormous total, making it inevitable there would be no chance of a second innings. The cherry on the cake was that my knee started playing up as I was fielding on the boundary. My mind was all over the place and I am sure there was a psychological element to the way that I started to feel pain. You always suffer more aches when things are going against you and it was as if the mental barrier I had built up around the knee had come tumbling down.

In the twilight months of my career it became a recurring pattern that I would enjoy the one-day games much more than their first-class equivalents, which was strange as I had always preferred the latter to the former, and been more successful in them. To try and counteract this, I had a long think before the Championship match against Warwickshire starting on 6 May at Edgbaston. I told myself I had to regroup and regain my focus, knuckle down in the gym and keep my resolve, otherwise it was going to be a dire summer and things would fizzle out very quickly. My pep talk did the trick, I stopped feeling sorry for myself and went to Birmingham full of hope.

This positive mindset did not last long, however, and I was dismissed for 16 with a blinding catch taken by Jim Troughton, one of the XI who had featured in my first one-dayer as captain of England six years previously. This match coincided with the first Test at Lord's, and seeing my former colleagues made me reflective enough to reach for my diary and make the first entry in a long while:

> Made 16 runs and then smashed one to backward point low down. Fourth low score of the season, felt good but it is just not happening. Is someone trying to tell me something? As I watched the lads at Lord's on TV in the big open dressing room I have to say I will be amazed if I get the chance to walk out at Lord's playing for England again. Ravi looks a class player and his temperament very sound. He should be given an extended run. He is now the future. Are my recent dismissals fate? County cricket: the schedule is madness. I have never been in the *Big Brother* house, but it must be like this. Crying out for the Diary Room!

A clue to my mindset was that when I was watching the Test from afar I was not sitting there urging Ravi to fail. I was thinking they really ought to be playing him instead of me. In cricket, if people are honest, there is often an element of hoping that somebody does not get too many if you are contesting the same spot, even if it is nothing personal. But I had stopped thinking that way. When I was injured I sometimes used to sit there wishing my replacement would nick it. When there was no vested interest I always enjoyed watching young players develop, and now I was taking pleasure in seeing Ravi take his chance.

I had always thought I was worth a swansong against Australia, especially given my record against them, but I knew that if I was captain I would be thinking that it was time to move on, however valuable my experience might have been against the old enemy. That's why Sir Alex Ferguson is such a genius, he virtually always gets it right when it comes to moving players on.

In that Edgbaston match I also did something to my hamstring which, following on from the knee discomfort against Worcestershire, again sent me into introspective mood. I began thinking that I was spending more time in the gym and on the treatment bench than out in the middle and also seemed to be getting out to questionable decisions and brilliant catches more often than was normal.

The injury caused me to miss the next two one-day matches while the Championship went into one of its baffling hibernations. I was still not finished, however, and after regaining fitness made a 66 in a Friends Provident match at Hove and then 74 against Surrey in a brilliant game in which we successfully chased 329. On the morning of the Surrey match at The Oval we were about to have a team meeting in the dressing room when the phone rang. It was Nichola, and therefore I took it, as she would not be ringing at that time for any trivial reason. She told me that Geoff Miller was at the house wanting to speak to me, even though I was 160 miles away at a long-standing fixture with Yorkshire. Apparently he did not realise.

The Magical Mystery Tour of the domestic cricketer then took us into the Twenty20 Cup, and I was quickly out to another amazing catch, this time by Steven Croft of Lancashire in our Roses encounter at Old Trafford. It was mind-boggling the way we had to switch from one format to the other with barely a day's preparation in between. The mentality that kind of schedule breeds is totally at odds with that required in a top-class international cricketer.

It was interesting to feel the buzz and energy around the dressing room during the Twenty20 competition. I noticed how the players and coaches were now treating it as something special, approaching the whole thing with more urgency than the Championship. For the first time we were examining videos as a team, exploring the ways of executing specific shots, looking at things like relay throws when we were fielding, the bowlers talking about when to come up with slower balls in particular situations. It felt very much like the focus of the season.

What was helping sustain my own enthusiasm through the Twenty20s, apart from the surprising amount of enjoyment and relative success I was having in the shorter forms, was the thought of four Championship games looming. From 6 June to 3 July we would face Sussex and Somerset at Headingley and then Worcestershire at New Road, before going to Somerset at Taunton. I was thinking that the last two games, in particular, offered the chance of posting some big scores to make a last-ditch case for inclusion against Australia.

My optimistic outlook receded, however, during the first game against Sussex. I got a duck in the first innings before making a brisk 39 in the second and then, in the final innings of the match, my knee suffered its first serious problem in quite a while. I was fielding on the boundary when, without warning, it suddenly locked out completely. That had not happened for a couple of years, and as I traipsed off I knew there was no prospect of being fit for the Somerset home game, as there were just 48 hours between the two matches and it would take several days' rest and rehabilitation at best to get it right.

I knew that there was still the Worcestershire game to come, and that shortly after that the squads for the preparation matches ahead of the Ashes would be announced. I did not entertain hopes of making the England XI to play Warwickshire, but thought there might have been a chance to play for the England Lions against the Aussies at the start of July. Apart from anything, I would have loved to have played in that match just to see for myself if I could still do it, although a big hundred would also have shown that I was ready for duty, if needed, when the really important stuff started. The knee was completely fine by the time of the Championship game at Worcester on 16 June and I felt good at the crease before getting to 43 and being caught by my old mate Gareth Batty. Too often I was making it into the thirties and forties and then being dismissed – this was clearly not going to be enough.

Geoff Miller turned up at the Worcestershire game, although I do not think it was specifically to see me. We had quite a long chat on the second day, discussing issues such as Twenty20, the mentality of the county game compared with international level and how other players were shaping up, but there was virtually no talk about me or how I was getting on. I took this to mean that there was no impending call-up for the Lions match, even though I thought I would be well-qualified to give the tourists a hard time, which looked to be the object of the exercise. I was quite amused that when I was overlooked for the Lions Geoff told the media that he had had a chat with me at Worcestershire. Strictly speaking, that was true, although my situation had barely figured in the discussion.

At Worcester there was another small signal that my Ashes dream was not going to become reality. I was hit on the wrist while fielding and needed to go off the field to get some ice on it. One of our younger players, Andrew Gale, told me only half-jokingly that I was a weak dick because I was always off the pitch getting treatment. I just looked at him and thought, 'I wish you knew what I'm going through, because I'm about to give all this away and it's bloody hard.' A certain smart-alec mentality among the younger players at Yorkshire, and probably at other counties, is quite a problem in our cricket, because they think they know it all at a young age, and possibly it is bred by having such a big professional system. In fairness, Gale could not have known the real circumstances in this case, because I had been keeping my thoughts to myself.

I left New Road planning my exit strategy from the game, reminding myself that I needed to be as professional about it as possible. I had already told Martyn, and at some point my employers at the ECB needed to be informed as well. The feeling was one of confusion, excitement and nervousness, all at the same time. Who do you ring when you are about to give up the thing that has anchored your working life ever since you can remember? There is no instruction manual, and it felt weird. The ritual of training, netting, touring, playing, time off, holidays – all that was about to go. Most difficult of all, I knew, would be leaving behind the four walls of the dressing room, which is the most special place. The strain I would not miss, that familiar experience of turning the light off at night and wondering why your hands did not feel quite right that day, but the feeling of winning and knowing what you have put yourself through to get there in the company of team-mates cannot be bettered.

There was barely any time to think, however, because we were now swerving from the longest form of the domestic game to the shortest, from the Championship back to Twenty20. There were four games left in the qualifying stages and I wanted to help us get through. The first match against Nottinghamshire on Monday 22 June was quietly significant because it was the first time that we had four players of Asian heritage featuring for Yorkshire, Pakistan's Rana Naved-ul-Hasan and the home-grown Ajmal Shahzad, Adil Rashid and Azeem Rafiq. This is going to be the shape of things to come for Yorkshire, as many of our most promising players come from the Asian community and it ought to be a good thing for our cricket.

Having talked to Martyn, the plan was to finish off the Twenty20s that coming Sunday against Derbyshire, then announce my retirement from first-class cricket but stay on to play in the NatWest Pro40 competition, which began in mid-July. The idea was that a few senior players would have to be rested for that, and that my presence would add useful experience to the team in their absence. I would do my bit and then ride off into the sunset.

We went up to Durham on the Wednesday and got hammered, and then came what turned out to be my final game of professional cricket, against Leicestershire at Grace Road on the Friday, where we lost again. Unsurprisingly, there had been speculation about my future following my omission from the England Lions squad earlier that week. The day after getting back from Leicester I got a call from Scyld Berry of the *Sunday Telegraph*, the paper I was writing a column for. Contrary to what the wider media thought, I had not told them of my plans, but they had got wind of it anyway. Earlier that week a well-known former player-turned-journalist from another outlet had rung to ask about my future and I had not denied that retirement was on my mind, as I was evidently not in England's plans. Now Scyld was telling me he had heard from a strong source that I was quitting, and I was not going to lie to him.

So it came out in the *Telegraph* and a couple of other

papers on the Sunday morning that I was retiring from first-class cricket and formally abandoning any hopes of trying to take on the Australians. That inevitably caused some interest and at 7.30 on the Sunday morning I received a text from Stewart Regan, Yorkshire's chief executive, saying that the club needed to make a comment on the matter. I replied that we should sit down when I got to the ground at 11 a.m., with Martyn there as well, to discuss how we were going to go forward.

Five minutes later, I had a text back from Regan saying that he had already told the BBC that this was going to be my last game for Yorkshire, which was not my understanding at all. As I drove to the ground the radio was saying that it was my final outing for the county and that people should get down to the ground for a last chance to see me, drumming up interest in what was otherwise a dead match against Derbyshire, because we were both already out of the competition.

The first thing I did when I got there was tell Martyn that I was not playing. I did not want Regan using me as some sort of cheap device to get people through the turnstiles. I was still quite happy to play in the Pro40, as promised, but that day had already got out of hand. Having seen the commotion the issue was causing, Martyn reflected and thought that it would be best to make a clean break and avoid any distractions for the lads further down the line. I respected that point of view and accepted that it was all over.

I was incensed when my attention was drawn to a piece in the *Guardian* the next day saying that I had tried to manufacture some kind of grandstanding farewell for the rest of the season, when the opposite was the truth. Far from being 'embittered' about my exit from the game, as he insinuated, I actually felt remarkably serene once the mess created by Regan had been cleared up on the Sunday. I went into the dressing room and talked to the players about an hour and half before the match, partly to say goodbye and partly to try and give an honest appraisal of where we were as a team.

I said that a few of them needed to change their attitudes, and that they should always remember that Yorkshire was a great club and they should be very proud to play for it. I said they should still be aiming high in the Championship and look to win the Pro40, because I did not think we were lacking in talent. I told them how important it was to keep your love of the game. I am an example, I said, of someone who has lost a little bit of his zest, but then I had been around an awful lot longer than them. If you do not have that fundamental love for the game, you have a serious problem. I got a bit emotional at one point when it came to wishing them well and, as had happened in the Caribbean with Duncan just over two years before, that brought out some emotion from a few of the players too.

That came to an end when Adam Lyth, one of our younger lads, asked what I was going to do with my bats. So I started handing them out, and then all my kit, training and everything. I made sure that my thigh pad and inner thigh pad were kept behind for a lad called Joe Root, who came through Sheffield Collegiate, same as me, and was now in the second XI. Martyn had once handed down Geoff Boycott's chest pad to me when I was starting out, and it had meant a lot.

My son Archie was there and so were my mum and dad, but after I had finished clearing up there really did not seem much point in hanging around. So after ten overs I got into my car and drove out of the car park, and it felt strange but perfectly comfortable, the right way to go. I did not miss any fanfare, but, two months on, it was disappointing that I had still not received any kind of letter or communication from the club.

The next day I met with Hugh Morris to talk about the details of winding up my contract and a press conference was planned for Tuesday, because on Monday the ECB were publicising the England team's trip to the war graves in Flanders. But on Tuesday there turned out to be the counter-attraction of the story emerging of Freddie missing the bus while they were away on the trip – there was something wonderfully ironic about that.

I found myself making one last entry in the diary:

Spoke to all the Yorkshire players, emotional. Handed out my bats to some of them and all the other kit. Felt very strange and almost surreal, what was happening. Mentally knew I had run out. The strain you have to go through to get out on the pitch for me had taken its toll. The gym, the physio, the batting, training, fielding, everything. Time to move on.

28

The Final Chapter

When Andrew Strauss and Ricky Ponting walked out at Cardiff for the toss on the first morning of the 2009 Ashes I was there purely as a spectator, nothing more and nothing less. And through all the atmosphere of heady expectation and the anthems it actually felt very normal. I thoroughly enjoyed my visit to the Welsh capital for the first two days of the match, and there was no desperate longing to be involved. Coming to terms with my new life was not difficult at all, and I am sure it was partly because I had been able to walk away from the game satisfied that I had given everything I could to make the best of my career.

Would I recommend the life of a cricketer to a sporty young-ster? Absolutely. There were times when, clearly, I found it immensely tough and challenging, but the rich experiences far outweighed the angst and bad times. In fact, in some ways I wish cricket was like golf, where you can pack it in after you have passed your prime and go on to a senior tour with your old buddies and relive it all. But you cannot, so when I walked up to the gates of the old Sophia Gardens I was pretty much like any ordinary member of the public. That is, if you exclude the hovering TV camera that had spotted my mate and me and followed us to the turnstile, where – very much like any member of the public – I was turned away and told I needed to enter somewhere else.

All very polite, of course. In fact, it was the warm welcome in Cardiff that helped make it such a success. People went there ready to criticise it as an inadequate Test venue but were pleasantly surprised by what a good show was put on and how smoothly the whole operation went. The wicket was a bit slow yet provided a classic finish, with Monty Panesar and James Anderson holding on after Paul Collingwood had batted fantastically through most of the afternoon to help save the match.

My expectation at the time was that these would be two very evenly matched teams. But while the Australians were not as strong as four years previously, especially in the bowling department, it was still imprinted on my brain that you should never underestimate them.

There is no doubt that Ricky would have left the ground after five days much the unhappier of the two captains. I could remember that gnawing feeling when you know you should have finished off the opposition and how it bugs you for days after a match. England, on the other hand, would have realised that they had got away with it, and there is always a psychological comfort in knowing that you cannot play any worse, particularly when you have somehow managed to avoid defeat.

Cardiff had shown, not for the first or the last time, that English teams tend to struggle when there is no movement on offer. There were other familiar traits in evidence, too, such as us playing well when backs are against the wall, and being unpredictable, as we were in pulling out a draw on the last afternoon. We had not bowled well, but then their attack did not look that special either.

At the second Test at Lord's a few days later I again went as a spectator, accepting an invitation, as I had in Cardiff, to watch from the comfort of Vodafone's corporate box. On the first morning I also ventured into the stands to sit with some mates, much to the surprise of the paying punters.

It was a great toss for Straussy to win at Lord's, particularly as the sun was out, as there is no place better to take advantage of that and post a big first-innings score. Playing at the game's spiritual headquarters often lifts the great players, but it can have an adverse effect on those who are new to it. One technical reason is that the slope takes a bit of getting used to, and another more general one is that the history can have an intimidating effect, and probably some of the less experienced Aussies were a little overawed. We tend to look hard at our own players who struggle in Ashes series, but the opposition are only human as well, as they showed on the first day.

It would have been a massive boost to Andrew to get that big hundred early in the series, as it improves your air of authority, and that benefits your captaincy as well. I thought back to four years previously, when I had felt so much pressure before landing a big one of my own in the third game at Old Trafford. I thought that Straussy was playing as well as I had ever seen him; his balance and alignment was perfect, his movement at the crease very consistent.

Another player at the peak of his powers at Lord's was Freddie Flintoff, despite having announced his retirement from the Test game just before the match. His spell on the fifth morning, when Australia resumed needing 209 for victory with five wickets standing, was about the best I had ever seen him bowl. Without him I think they might well have made the 522 they had been set to win.

It is one of the new realities in cricket that the old batting statistics are becoming increasingly irrelevant and records are getting broken all the time. Even halfway through my Test career the idea that a side could chase more than 500 in the fourth innings to win a Test would have been seen as pure pie in the sky. Now it seems eminently possible and a team will probably do it before long.

You would have to say we had our share of luck to win the Lord's Test. The toss went England's way, the sun came out and then the clouds arrived with excellent timing, and there were several key umpiring decisions that went to the home side. But then that is what the game is about, taking advantage when the circumstances are in your favour, and that is what England did to go 1–0 up.

When I heard they had won – I had gone to play golf after Freddie got Brad Haddin out, knowing that it was surely over – I would admit to having had a pang of wishing I was there. I used to find that time in the afterglow of victory magical. I pictured the players sitting around on those comfortable seats in the Lord's dressing room, drinking a few beers with their mates and sharing the moment of having beaten Australia, talking general rubbish about life, Fred having a fag on the balcony, music blaring. Then you think of all the training and preparation and discipline and snap out of it.

I felt no need to attend every day of every Ashes Test, far from it, and I made only a passing visit to Edgbaston at the end of July, where the rain was to interfere badly. It had been the scene of the most dramatic encounter of all four years previously, and I think the memories might have been burning brighter for Ricky than they were for me. I cannot really find any other explanation for his decision to bat first, which was the opposite of what he had fatefully chosen in 2005. When there is a rain delay you should be looking to bowl first, because the best way to win the match is to get 20 wickets. In this case there had been a huge amount of rain in the days leading up to the game and there was bound to be moisture in the wicket, coupled with forecast cloud cover.

Jimmy Anderson and Graham Onions exploited the favourable conditions brilliantly, showing again what a different team we are when the ball is doing something. Australia conceded a 113-run first-innings lead, so by the Sunday night there was only one team that could win it. Then came the reverse Cardiff effect, because on the last day the ball did not swing as much and Graeme Swann, who had got Ponting with a brilliant off-break the day before, perhaps tried too hard to replicate that under pressure. By the end, the tourists batted it out with consummate ease, and it was not just Aussie propaganda when they claimed they had taken far more from the match.

With only three days between the third and fourth Tests it was always going to be difficult for Freddie to make it, having had to give his knee another pounding on a very unresponsive pitch at Birmingham. He duly missed out at Headingley, which was bound to have a big effect on the atmosphere the match was played in.

One of the most interesting things to me as I watched from the sidelines was how much of a buzz Fred brought to the crowd whenever he came out to bat or was brought on to bowl. I had not noticed it to the same extent as a player, caught up with everything as I was, and it was clear that this ability to pump up the spectators was missed in that game, along with the potential runs and wickets. The only other player who can stir up the stands is, strangely, Monty Panesar. I guess it has to do with the fact that they are easy to identify with, Fred the man of the people and Monty having such an endearing manner about him.

I was in Leeds prior to the Test at Headingley, which is not a ground where the present England team seem to be comfortable on the whole. Unfortunately, there was a degree of history repeating itself in the build-up with all the uncertainty about the make-up of the team, as there had been before the Test there against South Africa in 2008, and I detected a bit of negativity in the air. The subsequent crushing defeat went to show that there is nothing teams dislike so much as a bit of instability during the preparations for a big match.

I had feared the worst when Australia finally decided to call up Stuart Clark, who was a bowler our lads would not have been pleased to see. Frankly, given his record against us and what he had done in the last series, I was amazed it had taken them so long to pick him. In fact, the Australian think tank did not seem to be the sharpest all series and I could not help feeling they also got it wrong in selecting their final XI at The Oval. It was pretty obvious that they misread the wicket in failing to choose a specialist spinner in Nathan Hauritz. I would also have gone with a fit-again Brett Lee for the decider, given the dryness of the surface, his ability to reverse-swing the ball and the problems he had caused our batsmen in the past.

Once the Headingley Test had started, I disappeared off to Portugal on holiday, as I was always conscious of the importance of not having too high a profile during the series, especially at what had been my home ground. The flak our players took in the Test was added to by the revelation of the dossier compiled for the Australians by Justin Langer, which was reprinted in a newspaper on the Sunday and featured some colourful language. But getting a dossier on the opposition is fairly standard practice and, broadly speaking, there was a lot in it that I could recognise, even if a few comments were over the top.

The swashbuckling lower-order stand between Graeme Swann and Stuart Broad on the Sunday morning, while futile in the context of the match, was quite an important statement nonetheless. The criticism of the team that followed Headingley was also beneficial in some ways, because it backed England into a corner, and we always seem to be at our best when that is the case.

Sadly Ravi Bopara was dropped for the final Test, with Belly promoted to number three, the position I had hoped to occupy for the series at one point. I had always felt it was a lot to ask of a young player like Ravi to bat that high in an Ashes series, but I have absolutely no doubt that he will become a fine Test match player for England.

I was in London ahead of the Oval match and saw a few of the players, including Straussy, who seemed in a good frame of mind. I said to him, 'You'll know by 10.31 on the morning of the game whether the Gods are with you.' When that hour came it seemed that they were, because it was another great toss to win. Also, the selection of Jonathan Trott after much fevered speculation proved an excellent decision. He immediately had that look about him of being comfortable at the highest level, and could prove to be a more stubborn version of Kevin Pietersen. I suppose you might wish that Trott was a bit more English, but after such a brilliant debut it appeared we had found another high-quality batsman.

I spent a day at The Oval before heading to Ireland for the wedding of the son of businessman Dermot Desmond, with whom I have become friends over the years. I actually attended only five days of the whole series in person, although I was mostly glued to it on the television and would watch replays when necessary. Anyway, on the Friday I went into the church service with Australia 73–1 in reply to our 332, and when I came out I quickly switched on my BlackBerry to get a score update. Martin O'Neill, the Aston Villa football manager, was standing next to me and I told him it was now 109–6! The word spread quickly among the wedding guests, and it was notable how many Irish people sought out televisions to keep up with the game. It was pleasing, on that occasion and many others, when someone told you that their interest in cricket had been started by what happened in 2005.

England bounced back brilliantly in that match, and showed the greater poise under huge pressure. Again Australia's batting proved vulnerable in the first innings, and while we had the greater portion of luck, there can be no disputing that the better team wins over a five-match Test series. I was especially pleased for Andrew Strauss, who led the team superbly as captain and batsman. The tightness of the unit he had forged with Andy Flower was a major part of the success, and it seemed to me that the whole backroom staff, as in 2005, had played their part, just getting on with the job and not seeking glory for themselves. My only twinge of envy came when I thought about the boys enjoying the celebration of their great achievement in the immediate aftermath. But it was good to look on with no regrets.

This time the England team had no chance of an open-top bus ride even if they had wanted one, which sensibly they did not. Within a day or so of the Oval triumph they were off to Ireland for a one-day international, part of a run of at least 11 ODIs in three countries over four weeks. The middle bit was a one-day series against the Aussies spread over seven matches, which made no sense at all.

That was far from satisfactory, but I do think it was probably for the best that there was no time to stop and dwell too much on the Ashes triumph, as we did in 2005. Those six vacant weeks back then were great while they lasted but ultimately not very helpful. We felt that by beating Australia we had reached the top of the mountain, and although injuries played a big part in our failure to follow up, there were other factors as well. The big challenge now is to try to beat Australia in Australia, and I think there is a real chance to do that in 2010–11. When Freddie led the team there in 2006–07 there was a superb raft of senior Aussie players waiting for revenge and wanting to end their careers on a high note. That will not be the case this time, and we have some exciting young players who will have improved by then. The 2009 Ashes showed that statistics only tell part of the story in cricket, particularly when playing in English conditions. Their averages in both batting and bowling matched up very favourably against ours as a whole, but no figures could tell you who produced the best cricket at the most important points of the five Tests.

A couple of sobering thoughts also struck me in the Ashes aftermath. The first was that, despite the quality of the coverage, many people will simply not have seen the 2009 triumph on television because it was not as widely available as before, and therefore fewer will have been inspired. A second worry was the reminder that not everything in our game works towards the betterment of the England side, with the counties trying to scrap the 50-over domestic competition, despite that being the format used in the World Cup, in which we have performed so poorly recently.

Not for the first time, after the Ashes I had cause to reflect on how small the difference is between being a hero and a zero when it comes to cricket. Maybe if we had lost the toss at The Oval, or if Monty and Jimmy had not held out at Cardiff, there would have been all sorts of inquests going on into the way our game is structured. As it was, there were celebrations all round, and well deserved from the team's perspective.

The conclusion of the Ashes series also marked the end of the mini sabbatical I had given myself after retiring earlier in the summer, as I resolved it was time to address what I will do from now on. I see my future, broadly speaking, as being within the game of cricket, and it would be nice to think I could do some coaching and broadcasting. Yet I also want to expand my horizons and take on challenges in areas that are well away from the game that has been so good to me. I am not the sort of person who will be happy sitting around the house or just playing golf the whole time. I function best when I am busy and stimulated.

Among the things I may get involved in is the golf and sports business side of things with International Sports Management, who have looked after my affairs since I became an England player. I also have some property interests, which date back to when I first started earning some reasonable money. While some of my contemporaries went for fast cars to go along with their England contracts, I preferred to keep my old Volkswagen and invest instead in some student flats, helped by the advice of my brother David.

In a totally different direction, I have found Artballing a very interesting world to be in, and while I do not take it too seriously, I am keen to develop it. In the summer of 2009 I went into partnership with Sacha Jafri, one of the real up-and-coming artists, to do a joint venture, with me creating the splats and him doing montages around them.

Back with cricket, I have developed cricket camps for five- to eight-year-olds, which will hopefully provide them with an introduction to the game and then point them in the direction of cricket clubs in their area. Who knows, one of them may even get set on the same path that I have been fortunate enough to tread in my life.

Even when the pressures got me down I always tried to remember how lucky I was to play this extraordinary sport that makes so many demands on you. Aside from the memories of battles on the field, what stays with you are the friendships cricket provides. Of course, it is not possible to get on perfectly with everyone you meet, but my life has been enriched by the travelling and the bonds forged with fellow players, opponents, coaches, officials, supporters, people in the media and those from such a diverse range of countries and cultures who share an interest in the game.

Before the Headingley Test I had a beer with Matthew Hayden, a brutally tough opponent with whom I had plenty of battles, some of them pretty edgy. But it was a pleasure to spend a bit of time with him, as it was with other Australians like Jason Gillespie and Dean Jones. It is funny how you can talk on a much more relaxed and natural basis on these occasions than when you were still foes on the field and were always holding something back.

A recurring theme in our conversations, and perhaps a sign of us all knocking on, was how much the sport has changed in the last decade and a half. When I first started there were cans of lager on the table at lunchtime, whereas now there are smoothies. Everybody loved a fry-up in the morning and bacon sandwiches were eagerly consumed (they remained a guilty treat for me) and it was party time most nights. Now you have muesli and training diaries, as a better class of athlete is produced.

Twenty20 cricket has hit the sport like a freight train – mostly having a positive effect – and it continues to cause reappraisals of thought processes and changes in everything from technical ideas to the economics of the sport. What we have to remember, though, is that less can be more, and that there has to be a grand plan that allows every form of the game to take its rightful place, with the bottom line not driving absolutely everything. We want our best players preserved in the game and playing every form of it, including Test cricket, which still provides the platform for the greatest deeds to be seen in the sport.

I also worry about the West Indies and New Zealand, at least in Test cricket, and the long form has to be nurtured there, otherwise we will be down to just a hard core of Test nations. Day-night Test matches need to be looked at seriously and pitches have to be conducive to exciting cricket, not just prepared to make a match last five days to get a few more quid in the bank. And a format must be devised whereby every Test counts, regardless of how an individual series is standing, because you cannot have dead rubbers in this day and age. The answer has to be some kind of Test championship.

More profoundly, an eye must be kept on the balance between bat and ball, as bats are much bigger and more powerful than they were 20 years ago. A sharp eye, too, is needed to guard against corruption rearing its head again on a widespread scale as Twenty20 tournaments proliferate. And I am not just talking about abroad, either.

Yet I still feel that cricket is a better game for the most part, both to play and to watch. The fielding has improved massively since I started playing, from athleticism in the outfield to catching. In the 50-over format you used to see the occasional six in an innings; now you are looking at tallies that often go into double figures. Tail-enders used to get rolled over; now most of them are able to smash it. Facilities have improved enormously, from those for the players to the infrastructure for the paying public. There are many more decent stadiums and those who perform in them are increasingly well rewarded.

I was lucky enough to travel the world and have my ticket paid. I was happy when someone once said I possessed a combination of Yorkshire grit and Lancashire flair, and I tried to draw on those virtues wherever I went. Earning money to play cricket? It still has to be the best job in the world.

Michael Vaughan in Test Cricket

Compiled by
Victor and Richard V. Isaacs

Test Career Record (1999/2000–2008)

up to and including Third Test v South Africa at Birmingham 2008

M	I	NO	Runs	HS	Avge	S/R	100s	50s
82	**147**	**9**	**5719**	**197**	**41.44**	**51.13**	**18**	**18**

1. v South Africa at Johannesburg 25-28 November 1999 –
    lost by an innings and 21 runs
    Toss: South Africa
    England 122 (A.A.Donald 6-53) & 260 (A.A.Donald 5-74);
    South Africa 403-9dec (D.J.Cullinan 108, D.Gough 5-70)

1st innings	c M.V.Boucher b S.M.Pollock	33	11-2-39-0
2nd innings	lbw b A.A.Donald	5	

    Notes:
    Made his Test match debut aged 25 years and 27 days.

2. v South Africa at Port Elizabeth 9-13 December 1999 –
    match drawn
    Toss: England
    South Africa 450 (L.Klusener 174) & 224-4dec;
    England 373 (M.A.Atherton 108) & 153-6

1st innings	b M.Hayward	21	3-0-16-0
2nd innings	c M.V.Boucher b J.H.Kallis	29	2-0-9-0

3. v South Africa at Cape Town 2-5 January 2000 –
    lost by an innings and 37 runs
    Toss: England
    England 258 (A.A.Donald 5-47) & 126;
    South Africa 421 (J.H.Kallis 105, D.J.Cullinan 120,
    C.E.W.Silverwood 5-91)

1st innings	c G.Kirsten b A.A.Donald	42	
2nd innings	c M.V.Boucher b L.Klusener	5	

4. v South Africa at Centurion 14-18 January 2000 –
    won by 2 wickets
    Toss: England
    South Africa 248-8dec & innings forfeited; England 0-0dec & 251-8

1st innings	did not bat		2-0-9-0
2nd innings	b M.Hayward	69	

    *Notes: Because it was not allowed to have forfeited first innings at this
    time in Test cricket, the match referee declared England's first innings as
    0-0dec, despite no batsmen stepping onto the field. Added 126 with
    A.J.Stewart for the second innings fifth wicket.*

5. v West Indies at Lord's 29 June-1 July 2000 – won by 2 wickets
    Toss: England
    West Indies 267 & 54 (A.R.Caddick 5-16);
    England 134 & 191-8 (C.A.Walsh 6-74)

1st innings	b C.E.L.Ambrose	4	3-1-10-0
2nd innings	c R.D.Jacobs b C.A.Walsh	41	

6. v West Indies at Old Trafford 3-7 August 2000 – match drawn
    Toss: West Indies
    West Indies 157 & 438-7dec (B.C.Lara 112);
    England 303 (A.J.Stewart 105) & 80-1

1st innings	c B.C.Lara b C.E.L.Ambrose	29	
2nd innings	did not bat		2-1-3-0

7. v West Indies at Headingley 17-18 August 2000 –
    won by an innings and 39 runs
    Toss: West Indies
    West Indies 172 (C.White 5-57) & 61 (A.R.Caddick 5-14);
    England 272

1st innings	c R.D.Jacobs b C.E.L.Ambrose	76

8. v West Indies at The Oval 31 August-4 September 2000 –
    won by 158 runs
    Toss: West Indies
    England 281 & 217 (M.A.Atherton 108);
    West Indies 125 (C.White 5-32) & 215

1st innings	lbw b C.E.L.Ambrose	10	
2nd innings	lbw b C.A.Walsh	9	3-1-12-0

9. v Sri Lanka at Colombo (SSC) 15-17 March 2001 –
    won by 4 wickets
    Toss: Sri Lanka
    Sri Lanka 241 & 81; England 249 (G.P.Thorpe 113*,
    W.P.U.J.C.Vaas 6-73) & 74-6

1st innings	c K.C.Sangakkara b W.P.U.J.C.Vaas	26
2nd innings	b M.Muralitharan	8

10. v Pakistan at Lord's 17-20 May 2001 – won by an innings and 9 runs
    Toss: Pakistan
    England 391; Pakistan 203 (D.Gough 5-61) & 179

1st innings	c Rashid Latif b Azhar Mahmood	32	
2nd innings			1-0-12-0

11. v Pakistan at Old Trafford 31 May-4 June 2001 – lost by 108 runs
    Toss: Pakistan
    Pakistan 403 (Inzamam-ul-Haq 114) & 323;
    England 357 (M.P.Vaughan 120, G.P.Thorpe 138) & 261
    (M.E.Trescothick 117)

1st innings	c Rashid Latif b Waqar Younis	120	2-0-21-0
2nd innings	c Rashid Latif b Abdul Razzaq	14	

    *Notes: Scored his first Test century in his 17th Test innings. Passed 500
    Test runs when he reached 61 in the first innings. Added 267 with
    G.P.Thorpe for the third wicket in England's first innings.*

12. v India at Ahmedabad 11-15 December 2001 – match drawn
    Toss: England
    England 407 (C.White 121, A.Kumble 7-115) & 257
    (Harbhajan Singh 5-71); England 291 (S.R.Tendulkar
    103, A.F.Giles 5-67) & 198-3

1st innings	c V.Sehwag b A.Kumble	11
2nd innings	not out	31

13. v India at Bangalore 19-23 December 2001 – match drawn
    Toss: England
    England 336 & 33-0; India 238

1st innings	handled the ball	64
2nd innings	did not bat	

    *Notes: Added 113 for the fourth wicket with M.R.Ramprakash. Became
    the seventh player in Test cricket history to be dismissed handled the ball
    (after W.R.Endean, A.M.J.Hilditch, Mohsin Khan, D.L.Haynes, G.A.Gooch
    and S.R.Waugh).*

14. v New Zealand at Christchurch 13-16 March 2002 – won by 98 runs
    Toss: New Zealand
    England 228 (N.Hussain 106) & 468-6dec (G.P.Thorpe 200*,
    A.Flintoff 137); New Zealand 147 (M.J.Hoggard 7-63)
    & 451 (N.J.Astle 222, A.R.Caddick 6-122)

1st innings	c A.C.Parore b C.L.Cairns	27
2nd innings	b I.G.Butler	0

15. v New Zealand at Wellington 21-25 March 2002 – match drawn
    Toss: New Zealand
    England 280 & 293-4dec; New Zealand 218 (A.R.Caddick 6-63)
    & 158-4

1st innings	c S.P.Fleming b C.J.Drum	7	
2nd innings	c C.J.Drum b D.L.Vettori	34	5-1-15-0

16. v New Zealand at Auckland 30 March-3 April 2002 – lost by 78 runs
    Toss: New Zealand
    New Zealand 202 & 269-9dec; England 160 (D.R.Tuffey 6-54) & 233

1st innings	c A.C.Parore b A.R.Adams	27
2nd innings	c S.P.Fleming b C.J.Drum	36

17. v Sri Lanka at Lord's 16-20 May 2002 – match drawn
    Toss: Sri Lanka
    Sri Lanka 555-8dec (M.S.Atapattu 185, D.P.M.D.Jayawardene 107)
    & 42-1; England 275 & 529-5dec (following on) (M.P.Vaughan 115,
    M.A.Butcher 105)

1st innings	c D.N.T.Zoysa b P.D.R.L.Perera	64	14-2-35-0
2nd innings	c K.C.Sangakkara b P.D.R.L.Perera	115	

    *Notes: Recorded his second Test century. Also passed 10,000 First-class
    runs when he reached 99 in the second innings. Added 106 for the first
    innings third wicket with N.Hussain. Added 168 for the second innings
    first wicket with M.E.Trescothick.*

18. v Sri Lanka at Edgbaston 30 May-2 June 2002 –
    won by an innings and 111 runs
    Toss: England
    Sri Lanka 162 & 272 (M.J.Hoggard 5-92);
    England 545 (M.E.Trescothick 161, G.P.Thorpe 123)

1st innings	c S.T.Jayasuriya b M.Muralitharan	46

    Notes: Passed 1,000 Test runs when he reached 11.

19. v Sri Lanka at Old Trafford 13-17 June 2002 – won by 10 wickets
    Toss: England
    England 512 (M.A.Butcher 123, A.J.Stewart 123) & 50-0;
    Sri Lanka 253 & 308 (following on) (R.P.Arnold 109)

1st innings	c W.P.U.J.C.Vaas b C.R.D.Fernando	36	
2nd innings	not out	24	2-0-9-0

20. v India at Lord's 25-29 July 2002 – won by 170 runs
Toss: England
England 487 (N.Hussain 155) & 301-6dec (M.P.Vaughan 100,
J.P.Crawley 100*); India 221 & 397 (A.B.Agarkar 109*)

1st innings	lbw b Z.Khan	0	6-2-12-1
2nd innings	c W.Jaffer b A.Nehra	100	

*Notes: Recorded his third Test century. Became the 108th Test batsman
to score a century and a duck in the same Test. Claimed his first Test
wicket (W.Jaffer c N.Hussain b M.P.Vaughan 53). Added 137 for the
second innings fourth wicket with J.P.Crawley.*

21. v India at Trent Bridge 8-12 August 2002 – match drawn
Toss: India
India 357 (V.Sehwag 106) & 424-8dec (R.Dravid 115);
England 617 (M.P.Vaughan 197)

1st innings	c P.A.Patel b A.B.Agarkar	197	
2nd innings			21-5-71-2

*Notes: Recorded his fourth Test century. To date, this is Vaughan's
highest Test and First-class score with the bat. Won the man of the
match award. Added 165 for the second wicket with M.A.Butcher.*

22. v India at Headingley 22-26 August 2002 –
lost by an innings and 46 runs
Toss: India
India 628-8dec (R.Dravid 148, S.R.Tendulkar 193, S.C.Ganguly 128);
England 273 & 309 (N.Hussain 110)

1st innings	c V.Sehwag b A.B.Agarkar	61	1-0-1-0
2nd innings	lbw b A.B.Agarkar	15	

23. v India at The Oval 5-9 September 2002 – match drawn
Toss: England
England 515 (M.P.Vaughan 195, Harbhajan Singh 5-115) & 114-0;
India 508 (R.Dravid 217)

1st innings	c A.Ratra b Z.Khan	195	12-1-36-1
2nd innings	not out	47	

*Notes: Recorded his fifth Test century. Passed 1,500 Test runs when he
reached 32 in the first innings. Added 174 with M.A.Butcher for the first
innings second wicket. Added 114* with M.E.Trescothick in the second
innings first wicket.*

24. v Australia at Brisbane 7-10 November 2002 – lost by 384 runs
Toss: England
Australia 492 (M.L.Hayden 197, R.T.Ponting 123) &
296-5 (M.L.Hayden 103); England 325 & 79

1st innings	c A.C.Gilchrist b G.D.McGrath	33
2nd innings	lbw b G.D.McGrath	0

25. v Australia at Adelaide 21-24 November 2002 –
lost by an innings and 51 runs
Toss: England
England 342 (M.P.Vaughan 177) & 159; Australia 552-9dec
(R.T.Ponting 154)

| 1st innings | c S.K.Warne b A.J.Bichel | 177 |
| 2nd innings | c G.D.McGrath b S.K.Warne | 41 |

Notes: Recorded his sixth Test century. Passed 11,000 First-class runs when he passed 27 in the first innings. Added 140 for the first innings third wicket with N.Hussain.

26. v Australia at Perth 29 November-1 December 2002 –
lost by an innings and 48 runs
Toss: England
England 185 & 223; Australia 456 (C.White 5-127)

| 1st innings | c A.C.Gilchrist b G.D.McGrath | 34 |
| 2nd innings | run out | 9 |

Notes: Passed 2,000 Test runs when he passed 5 in the second innings.

27. v Australia at Melbourne 26-30 December 2002 – lost by 5 wickets
Toss: Australia
Australia 551-6dec (J.L.Langer 250, M.L.Hayden 102) & 107-5;
England 270 & 387 (M.P.Vaughan 145, S.C.G.MacGill 5-152)

| 1st innings | b G.D.McGrath | 11 |
| 2nd innings | c M.L.Love b S.C.G.MacGill | 145 |

Notes: Recorded his seventh Test century. Added 189 for the second innings third wicket with N.Hussain.

28. v Australia at Sydney 2-6 January 2003 – won by 225 runs
Toss: England
England 362 (M.A.Butcher 124) & 452-9dec (M.P.Vaughan 183);
Australia 363 (S.R.Waugh 102, A.C.Gilchrist 133) &
226 (A.R.Caddick 7-94)

| 1st innings | c A.C.Gilchrist b B.Lee | 0 |
| 2nd innings | lbw b A.J.Bichel | 183 |

Notes: Recorded his eighth Test century. Became the 110th player to record a century and a duck in the same Test and the second time he achieved this mark. Added 189 with N.Hussain for the second innings third wicket. Won the man of the match award.

29. v Zimbabwe at Lord's 22-24 May 2003 – won by an innings and 92 runs
Toss: Zimbabwe
England 472 (M.A.Butcher 137); Zimbabwe 147 (J.M.Anderson 5–73)
& 233

| 1st innings | b H.H.Streak | 8 |

30. v Zimbabwe at Chester-le-Street 5-7 June 2003 –
     won by an innings and 69 runs
     Toss: England
     England 416; Zimbabwe 94 (R.L.Johnson 6-33) & 253

     1st innings   c S.M.Ervine b H.H.Streak   20

31. v South Africa at Edgbaston 24-28 July 2003 – match drawn
     Toss: South Africa
     South Africa 594-5dec (G.C.Smith 277, H.H.Gibbs 179) & 134–4dec;
     England 408 (M.P.Vaughan 156) & 110-1

     1st innings   c M.V.Boucher b D.Pretorius   156   8-0-26-1
     2nd innings   c S.M.Pollock b R.J.Peterson   22

     Notes: Recorded his ninth Test century. Passed 2,500 Test match runs when he passed 129 in the first innings. Passed 12,000 First-class runs when he passed 136 in the first innings.

32. v South Africa at Lord's 31 July-3 August 2003 –
     lost by an innings and 92 runs
     Toss: South Africa
     England 173 (M.Ntini 5-75) & 417 (A.Flintoff 142, M.Ntini 5-145);
     South Africa 682-6dec (G.C.Smith 259, G.Kirsten 108)

     1st innings   c sub b M.Ntini   33
     2nd innings   c S.M.Pollock b A.J.Hall   29

     Notes: Captained England for the first time, becoming the 74th player to do so.

33. v South Africa at Trent Bridge 14-18 August 2003 – won by 70 runs
     Toss: England
     England 445 (M.A.Butcher 106, N.Hussain 116) & 118
     (S.M.Pollock 6-39); South Africa 362 (J.M.Anderson 5-102) &
     131 (R.J.Kirtley 6-34)

     1st innings   c H.H.Gibbs b S.M.Pollock   1   1-1-0-0
     2nd innings   c M.V.Boucher b S.M.Pollock   5
     Notes: England captain.

34. v South Africa at Headingley 21-25 August 2003 – lost by 191 runs
     Toss: South Africa
     South Africa 342 (G.Kirsten 130) & 365; England 307 & 209
     (J.H.Kallis 6-54)

     1st innings   b M.Ntini   15
     2nd innings   c H.H.Gibbs b J.H.Kallis   21   5-1-13-0
     Notes: England captain.

35. v South Africa at The Oval 4-8 September 2003 – won by 9 wickets
Toss: South Africa
South Africa 484 (H.H.Gibbs 183) & 229;
England 604-9dec (M.E.Trescothick 219, G.P.Thorpe 124) & 110-1

| 1st innings | c H.H.Gibbs b S.M.Pollock | 23 | 5-0-24-0 |
| 2nd innings | c M.V.Boucher b J.H.Kallis | 13 | |

Notes: England captain. Vaughan was S.M.Pollock's 300th Test dismissal.

36. v Bangladesh at Dhaka 21-25 October 2003 – won by 7 wickets
Toss: Bangladesh
Bangladesh 203 (S.J.Harmison 5-35) & 255; England 295
(M.E.Trescothick 113) & 164-3

| 1st innings | b Mohammad Rafique | 48 |
| 2nd innings | not out | 81 |

Notes: England captain. Added 137 for the second innings first wicket with M.E.Trescothick.

37. v Bangladesh at Chittagong 29 October-1 November 2003 –
won by 329 runs
Toss: Bangladesh
England 326 & 293-5dec; Bangladesh 152 (R.L.Johnson 5-49) & 138

| 1st innings | c Khaled Mashud b Mashrafe Mortaza | 60 |
| 2nd innings | run out | 25 |

Notes: England captain. Added 126 for the first innings first wicket with M.E.Trescothick.

38. v Sri Lanka at Galle 2-6 December 2003 – match drawn
Toss: Sri Lanka
Sri Lanka 331 & 226; England 235 (M.Muralitharan 7-46) & 210-9

| 1st innings | b M.Muralitharan | 24 | |
| 2nd innings | c H.P.Tillakaratne b K.A.D.M.Fernando | 8 | 1-0-2-0 |

Notes: England captain.

39. v Sri Lanka at Kandy 10-14 December 2003 – match drawn
Toss: Sri Lanka
Sri Lanka 382 (A.F.Giles 5-116) & 279-7dec (T.M.Dilshan 100);
England 294 & 285-7 (M.P.Vaughan 105)

| 1st innings | c D.P.M.D.Jayawardene b M.Muralitharan | 52 | 5-0-9-0 |
| 2nd innings | c T.M.Dilshan b M.Muralitharan | 105 | 3-0-11-0 |

Notes: England captain. Recorded his tenth Test century. Became the 86th player in Test history to score ten centuries and the 22nd Englishman.

40. v Sri Lanka at Colombo (SSC) 18-21 December 2003 –
lost by an innings and 215 runs
Toss: England
England 265 & 148; Sri Lanka 628-8dec (T.T.Samaraweera 142,
D.P.M.D.Jayawardene 134)

1st innings	c D.P.M.D.Jayawardene b U.D.U.Chandana	18	1-0-5-0
2nd innings	c S.T.Jayasuriya b C.R.D.Fernando	14	

Notes: England captain.

41. v West Indies at Kingston 11-14 March 2004 – won by 10 wickets
Toss: West Indies
West Indies 311 (D.S.Smith 108) & 47 (S.J.Harmison 7-12);
England 339 & 20-0

1st innings	c B.C.Lara b F.H.Edwards	15	1-0-2-0
2nd innings	not out	11	

Notes: England captain.

42. v West Indies at Port-of-Spain 19-23 March 2004 – won by 7 wickets
Toss: West Indies
West Indies 208 (S.J.Harmison 6-61) & 209 (S.P.Jones 5-57);
England 319 & 99-3

1st innings	lbw b P.T.Collins	0
2nd innings	lbw b A.Sanford	23

Notes: England captain.

43. v West Indies at Bridgetown 1-3 April 2004 – won by 8 wickets
Toss: England
West Indies 224 (A.Flintoff 5-58) & 94; England 226
(G.P.Thorpe 119*) & 93-2

1st innings	c R.D.Jacobs b F.H.Edwards	17
2nd innings	c R.D.Jacobs b C.D.Collymore	32

Notes: England captain.

44. v West Indies at St John's 10-14 April 2004 – match drawn
Toss: West Indies
West Indies 751-5dec (B.C.Lara 400*, R.D.Jacobs 107*);
England 285 (A.Flintoff 102*) & 422-5 (M.P.Vaughan 140)

1st innings	c R.D.Jacobs b P.T.Collins	7	13-0-60-0
2nd innings	c R.D.Jacobs b R.R.Sarwan	140	

Notes: England captain. Recorded his eleventh Test century. Added 182 for the second innings first wicket with M.E.Trescothick.

45. v New Zealand at Headingley 3-7 June 2004 – won by 9 wickets
Toss: England
New Zealand 409 & 161; England 526 (M.E.Trescothick 132,
G.O.Jones 100) & 45-1

| 1st innings | c S.P.Fleming b S.B.Styris | 13 | 2-0-3-0 |
| 2nd innings | lbw b C.L.Cairns | 61 | 1-0-5-0 |

Notes: England captain.

46. v New Zealand at Trent Bridge 10-13 June 2004 – won by 4 wickets
Toss: New Zealand
New Zealand 384 (S.P.Fleming 117, S.B.Styris 108) & 218;
England 319 (C.L.Cairns 5-79) & 284-6 (G.P.Thorpe 104*)

| 1st innings | lbw b C.L.Cairns | 61 | 1-0-5-0 |
| 2nd innings | lbw b C.L.Cairns | 10 | |

*Notes: England captain. Passed 13,000 First-class runs when he passed 4
in the second innings. Added 110 for the first innings third wicket with
M.E.Trescothick.*

47. v West Indies at Lord's 22-26 July 2004 – won by 210 runs
Toss: West Indies
England 568 (A.J.Strauss 137, R.W.T.Key 221, M.P.Vaughan 103)
& 325-5dec (M.P.Vaughan 101*); West Indies 416
(S.Chanderpaul 128*) & 267 (A.F.Giles 5-81)

| 1st innings | c D.S.Smith b P.T.Collins | 103 |
| 2nd innings | not out | 101 |

*Notes: England captain. Became the 55th Test batsman to record twin
centuries in the same game and the 9th English batsman to achieve this
feat. These centuries were his twelfth and thirteenth in Test cricket.
Passed 13,000 First-class runs when he passed 4 in the second innings.
Added 116 for the first innings fourth wicket with G.P.Thorpe. Added
146 for the second innings third wicket with R.W.T.Key.*

48. v West Indies at Birmingham 29 July-1 August 2004 –
won by 256 runs
Toss: England
England 566-9dec (M.E.Trescothick 105, A.Flintoff 167) &
248 (M.E.Trescothick 107, C.H.Gayle 5-34);
West Indies 336 (R.R.Sarwan 139) & 222 (A.F.Giles 5-57)

| 1st innings | c and b D.J.Bravo | 12 | 1-0-8-0 |
| 2nd innings | c C.H.Gayle b J.J.C.Lawson | 3 | 3-0-9-0 |

Notes: England captain.

49. v West Indies at Old Trafford 12-16 August 2004 – won by 7 wickets
Toss: West Indies
West Indies 395 & 165; England 330 (G.P.Thorpe 114,
D.J.Bravo 6-55) & 231-3

| 1st innings | b D.J.Bravo | 12 |
| 2nd innings | c B.C.Lara b C.H.Gayle | 33 |

Notes: England captain.

50. v West Indies at The Oval 19-21 August 2004 – won by 10 wickets
Toss: England
England 470 & 4-0; West Indies 152 (S.J.Harmison 6-46) &
318 (C.H.Gayle 105)

| 1st innings | c B.C.Lara b D.J.Bravo | 66 |
| 2nd innings | did not bat | |

Notes: England captain. Became the 50th English player to appear in 50 Tests. Added 146 for the first innings fourth wicket with I.R.Bell.

51. v South Africa at Port Elizabeth 17-21 December 2004 –
won by 7 wickets
Toss: South Africa
South Africa 337 (H.H.Dippenaar 110) & 229;
England 425 (A.J.Strauss 126) & 145-3

| 1st innings | c G.C.Smith b A.J.Hall | 10 |
| 2nd innings | b D.W.Steyn | 15 |

Notes: England captain.

53. v South Africa at Durban 26-30 December 2004 – match drawn
Toss: South Africa
England 139 & 570-7dec (M.E.Trescothick 132, A.J.Strauss 136,
G.P.Thorpe 118*); South Africa 332 (J.H.Kallis 162) & 290-8

| 1st innings | lbw b M.Ntini | 18 | 10-2-29-1 |
| 2nd innings | c A.B.deVilliers b M.Ntini | 10 | 1-1-0-0 |

Notes: England captain.

53. v South Africa at Cape Town 2-6 January 2005 – lost by 196 runs
Toss: South Africa
South Africa 441 (J.H.Kallis 149) & 222-8dec;
England 163 (C.K.Langeveldt 5-46) & 304

| 1st innings | c A.B.deVilliers b C.K.Langeveldt | 11 |
| 2nd innings | c J.A.Rudolph b M.Ntini | 20 |

Notes: England captain.

54. v South Africa at Johannesburg 13-17 January 2005 –
     won by 77 runs
     Toss: England
     England 411-8dec (A.J.Strauss 147) & 332-9dec (M.E.Trescothick
     180); South Africa 419 (H.H.Gibbs 161, M.J.Hoggard 5-144) &
     247 (M.J.Hoggard 7-61)

     1st innings   not out   82
     2nd innings   c M.V.Boucher b S.M.Pollock   54

     *Notes: England captain. Added 124 for the first innings third wicket
     with M.E.Trescothick.*

55. v South Africa at Centurion 21-25 January 2005 – match drawn
     Toss: England
     South Africa 247 & 296-6dec (A.B.deVilliers 109, J.H.Kallis 136*);
     England 359 (A.Nel 6-81) & 73-4

     1st innings   c J.A.Rudolph b S.M.Pollock   0
     2nd innings   not out   26

     *Notes: England captain. Passed 4,000 Test runs when he passed 3 in the
     second innings.*

56. v Bangladesh at Lord's 26-28 May 2005 –
     won by an innings and 261 runs
     Toss: England
     Bangladesh 108 & 159; England 528-3dec (M.E.Trescothick 194,
     M.P.Vaughan 120)

     1st innings   c Khaled Mashud
                    b Mashrafe Mortaza   120

     *Notes: England captain. Recorded his fourteenth Test century. Added
     255 for the first innings second wicket with M.E.Trescothick.*

57. v Bangladesh at Chester-le-Street 3-5 June 2005 –
     won by an innings and 27 runs
     Toss: England
     Bangladesh 104 (S.J.Harmison 5-38) & 316 (M.J.Hoggard 5-73);
     England 447-3dec (M.E.Trescothick 151, I.R.Bell 162*)

     1st innings   c Khaled Mashud
                    b Mashrafe Mortaza   44

     Notes: England captain.

58. v Australia at Lord's 21-24 July 2005 – lost by 239 runs
     Toss: Australia
     Australia 190 (S.J.Harmison 5-43) & 384;
     England 155 (G.D.McGrath 5-53) & 180

     1st innings   b G.D.McGrath   3
     2nd innings   b B.Lee   4

     Notes: England captain. Vaughan became B.Lee's 300th Test wicket.

59.	v Australia at Edgbaston 4-7 August 2005 – won by 2 runs
	Toss: Australia
	England 407 & 182 (S.K.Warne 6-46); Australia 308 & 279

	1st innings	c B.Lee b J.N.Gillespie		24
	2nd innings	b B.Lee				1

	Notes: England captain.

60.	v Australia at Old Trafford 11-15 August 2005 – match drawn
	Toss: England
	England 444 (M.P.Vaughan 166) & 280-6dec (A.J.Strauss 106,
	G.D.McGrath 5-115); Australia 302 (S.P.Jones 6-53) &
	371-9 (R.T.Ponting 156)

	1st innings	c G.D.McGrath b S.M.Katich	166
	2nd innings	c sub b B.Lee			14	5-0-21-0

	*Notes: England captain. Recorded his fifteenth Test century. Passed
	14,000 First-class runs when he passed 22 in the first innings. Added
	137 for the first innings second wicket with M.E.Trescothick. Added 127
	for the first innings third wicket with I.R.Bell.*

61.	v Australia at Trent Bridge 25-28 August 2005 – won by 3 wickets
	Toss: England
	England 477 (A.Flintoff 102) & 129-7; Australia 218
	(S.P.Jones 5-44) & 387 (following on)

	1st innings	c A.C.Gilchrist b R.T.Ponting	58
	2nd innings	c M.L.Hayden b S.K.Warne		0

	Notes: England captain.

62.	v Australia at The Oval 8-12 September 2005 – match drawn
	Toss: England
	England 373 (A.J.Strauss 129, S.K.Warne 6-122) &
	335 (K.P.Pietersen 158, S.K.Warne 6-124); Australia 367 (J.L.Langer
	105, M.L.Hayden 138, A.Flintoff 5–78) & 4–0

	1st innings	c M.J.Clarke b S.K.Warne		11
	2nd innings	c A.C.Gilchrist b G.D.McGrath	45

	*Notes: England captain. Became the first English captain since 1987 to
	lift the Ashes.*

63.	v Pakistan at Faisalabad 20-24 November 2005 – match drawn
	Toss: Pakistan
	Pakistan 462 (Inzamam-ul-Haq 109) & 268-9dec (Inzamam-ul-Haq
	100*); England 446 (I.R.Bell 115, K.P.Pietersen 100) & 164-6

	1st innings	b Naved-ul-Hasan			2
	2nd innings	lbw b Naved-ul-Hasan		9

	Notes: England captain.

64. v Pakistan at Lahore 29 November-3 December 2005 –
lost by an innings and 100 runs
Toss: England
England 288 & 248 (Shoaib Akhtar 5-71); Pakistan 636-8dec
(Mohammad Yousuf 223, Kamran Akmal 154)

1st innings   c Mohammad Yousuf b Shoaib Malik 58
2nd innings   c and b Shoaib Akhtar   13

*Notes: England captain. Added 101 for the first innings first wicket with
M.E.Trescothick.*

65. v West Indies at Headingley 25-28 May 2007 –
won by an innings and 283 runs
Toss: England
England 570-7dec (M.P.Vaughan 103, K.P.Pietersen 226);
West Indies 146 & 141

1st innings   c R.S.Morton b J.E.Taylor   103

*Notes: England captain. Recorded his sixteenth Test century. Joined
P.B.H.May as the most successful captain of England, this being
Vaughan's 20th Test win in charge. Added 163 for the first innings third
wicket with K.P.Pietersen.*

66. v West Indies at Old Trafford 7-11 June 2007 – won by 60 runs
Toss: England
England 370 & 313 (A.N.Cook 106, D.J.G.Sammy 7-66);
West Indies 229 & 394 (S.Chanderpaul 116*, M.S.Panesar 6-137)

1st innings   b C.D.Collymore   41
2nd innings   c and b D.J.G.Sammy   40

*Notes: England captain. Passed P.B.H.May as the most successful captain
of England, this being Vaughan's 21st Test win in charge. Added 104 for
the second innings second wicket with A.N.Cook.*

67. v West Indies at Chester-le-Street 15-19 June 2007 –
won by 7 wickets
Toss: England
West Indies 287 (S.Chanderpaul 136*, R.J.Sidebottom 5-88)
& 222 (M.S.Panesar 5-46); England 400 (P.D.Collingwood 128,
F.H.Edwards 5-112) & 111-3

1st innings   c D.J.Bravo b F.H.Edwards   19
2nd innings   not out   48

Notes: England captain.

68. v India at Lord's 19-23 July 2007 – match drawn
     Toss: England
     England 298 & 282 (K.P.Pietersen 134, R.P.Singh 5-59);
     India 201 (J.M.Anderson 5-42) & 282-9

     1st innings   c M.S.Dhoni b R.P.Singh   79
     2nd innings   b R.P.Singh   30   4-0-18-0

     *Notes: England captain. Passed 15,000 First-class runs when he passed
     32 in the first innings. Added 142 for the first innings second wicket
     with I.R.Bell.*

69. v India at Trent Bridge 27-31 July 2007 –
     lost by 7 wickets
     Toss: India
     England 198 & 355 (M.P.Vaughan 124); India 481 & 73-3

     1st innings   c S.R.Tendulkar b Z.Khan   9
     2nd innings   b Z.Khan   124

     *Notes: England captain. Recorded his seventeenth Test century. Passed
     5,000 Test runs when he passed 36 in the second innings. Added 112 for
     the second innings fourth wicket with P.D.Collingwood.*

70. v India at The Oval 9-13 August 2007 – match drawn
     Toss: India
     India 664 (A.Kumble 110) & 180-6dec; England 345 &
     369-6 (K.P.Pietersen 101)

     1st innings   c and b A.Kumble   11
     2nd innings   c M.S.Dhoni b S.Sreesanth   42

     Notes: England captain.

71. v Sri Lanka at Kandy 1-5 December 2007 –
     lost by 88 runs
     Toss: Sri Lanka
     Sri Lanka 188 & 442-8dec (K.C.Sangakkara 152); England 281
     (M.Muralitharan 6-55) & 261

     1st innings   c L.P.C.Silva b M.Muralitharan   37
     2nd innings   c H.A.P.W.Jayawardene
                    b W.P.U.J.C.Vaas   5   3-0-6-0

     Notes: England captain.

72. v Sri Lanka at Colombo (SSC) 9-13 December 2007 –
     match drawn
     Toss: England
     England 351 (M.Muralitharan 5-116) & 250-3;
     Sri Lanka 548-9dec (M.G.Vandort 138, D.P.M.D.Jayawardene 195)

     1st innings   c J.Mubarak b M.Muralitharan   87
     2nd innings   c and b C.R.D.Fernando   61

     *Notes: England captain. Added 133 for the first innings first wicket with
     A.N.Cook. Added 107 for the second innings first wicket with A.N.Cook.*

73. v Sri Lanka at Galle 18-22 December 2007 –
match drawn
Toss: England
Sri Lanka 499-8dec (D.P.M.D.Jayawardene 213*);
England 81 & 251-6 (A.N.Cook 118)

1st innings	lbw b W.P.U.J.C.Vaas	1
2nd innings	c D.P.M.D.Jayawardene	
	b U.W.M.B.C.A.Welagedara	24

Notes: England captain.

74. v New Zealand at Hamilton 5-9 March 2008 –
lost by 189 runs
Toss: New Zealand
New Zealand 470 (L.R.P.L.Taylor 120) & 177-9dec
(R.J.Sidebottom 6-49); England 348 & 110

| 1st innings | c B.B.McCullum b J.S.Patel | 63 |
| 2nd innings | lbw b K.D.Mills | 9 |

Notes: England captain.

75. v New Zealand at Wellington 13-17 March 2008 –
won by 126 runs
Toss: New Zealand
England 342 (T.R.Ambrose 102) & 293; New Zealand 198
(J.M.Anderson 5-73) & 311 (R.J.Sidebottom 5-105)

| 1st innings | b J.D.P.Oram | 32 |
| 2nd innings | c B.B.McCullum b K.D.Mills | 13 |

Notes: England captain.

76. v New Zealand at Napier 22-26 March 2008 – won by 121 runs
Toss: England
England 253 (K.P.Pietersen 129, T.G.Southee 5-55) & 467-7dec
(A.J.Strauss 177, I.R.Bell 110); New Zealand 168
(R.J.Sidebottom 7-47) & 431 (M.S.Panesar 6-126)

| 1st innings | lbw b T.G.Southee | 2 |
| 2nd innings | c B.B.McCullum b C.S.Martin | 4 |

Notes: England captain.

77. v New Zealand at Lord's 15-19 May 2008 – match drawn
Toss: England
New Zealand 277 & 269-6 (J.D.P.Oram 101); England 319
(M.P.Vaughan 106, D.L.Vettori 5-69)

| 1st innings | c J.A.H.Marshall b D.L.Vettori | 106 |

Notes: England captain. Recorded his eighteenth and final Test century to date.

78. v New Zealand at Old Trafford 23-26 May 2008 – won by 6 wickets
     Toss: New Zealand
     New Zealand 381 (L.R.P.L.Taylor 154*) & 114 (M.S.Panesar 6-37);
     England 202 (D.L.Vettori 5-66) & 294-4 (A.J.Strauss 106)

| 1st innings | lbw b D.L.Vettori | 30 |
| 2nd innings | c B.B.McCullum b C.S.Martin | 48 |

     Notes: England captain.

79. v New Zealand at Trent Bridge 5-8 June 2008 –
     won by an innings and 9 runs
     Toss: New Zealand
     England 364 (K.P.Pietersen 115); New Zealand 123
     (J.M.Anderson 7-43) & 232 (R.J.Sidebottom 6-67)

| 1st innings | b I.E.O'Brien | 16 |

     Notes: England captain.

80. v South Africa at Lord's 10-14 July 2008 – match drawn
     Toss: South Africa
     England 593-8dec (K.P.Pietersen 152, I.R.Bell 199);
     South Africa 247 (A.G.Prince 101) & 393-3dec (G.C.Smith 107,
     N.D.McKenzie 138, H.M.Amla 104*)

| 1st innings | b D.W.Steyn | 2 |

     Notes: England captain.

81. v South Africa at Headingley 18-21 July 2008 – lost by 10 wickets
     Toss: South Africa
     England 203 & 327; South Africa 522 (A.G.Prince 149,
     A.B.deVilliers 174) & 9-0

| 1st innings | c G.C.Smith b D.W.Steyn | 0 |
| 2nd innings | c M.V.Boucher b M.Ntini | 21 |

     Notes: England captain.

82. v South Africa at Edgbaston 30 July-2 August 2008 – lost by 5 wickets
     Toss: England
     England 231 & 363 (P.D.Collingwood 135);
     South Africa 314 & 283-5 (G.C.Smith 154*)

| 1st innings | c M.V.Boucher b A.Nel | 0 |
| 2nd innings | c H.M.Amla b A.Nel | 17 |

     *Notes: England captain. Vaughan resigned the captaincy the next day
     with a record of 51 matches, 26 wins, 11 defeats and 14 draws. Has not
     played since.*

Michael Vaughan in One-Day International Cricket

Compiled by
Victor and Richard V. Isaacs

One-Day International Career Record (2000/01–2006/07)

up to and including West Indies at Bridgetown 2007

M	I	NO	Runs	HS	Avge	S/R	100s	50s
86	83	10	1983	90*	27.15	68.39	0	16

1. v Sri Lanka at Dambulla 23 March 2001 – lost by 5 wickets
   Toss: England
   England 143 (48.5 overs) (G.P.Thorpe 62*, M.Muralitharan 4-29);
   Sri Lanka 144-5 (40.5 overs)
   st R.S.Kaluwitharana b M.Muralitharan   9   (20 balls)   1-0-3-0

2. v Sri Lanka at Colombo (RPS) 25 March 2001 – lost by 66 runs
   Toss: Sri Lanka
   Sri Lanka 226-6 (50 overs) (D.P.M.D.Jayawardene 101*,
   M.S.Atapattu 57); England 160 (A.J.Stewart 55)
   c R.P.Arnold b M.Muralitharan   26   (53 balls)

3.   v Pakistan at Edgbaston 7 June 2001 – lost by 108 runs
     Toss: Pakistan
     Pakistan 273-6 (50 overs) (Inzamam-ul-Haq 79, Saeed Anwar 77);
     England 165 (47.2 overs) (N.V.Knight 59*)
     c Saeed Anwar b Azhar Mahmood   5   (14 balls) 2-0-17-0

4.   v Pakistan at Lord's 12 June 2001 – lost by 2 runs
     Toss: England
     Pakistan 242-8 (50 overs) (Yousuf Youhana 81); England 240
     (M.E.Trescothick 137, O.A.Shah 62)
     c Azhar Mahmood b Waqar Younis   0   (4 balls)

5.   v Australia at Old Trafford 14 June 2001 – lost by 125 runs
     (D/L method)
     Toss: Australia
     Australia 208-7 (48 overs) (S.R.Waugh 64, D.R.Martyn 51*);
     England 86 (32.4 overs)
     b J.N.Gillespie   0   (1 ball)

6.   v Pakistan at Headingley 17 June 2001 – lost on a concession
     (after a pitch invasion)
     Toss: Pakistan
     England 156 (45.2 overs) (B.C.Hollioake 53, Waqar Younis 7-36);
     Pakistan 153-4 (39.5 overs) (Abdul Razzaq 75)
     c Younis Khan b Waqar Younis   2   (17 balls)

7.   v India at Kolkata 19 January 2002 – lost by 22 runs
     Toss: India
     India 281-8 (50 overs) (D.Mongia 71); England 259 (44 overs)
     (M.E.Trescothick 121)
     c A.B.Agarkar b A.Kumble   14   (26 balls)   1-0-8-0

8.   v India at Cuttack 22 January 2002 – won by 16 runs
     Toss: India
     England 250-7 (50 overs) (P.D.Collingwood 71*, M.P.Vaughan 63);
     India 234 (48.4 overs)
     run out (H.K.Badani/Harbhajan Singh)   63   (80 balls)

9.   v India at Chennai 25 January 2002 – lost by 4 wickets
     Toss: England
     England 217 (48 overs) (A.B.Agarkar 4-34); India 221-6
     (46.4 overs) (S.R.Tendulkar 68, V.Sehwag 51)
     c S.R.Tendulkar b A.Kumble   43   (59 balls)   0.4-0-7-0

10. v India at Kanpur 28 January 2002 – lost by 8 wickets
     Toss: England
     England 218-7 (39 overs) (N.V.Knight 74); India 219-2 (29.4 overs)
     (S.R.Tendulkar 87*, V.Sehwag 82)
     b S.C.Ganguly   4   (6 balls)

11.   v India at Delhi 31 January 2002 – won by 2 runs
      Toss: India
      England 271-5 (50 overs) (N.V.Knight 105, A.Flintoff 52);
      India 269-8 (50 overs) (S.C.Ganguly 74, A.F.Giles 5-57)
      not out   7   (5 balls)   7-0-40-0

12.   v India at Mumbai 3 February 2002 – won by 5 runs
      Toss: England
      England 255 (49.1 overs) (M.E.Trescothick 95, Harbhajan Singh
      5-43); India 250 (49.5 overs) (S.C.Ganguly 80)
      st A.Ratra b S.C.Ganguly   16   (27 balls)   10-1-37-2

13.   v New Zealand at Auckland 23 February 2002 –
      won by 33 runs (D/L method)
      Toss: England
      England 193-6 (40 overs) (G.P.Thorpe 59, M.P.Vaughan 59);
      New Zealand 189 (38 overs) (C.L.Cairns 58, A.Flintoff 4-17)
      run out (D.L.Vettori)   59   (53 balls)

14.   v India at Chester-le-Street 4 July 2002 – no result
      Toss: India
      India 285-4 (50 overs) (S.R.Tendulkar 105, R.Dravid 82);
      England 53-1 (12.3 overs)
      did not bat

15.   v Sri Lanka at Old Trafford 7 July 2002 – lost by 23 runs
      Toss: Sri Lanka
      Sri Lanka 229 (49.4 overs) (K.C.Sangakkara 70, M.P.Vaughan 4–22);
      England 206 (47.4 overs)
      c and b U.D.U.Chandana   14   (15 balls)

16.   v India at The Oval 9 July 2002 – won by 64 runs
      Toss: India
      England 229-8 (R.C.Irani 53, A.Flintoff 51);
      India 165 (R.C.Irani 5-26)
      c Yuvraj Singh b Z.Khan   30   (17 balls)

17.   v India at Lord's 13 July 2002 – lost by 2 wickets
      Toss: England
      England 325-5 (50 overs) (N.Hussain 115, M.E.Trescothick 109);
      India 326-8 (M.Kaif 87*, Yuvraj Singh 69, S.C.Ganguly 60)
      c D.Mongia b Z.Khan   3   (5 balls)

18.   v Sri Lanka at Adelaide 17 January 2003 – won by 19 runs
      Toss: England
      England 279-7 (50 overs) (N.V.Knight 88, A.J.Stewart 51);
      Sri Lanka 260 (49.2 overs) (S.T.Jayasuriya 99, K.C.Sangakkara 56,
      A.R.Caddick 4-35)
      c W.P.U.J.C.Vaas b C.R.D.Fernando   28   (35 balls)   7-0-35-1

19. v Australia at Adelaide 19 January 2003 – lost by 4 wickets
Toss: England
England 152 (48.3 overs) (P.D.Collingwood 63*);
Australia 153-6 (D.R.Martyn 59)
c A.C.Gilchrist b B.A.Williams   21   (22 balls)   5-0-20-1

20. v Australia at Sydney 23 January 2003 – lost by 10 wickets
Toss: England
England 117 (A.J.Bichel 4-18); Australia 118-0 (12.2 overs)
(A.C.Gilchrist 69*)
lbw b A.J.Bichel   21   (48 balls)

21. v Australia at Melbourne 25 January 2003 – lost by 5 runs
Toss: Australia
Australia 229-7 (50 overs) (G.B.Hogg 71*, M.L.Hayden 69);
England 224 (49.3 overs) (M.P.Vaughan 60, A.J.Stewart 60,
B.Lee 5-30)
c R.T.Ponting b S.K.Warne   60   (81 balls)   1-0-12-0

22. v Netherlands at East London 16 February 2003 – won by 6 wickets
Toss: England
Netherlands 142-9 (50 overs) (T.B.M.de Leede 58*,
J.M.Anderson 4-25); England 144-4 (23.2 overs) (N.V.Knight 51,
M.P.Vaughan 51)
c T.B.M.de Leede b D.L.S.van Bunge   51   (47 balls)

23. v Namibia at Port Elizabeth 19 February 2003 – won by 55 runs
Toss: Namibia
England 272 (50 overs) (A.J.Stewart 60, M.E.Trescothick 58,
R.J.van Vuuren 5-43); Namibia 217-9 (50 overs) (A.J.Burger 85)
c L.J.Burger b R.J.van Vuuren   14   (18 balls)   6-0-31-0

24. v Pakistan at Cape Town 22 February 2003 – won by 112 runs
Toss: England
England 246-8 (50 overs) (P.D.Collingwood 66*, M.P.Vaughan 52);
Pakistan 134 (31 overs) (J.M.Anderson 4-29)
c Younis Khan b Shoaib Akhtar   52   (64 balls)

25. v India at Durban 26 February 2003 – lost by 82 runs
Toss: India
India 250-9 (50 overs) (R.Dravid 62, S.R.Tendulkar 50);
England 168 (45.3 overs) (A.Flintoff 64, A.Nehra 6-23)
c R.Dravid b A.Nehra   20   (47 balls)

26. v Australia at Port Elizabeth 2 March 2003 – lost by 2 wickets
Toss: England
England 204-8 (50 overs) (A.J.Bichel 7-20); Australia 208-8
(M.G.Bevan 74*, A.R.Caddick 4-35)
c A.C.Gilchrist b A.J.Bichel   2   (5 balls)   2-0-10-0

27. v Pakistan at Old Trafford 17 June 2003 – lost by 2 wickets
     Toss: England
     England 204-9 (50 overs); Pakistan 208-8 (49.2 overs)
     (Mohammad Hafeez 69)
     c Rashid Latif b Umar Gul   27   (34 balls)   2-0-9-0

28. v Pakistan at The Oval 20 June 2003 – won by 7 wickets
     Toss: Pakistan
     Pakistan 185 (44 overs) (Yousuf Youhana 75*, J.M.Anderson 4-27);
     England 189-3 (M.E.Trescothick 86)
     c Younis Khan b Shoaib Akhtar   10   (14 balls)

29. v Pakistan at Lord's 22 June 2003 – won by 4 wickets
     Toss: England
     Pakistan 229-7 (50 overs) (Abdul Razzaq 64, Younis Khan 63,
     A.Flintoff 4-32); England 231-6 (48.3 overs) (M.E.Trescothick 108*)
     c Mohammad Hafeez b Azhar Mahmood   29   (41 balls)

30. v Zimbabwe at Trent Bridge 26 June 2003 – lost by 4 wickets
     Toss: Zimbabwe
     England 191-8 (50 overs) (A.Flintoff 53), Zimbabwe 195-6 (48 overs)
     (G.W.Flower 96*)
     c T.Taibu b S.M.Ervine   13   (22 balls)

31. v Zimbabwe at Headingley 1 July 2003 – no result
     Toss: Zimbabwe
     England 81-4 (16.3 overs)
     not out   35   (45 balls)

32. v South Africa at Old Trafford 3 July 2003 – lost by 7 wickets
     Toss: England
     England 223-7 (50 overs) (M.E.Trescothick 60, A.McGrath 52);
     South Africa 227-3 (47.3 overs) (J.H.Kallis 82*, J.A.Rudolph 71*)
     c M.V.Boucher b S.M.Pollock   3   (4 balls)   5-0-27-0

33. v Zimbabwe at Bristol 6 July 2003 – won by 6 wickets
     Toss: England
     Zimbabwe 92 (D.Gough 4-26); England 95-4 (17.5 overs)
     (H.H.Streak 4-21)
     not out   11   (34 balls)

34. v South Africa at Edgbaston 8 July 2003 – won by 4 wickets
     Toss: South Africa
     South Africa 198-9 (50 overs) (J.M.Anderson 4-38);
     England 199-6 (39 overs) (M.P.Vaughan 83, A.Flintoff 54)
     lbw b A.J.Hall   83   (115 balls)

35.   v South Africa at Lord's 12 July 2003 – won by 7 wickets
      Toss: England
      South Africa 107 (32.1 overs); England 111-3 (20.2 overs)
      (V.S.Solanki 50)
      c M.Ntini b A.Nel   30   (29 balls)

36.   v Bangladesh at Chittagong 7 November 2003 – won by 7 wickets
      Toss: Bangladesh
      Bangladesh 143 (A.Flintoff 4-14); England 144-3 (25.3 overs)
      (A.Flintoff 55*)
      st Khaled Mashud b Manjural Islam   9   (9 balls)

37.   v Bangladesh at Dhaka 10 November 2003 – won by 7 wickets
      Toss: Bangladesh
      Bangladesh 134-9 (50 overs); England 137-3 (27.4 overs)
      (A.Flintoff 70*)
      not out   37   (69 balls)

38.   v Bangladesh at Dhaka 12 November 2003 – won by 7 wickets
      Toss: Bangladesh
      Bangladesh 182 (49.1 overs); England 185-3 (39.3 overs)
      (A.Flintoff 52*, M.E.Trescothick 50)
      lbw b Mushfiqur Rahman   29   (46 balls)

39.   v Sri Lanka at Dambulla 18 November 2003 – lost by 10 wickets
      Toss: England
      England 88 (46.1 overs); Sri Lanka 89-0 (13.5 overs)
      b K.A.D.M.Fernando   2   (19 balls)

40.   v West Indies at Georgetown 18 April 2004 – won by 2 wickets
      Toss: England
      West Indies 156-5 (30 overs) (S.Chanderpaul 84);
      England 157-8 (29.3 overs)
      c R.D.Jacobs b M.Dillon   0   (3 balls)

41.   v West Indies at Port of Spain 24 April 2004 – no result
      Toss: West Indies
      West Indies 57-2 (16 overs); England did not bat

42.   v West Indies at Gros Islet 1 May 2004 – lost by 5 wickets
      Toss: West Indies
      England 281-8 (50 overs) (M.E.Trescothick 130, A.Flintoff 59);
      West Indies 284-5 (48 overs) (R.R.Sarwan 73*)
      c R.D.Jacobs b I.D.R.Bradshaw   25   (29 balls)

43.   v West Indies at Gros Islet 2 May 2004 – lost by 4 wickets
      Toss: West Indies
      England 280-8 (50 overs) (M.P.Vaughan 67, A.J.Strauss 67);
      West Indies 282-6 (47.1 overs) (S.Chanderpaul 63, B.C.Lara 57)
      run out (R.L.Powell)   67   (78 balls)

44. v West Indies at Bridgetown 5 May 2004 – won by 5 wickets
     Toss: England
     West Indies 261-6 (50 overs) (R.R.Sarwan 104*);
     England 262-5 (47.2 overs) (M.E.Trescothick 82, A.J.Strauss 66)
     c R.D.Jacobs b R.Rampaul   14   (16 balls)

45. v West Indies at Trent Bridge 27 June 2004 – lost by 7 wickets
     Toss: West Indies
     England 147 (38.2 overs); West Indies 148-3 (32.2 overs)
     (C.H.Gayle 60*)
     c R.R.Sarwan b I.D.R.Bradshaw   1   (6 balls)

46. v New Zealand at Riverside 29 June 2004 – lost by 7 wickets
     Toss: New Zealand
     England 101 (32.5 overs) (J.E.C.Franklin 5-42);
     New Zealand 103-3 (17.2 overs)
     b J.E.C.Franklin   12   (18 balls)

47. v West Indies at Headingley 1 June 2004 – won by 7 wickets
     Toss: England
     West Indies 159 (40.1 overs); England 160-3 (22 overs)
     (M.E.Trescothick 55)
     c C.H.Gayle b D.J.Bravo   14   (25 balls)

48. v New Zealand at Bristol 4 July 2004 – lost by 6 wickets
     Toss: New Zealand
     England 237-7 (50 overs) (A.Flintoff 106, A.J.Strauss 61);
     New Zealand 241-4 (47.2 overs) (S.P.Fleming 99, H.J.H.Marshall 55,
     N.J.Astle 53)
     c C.Z.Harris b J.D.P.Oram   12   (31 balls)   5-0-29-0

49. v West Indies at Lord's 6 July 2004 – lost by 7 wickets
     Toss: West Indies
     England 237-7 (50 overs) (A.Flintoff 123, A.J.Strauss 100);
     West Indies 286-3 (49.1 overs) (C.H.Gayle 132*, R.R.Sarwan 89)
     c R.D.Jacobs b T.L.Best   8   (21 balls)   1-0-10-0

50. v India at Trent Bridge 1 September 2004 – won by 7 wickets
     Toss: England
     India 170 (43.5 overs) (M.Kaif 50);
     England 171-3 (32.2 overs) (V.S.Solanki 52)
     b L.Balaji   0   (7 balls)

51. v India at The Oval 3 September 2004 – won by 70 runs
     Toss: India
     England 307-5 (A.Flintoff 99, P.D.Collingwood 79*);
     India 237 (46.3 overs) (M.Kaif 51, D.Gough 4-50)
     c R.Dravid b Harbhajan Singh   4   (12 balls)   5-0-32-0

52.   v India at Lord's 5 September 2004 – lost by 23 runs
      Toss: India
      India 204 (49.3 overs) (S.C.Ganguly 90, R.Dravid 52,
      S.J.Harmison 4-22); England 181 (48.2 overs) (M.P.Vaughan 74)
      st K.D.Karthik b Harbhajan Singh   74   (141 balls)   5-0-23-0

53.   v Zimbabwe at Edgbaston 10 September 2004 – won by 152 runs
      Toss: Zimbabwe
      England 299-7 (50 overs) (P.D.Collingwood 80*, V.S.Solanki 62);
      Zimbabwe 147 (39 overs)
      c M.A.Vermeulen b E.C.Rainsford   17   (13 balls)

54.   v Sri Lanka at Rose Bowl 17 and 18 September 2004 –
      won by 49 runs (D/L)
      Toss: Sri Lanka
      England 251-7 (50 overs) (A.Flintoff 104, M.E.Trescothick 66);
      Sri Lanka 95-5 (24 overs)
      b D.N.T.Zoysa   5   (11 balls)

55.   v Australia at Edgbaston 21 September 2004 – won by 6 wickets
      Toss: England
      Australia 259-9 (50 overs) (D.R.Martyn 65); England 262-4
      (46.3 overs) (M.P.Vaughan 86, M.E.Trescothick 81, A.J.Strauss 52*)
      c M.L.Hayden b B.Lee   86   (122 balls)   10-0-42-2
      Highlights: Won the man of the match award

56.   v West Indies at The Oval 25 September 2004 – lost by 2 wickets
      Toss: West Indies
      England 217 (49.4 overs) (M.E.Trescothick 104);
      West Indies 218-8 (48.5 overs)
      b I.D.R.Bradshaw   7   (18 balls)

57.   v Zimbabwe at Harare 28 November 2004 – won by 5 wickets
      Toss: England
      Zimbabwe 195 (49.3 overs) (E.Chigumbura 52); England 197-5
      (47.4 overs) (I.R.Bell 75, M.P.Vaughan 56)
      c E.Chigumbura b S.Matsikenyeri   56   (75 balls)

58.   v Zimbabwe at Harare 1 December 2004 – won by 161 runs
      Toss: England
      England 263-6 (50 overs) (K.P.Pietersen 77*, G.O.Jones 66);
      Zimbabwe 102 (36 overs) (A.G.Wharf 4-24)
      lbw b T.Panyangara   11   (21 balls)

59.   v Zimbabwe at Bulawayo 4 December 2004 – won by 8 wickets
      Toss: Zimbabwe
      England 238-7 (50 overs) (S.Matsikenyeri 73, D.D.Ebrahim 65);
      England 239-2 (43.1 overs) (V.S.Solanki 100, M.P.Vaughan 54*,
      I.R.Bell 53)
      not out   54   (75 balls)   8-0-35-1

60.   v Zimbabwe at Bulawayo 5 December 2004 – won by 74 runs
      Toss: England
      England 261-6 (50 overs) (M.P.Vaughan 90*, G.O.Jones 80);
      Zimbabwe 187 (48.4 overs) (H.Masakadza 66, D.Gough 4-34)
      not out   90   (99 balls)

61.   v South Africa at Johannesburg 30 January 2005 –
      won by 26 runs (D/L)
      Toss: England
      South Africa 175-9 (50 overs); England 103-3 (25.1 overs)
      not out   44   (70 balls)
      Highlights: Won the man of the match award

62.   v South Africa at Bloemfontein 2 February 2005 – match tied
      Toss: South Africa
      England 270-5 (50 overs) (K.P.Pietersen 108*);
      South Africa 270-8 (50 overs) (H.H.Gibbs 78, J.H.Kallis 63)
      run out (A.B.de Villiers)   42   (82 balls)

63.   v South Africa at Cape Town 6 February 2005 – lost by 108 runs
      Toss: England
      South Africa 291-5 (50 overs) (H.H.Gibbs 100, J.H.Kallis 71,
      J.M.Kemp 57); England 183 (41.2 overs) (K.P.Pietersen 75)
      c J.H.Kallis b S.M.Pollock   0   (6 balls)   4-0-21-0

64.   v South Africa at East London 9 February 2005 – lost by 7 runs
      Toss: South Africa
      South Africa 311-7 (50 overs) (G.C.Smith 115*, J.M.Kemp 80);
      England 304-8 (50 overs) (K.P.Pietersen 100*, M.P.Vaughan 70)
      c A.G.Prince b N.Boje   70   (94 balls)

65.   v South Africa at Durban 11 February 2005 – no result
      Toss: South Africa
      South Africa 211 (46.3 overs) (H.H.Gibbs 118);
      England 7-2 (3.4 overs)
      not out   2   (6 balls)   5-0-24-0

66.   v South Africa at Centurion 13 February 2005 – lost by 3 wickets
      Toss: South Africa
      England 240 (49.5 overs) (K.P.Pietersen 116);
      South Africa 241-7 (49 overs) (A.G.Prince 62*)
      b M.Ntini   1   (5 balls)   5-0-22-1

67.   v Bangladesh at The Oval 16 June 2005 – won by 10 wickets
      Toss: England
      Bangladesh 190 (45.2 overs) (Aftab Ahmed 51, S.J.Harmison 4-39);
      England 192-0 (24.5 overs) (M.E.Trescothick 100*, A.J.Strauss 82*)
      did not bat

68.　v Australia at Bristol 19 June 2005 – won by 3 wickets
　　Toss: Australia
　　Australia 252-9 (50 overs) (M.E.K.Hussey 84, S.J.Harmison 5-33);
　　England 253-7 (47.3 overs) (K.P.Pietersen 91*, M.P.Vaughan 57)
　　lbw b G.B.Hogg　57　(92 balls)　6-0-33-0

69.　v Bangladesh at Trent Bridge 21 June 2005 – won by 168 runs
　　Toss: England
　　England 391-4 (50 overs) (A.J.Strauss 152, P.D.Collingwood 112*,
　　M.E.Trescothick 85); Bangladesh 223 (45.2 overs) (Mohammad
　　Ashraful 94, Javed Omar 59, P.D.Collingwood 6-31,
　　C.T.Tremlett 4-32)
　　b Nazmul Hossain　0　(8 balls)

70.　v Australia at Edgbaston 28 June 2005 – no result
　　Toss: Australia
　　Australia 261-9 (50 overs) (A.Symonds 74); England 37-1 (6 overs)
　　not out　0　(0 balls)　1-0-13-0

71.　v Australia at Lord's 2 July 2005 – match tied
　　Toss: England
　　Australia 196 (48.5 overs) (M.E.K.Hussey 62*),
　　England 196-9 (50 overs) (G.O.Jones 71, P.D.Collingwood 53)
　　b G.D.McGrath　0　(7 balls)

72.　v Australia at Headingley 7 July 2005 – won by 9 wickets
　　Toss: England
　　Australia 219-7 (50 overs) (P.D.Collingwood 4-34);
　　England 221-1 (46 overs) (M.E.Trescothick 104*, M.P.Vaughan 59*)
　　not out　59　(65 balls)

73.　v Australia at Lord's 10 July 2005 – lost by 7 wickets
　　Toss: Australia
　　England 223-8 (50 overs) (A.Flintoff 87, B.Lee 5-41);
　　Australia 224-3 (44.2 overs) (R.T.Ponting 111)
　　lbw b G.D.McGrath　1　(3 balls)

74.　v Australia at The Oval 12 July 2005 – lost by 8 wickets
　　Toss: Australia
　　England 228-7 (50 overs) (K.P.Pietersen 74, V.S.Solanki 53*);
　　Australia 229-2 (34.5 overs) (A.C.Gilchrist 121*)
　　run out (R.T.Ponting)　15　(30 balls)

75.　v Australia at Melbourne 12 January 2007 – lost by 8 wickets
　　Toss: England
　　England 242-8 (K.P.Pietersen 82); Australia 246-2 (45.2 overs)
　　(R.T.Ponting 82*, A.C.Gilchrist 60, M.J.Clarke 57*)
　　c M.L.Hayden b N.W.Bracken　26　(32 balls)

76.   v New Zealand at Hobart 16 January 2007 – won by 3 wickets
      Toss: New Zealand
      New Zealand 205-9 (50 overs) (J.M.Anderson 4-42);
      England 206-7 (49.5 overs) (A.Flintoff 72*)
      c L.R.P.L.Taylor b J.E.C.Franklin   17   (29 balls)

77.   v Australia at New Zealand at Brisbane 6 February 2007 –
      won by 14 runs
      Toss: England
      England 270-7 (50 overs) (P.D.Collingwood 106, A.J.Strauss 55,
      S.E.Bond 4-46); New Zealand 256-8 (50 overs) (S.P.Fleming 106)
      b S.E.Bond   0   (1 ball)

78.   v New Zealand at Gros Islet 16 March 2007 – lost by 6 wickets
      Toss: New Zealand
      England 209-7 (50 overs) (K.P.Pietersen 60);
      New Zealand 210-4 (41 overs) (S.B.Styris 87*, J.D.P.Oram 63*)
      b J.E.C.Franklin   26   (52 balls)

79.   v Canada at Gros Islet 18 March 2007 – won by 51 runs
      Toss: Canada
      England 279-6 (50 overs) (E.C.Joyce 66, P.D.Collingwood 62*);
      Canada 228-7 (50 overs) (A.A.Mulla 58)
      c J.M.Davison b A.M.Samad   45   (64 balls)

80.   v Kenya at Gros Islet 24 March 2007 – won by 7 wickets
      Toss: Kenya
      Kenya 177 (43 overs) (S.O.Tikolo 76); England 178-3 (33 overs)
      (E.C.Joyce 75, K.P.Pietersen 56*)
      c C.O.Obuya b P.J.Ongondo   1   (4 balls)

81.   v Ireland at Providence 30 March 2007 – won by 48 runs
      Toss: England
      England 266-7 (50 overs) (P.D.Collingwood 90); Ireland 218 (48.1
      overs) (N.J.O'Brien 63, A.Flintoff 4-43)
      c N.J.O'Brien b W.B.Rankin   6   (13 balls)

82.   v Sri Lanka at North Sound 4 April 2007 – lost by 2 runs
      Toss: England
      Sri Lanka 235 (50 overs) (W.U.Tharanga 62, D.P.M.D.Jayawardene
      56, S.I.Mahmood 4-50); England 233-8 (K.P.Pietersen 58,
      R.S.Bopara 52)
      c K.C.Sangakkara b W.P.U.J.C.Vaas   0   (3 balls)   3-0-14-0

83.   v Australia at St Peter's 8 April 2007 – lost by 7 wickets
      Toss: England
      England 247 (49.5 overs) (K.P.Pietersen 104, I.R.Bell 77);
      Australia 248-3 (47.2 overs) (R.T.Ponting 86, M.J.Clarke 55*)
      b S.W.Tait   5   (8 balls)

84. v Bangladesh at Bridgetown 11 April 2007 – won by 4 wickets
    Toss: England
    Bangladesh 143 (37.2 overs) (Saqibul Hasan 57);
    England 147-6 (44.5 overs)
    c Habibul Bashar b Abdur Razzak   30   (59 balls)

85. v South Africa at Bridgetown 17 April 2007 – lost by 9 wickets
    Toss: England
    England 154 (48 overs) (A.J.Hall 5-18); South Africa 157-1
    (19.2 overs) (G.C.Smith 89*)
    lbw b A.Nel   17   (38 balls)

86. v West Indies at Bridgetown 21 April 2007 – won by 1 wicket
    Toss: England
    West Indies 300 (49.5 overs) (C.H.Gayle 79, D.S.Smith 61,
    M.N.Samuels 51); England 301-9 (49.5 overs) (K.P.Pietersen 100,
    M.P.Vaughan 79)
    run out (D.J.Bravo)   79   (68 balls)   10-0-39-3

Michael Vaughan in International Twenty20 Matches

Compiled by
Victor and Richard V. Isaacs

International Twenty20 Career Record (2005–2006/07)

M	I	NO	Runs	HS	Avge	S/R	100s	50s
2	2	0	27	27	13.50	122.72	0	0

1. v Australia at Rose Bowl 13 June 2005 – won by 100 runs
   Toss: England
   England 179-8 (20 overs); Australia 79 (14.3 overs) (J.Lewis 4-24)
   c R.T.Ponting b A.Symonds   0   (1 ball)

2. v Australia at Sydney 9 January 2007 – lost by 77 runs
   Toss: Australia
   Australia 221-5 (20 overs); England 144-9 (20 overs)
   lbw b A.Symonds   27   (21 balls)

Michael Vaughan
Full Career Records

Compiled by
Victor and Richard V. Isaacs

First-class (1998–2009)

up to and including Warwickshire v Yorkshire at Edgbaston 6-9 May 2009

M	I	NO	Runs	HS	Avge	100s	50s
267	466	27	16213	197	36.93	42	68

Balls	Mdns	Runs	Wkts	Avge	BB	5wI	Econ
9342	293	5245	114	46.00	4-39	0	3.36

List-A (Limited Overs matches) (1997–2009)

up to and including Surrey v Yorkshire at The Oval 20 May 2009

M	I	NO	Runs	HS	Avge	100s	50s
282	273	25	7238	125*	29.18	3	46

Balls	Mdns	Runs	Wkts	Avge	BB	4wI	Econ
3381	16	2604	78	33.38	4-22	4	4.62

Test Centuries

197	v India	Nottingham	2002
195	v India	The Oval	2002
183	v Australia	Sydney	2002/2003
177	v Australia	Adelaide	2002/2003
166	v Australia	Manchester	2005
156	v South Africa	Birmingham	2003
145	v Australia	Melbourne	2002/2003
140	v West Indies	St John's	2003/2004
124	v India	Nottingham	2007
120	v Bangladesh	Lord's	2005
120	v Pakistan	Manchester	2001
115	v Sri Lanka	Lord's	2002
106	v New Zealand	Lord's	2008
105	v Sri Lanka	Kandy	2003/2004
103	v West Indies	Leeds	2007
103	v West Indies	Lord's	2004
101*	v West Indies	Lord's	2004
100	v India	Lord's	2002

Index

9/11 attacks 66, 80–81

Adams, Chris 48, 51
Adams, Jimmy 60
Afridi, Shahid 268
Agarkar, Ajit 93
Agnew, Jonathan 4
Ahmed, Mushtaq 274, 368
Akhtar, Shoaib 74, 120, 268, 339
Akram, Wasim 31, 32, 35, 40, 74, 76
Ali, Kabir 375
Ambrose, Curtly 36, 59, 60, 63, 65
Ambrose, Tim 350, 370, 385
Amla, Hashim 373, 377, 384
Anderson, James 121–2, 132, 139, 183, 200, 251, 298, 320, 325, 348, 350, 351, 367–8, 372, 374, 375, 417, 420, 424
Artballing 425
Arthur, Mickey 377
Ashes
    (1981) 378
    (2001) 77–8
    (2002/2003) 99–116, 219
    (2005) 1–2, 8, 122, 151, 179, 208, 219, 235–61, 290
        the aftermath 260–61, 262–6, 361
    (2006) 273, 275, 283–9, 291, 389
    (2009) 329, 359–60, 366, 416–24
Astle, Nathan 86
Atherton, Mike 8, 13, 45, 47, 49, 50, 53, 60, 65, 66, 67, 93, 151, 215–16, 348, 354, 386
Australia
    Ashes (1981) 378; (2001)

77–8; (2002/2003) 99–116, 219; (2005) 1–2, 8, 122, 151, 179, 208, 219, 235–61, 290; (2006) 273, 275, 283–9, 291; (2009) 329, 359–60, 366, 416–24
    Twenty20 matches v England (2005) 223–5; (2007) 292
Australia ODIs
    v Bangladesh (2005) 226
    v England (2004) 186–7, 189; (2005) 226–9; (2007) 301–2
Avery, James 314

back-room team 214
Bairstow, David 10
Bangladesh ODIs
    v Australia (2005) 226
    v England (2003) 164; (2005) 222–3; (2007) 302–3
Bangladesh v England (2003) 162–3
Bashar, Habibul 302
Batty, Gareth 165, 173, 174, 410
Batty, George 174
Batty, Jeremy 27
BBC 4, 191, 306, 397, 413
Bell, Ian 180, 182, 183, 189, 211, 216, 222, 223, 245, 257, 287, 298, 302, 335, 339, 347, 354, 373, 422
Benjamin, Kenny 17
Benson & Hedges Cup 39, 40, 75
Benson & Hedges Super Cup 40
Berry, Scyld 115, 412, 413
Best, Tino 169

Bethel, Jack 15, 24, 26
Bethel, Steve 24, 26, 27
Bevan, Michael 39, 121
Bevan, Richard 3, 6, 159, 192–3, 359
Bichel, Andy 108, 121, 122
Bicknell, Martin 110, 145–6
bin Laden, Osama 66–7
Bishop, Ian 17
Blackwell, Ian 120, 121
Blackwell, Kevin 279
Blair, Euan 263
Blair, Tony 1, 252, 263, 396
Board President's XI 271
Boon, Tim 214
Bopara, Ravi 301, 405, 407, 422
Bore, Mike 25
Botham, Sir Ian 13, 139, 174, 294
Boucher, Mark 51, 196, 198, 383, 385
Bowden, Billy 242–3, 257
bowlers, preferred number of 368
bowling changes 206, 377
Boycott, Geoff 78, 79–80, 140, 240, 273, 389, 414
Bradshaw, Ian 188
Bransgrove, Rod 174
Brearley, Mike 139
Bresnan, Tim 370, 398
Broad, Stuart 227, 288, 340, 348, 375, 378, 392
Broadhurst, Mark 29
Browne, Courtney 188
Buchanan, John 234
Bucknor, Steve 321
Bull, Steve 282
Bunbury Festival 18–19
Butcher, Alan 110
Butcher, Mark 46, 48, 49, 50, 78, 86, 90, 91, 101, 109, 110, 111, 115,

124, 136, 138, 141–4,
162, 168, 169, 182,
189, 194–8, 216, 222
Byas, Bingo 39–40, 78–9, 80
Byas, David 39, 78, 218

C&G Trophy games 273
Caddick, Andy 59, 62, 63, 64,
67, 74, 81, 104–5, 106,
114, 121, 227
Cairns, Chris 179
Canada ODI v England
(2007) 298, 300
Caprice 265
captains
international 218–19
Yorkshire 218–19
Carr, John 192
Carrick, Phil 28, 29
Cassar, Matt 58
central-contracts system 221
Chambers, Alan 231
Chanderpaul, Shivnarine 318
Chandler, Chubby 125
Channel Four television 95–6
Chapple, Glen 30, 32
Clark, Stuart 309, 421
Clark, Wayne 79, 80
Clarke, Darren 117, 125
Clarke, Giles 163, 339, 344,
399
Clarke, Matthew 224
Clarke, Michael 224, 241,
255
Clarke, Rikki 127
Close, Brian 26, 80
coaching 155–6
Collier, David 367
Collingwood, Paul 1, 5, 6, 86,
114, 124, 157, 164,
165, 226, 251, 252,
255, 256, 258, 259,
263, 295, 301, 302,
307, 318, 319, 320,
322, 324, 327, 329,
340, 342, 350, 356,
357, 358, 365, 367,
370, 372, 376, 381–5,
392, 395, 417
Commonwealth Bank series
(2007) 293, 295
Conway, Dean 34, 37–8, 68
Cook, Alastair 272, 287, 317,
324, 339, 350
Cook, Geoff 152
Cook, Nick 402
Cooley, Troy 170
Cork, Dominic 59, 60, 61, 64,
309
County Championship 374
(2001) 78–80

(2008) 151, 152, 402–3,
404–5
Coverdale, Steve 16–17
Crawley, John 62, 101,
114–15
Cricket Reform Group 151
Croft, Robert 71, 81
Croft, Steven 408
Cronje, Wessel Johannes
(Hansie) 51, 56, 57,
201
Crowe, Martin 218
Cumbes, Jim 315

Dawson, Matt 164
Dawson, Richard 78, 109,
111, 115
de Silva, Aravinda 90
de Villiers, AB 377, 378, 385
DeFreitas, Phil 31, 32
Derbyshire CCC v Yorkshire
(2000) 58; (2008) 413
Desmond, Dermot 422
Devonshire, Duke and
Duchess of 21
Dickason, Reg 298
Dickson, Mike 207
Donald, Allan 49, 50, 51–2,
54
doosra 70–71, 94
Dravid, Rahul 97, 218–19,
321, 323, 396
Duckworth-Lewis method
120, 202
Dunhill Links golf
championship, St
Andrews 328
Durham CCC
County Championship
(2008) 152
v Yorkshire (1998) 39;
(2008) 371, 402–3, 412

Edwards, Fidel 169
Elizabeth II, Queen 1, 252
England
Ashes (1981) 378; (2001)
77–8; (2002/2003)
99–116, 219; (2005)
1–2, 8, 122, 151, 179,
208, 219, 235–61, 290;
(2006) 273, 275,
283–9, 291, 389;
(2009) 329, 359–60,
366, 416–24
Twenty20 matches v
Australia (2005) 223–5;
(2007) 292
v Bangladesh (2003) 162–3
v India (2001/2002) 81–4;
(2002) 92–7, 98;

(2006) 272; (2007)
320–25
v New Zealand (1999) 41;
(2002) 86–8; (2004)
176–80; (2009)
347–56, 358, 363–8
v Pakistan (2000) 68–9;
(2001) 74–7; (2005)
267–8; (2006) 279–80
v South Africa (1999/2000)
49–57; (2003) 131–47,
148, 149, 150, 162;
(2004/2005) 195–201;
(2008) 372–3, 374–85,
421
v Sri Lanka (2001) 69–71;
(2002) 89–91; (2003)
164–7, 328–9; (2007)
330–41
v West Indies (2000) 59–66;
(2004) 131, 168–74,
181–4; (2007) 309–19;
(2008) 405
v Zimbabwe (2000) 58,
59
England and Wales Cricket
Board (ECB) 117, 118,
119, 150, 156, 158,
159, 163, 178, 185,
192, 207, 221, 227,
252, 258, 262, 269,
275, 287, 289, 297,
314, 339, 343–4, 359,
360, 363, 367, 393,
395, 399, 411, 415
England Lions 395–8, 410,
412
England ODIs
v Australia (2004) 186–7,
189; (2005) 226–9;
(2007) 301–2
v Bangladesh (2003) 164;
(2005) 222–3; (2007)
302–3
v Canada (2007) 298, 300
v India (2002) 84, 91–2;
(2004) 184
v Ireland (2007) 301;
(2009) 423
v Kenya (2007) 300
v New Zealand (2002)
85–6; (2007) 295,
297–8; (2008) 346
v Pakistan (2003) 126–9,
130
v South Africa (2003)
129–30; (2005) 202,
203; (2007) 303–4
v Sri Lanka (2001) 71–2;
(2002) 91; (2004)
185–6; (2007) 301

v West Indies (2004) 188–9;
(2007) 306
v Zimbabwe (2003) 129;
(2004) 184–6, 191–5
English, David 19
English Premier League (EPL)
154
Essex CCC v Yorkshire
(1998) 40; (1999) 42
Etheridge, John 352
Evans, Chris 260

Fairbrother, Neil 'Harvey' 32,
304, 316, 359
Faldo, Nick 153
Ferguson, Sir Alex 408
Fernando, Dilhara 91, 301
field-setting 170, 206, 215,
377
Fleming, Stephen 218, 297,
355
Fletcher, Duncan 1, 6, 38, 41,
42, 44–7, 50, 53,
58–61, 64–5, 68, 69,
71, 74, 76, 79–80, 81,
83, 84, 86, 87, 95, 96,
97, 106, 110, 119, 124,
125, 127, 135, 137,
140, 156, 159, 162,
163, 166, 168, 171,
172, 176, 178–81, 185,
192–5, 197, 200, 202,
216, 224, 229–30, 238,
244, 249, 250, 258,
260, 265, 268, 270,
271, 277, 281, 282,
286, 290, 291–7, 299,
304–7, 308–11, 324–5,
329, 332, 333, 334,
342, 344–7, 353, 354,
382, 414
Flintoff, Andrew (Freddie) 1,
5, 6, 41, 51, 55, 68–9,
85, 86, 91, 92, 94, 99,
102, 117, 121, 128–9,
132, 139, 143, 144,
146, 164, 170, 171,
180, 182, 185, 187,
188, 194, 196, 197,
200, 201, 203, 211–14,
216, 236, 237, 240,
241, 242, 246, 247–8,
250, 251, 253, 254,
255, 258, 261, 265,
272, 277–8, 281, 282,
283, 287, 288, 289,
294–5, 298, 299, 302,
314–16, 317, 332, 336,
348, 368, 372–6, 383,
384, 415, 418, 419,
420, 424

Flower, Andy 368, 382, 394,
404, 423
forward press 69, 92–3
Foster, James 81, 115, 189
Fraser, Gus 7
'Fredalo' incident 294–5,
314–15
Friends Provident Trophy
151, 308, 371, 402,
404, 408

Gale, Andrew 410–11
Ganguly, Sourav 92, 94
Garaway, Mark 5, 340–41
Gatting, Mike 37, 126
Gayle, Chris 319, 405
Gaywood, Nick 17
Gibbs, Herschelle 132, 199
Gibson, Colin 227
Gibson, Ottis 382, 392
Gilchrist, Adam 155, 216,
229, 233, 236, 243,
245, 257, 338
Giles, Ashley 5, 68, 71, 82, 83,
91, 106, 124, 165, 170,
174, 179, 181–2, 196,
200, 212, 225, 230,
231–2, 238, 245, 250,
255, 258, 259, 263,
266, 286, 338, 379
Gillespie, Jason 100, 101,
108, 109, 170, 226,
229, 247
Glamorgan CCC 149
v Yorkshire (1998) 44;
(2001) 79
Gloucestershire CCC v
Yorkshire (1999) 40
Gooch, Graham 83, 95, 155,
297
Gough, Darren 28, 31, 47,
56, 57, 60, 63, 64, 71,
74, 81, 84, 99, 102,
127–8, 133, 136, 137,
139, 142, 214, 225,
227, 296–7, 369–70
Gower, David 155
Graveney, David 37, 38, 42,
125, 172, 230, 281–4,
334, 343–5
Grayson, Paul 27
Gregory, Peter 270–71

Haddin, Brad 420
Hair, Darrell 173, 279, 281
Hall, Andrew 304
Halsall, Richard 382
Hamilton, Gavin 24, 45, 47,
51
Hampshire CCC v Yorkshire
(2007) 309

Harbottle & Lewis 367
Harmison, Steve 39, 41, 93,
106, 112, 145, 146,
163–4, 167, 169, 170,
173, 183, 185–8, 194,
196, 197, 198, 200,
213, 226, 229, 235,
237, 241, 242, 251,
265, 297, 325, 326,
340, 348, 350, 366,
368, 371–5, 380–81,
383, 392, 402
Harris, Andrew xii
Harris, Paul 384
Hartley, Peter 31
Hassall, Chris 16
Hauritz, Nathan 422
Hayden, Matthew 98, 100,
104, 105, 112, 224,
226, 227, 233, 236,
240, 249, 253, 260,
295, 338, 426
Hayward, Nantie 46
Headley, Dean 45
Healey, Austin 387
Hegg, Warren 32
Hick, Graeme 62, 63, 70,
88
Hillside Golf Club, Southport
125
Hodge, Brad 248–9
Hoggard, Matthew 68–9,
112, 113–14, 157, 170,
171, 196, 200–201,
212, 227, 236, 238,
240, 241, 250, 253,
255, 263, 348, 349,
368, 370
Hoggard family 113
Hollioake, Adam 37, 124,
218
Hollioake, Ben 86–7
Houghton, Dave 238
Humewood golf course, Port
Elizabeth 123
Hurst, David 155
Hussain, Nasser 7, 8, 41, 42,
45, 47–50, 53, 54, 56,
59, 61, 64, 65, 67, 68,
70, 71, 74, 82, 83, 86,
87, 91–6, 101, 103,
106, 107, 108, 112,
113, 114, 117–18, 120,
121, 123, 124, 127,
128, 131–7, 139–42,
145, 162, 165–9,
177–8, 200, 208, 209,
210, 216–19, 316, 320,
331–2, 344–5, 385,
386, 394
Hussey, Mike 155

ICC Trophy
  (2001) 66
  (2003) 98–9
  (2004) 122, 184, 185
Illingworth, Ray 80, 140, 218
India ODIs v England (2002) 84, 91–2; (2004) 184
India v England (2001/2002) 81–4; (2002) 92–7, 98; (2006) 272; (2007) 320–25
Indian Cricket League (ICL) 344
Indian Premier League (IPL) 154, 362, 363
Innes, Kevin 34–5
International Cricket Council (ICC) 118, 193, 264, 265, 279–80, 302, 327
International Sport Management 117, 125, 425
Irani, Ronnie 118
Ireland ODI v England (2007) 301; (2009) 423

Jacobs, David 230
Jacobs, Sheila 230
Jafri, Sacha 425
Jaguar 136
Jarvis, David 25
Jayawardene, Mahela 335–6, 338, 342
Jellybeangate 322, 323, 324, 325
John, Elton 1
Johnson, Martin 164
Johnson, Richard 81
Jones, Geraint 171–2, 173, 212, 243, 245, 247–8, 259, 338
Jones, Simon 93, 104, 170, 180, 183, 196, 200, 212–13, 226–7, 240, 242, 245–8, 251, 272, 288, 357, 375
Joyce, Ed 297

Kaif, Mohammad 84
Kallis, Jacques 51, 146, 372, 383, 384
Kashmir earthquake (2005) 266
Kasprowicz, Michael 241, 242, 247
Katich, Simon 245
Keedy, Gary 26
Kellett, Simon 29
Kent, v Yorkshire (1999) 43
Kent, Paul 22

Kenya ODI v England (2007) 300
Kettleborough, Richard 20, 26
Key, Robert 94, 106, 181, 183, 199, 402
Khan, Zaheer 92, 95, 322, 323, 324
King, Reon 60
Kirby, Steve 78
Kirsten, Gary 51, 54–5, 146
Kirtley, James 142, 143, 145
Klusener, Lance 51, 52, 55, 56
Knight, Nick 120
Koertzen, Rudi 281
Kolpak players 152, 157–8
Kruger, Garnett 54
Kruis, Deon 157
Kumble, Anil 95, 325
KwaZulu-Natal 52

Lancashire CCC v Yorkshire (1993) 31–2, 35; (1995) 39; (2007) 319; (2008) 369; (2008) 408
Langer, Justin 107, 108, 155, 235, 241, 260, 338, 357, 421
Lara, Brian 61, 64, 173–4, 183, 219, 306
Laud, Medha 258
League Managers Association 359
Lee, Brett 100, 109, 110, 114, 237, 241, 242, 245, 246, 250, 257, 258, 259, 421
Leeds United FC 279
Lehmann, Darren 63, 78, 79, 107–8, 232, 236, 283
Leicestershire CCC xi v Yorkshire (2008) 412
Leverock, Dwayne 296
Lewis, Jon 298
Lister, Joe 16
Lloyd, Clive 167, 198, 199
Lloyd, David 41, 273
London, Nick 275, 313
Love, Martin 102–3, 106
Loye, Mal 297
Lyth, Adam 414

McAllister, Scott 274, 275
McCullum, Brendon 355
McGee, Bert 12
McGrath, Anthony 109, 127, 132, 135–6, 139, 140–41, 150, 370
McGrath, Glenn 97, 99–100, 101, 105–9, 170, 176,

203, 205, 208, 209–10, 226, 228, 237, 239, 244–7, 253, 256, 257
McIlroy, Rory xii
McKenzie, Neil 373, 384
McLean, Nixon 63
McRae, Donald 314, 315
Maddy, Darren 45, 48
Madugalle, Ranjan 232
Mahmood, Sajid 287
Mallender, Neil 281
Marks, Vic 93
Marron, Peter 317, 366
Marsh, Rod 172
Martin, Peter 31
Martyn, Damien 241
May, Peter 93, 115, 318
Maynard, Matthew 44, 214
MCC (Marylebone Cricket Club) 177, 401
Metcalfe, Ashley 29
Middlesex CCC v Yorkshire (2006) 274
Miller, Geoff 7, 29–30, 281, 317, 343, 344, 345, 376, 379, 381, 390, 401, 403, 406, 408, 410
Moores, Peter 2, 4, 6, 7, 84, 183, 214, 285, 307–10, 325, 329–34, 337–8, 342, 345–9, 351, 353–8, 365, 366, 368, 379–81, 386, 387, 390, 399
Morgan, David 185, 192
Morkel, Morne 372–3
Morris, Alex 26
Morris, Hugh 7, 159, 356, 357, 359, 383–4, 395, 415
Morris, Karl 247, 359
Morton, Runako 313
Morton, Wayne 273, 275, 278, 279
Moxon, Martyn xii, 16, 31, 32, 35, 36, 218, 308, 371, 389, 400, 411, 412, 413, 414
Mugabe, Robert 118, 120
Mullally, Alan 45, 51–2
Muralitharan, Muttiah 70–71, 89, 90, 91, 163, 164, 166–7, 215, 332, 335, 339, 368
Murphy, Pat 306
Murray, Andy 153
Mustard, Phil 'Colonel' 370, 402
Myles, Simon 17

Namibia 190–91
National Academy,
    Loughborough 404
NatWest Pro40 competition
    xi, 412, 413, 414
NatWest triangular series 226
NatWest Trophy 39
Naved-ul-Hasan, Rana 412
Navratilova, Martina 398
Neale, Phil 13, 179, 192, 233,
    250, 284
Neville, Gary 19
Neville, Phil 19
New Zealand, v England
    (1999) 41; (2002)
    86–8; (2004) 176–80;
    (2008) 347–56, 358,
    363–8
New Zealand ODIs v England
    (2002) 5–6; (2007)
    295, 297–8; (2008) 346
Newcastle United FC 169
Nicholas, Mark 224, 232,
    364
Nicky Oppenheimer's XI
    45–6
Nixon, Paul 289, 292, 301,
    302
Noffke, Ashley 406
Northamptonshire CCC v
    Yorkshire (1995) 39
Northerns/Gauteng team 48
Norton College, Sheffield 22
Nottinghamshire CCC v
    Yorkshire (1999) 42;
    (2008) 411–12
npower 221, 324, 329, 345

Oldham, Steve 16, 29, 31, 33,
    36
O'Leary, David 125
Olympics (2008) 153
one-day internationals
    Australia (2004) 106–7;
        (2005) 226–9; (2007)
        301–2
    Bangladesh (2003) 164;
        (2005) 222–3; (2007)
        302–3
    Canada (2007) 300
    India (2002) 84, 91–2;
        (2004) 184
    Ireland (2007) 301
    Kenya (2007) 300
    New Zealand (2002) 85–6;
        (2007) 295, 297–8;
        (2008) 346
    Pakistan (2003) 126–9, 130
    Sri Lanka (2001) 71–2;
        (2002) 91; (2004)
        185–6; (2007) 301

West Indies (2004) 188–9;
    (2007) 306
Zimbabwe (2003) 129;
    (2004) 184–5
O'Neill, Martin 423
Onions, Graham 398, 420
Oppenheimer, Nicky 45
Oram, Jacob 355, 364
Ormond, Jimmy 81
Owen, Michael 97

Padgett, Doug 16, 26–7, 157
Pakistan ODIs v England
    (2003) 126–9, 130
Pakistan v England (2000)
    68–9; (2001) 74–7;
    (2005) 267–8; (2006)
    279–80
Panesar, Monty 285–6, 317,
    320, 336, 340, 354,
    366, 372, 380, 383,
    385, 417, 420, 424
Pattinson, Darren 374–7, 380
Pietersen, Jessica 356
Pietersen, Kevin (KP) 5, 7, 8,
    52–3, 139, 142, 162,
    180, 183, 189, 191,
    193, 202–4, 211, 222,
    225, 226, 230, 237,
    250, 257, 258–9, 265,
    268, 302, 312–13,
    319–22, 339, 354, 356,
    367, 373, 384, 386,
    390, 394, 395, 398,
    399, 422
player management committee
    333–4, 349
Plunkett, Liam 298
Pollock, Shaun 49, 50, 51,
    144
Ponting, Ricky 174, 212, 219,
    229, 231, 232, 234,
    235, 236, 239, 240,
    246, 248, 249, 252–5,
    323, 416, 417, 419,
    420
Porter FC 12, 14
Pratt, Gary 248
Priestley, Neil 17
Pringle, Derek 8
Prior, Matt 323–4, 335
Professional Cricketers'
    Association 159, 178,
    359, 363, 367
    player-of-the-year award 98
Pura Cup 80

Question of Sport, A (TV
    programme) 53

Rafiq, Azeem 412

Ramprakash, Mark 36, 60,
    62, 83, 88, 328
Rashid, Adil 370, 412
Razzaq, Abdul 128
Read, Chris 48, 165–6, 168,
    171, 172, 189, 281,
    346
Redgrave, Sir Steve 303–4
referrals system 280
Regan, Stewart 371, 413, 414
Richardson, Richie 31, 36
Riddle, Dean 279
Ripley, David 17
Rocky (dressing room
    attendant) 113
Root, Joe 414
Rose, Franklyn 60
Rose, Graham 36
Rudolph, Jacques 157, 370
Russell, Kirk 250, 275, 283

Sackfield, Craig 3, 6, 381
Saggers, Martin 180
Salford Boys football teams
    11
Sami, Mohammad 128
Samuels, Marlon 323
Sanderson, Matt 20, 98, 161
Sanderson, Tom 19
Sangakkara, Kumar 105, 335
Saxby, Mark 5, 340–41, 356
Schofield, Chris 58
Schofield Report 53, 158–9,
    289–90, 344, 349, 357
Shah, Owais 310, 350, 351,
    352, 401
Shahzad, Ajmal 412
Shannon, Ray 360–61, 362,
    387
Sharp, Kevin 29
Shaw, Connor 244–5
Sheffield Collegiate CC 11,
    15–16, 17, 18, 414
Sheffield United FC 279
Sheffield Wednesday FC 12,
    14, 15, 22, 98
Shepherd, David 76
Shine, Kevin 299
Sidebottom, Ryan 75, 313,
    320, 325, 340, 351,
    354, 368, 372, 374,
    375–6, 392
Silverdale Comprehensive
    School, Sheffield 18,
    19–23
Silverwood, Chris 26
Singh, Harbhajan 95, 323
Singh, Sarandeep 83
Sir Allen Stanford week
    392
Sky News 387

Sky television 154, 268, 310
Smith, Devon 168
Smith, Ed 141, 142
Smith, Graeme 3, 132, 137,
    139, 140, 198–9, 219,
    304, 327, 372, 373,
    385
Smith, Mike 59
Smith, Dr Tom 14
Snape, Jeremy 299
Somerset CCC v Yorkshire
    (1993) 36; (2001) 75;
    (2008) 390, 409
Sons and Daughters of
    Zimbabwe 119
South Africa ODIs v England,
    (2003) 129–30; (2005)
    202, 203; (2007) 303–4
South Africa v England
    (1999/2000) 49–57;
    (2003) 131–47, 148,
    149, 150, 162;
    (2004/2005) 195–201;
    (2008) 372–3, 374–85,
    421
Southee, Tim 353, 354
Speed, Malcolm 118
spinners, playing 69, 97
Spivey, Mark 350–51
Sreesanth 321–4
Sri Lanka ODIs v England
    (2001) 71–2; (2002)
    91; (2004) 185–6;
    (2007) 301
Sri Lanka v England (2001)
    69–71; (2002) 89–91;
    (2003) 164–7, 328–9;
    (2007) 330–41
Srinath, Javagal 85
Stanford, Sir Allen 362, 363,
    367
Stanford debacle (2008)
    392–5
Statham, Brian 64
Stewart, Alec 41, 50, 56, 59,
    61, 81, 91, 101, 104,
    110, 120, 121, 135,
    136, 138, 139, 145,
    146, 169, 216
Steyn, Dale 372
Stockill, Nigel 92, 141
Strauss, Andrew 5, 157, 168,
    177, 178, 187, 196,
    199, 201, 211, 227,
    231, 234, 240, 245,
    253, 255, 266, 268,
    277, 279, 281, 295,
    310, 317, 318–19, 331,
    338, 339, 342, 350,
    354, 357, 363, 364,
    366, 377, 390, 394,

396, 404–5, 416, 418,
    422, 423
Strydom, Pieter 56
Styris, Scott 297–8
'Super Sixes' 119
Surrey CCC v Yorkshire
    (2003) 145; (2008) 408
Sussex CCC v Yorkshire
    (2006) 274–5; (2008)
    404; (2008) 409
Swann, Graeme 45, 420,
    421–2
Symcox, Pat 46
Symonds, Andrew 187, 225,
    226

Tait, Shaun 247, 302, 339
Tapler, Simon 387–8
Tasker, Andy 17
Taufel, Simon 281
Taylor, Jerome 313
Taylor, Ross 365
Taylor, Zac 177
Tendulkar, Sachin 22, 83,
    93–4, 97, 323, 325
Thomas, Darren 34
Thomas, Dr Neil 274
Thorpe, Graham 70, 71, 82,
    86, 90, 93, 141, 145,
    162, 168, 171, 179,
    182, 189, 196, 216,
    222–3, 225, 230
toss, the 214–15
Tremlett, Chris 230, 288,
    320, 321, 325–6, 374,
    376, 380, 381
Trescothick, Marcus
    ('Banger') 34, 70, 76,
    86, 90, 91, 93, 95, 101,
    105, 106, 109, 120,
    123–5, 128, 132, 143,
    145, 163, 174, 185,
    187, 194, 196, 200,
    201, 211, 228, 231,
    233, 234, 240, 245,
    255, 257–8, 266, 267,
    270–72, 288, 297, 342,
    357, 387, 390
Trott, Jonathan 386, 422
Troughton, Jim 127, 407
Trueman, Fred 26, 64, 80
Tsunami (2004) 333, 337
Tudor, Alex 109, 110
Tufnell, Phil 46, 53
Twenty20 cricket 85, 151,
    154, 158, 223, 225–6,
    292, 327, 362, 363,
    369–71, 375, 381,
    408–12, 426, 427
    Stanford debacle (2008)
    392–5

v Australia (2005) 223–5
v Australia (2007) 292
Tyldesley, Ernest 10–11
Tyldesley, J.T. 10
Tyldesley family 10, 11

umpires 279–81

Vaughan, Archie (son) 269,
    278, 361, 387, 415
Vaughan, David (brother) 10,
    11, 12, 14, 19, 20, 426
Vaughan, Dee (mother)
    10–11, 14, 23, 31, 49,
    75, 128, 244, 415
Vaughan, Graham (father) 3,
    10–19, 23, 31, 49, 75,
    128, 244, 415
Vaughan, Michael Paul, OBE
    first interest in cricket 9–10
    first bat 10, 13
    sporting genes 10–11
    surgery for hereditary toe
        condition 13–14
    at Sheffield Collegiate
        15–18
    coaching at Headingley 16,
        17
    first XI debut 17
    Daily Telegraph Under-15
        player of the year 18
    education 19–23
    meets Nichola 20–21
    signs contract with
        Yorkshire (1991) 24
    cricket academy 25–6
    debut for second team 27
    England Under-19s debut
        30–31
    joins the first team 31–3
    maiden century 36
    awarded his Yorkshire cap
        37
    Test debut 49–52
    ODI debut 71–2
    dismissed for handling the
        ball 83
    dropping catches 84–5
    player-of-the-year award 98
    becomes one-day captain
        125–7
    appointed England captain
        134–6
    Daily Mail article (2003)
        148–50, 151
    marriage (2003) 21, 161
    bodysurfing incident 165
    birth of his daughter 179
    on the art of captaincy
        205–20
    euphoria after winning the

Ashes (2005) 260–61, 262–4
given the freedom of Sheffield 264
knee injury and recuperation 266–7, 269–76, 277, 278, 282–3
awarded OBE 135, 269
in the one-day squad 287–8
resumes his captaincy 290
achieves his sixteenth Test century 312–13
interview referring to the 'Fredalo' incident 314–16
decision to stand down as one-day captain 317–18
England's most successful captain 318
'therapeutic' diary 329, 330, 335–41, 343–4, 348, 352–3, 357, 359, 362–3, 377, 386–7, 389, 391, 407, 415
as a perfectionist 362
sixth Lord's hundred 364
starts to hate the game 380
decision to give up England captaincy 379, 383
resigns the England captaincy 3–8, 386
visits a homeopath 387–8
plans his comeback 395, 401–3
decision to retire from first-class cricket xi-xii, 411–15
final game of professional cricket 412
plans for the future 424–5
full career records 458–59
International Twenty20 Matches 457
one-day-international cricket record 445–56
Test career record 428–44
Vaughan, Nichola (née Shannon; wife) 3, 6, 8, 20–21, 54, 111, 113, 134, 161, 179, 262, 269, 274, 278, 287, 343, 360, 379, 383, 387, 408
Vaughan, Talulla Grace (daughter) 179, 361
Vettori, Daniel 366

Vodafone 2, 47, 113, 364, 381, 417

Waddle, Chris 155
Walker, Matthew 30
Walpole, Andrew 207, 284
Walsh, Courtney 59, 60, 63, 65
Warne, Shane 2, 77–8, 100, 104–9, 170, 176, 203, 215, 224, 237, 239, 241–5, 247–50, 254–9, 285, 288, 339, 368
Warwickshire CCC v Yorkshire (2008) 406–8
Waugh, Steve 77, 100, 103, 105, 108, 112, 114, 218, 240
West Indies ODIs v England (2004) 188–9; (2007) 306
West Indies v England (2000) 59–66; (2004) 131, 168–74, 181–4; (2007) 309–19; (2008) 405
Westwood, Lee xii
Whitaker, James 210, 349, 379
White, Craig ('Chalky') 24, 64, 65, 68, 82, 88, 101, 107–8, 110
wicketkeepers 168–9
Wilkinson, Jonny 88, 153
Willis, Bob 151, 378
Wilson, Dean 337
Wisden Cricketers' Almanack 115
Wisden Trophy 64, 66
Wood, Barry 33
Wood, Matthew 78, 161
Woods, Tiger 120
Woodward, Sir Clive 354
Worcestershire CCC xii
Worcestershire CCC v Yorkshire (2008) 404, 405–6, 408, 409, 410
World Cup 217
(1999) 41, 45, 54
(2003) 111, 117–24
(2007) 126, 296, 298–307, 314
(2010) 119
World Cup (rugby) 164
World Test Team of the Year (2007) 327
Worsley CC 11, 154
Wright, Luke 370, 392

Yorkshire CCC
MV is coached at Headingley 16, 17
MV is spotted by Yorkshire 16
academy 25–6, 156, 181
change in attitudes 16, 22
Leeds/Bradford university side 360
v Derbyshire (2000) 58; (2008) 413
v Durham (1998) 39; (2008) 371, 412
v Essex (1998) 40; (1999) 42
v Glamorgan (1998) 44; (2001) 79
v Gloucestershire (1999) 40
v Hampshire (2007) 309
v Kent (1999) 43
v Lancashire (1993) 31–2, 35; (1995) 39; (2007) 319; (2008) 369; (2008) 408
v Leicestershire 412
v Middlesex (2006) 274
v Northamptonshire (1995) 39
v Nottinghamshire (1999) 42; (2008) 411–12
v Somerset (1993) 36; (2001) 75; (2008) 390, 409
v Surrey (2003) 145; (2008) 408
v Sussex (2006) 274–5; (2008) 404, 409
v Warwickshire (2008) 406–8
v Worcestershire (2008) 404, 405–6, 408, 409, 410
wins County Championship (2001) 78–80
Yorkshire Legends 26
Yorkshire Premier League 156
Younis, Waqar 74
Yousuf, Mohammad 313

Zimbabwe ODIs v England (2003) 129; (2004) 184–6, 191–5
Zimbabwe v England (2000) 58, 59